Publisher's Cataloging-in-Publication data

Names: Nelson, Eric S.,1950-, author. | Yule, George, 1947-, author.
Title: Grammar Advantage: A course text and self-study tool for advanced learners of English for academic purposes / Eric S. Nelson; George Yule.

Description: Tucson, AZ; Minneapolis, MN: A3D Impressions a division of Awareness3D LLC, 2019

Identifiers: ISBN 978-1-7320677-5-2 (paper); 978-1-7320677-4-5 (ebook)

Subjects: LCSH English language—Grammar—Problems, Exercises, etc. | English language—Grammar--Study guides. | English language—Textbooks for foreign speakers. | English language—Study and teaching—Foreign speakers. | BISAC FOREIGN LANGUAGE STUDY / English as a Second Language | LANGUAGE ARTS & DISCIPLINES / Grammar & Punctuation

Classification: LCC PE1128 .N45 2019 | DDC 428.2/4—dc23

Library of Congress Control Number: 2018965135

Grammar Advantage

Eric S. Nelson
George Yule

A3D Impressions
Tucson | Minneapolis

To the student

Welcome to *Grammar Advantage*. Here are some tips for getting the most out of this book.

- Be sure you understand how the book is organized. See Chapter 1, especially section 1.5, *How can you get use* Grammar Advantage *effectively?*
- Pay attention to both the explanatory parts and the examples. If you have a hard time understanding a rule, often the examples will help. Some students, when they first look at a chapter, look at the examples first.
- Pay attention to **lexical grammar** as well as regular grammar. Regular grammar is the grammar that always (or almost always) applies. Lexical grammar is the grammar of individual words. For example, we say *enjoy doing* but not usually *enjoy to do*. In contrast, both *like doing* and *like to do* are correct. That's lexical grammar. Lexical grammar is often especially important with verbs. Many of the charts in this book show lexical grammar information.
- Use the glossary — the explanations of grammar terms at the end of the book. Sometimes the glossary includes information that goes beyond the scope of the chapters.
- Pay special attention to exercises marked *High priority*. Go to GrammarAdvantage.com for an answer key to odd-numbered items in the exercises. Checking the key will let you know if you're on the right track.

To the teacher

Grammar Advantage, based on the authors' decades of experience teaching and investigating English grammar, is a course text and self-study tool for advanced learners of English as a second language (C-TOEFL score of at least 190 or equivalent). It highlights topics of special importance to academic writing. The explanatory parts and examples are designed to be easy for teachers to use in guiding students to explanations and helping them edit their work. The explanations and exercises feature real-world content along with everyday conversational English and focus on meaning and usage as well as form.

Coverage of basic rules and finer points of usage help students understand not just basic grammar but how individual words are used (lexical grammar). An important feature of many of the charts is the use of words in phrases. For example, a display of verbs that are often followed by a gerund (Chapter 6) lists verbs in phrases like *enjoy visiting museums, finish getting dressed*, and *regret not studying*. These are a reminder to students (they are less likely to forget what the list is supposed to show) and they often suggest questions that can be raised in class, such as *Do you enjoy visiting museums?*

Sections at the end of each chapter marked *Usage guide* include lexical grammar and finer points of usage, often related to writing. Sections on errors to avoid — at the ends of chapters – provide summaries of key points.

For an answer key and ideas about to use *Grammar Advantage*, visit GrammarAdvantage.com.

Grammar Advantage
Contents

Chapter 1	**Thinking about grammar**	.1
Chapter 2	**Sentence structure**	.9
Chapter 3	**Transition expressions and sentence flow**	.65
Chapter 4	**Tenses**	.91
Chapter 5	**Active and passive voice**	.135
Chapter 6	**Gerunds and infinitives**	.157
Chapter 7	**Noun clauses and reporting**	.195
Chapter 8	**Relative clauses**	.231
Chapter 9	**Adverbial clauses**	.269
Chapter 10	**Conditionals**	.303
Appendix A	**Tense overview: a summary of forms and meanings**	325
Appendix B	**Basic punctuation for joining clauses**	.329
Appendix C	**Transition expressions word by word**	.331
Appendix D	**Principles for ordering information in sentences**	.337
	Glossary of grammar terms	.339
	Editing Guide	.349
	Index	.351

Detailed contents on following pages

Detailed contents

Chapter 1: Thinking About Grammar 1

    1.1   The Invisible gorilla 1
    1.2   Why pay attention to grammar? 1
    1.3   Exercising your grammar brain 2
    1.4   Grammar terms 5
    1.5   How can you use *Grammar Advantage* effectively? 5

Chapter 2: Sentence structure 9

    2.1   What is sentence structure? 12
    2.2   Subjects and verbs 13
        2.2.1   Don't omit the subject 14
        2.2.2   Don't add an extra subject 14
        2.2.3   Don't omit the verb 14
        2.2.4   Avoid mismatches 14
        2.2.5   Subject-verb agreement 16
    2.3   Word forms and parts of speech 17
        2.3.1   Word forms 17
        2.3.2   Parts of speech 18
        2.3.3   Avoiding word form mistakes 19
    2.4   Completing the meaning of a verb: object or prepositional phrase? 21
        2.4.1   Verbs with objects (transitive verbs) 21
        2.4.2   Necessary objects 22
        2.4.3   Verbs without objects (intransitive verbs) 23
        2.4.4   Common intransitive verbs with typical prepositional phrases ...23
        2.4.5   Sometimes transitive, sometimes intransitive 26
    2.5   Prepositions after nouns but not verbs: *contact* or *contact with*? 27
    2.6   Two-object verbs 30
        2.6.1   *Give someone something / give something to someone* 30
        2.6.2   *Buy someone something / buy something for someone* 30
        2.6.3   Typical patterns for the verb *ask* 30
        2.6.4   *Cost, save,* and *take* 30
    2.7   Avoiding verb completion mistakes 33
    2.8   Linking verbs 34
        2.8.1   Linking verbs followed by adjectives and other structures 34
        2.8.2   Sentences like *Mozart died young* 34
        2.8.3   BE *like* 34
    2.9   *Look like, seem like, sound like* 35
    2.10   Phrasal verbs (*go on, put off, run out of,* etc.) 36
    2.11   Empty *it* subjects 38
    2.12   *There is* (existential *there*) 39
    2.13   Inversion 41
        2.13.1   Reversing the order of a subject and auxiliary 41
        2.13.2   Inversion with fronted negative elements 41
    2.14   Questions 42
        2.14.1   *Yes/no* questions 42
        2.14.2   *Wh* questions 42
        2.14.3   No inversion in subordinate clauses 42
        2.14.4   *What is it like? / How is it?* 43
        2.14.5   Problems with questions 44
    2.15   Commands, requests, and exclamatory sentences 46
        2.15.1   Three sentence types 46
        2.15.2   Commands 46
        2.15.3   Exclamatory sentences 46

2.16	Pronouns and reference	47
	2.16.1 Reference	47
	2.16.2 Pronoun forms	47
	2.16.3 Pronoun agreement	47
	2.16.4 Clear reference	47
	2.16.5 Avoiding repetitiveness	48
2.17	Sentences and clauses	49
	2.17.1 Two kinds of clauses: Independent and subordinate	49
	2.17.2 Building sentences with subordination	49
	2.17.3 Building sentences with coordination	50
2.18	Parallelism (parallel structure)	52
	2.18.1 *And*	52
	2.18.2 Avoid faulty parallelism	52
	2.18.3 The algebra of coordination	53
	2.18.4 *But* and *or* with a variety of structures	53
2.19	Fragments, run-ons, and comma splices	55
2.20	Adverbs	56
2.21	Time expressions in the form of noun phrases	57
2.22	Usage guide Beginning and ending sentences	58
	2.22.1 Beginning with an adverbial	58
	2.22.2 Old before new	58
	2.22.3 Beginning with a noun phrase	59
	2.22.4 Beginning with *For*	59
	2.22.5 Beginning with an *–ing* word	59
2.23	Usage guide Sentence variety in your writing	60
	2.23.1 Traditional sentence types	60
	2.23.2 Avoiding choppiness	60
2.24	Usage guide Avoiding gender bias in pronoun choice	61
2.25	Usage guide Impersonal *you* and *one* in generalizations	61
2.26	Usage guide Avoiding shifting points of view	61
2.27	Problems with sentence structure	62

Chapter 3: **Transition expressions and sentence flow**   ...65

3.1	Transition expressions in context	67
3.2	What are transition expressions?	67
3.3	Transition expressions listed alphabetically	68
3.4	Expanded transition expressions	69
3.5	Placement and punctuation of transition expressionss	70
3.6	Transition expressions and conjunctions	71
3.7	Meanings that transition expressions express	72
3.8	Addition, examples, details, and restatement	74
3.9	Result, time, and text structure	76
3.10	Contrast	77
3.11	Correcting a misconception	78
3.12	Concession	79
3.13	Condition	80
3.14	Usage guide Punctuation with *so* and *yet*	81
3.15	Usage guide Placing *however* and *for example* between sentence parts	81
3.16	Usage guide Using expanded transition expressions for conciseness	82
3.17	Usage guide Old before new information	82
3.18	Usage guide Parallel structure and repetition	83
3.19	Usage guide Review: Five ways of achieving good sentence flow	83
3.20	Problems with transition expressions	87

Chapter 4: Tenses 91

- 4.1 Tenses in context 93
- 4.2 Tense chart 94
- 4.3 Tenses in passive verb phrases 94
- 4.4 Modal auxiliaries and semi-modals 95
  - 4.4.1 Modal auxiliaries 95
  - 4.4.2 Semi-modals 95
  - 4.4.3 Avoiding errors with modals 95
- 4.5 Verbs with no tense: infinitives, gerunds, and participles 96
  - Tense chart with negative sentences and questions (Exercise 5) 98
- 4.6 Simple present 99
- 4.7 Present continuous 100
- 4.8 Simple present and present continuous in contrast 101
- 4.9 Simple past 104
- 4.10 Past continuous 106
- 4.11 *Used* to and *would* for past actions 107
- 4.12 Present perfect 108
- 4.13 Present perfect and simple past in contrast 113
- 4.14 Present perfect continuous 115
- 4.15 Past perfect 116
- 4.16 Past perfect continuous 117
- 4.17 Past tenses in contrast 117
- 4.18 Future with *will* and BE *going to* 117
- 4.19 Present tenses for future time 118
- 4.20 Present tense for future time in subordinate clauses 119
- 4.21 Future continuous 120
- 4.22 Future perfect 120
- 4.23 Future perfect continuous 120
- 4.24 Future in the past 121
- 4.25 Tense choice and verb choice 122
- 4.26 Usage guide Simple present for reporting what an author says 124
- 4.27 Usage guide Simple present with performative verbs 124
- 4.28 Usage guide Avoiding unanchored past tenses 124
- 4.29 Usage guide Past forms in unreal conditionals and after *wish* 124
- 4.30 Usage guide Continuous tenses with stative verbs 125
- 4.31 Usage guide Continuous tenses for change over time 125
- 4.32 Usage guide Continuous tenses with verbs that describe momentary actions 125
- 4.33 Usage guide Continuous tenses with *always* to express emotion 125
- 4.34 Usage guide Place adverbials and *-ing* phrases indicating "at the same time" 126
- 4.35 Usage guide Using future-oriented verbs 126
- 4.36 Usage guide Understanding time reference in reduced clauses 126
- 4.37 Usage guide Tenses in generalizations 127
- 4.38 Usage guide Marking tense shifts 128
- Test yourself 128
- 4.39 Problems with tenses 130

Chapter 5: Passive and active voice 135

- 5.1 Passive and active voice in context 137
- 5.2 Comparing active and passive 137
- 5.3 Passive voice in different tenses and with modal auxiliaries 138
- 5.4 Indicating the agent with a *by* phrase 139
- 5.5 Visualizing the relationship between active and passive 140

5.6	Which verbs can be passive?	142
5.7	Verbs that are never passive	143
	5.7.1 Intransitive verbs to avoid using in the passive voice	143
	5.7.2 Verb + preposition combinations that allow passive voice	143
5.8	Avoiding the extra BE problem	144
5.9	Ergative verbs	145
5.10	Uses of the passive voice	145
5.11	Stative passives	147
5.12	Words like *bore, bored,* and *boring*	149
	5.13 Usage guide Passive voice and the dictionary	151
	5.14 Usage guide Choosing passive or active	152
	5.15 Usage guide Phrases like *is said to be*	153
5.16	Problems with passive and active voice	154

Chapter 6: Gerunds and infinitives 157

6.1	Gerunds and infinitives in context	159
6.2	What are gerunds and infinitives?	159
6.3	Gerunds and infinitives in sentences	160
6.4	Gerund subjects	161
6.5	Gerunds after prepositions	162
6.6	Gerunds after verbs: *enjoy doing something*	163
6.7	Infinitive subjects, delayed infinitive subjects, and infinitives after BE	165
6.8	Common expressions with empty *it*	165
6.9	Empty it as an object	165
6.10	Verb (+ object) + infinitive: *tend to do something, allow someone to*	168
6.11	Verbs + gerund OR infinitive: *remember, try, like,* etc.	171
6.12	Verb + object + bare infinitive	171
6.13	Causative HAVE	172
	6.13.1 *Have someone do something*: active complements	172
	6.13.2 *Have something done*: passive complements	172
	6.13.3 *Get someone to do something, get something done*	172
6.14	Perception verbs + object + bare infinitive	174
6.15	*Too* and *enough* + infinitive	178
6.16	Adjectives like *easy* + infinitive	179
6.17	*Wh* words + infinitives	179
6.18	Relative clause type infinitives	180
6.19	Implied subjects and phrases like *for someone to do something*	180
6.20	Passive gerunds and infinitives	183
6.21	Perfect gerunds and infinitives	183
6.22	Noun + *of* + gerund: *The process of learning*	185
6.23	Nouns and adjectives with infinitive complements	185
6.24	Usage guide Expressing probability: *be likely to* and *be sure to*	186
6.25	Usage guide *Prevent someone from doing* something, *look forward to doing something*	188
6.26	Usage guide Three patterns: *Have difficulty walking, go shopping, stand waiting*	188
6.27	Usage guide Implied subjects of gerunds: *I appreciate your asking*	188
6.28	Usage guide Gerunds and infinitives and lexical grammar	190
6.29	Problems with gerunds and infinitives	191

Chapter 7: **Noun clauses and reporting** 195

7.1	Noun clauses in context	197
7.2	What are noun clauses?	197
7.3	Noun clauses with *that* or no marker	198
7.4	Noun clauses beginning with *wh* words	199
	7.4.1 Embedded questions	199
	7.4.2 *Whether* and *if*	199
	7.4.3 Punctuation	199
	7.4.4 Noun clauses that are like relative clauses	199
	7.4.5 Grammatical roles of *wh* clauses	199
	7.4.6 *Wh* words + infinitives	200
	7.4.7 Verbs that often introduce *wh* clauses	200
7.5	Noun clauses as subjects and delayed subjects	203
7.6	*That* clauses after BE	204
7.7	*That* clauses after verbs	206
	7.7.1 Verb + *that* clause: *know that you're ready*	206
	7.7.2 Verb + indirect object + *that* clause: *tell them that you're ready*	206
	7.7.2a Verbs with an optional indirect object after *to*	206
	7.7.2b Verbs with an optional or required indirect object	206
	7.7.3 Verbs followed by a subjunctive *that* clause: *ask that he leave*	208
	7.7.4 Noun clauses after *wish* and *hope*	208
7.8	*The fact that* and other nouns and adjectives followed by *that* clauses	211
	7.8.1 Nouns that can be followed by a *that* clause – in typical phrases	211
	7.8.2 Adjectives that can be followed by a *that* clause	211
7.9	Reporting with noun clauses and other structures	213
7.10	Tenses, modals, and adverbials in reporting	215
7.11	Reporting questions	216
7.12	Reporting commands and requests	218
7.13	Verbs that are not followed by a *that* clause	218
7.14	Usage guide Reporting special types of speech indirectly	220
7.15	Usage guide *According to* and other phrases for attribution	222
7.16	Usage guide Directly reporting parts of sentences	222
7.17	Usage guide When to include *that*	223
7.18	Usage guide *Feel like, look like, sound like, seem like*	223
7.19	Usage guide *Like it that..., make it clear that...* etc.	223
7.20	Usage guide *Consider, find, regard,* and *see*	223
7.21	Usage guide Recreated or typical speech in academic writing	225
	7.21.1 Usage guide Direct reporting for recreated speech	225
	7.21.2 Usage guide Direct reporting for typical speech	225
7.22	Usage guide Indirect reporting and paraphrasing	225
7.23	Usage guide Noun clauses and lexical grammar	226
7.24	Usage guide Noun clauses and relative clauses	226
7.25	Usage guide Using noun clauses to make your writing more precise	226
7.26	Problems with noun clauses and reporting	227

Chapter 8: **Relative clauses** 231

8.1	Relative clauses in context	233
8.2	What are relative clauses?	233
8.3	Subjects: *a woman who was lost*	234
8.4	Objects: *the woman (whom) we helped*	234
8.5	Objects of a preposition: *the friends we stayed with*	235

8.6	Whose: *a woman whose name I've forgotten*	238
8.7	*Where, when, why and the way*	239
8.8	Restrictive and nonrestrictive clauses	242
8.9	Relative clauses that modify a sentence	244
8.10	Clauses with *of whom* or *of which*	244
8.11	Relative clauses like (*the candidate*) *they say will win*	244
8.12	Reduced relative clauses	245
8.13	Phrases like *a book belonging to the library*	247
8.14	Past participle or *–ing* form?	248
8.15	Appositives	249
8.16	Adjectives and prepositional phrases after nouns	250
8.17	Nonrestrictive reduced clauses	250
8.18	Relative clauses that modify pronouns	251
8.19	Headless relative clauses	252
8.20	Infinitive relatives	252
8.21	Relative clauses and sentence structure	255
8.22	Relative clauses compared to other structures that modify nouns	256
8.23	Usage guide Grammar checkers' advice on *that* and *which*	257
8.24	Usage guide Using relative clauses to express details	257
8.25	Usage guide Avoiding wordy relative clauses	257
8.26	Usage guide Relative clauses in definitions	258
8.27	Usage guide Using relative clauses for a tight writing style	259
8.28	Problems with relative clauses	264

Chapter 9: **Adverbial clauses** 269

9.1	Adverbial clauses in context	271
9.2	Meanings that adverbial clauses express	271
9.3	How do you introduce an adverbial clause?	272
9.4	Conjunctions or prepositions?	272
9.5	Connecting an adverbial clause and a main clause	273
9.6	Avoiding fragments with adverbial clauses	273
9.7	Time clauses	277
	9.7.1 *When, whenever, while, as*	277
	9.7.2 *After, as soon as, before, by the time, since, until*	277
	9.7.3 Reduced adverbial clauses like *after finishing*	278
	9.7.4 Time clauses about the future: *When I will*	278
	9.7.5 Usage guide *When* or *while* or *as*?	279
	9.7.6 Usage guide *Before* and *until*	279
	9.7.7 Usage guide *By the time* and *before*	279
	9.7.8 Usage guide *Two years after* and similar expressions	279
	9.7.9 Usage guide *Since before* and *until after*	280
	9.7.10 Usage guide *Once* and *now that* for stylistic variety	280
9.8	Reason, result and purpose	283
9.9	Reason clauses and phrases	283
	9.9.1 Reason clauses	283
	9.9.2 Reason phrases with prepositions	283
9.10	Result clauses with *so* and *so that*	284
9.11	Result clauses with separate parts	284
9.12	Purpose clauses and phrases: *to, in order to, so (that), so as to*	285
9.13	*For* and *to* in descriptions of the purpose of an object or action	286
9.14	Usage guide *So little* and *so few...that* before a result clause	286
9.15	Usage guide *Such a disaster* and similar expressions	286

9.16	Usage guide	Lexical grammar: *Thank you for not smoking*	287
9.17	Usage guide	Using subordination to write more tightly: *so/such*	288
9.18	Usage guide	Purpose infinitives in front position	288
9.19		Contrast and concession clauses	291
		9.19.1 Contrast clauses	291
		9.19.2 Concession clauses: *although, though, even though, even if*	291
9.20		Manner clauses: *as, just as, as if, as though, like*	292
9.21		Place clauses: *where, wherever, everywhere*	292
9.22	Usage guide	Four ways of expressing contrast	293
9.23	Usage guide	Lexical grammar: *look like / as if / as though*	293
9.24	Usage guide	Reduced clauses of contrast, manner, and place	294
9.25		Problems with adverbial clauses and related structures	298

Chapter 10: **Conditionals** 303

10.1		Conditionals in context	305
10.2		What are conditionals?	305
10.3		Real conditionals	306
10.4		Unreal conditionals	307
10.5		Contrasting real and unreal conditionals	308
10.6		Conditionals with *can, could, may,* and *might*	311
10.7		*Were* in unreal conditionals	312
10.8		*Should* in conditionals	312
10.9		Inversion in *if* clauses	312
10.10		Negative conditions	313
10.11		Limited conditions	313
10.12		*Assuming, given that, in case*	314
10.13		Continuous verb phrases in conditionals	315
10.14		Mixed times in conditionals	315
10.15		When there is no condition: *no matter* and words with *-ever*	316
10.16	Usage guide	Conditionals in paragraphs	317
10.17	Usage guide	*Suppose* and *What if*	317
10.18	Usage guide	Imperatives plus *and* or *or* to express conditions	318
10.19	Usage guide	Special uses of *will* and *would* in *if* clauses	319
10.20	Usage guide	*If I had ...* and *I wish (that) I had*	319
10.21		Problems with conditionals	321

Appendix A Tense overview: a summary of forms and meanings 325
Appendix B Basic punctuation for joining clauses 329
Appendix C Transition expressions word by word 331
Appendix D Principles for ordering information in sentences 337
Glossary of grammar terms 339
Editing guide 349
Index 351

Chapter 1
Thinking about grammar

Chapter 1: **Thinking About Grammar**	1
1.1 The Invisible gorilla	1
1.2 Why pay attention to grammar?	1
1.3 Exercising your grammar brain	2
1.4 Grammar terms	5
1.5 How can you use *Grammar Advantage* effectively?	5

IN THIS CHAPTER

Reflecting on grammar, grammar terms, and concepts that underlie grammar learning

1.1 The Invisible Gorilla

In a well-known experiment, two researchers — Christopher Chabris and Daniel Simons — asked participants to view a video of about 30 seconds. In the video, three people in light T-shirts and three in dark T-shirts pass basketballs back and forth. The participants in the experiment were asked to count the number of times a ball is passed by the players in the light T-shirts.

There is one very unexpected moment in the video: A person wearing a gorilla suit enters the scene, stays for a moment, and walks out. The gorilla is on camera for about nine seconds.

Surprisingly, about half of the participants did not notice the gorilla. The researchers concluded that when we are concentrating on a task it's hard to pay attention to other things.

1.2 Why pay attention to grammar?

Most people, when they speak or write, think mostly about content. Grammar is like the gorilla in the video. It's there, but you don't think about it and maybe don't even notice it.

There are times, however, when it's important to pay attention to grammar. Why? Consider the reasons below. Which do you consider most important?
   a. Inaccurate grammar may distract someone who is trying to understand you.
   b. A good understanding of grammar allows you to express ideas more clearly.
   c. Accurate grammar makes you sound more knowledgeable and professional.

Does inaccurate grammar distract listeners and readers? In casual conversation and writing, it may not. In academic or professional communication, it often does.

Does accurate grammar help you express your ideas more clearly?

Both structure and meaning are relevant

Does a good understanding of grammar contribute to clarity? Sometimes it does. Suppose a class is discussing an article they've read, and a student says, "I agree with the article." There is no mistake in that sentence, but it is not very clear. An article usually includes lots of ideas, so it would be clearer to say "I agree with the author that education should not be competitive," or "I agree that grading is too subjective," or "I agree that grades should be abolished." These more informative sentences use a grammar structure — noun clauses (see Ch. 7) — that allows for clearer communication.

Does accurate grammar make you sound more knowledgeable and professional? Most people would say yes. In the same way, inaccurate grammar may cause you to be judged negatively. Accurate grammar — especially in writing — is often important. On academic assignments, for example, when points may be deducted for grammar problems, accurate grammar is an advantage. To avoid distracting others, to express yourself clearly, and to present yourself well, you need that advantage. That is what *Grammar Advantage* is for.

KEY
Ch. 6 = Chapter 6
Ex. 23 = Exercise 23
5.2 = Chapter 5, section 2
2.14.3 = Chapter 2, section 14, subsection 3
(a) = an example

1.3 Exercising your grammar brain

Exercise your **grammar brain** by thinking about the questions below. The goal of this exercise is to call your attention to things — like the invisible gorilla — that may be easy to miss. Both structure and meaning are relevant.

1. *Talk* and *discuss* are very similar meaning, but they are not always interchangeable. How are they different grammatically? Imagine sentences with them, and you should be able to see a grammatical difference. For a hint, look at 2.4.

2. The first two sentences below are correct. The third and fourth sentences are odd. What is odd about (c) and (d)? How are they different from (a) and (b)? For a hint, look at 9.7.3.
    a. *While playing "Call of Duty" last night, I began to feel bored.*
    b. *After reading it twice, I still didn't understand the paragraph.*
    c. *While playing "Call of Duty" last night, my dog started barking.*
    d. *After reading it twice, the paragraph still wasn't clear.*

3. Match each sentence on the left with one on the right. Think about the meaning. To learn more, see 4.12.
    a. *Mark has worked as a nurse's aide.*   __ That's his job.
    b. *Todd works as a nurse's aide.*   __ It's a temporary job.
    c. *Alex is working as a nurse's aide.*   __ That was once his job.

4. When you learn certain words, you need to learn a preposition as well: *listen* **to**, *depend* **on**, etc. Do you see any examples of such words in these sentences?
    a. *Do you have much contact with your former roommate?*
    b. *In some cultures, people have great respect for the elderly.*
    Now how about these?
    c. *Contact your professor if you need help.*
    d. *We respect them because of their age and experience.*
    With words like *contact* and *respect*, when do you need a preposition and when do you not? For a hint, see 2.4.

5. Compare the ways *however* is used below. One of them is different from the others. Which one? For a hint, see 3.10 and 10.15.
    a. *People are social animals. However, that doesn't mean everyone is equally sociable.*
    b. *We usually eat at home. Recently, however, we've gone out a lot.*
    c. *Some people can't quit smoking, however they try.*

6. The sentences below are usually considered incorrect. Do you know how to correct them? Which mistakes are more serious, in your view? Which are sentences that a native speaker might say or write?
   a. *It don't make no difference.*
   b. *English grammar doesn't works like Spanish grammar.*
   c. *Why you don't listen when I'm talking to you?*
   d. *The lack of jobs in small towns make it necessary for young people to move to cities.*

7. You have probably heard the sentence *Time flies like an arrow.* As a joke, that sentence is sometimes followed by this one: *Fruit flies like a banana.* Does the second sentence make sense to you? Think about the structure.

8. Many words have different forms (2.3). For example, the verb BE includes *is* and *are*. How many other forms of BE can you think of?

   The eight forms of BE appear in the chart below, arranged according to their frequency in books published in the last century.

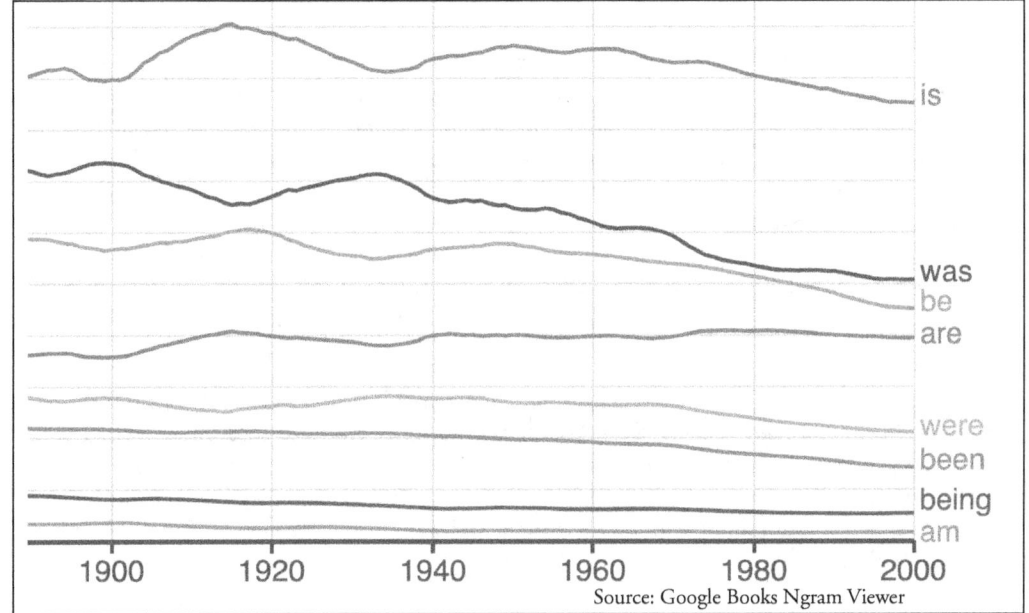

   a. Exercise your grammar brain by writing a paragraph that includes all eight forms. Try to do it with fewer than 100 words. Choose any topic: maybe your family, your interests, or the room you are sitting in right now.

   b. Then think about the grammar knowledge you have that allows you to do that. It's easy to use *is*, but *being* is harder. Why?

   c. Speculate about the ranking of forms in the chart. For example, why do you suppose *am* is so much less frequent than *is*?

Comments

1. To complete the meaning of *talk*, we usually need a preposition, like *about*: *Let's talk about our weekend plans*. *Discuss* does not require a preposition: *Let's discuss our weekend plans.* See 2.4.

2. In (c), it sounds like the dog was playing "Call of Duty." In (d), we expect a word like *I* after the first part: *After reading it twice, I still didn't understand the paragraph.* See 9.7.3.

3. *Mark has worked as a nurse's aide* is a good sentence if we are discussing his work experience; he once had that job. If we say *Todd works as a nurse's aide,* that is currently his job (or one of his jobs). If we say *Alex is working as a nurse's aide*, it's probably a temporary job or maybe he just started. See 4.12, 4.6, and 4.7.

4. When we use *contact* as a noun (*Do you have much contact…*), we use *with*. Similarly, when we use *respect* as a noun (*great respect)*, we use *for*. When these words are used as verbs, we don't use *with* or *for*. See 2.5.

5. *However* is usually used as it is in (a) and (b). See 3.10. *However* has another use in which it expresses the idea of "It doesn't matter" or "under any condition." See 10.15.

6. *It don't make no difference* is a very informal way of saying *It doesn't make any difference.* Though this usage is not appropriate in academic communication, you might hear it in a pop song. The correct version of (b) is *English grammar doesn't **work** like Spanish grammar*. This is not the kind of mistake native usually speakers make. They tend to follow this rule of tense formation (see 4.6) accurately and unconsciously. For (c), the correct way is *Why don't you…* Again, native speakers generally don't make mistakes like this (see 2.13) consistently. The correct version of (d) is *The lack of jobs in small towns makes it necessary for young people to move to cities.* If you don't see the difference, look again. (Don't miss the gorilla!) Also, see section 2.2.5 — especially example (a). Native speakers try to avoid errors like (d), but they don't always succeed.

7. In *Time flies like an arrow*, we are talking about time and how fast it goes. In *Fruit flies like a banana*, we are not talking about fruit. We are talking about fruit flies and something they like. (Try Googling these two sentences and select *images*.) These sentences are a good reminder that a sentence is not just a series of words. Some words go together to make larger units. Exercising your grammar brain — using *Grammar Advantage* — can help you notice things like that, along with other invisible gorillas.

8. a. An example paragraph: *My family **is** very important to me. We have always **been** close. We are not together very often nowadays, but last summer we **were** lucky enough to spend a week together. It **was** the best week of my year. **Being** with my family calms me. When I **am** with them, my worries go away. I hope we can **be** together soon.*

   b. Observations about the forms: The form *being* allows us to use the word as a subject (6.4). *Been* is necessary after *have,* to form a specific tense (section 4.12). *Be* is used because it's the only possible form after *can*. We use *is* after *my family* because *my family* is one thing. (In some varieties of English, it might be *My family are…* Varieties of English differ in many ways.)

   c. Observations about the ranking: Since we tend to talk a lot about ourselves and how things affect us, we might expect *am* to be higher in the ranking. However, this chart is based on books, which generally deal with larger topics in an impersonal way. The high ranking of *is* reminds us that in some ways it is the most versatile form of BE. For example, we use it is in expressions like *It's easy to…* (6.7 and 6.8) and *It's important that…* (7.5), and after subjects like *Being with my family* and *Living alone* (6.4).

1.4 Grammar terms

If you read a paragraph filled with words like *assets, liabilities, profit, valuation, cash flow*, and *bottom line,* you probably recognize the topic as finance. Grammar, like any topic, has its own terminology. There are terms for words (*noun, verb, preposition*), structures (*noun phrase, clause, relative clause*) and processes (*negation, modification*). Of course, the most important part of grammar is knowing how to use it, not knowing special terms. However, if you know some terminology you will have an easier time understanding the rules that can help you speak and write more accurately. And when you have a question about grammar, knowing some terminology may help you find the answer.

The word cloud below shows the most frequently used words in the glossary at the end of this book. Which grammar terms do you recognize? (There are ordinary words from examples as well.) What do they refer to? As you encounter terms in this book, consult the glossary for help.

[word cloud with terms including: another, people, comma, etc, parts, pronoun, object, idea, verb, words, before, phrases, person, continuous, clause, explained, forms, word, subject, tenses, noncount, form, know, Chapter, child, action, singular, attributive, some, time, Modify, See, work, example, worked, main, active, Perfect, though, Present, conjunctions, use, having, history, mistake, voice, written, after, adverbs, noun, term, more, different, infinitive, place, any, go, parallel, name, live, participle, adjectives, take, sometimes, stayed, adjective, refers, hard, idiomatic, agreement, wrong, plus, passive, followed, good, called, like, call, follows, past, information, Most, letter, pronouns, about, language, students, plural, clauses, nouns, used, relative, phrase, Possessive, because, meaning, preposition, parallelism, sentence]

1.5 How can you use Grammar Advantage effectively?

Understanding key features will help you get the most out of this book. Skim the table of contents. Notice the titles of the major parts, including the appendices at the end. Notice how the book is organized and try to identify key features. The questions that follow will call your attention to some of those features.

The answers are on the right — but try to answer each question without looking at the answer!

1. Look at Ch. 2, on sentence structure. What section is about linking verbs, and how many subdivisions are in that section? | Section 2.8 is about linking verbs, and it includes three subsections (2.8.1, 2.8.2, and 2.8.3). Sections of the book often have subsections, and some subsections are further subdivided. It's helpful to be aware of how the parts relate to each other.

KEY
Ch. 6 = Chapter 6
Ex. 23 = Exercise 23
5.2 = Chapter 5, section 2
2.14.3 = Chapter 2, section 14, subsection 3
(a) = an example

ANSWER KEY
For answers to exercises, go to grammaradvantage.com.

2. Here is a line of explanation from 2.8.2: After a verb at the end of a clause, we sometimes use an adjective (a), an adjective phrase (b), or a participial phrase (c, d), even if the verb is not usually used as a linking verb. What do the letters in parentheses refer to?

   The letters refer to the examples in the box below the explanation. An adjective, *young*, appears in (a). An adjective phrase, *ready to win*, appears in (b). A participial phrase, *satisfied with our efforts*, appears in (c), and another participial phrase, *wearing a gorilla suit*, appears in (d).

3. Look at Ch. 3, on transition expressions. What is the title of section 3.1?

   The title is "Transition expressions in context." Most of the chapters begin with a section like this, followed by a brief exercise intended to introduce the topic and remind you of what you may already know about it.

4. Look at Ch. 4, on tenses, and find section 4.26. What two words appear above the title of that section?

   Usage guide. In most chapters, the final sections are labeled *usage guide*. Usually these parts present information about how we use particular structures in writing. Sometimes they just present finer points about grammar. Sometimes they are about points of style or vocabulary.

5. Look at Ch. 5, on active and passive voice. What do you find in the very last section?

   Problems with active and passive voice. Each chapter ends with a section like this, based on errors students often make.

6. In Ch. 6, on gerunds and infinitives, find section 6.6. What do you see after each boldface verb in the box?

   After each boldface verb, there is a gerund (e.g. *winning*) or a gerund phrase (e.g. *registering early*) to remind you that the verbs in this box are gerund-taking verbs. Especially in Ch. 6 and 7, you will find boxes like these. Usually they are lists of verbs that are followed by particular structures.

7. In Ch.7, on noun clauses and reporting, find Ex. 20. What are you supposed to add in Ex. 20?

   You are supposed to add punctuation — that is, periods, commas, quotation marks, and so on, along with words in the blanks. The sentences come directly from the preceding section, 6.9, so this type of exercise may seem easy. However, it can be a useful way of testing yourself. It's also a good reminder that punctuation is important.

8. In Ch. 8, on relative clauses, find Ex. 25. There are eight sentences in this exercise. How many of them include a mistake?

   Only two or three include a mistake, so when you do this exercise, you are mostly reading correct sentences. That may seem odd. Why doesn't every sentence include a mistake, so that you get more practice? In fact, reading correct examples attentively is an important kind of practice. To remember correct patterns, it's helpful to see lots of examples.

9. In Ch. 9, on adverbial clauses, find Ex. 19. In item 1, which answer looks best to you? How about in item 2?

   Option (c) is the only correct answer for item 1. For item 2, the first three options are all possible. (That does not mean they are exactly the same, but they are all possible.) It's important to notice that in some multiple-choice exercises, more than one option is correct. Read all instructions carefully.

10. Look at Ch. 10, on conditionals. What kind of sentence do you see in the cartoon that begins the chapter?

    It's one kind of conditional sentence — that is, a sentence consisting of an *if* clause and a main clause. The illustrations that begin each chapter were developed as a connection to the topic of the chapter.

Chapter 2
Sentence Structure

IN THIS CHAPTER

Sentence parts and their arrangement

word forms

completing the meaning of a verb

avoiding fragments, comma splices, and run-ons

Chapter 2
Sentence Structure

Chapter 2: Sentence structure 9
- 2.1 What is sentence structure? 12
- 2.2 Subjects and verbs 13
  - 2.2.1 Don't omit the subject 14
  - 2.2.2 Don't add an extra subject 14
  - 2.2.3 Don't omit the verb 14
  - 2.2.4 Avoid mismatches 14
  - 2.2.5 Subject-verb agreement 16
- 2.3 Word forms and parts of speech 17
  - 2.3.1 Word forms 17
  - 2.3.2 Parts of speech 18
  - 2.3.3 Avoiding word form mistakes 19
- 2.4 Completing the meaning of a verb: object or prepositional phrase? 21
  - 2.4.1 Verbs with objects (transitive verbs) 21
  - 2.4.2 Necessary objects 22
  - 2.4.3 Verbs without objects (intransitive verbs) 23
  - 2.4.4 Common intransitive verbs with typical prepositional phrases ...23
  - 2.4.5 Sometimes transitive, sometimes intransitive 26
- 2.5 Prepositions after nouns but not verbs: *Contact* or *contact with*? 27
- 2.6 Two-object verbs 30
  - 2.6.1 *Give someone something / give something to someone* 30
  - 2.6.2 *Buy someone something / buy something for someone* 30
  - 2.6.3 Typical patterns for the verb *ask* 30
  - 2.6.4 *Cost, save,* and *take* 30
- 2.7 Avoiding verb completion mistakes 33
- 2.8 Linking verbs 34
  - 2.8.1 Linking verbs followed by adjectives and other structures 34
  - 2.8.2 Sentences like *Mozart died young* 34
  - 2.8.3 BE *like* 34
- 2.9 *Look like, seem like, sound like* 35
- 2.10 Phrasal verbs (*go on, put off, run out of,* etc.) 36
- 2.11 Empty *it* subjects 38
- 2.12 *There is* (existential *there*) 39
- 2.13 Inversion 41
  - 2.13.1 Reversing the order of a subject and auxiliary 41
  - 2.13.2 Inversion with fronted negative elements 41
- 2.14 Questions 42
  - 2.14.1 *Yes/no* questions 42
  - 2.14.2 *Wh* questions 42
  - 2.14.3 No inversion in subordinate clauses 42
  - 2.14.4 *What is it like? / How is it?* 43
  - 2.14.5 Problems with questions 44

2.15	Commands, requests, and exclamatory sentences	46
	2.15.1 Three sentence types	46
	2.15.2 Commands	46
	2.15.3 Exclamatory sentences	46
2.16	Pronouns and reference	47
	2.16.1 Reference	47
	2.16.2 Pronoun forms	47
	2.16.3 Pronoun agreement	47
	2.16.4 Clear reference	47
	2.16.5 Avoiding repetitiveness	48
2.17	Sentences and clauses	49
	2.17.1 Two kinds of clauses: Independent and subordinate	49
	2.17.2 Building sentences with subordination	49
	2.17.3 Building sentences with coordination	50
2.18	Parallelism (parallel structure)	52
	2.18.1 *And*	52
	2.18.2 Avoid faulty parallelism	52
	2.18.3 The algebra of coordination	53
	2.18.4 *But* and *or* with a variety of structures	53
2.19	Fragments, run-ons, and comma splices	55
2.20	Adverbs	56
2.21	Time expressions in the form of noun phrases	57
2.22	Usage guide Beginning and ending sentences	58
	2.22.1 Beginning with an adverbial	58
	2.22.2 Old before new	58
	2.22.3 Beginning with a noun phrase	59
	2.22.4 Beginning with *For*	59
	2.22.5 Beginning with an *–ing* word	59
2.23	Usage guide Sentence variety in your writing	60
	2.23.1 Traditional sentence types	60
	2.23.2 Avoiding choppiness	60
2.24	Usage guide Avoiding gender bias in pronoun choice	61
2.25	Usage guide Impersonal *you* and *one* in generalizations	61
2.26	Usage guide Avoiding shifting points of view	61
2.27	Problems with sentence structure	62

KEY

Ch. 6 = Chapter 6
Ex. 23 = Exercise 23
5.2 = Chapter 5, section 2
2.14.3 = Chapter 2, section 14, subsection 3
(a) = an example

2.1 What is sentence structure?

In this text, sentence structure includes:

- Parts of sentences and their arrangement
- Word forms (*cup, cups; succeed, succeeds, succeeded, succeeding*) and parts of speech (*succeed, success, successful, successfully*)
- Types of sentences, including questions
- Ways of joining sentences and sentence parts
- Relationships between parts: concepts like transitivity, reference, and agreement

This chapter uses grammar terms such as *subject, verb, noun,* and *clause*. Some terms are defined, but you may need to refer to the glossary at the end of the book.

HIGH PRIORITY

■ **Exercise 1** Read the passage. Based on what you already know, underline the verbs (like *imagine* and *are*) or verb phrases (like *are participating* and *is going to leave*). (If you prefer, read 2.2 first.)

The Marshmallow Experiment

Imagine that you are seven years old. You are participating in an experiment. A researcher greets you and shows you into a small room. In the room there is a marshmallow. The marshmallow is for you, but here is the interesting part: The researcher tells you that she is going to leave you alone in the room for a while. You can eat the marshmallow right away, or you can wait until she gets back. If you wait until she gets back, you will get a second marshmallow. What do you do? Do you eat the marshmallow right away?

An experiment like this, known informally as the marshmallow experiment, was conducted decades ago at Stanford University. It turned out that some children ate the marshmallow right away, while others were able to wait. In other words, some sought instant gratification, and some delayed it. Years later, the researchers followed up on the participants. They found that the children who delayed gratification were in general more successful than those who ate the marshmallow right away. By a variety of measures, including SAT scores, they seemed more competent. The experiment seemed to provide evidence that the ability to delay gratification may predict a child's success.

Over the years, the marshmallow experiment ranked among the most famous examples of research in the social sciences, a common topic in psychology textbooks.

As it turns out, however, the marshmallow experiment was flawed. A more recent study, similar in design, had a much larger sample of children and looked at many other factors that might influence success. One magazine report concluded:

> Ultimately the new study finds limited support for the idea that being able to delay gratification leads to better outcomes. Instead, it suggests that the capacity to hold out for a second marshmallow is shaped in large part by a child's social and economic background — and in turn, that background, not the ability to delay gratification, is what's behind kids' long-term success. — The Atlantic, June 2018

Still, the conclusion of the original experiment — that being able to delay gratification is linked to later success in life — remains fixed in the public mind. Even when research is supplanted by later research, it takes a while for the public to catch up.

2.2 Subjects and verbs

KEY
(a)-(f) = examples in the box below
Ch. 6 = Chapter 6

- Verbs name actions (*participate, work*), states (*believe, want*), and relationships (*correlate, own*).

- Usually a verb has a subject before it. In (a)-(f) the subjects are underlined.

- The subject names the person or thing that does (sometimes experiences) the action.

- The subject may be a noun (*children*), a noun phrase or noun clause (*an experiment like this, what I want*) or a subject pronoun (*you, it, they*).

- Gerunds (d) and infinitives (Ch. 6) can also be subjects.

- We use the term *clause* for a combination of subject + verb and accompanying words. Many sentences include more than one clause (e, f). Each clause has a subject and verb.

- You can often identify a subject by asking "Who or what does (causes, experiences) the action?"

a. <u>You</u> are participating in an experiment.	Who is participating? *You.*
b. <u>The researchers</u> followed up….	Who followed up…? *The researchers.*
c. <u>Common sense</u> tells us…	What tells us? *Common sense.*
d. <u>Arguing about this</u> is unproductive.	What is unproductive? *Arguing about this.*
e. <u>What happened next</u> surprised us.	What surprised us? *What happened next.*
f. <u>Kids</u> like art because <u>art</u> is fun.	Who likes art? *Kids.* What is fun? *Art.*

■ **Exercise 2** Underline the complete subjects in the sentences below, and double-underline the verbs that go with them. Identifying the subject means identifying the main word of the subject and the parts that modify it. (In the first two sentences, the main words are in **boldface**.) When you underline the verb, include both auxiliary verbs and main verbs (as in the first sentence, with *was…used*).

HIGH PRIORITY

In the 1960s and 70s, <u>the **term** "generation gap"</u> <u><u>was often used</u></u> to refer to the differences between young people in the U.S. and their parents' generation. <u>Many young **people**</u> felt distant from their parents because of differences in ideas about politics, social issues, and popular culture. Since then, conflicts between generations have diminished in many ways. Child-rearing experts in the late 20th century encouraged parents to be like friends to their children. Thanks to technology, young people and their parents are able to contact each other easily at any time. On any college campus, the students you see texting or talking on cell phones are often communicating with Mom or Dad. Fifty years ago, closeness of this kind was less common. In addition, the youth-centered nature of U.S. life has reduced many generational differences. In many families, parents and their teenaged children dress in similar ways, listen to the same music, and enjoy the same movies and videos on YouTube.

2.2.1 **Avoid the mistake of omitting a subject.** In sentences with more than one clause, remember that each verb needs a subject (except for nonfinite verbs; see Ch. 6). A single subject may go with more than one verb, however, and the subject does not need to be repeated (c).

a. The test was hard ~~because included~~ two essay questions.	➤ *it* included (9.9.)
b. People are always doing things ~~that shouldn't~~ be doing when they're driving, like texting.	➤ that they shouldn't... (8.3.)
c. Regular exercise builds strength and prolongs life.	*It* is not needed before *prolongs*.

2.2.2 **Avoid the mistake of adding an extra subject.** Even after long and complex subjects, don't add a pronoun (d). This mistake often occurs when the subject is a gerund (e); see 6.4. An appositive (8.15) may follow a subject (f), but do not include a subject pronoun after it.

d. The salaries of top executives at major companies have grown dramatically. (~~they~~ have)
e. Adapting to a new culture takes time. (~~Adapting to a new culture it takes time.~~)
f. Kemal Ataturk, the founder of the modern Turkish state, was born in 1881. (~~he~~ was born)

2.2.3. **Avoid the mistake of omitting the verb.** One common mistake involves omitting a BE verb (g, h, i). A word like *absent* (*afraid, aware, away, back*) is not a verb (i, j). Put a verb before it.

g. The earthquake that struck Nepal in April of 2015 one of the worst in memory.	➤ was one of...
h. Computer games are exciting. That why so many people play them.	➤ That is why / That's why
i. If you absent on the day of a test, you need to make it up.	➤ If you are absent...
j. When I back to my country, I plan to get a job.	➤ When I go back to / When I am back in

2.2.4 **Avoid mismatches.** The **predicate** of a sentence *is the part that follows the subject. It usually begins with a verb and may continue with other words that complete the meaning.* The subject and the predicate *must make sense together.* Otherwise, you *have a* **mismatch**. (The predicates in the preceding sentences are in italics.) More generally, the beginning of a sentence must match with the ending.

k. WRONG: Traveling abroad can learn about other cultures.	RIGHT: Traveling abroad can **teach you about** other cultures. Traveling abroad can **introduce you to** other cultures.	The subject *traveling abroad* (a gerund phrase, 6.4) works well with *teach you about* and *introduce you to*, but not with *learn about*.
	Traveling abroad, **you** can learn about other cultures.	The phrase *Traveling abroad* introduces the sentence as an adverbial phrase (Ch. 9). The subject *you* works well with *learn*.
l. WRONG: Working together is a great idea. Good teamwork can complete a project in a short time.	RIGHT: A good team can complete... With good teamwork, we can complete...	Teamwork cannot "complete" work. A team can. *We* provides a subject that works well with *complete*.

Chapter 2 — Sentence structure

■ Exercise 3

A. Identify places where a subject should be added (2.2.1), an extra subject should be omitted (2.2.2), or a verb should be added (2.2.3). Fix one problem in each item (1–8).

1. The best vacations are vacations that take you completely away from your work and other daily concerns, so that don't even think about your responsibilities and problems.

2. In this school, children start studying a foreign language at the age of six, because is much easier to learn a language at that age. Waiting until you are 12 or 13 makes learning a language much harder.

3. I really like talking to strangers. People that I have never met before they have such interesting experiences.

4. Lots of English words are hard to spell. For example, the word *know* it starts with a letter that is not even pronounced.

5. Growing up in a family with lots of brothers and sisters they helped me learn how to get along with others and speak up for myself.

6. Most U.S. states have a senate and a house of representatives, just like the national government. The only exception Nebraska, which has only one legislative body.

7. Are you the kind of person who likes following a routine, or do you prefer a life in which every day different from every other day?

8. Something is wrong with my laptop. I can't print. On the other hand, maybe something wrong with my printer.

B. Examine each predicate in *italics*. Most of the items have a mismatch; that is, the beginning of a sentence does not work well with the end (2.2.4). Identify the sentences with mismatches. Notice that some items have more than one sentence. Be prepared to discuss possible revisions.

9. Knowing a second language *will have lots of job opportunities*.

10. A different language sometimes *requires you to think in different ways*.

11. Better employment opportunities *can get a higher salary*.

12. A second language *can talk to a whole new world of people from other countries*.

13. Full-time students who have part-time jobs *might be difficult*.

14. Children *should learn to develop patience*. A patient person *works more carefully*. Impatience *is more likely to make mistakes*.

15. Writing a research paper *is not easy* and *sometimes need to spend a lot of time at the library*.

16. Minneapolis *gets cold in the winter* and *sometimes have to wear a heavy jacket even in March*.

17. The most challenging class I had in college *was taking my first philosophy course*.

18. After five years, I *quit my job* at IBM and *started my own business*. Running my own company *enjoyed my work much more*.

2.2.5 Subject-verb agreement

- In present tenses (and with *was* and *were*), verbs agree in number with subjects. Use plural verbs (*are, were, sit*) with plural subjects (*students, they, my sister and I*). Use singular verbs (*is, was, sits*) with singular subjects (*she, the earth*) and uncountable subjects (*information, homework*).
- To decide whether the verb should be plural or singular, look at the main noun in the subject, not necessarily the noun that is closest to the verb (a, b).
- Some nouns that look plural are not (c). Some nouns that look singular are not (d). *Everything, everyone*, and phrases like *every book* and *every student in the class* are singular (e).

a.	WRONG: *The lack of jobs cause many young people to leave rural areas.*	➤ *The lack...**causes**... Lack*, the main noun in the subject, is not plural.
b.	WRONG: *Weaknesses in the economy has led to a loss of population.*	➤ *Weaknesses...**have**.... Weaknesses*, the main noun in the subject, is plural.
c.	WRONG: *The news today are all about a hurricane.*	➤ *The news today **is** all about... News* is not plural. (It is uncountable.)
d.	WRONG: *The police is often in the news. Most people is honest.*	➤ *The police **are**... Most people **are**... Police* and *people* are plural.
e.	WRONG: *Everyone / Every book / Everything are / were / have...*	➤ *Every....**is / was / has**....* Use a singular verb with subjects like *everyone* and *every book*.

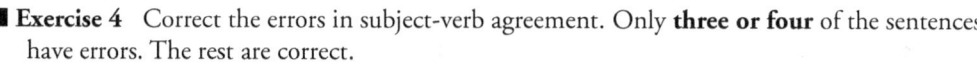

■ **Exercise 4** Correct the errors in subject-verb agreement. Only **three or four** of the sentences have errors. The rest are correct.

1. The cost of textbooks has risen a lot in recent years.
2. People in small towns are often quick to notice when a stranger appears.
3. If you call 911, sometimes the police is there within minutes.
4. The lack of job opportunities in small towns make it necessary for young people to move to cities.
5. The most important news in the newspaper is usually on the first page.
6. Although developments in technology have made it easier for people in rural areas to take advantage of higher education, people in those areas still generally lag behind urban people in education.
7. The average age at which young women get married has risen during the past several decades.
8. In 1969, the average age for young women to get married was 19; now it is closer to 30.
9. These days when an employee return to work after a vacation, he or she often finds an in-box full of hundreds of email messages.
10. Email has made office communication easier, but some employees feel that it has become a burden.

2.3 Word forms and parts of speech

2.3.1 Word forms Many mistakes involve choosing the wrong word. If you write *They said me to wait,* for example, you have a **word choice** mistake. A teacher may flag the error with WC or WW, for *wrong word*. It should be *They told me to wait*. (7.12)

Other mistakes have the right word but the wrong **form**. If you write *Thank you for tell me*, you have a **word form** mistake (sometimes marked WF). It should be *Thank you for telling me*. (6.5)

An important aspect of sentence structure is choosing the right forms. That applies to subject-verb agreement (2.2.5), verb tenses (Ch. 4), and many other topics. This section does not offer a comprehensive look at word forms (online resources can help), but word forms are relevant throughout the book. Here is some advice on using word forms correctly:

1. When you edit your work, look carefully for parts that mark word forms, especially *–ed*, *-ing*, and *-s*. Are they correct? Are there places where you need to add them?

2. Become aware of your word form "enemies" — mistakes you often make. Create a list of word form problems and solutions and make an effort to unlearn bad habits.

3. Learn the main forms of irregular verbs (verbs that don't use *-ed* for past tense): *speak, spoke spoken; fall, fell, fallen; feel, felt, felt; put, put, put,* etc. These forms are sometimes called principle parts. Dictionaries and online sources can help. Look for a list of the most common irregular verbs. A list of all irregular verbs will include some that you don't need.

4. Use spell-checking — as long as you use it with careful judgment. It will flag potential problems and sometimes offer correct suggestions. For example, the sentences in Exercise 4 in this chapter include two word-form mistakes related to subject-verb agreement. Microsoft Word's spelling and grammar check feature flags one of the two. Microsoft Word almost always has good advice for correcting mistakes like *are participate* (⟶ *participating*), *may has* (⟶ *may* have) want to *left* (⟶ *leave*). Google docs and Word both correctly pick out the problem in *Thank you for tell me*, suggesting *for telling*, the correct way. Sometimes the suggestions are wrong, but often they are helpful.

■ **Exercise 5** Find some of your written work — like a paper for a class — and check it with a grammar checker. Look especially at word forms (including subject-verb agreement). Does the program seem to offer useful suggestions? Discuss your results with a friend or a teacher.

2.3.2 Parts of speech *Parts of speech* is the traditional term for major categories of words, like nouns (*difference*), verbs (*differ*), adjectives (*different*), adverbs (*differently*), and prepositions (*at, in, of, to,* etc.). Part of learning a word is learning its part-of-speech category. When you learned the word *absent*, for example, you probably learned that it is an adjective and that it also has a noun form. So you can correctly say *I was absent* and *I've had three absences*. (Because *absent* is not a verb, you can't say *When did you absent?*) Some key points about part-of-speech categories appear below.

a. *Please make an **effort** to comply.* (N) (*Please ~~effort~~*) b. *I want to **succeed**.* (V) (*want to ~~success~~*) c. *Smoking is not a **healthy** habit.* (Adj) (*~~health~~*)	Use a dictionary to be sure you don't misuse a word because you have a mistaken idea about whether it is a noun, a verb, or an adjective.
d. *What's your **answer** to question 3?* (N) e. *Please **answer** the question.* (V)	Sometimes the same word is used for more than one category. Notice that the noun *answer* but not the verb *answer* is followed by a preposition. See 2.5.
f. *Keep your **focus** on the future.* (N) g. *You should **focus** on the future.* (V)	Sometimes the same word is used for more than one category, and both are followed by a preposition. See 2.4.4.
h. *What's your **analysis**?* (N) i. *How do you **analyze** the situation?* (V) j. *You need to be more **analytical**.* (Adj) k. *Try to think **analytically**.* (Adv)	Often different words are needed. The end (*sis, ize/yze, al, ally,* etc.) may give clues to what kind of word it is. Online sources have lists of these suffixes and words with them.
l. *You need to support your **argument**.* (N) m. *You need to **argue** effectively.* (V) n. *It's an **argumentative** essay.* (Adj) o. *That's an **arguable** point.* (Adj) p. *Read the chapter about **argumentation**.* (N)	The same part (like *argu*, called a root) can appear in more than one verb, noun, or adjective. To understand the differences, you need to consult a dictionary.
q. *What are the **effects** of this drug?* (N) r. *It **affects** appetite by suppressing it.* (V) s. *It's an **effective** drug.* (Adj) t. *The **effect** of an earthquake is widespread.* u. (N) v. *Earthquakes **affect** everything for miles.* (V) *Earthquakes are **powerful**. (~~effective~~)* (Adj)	Even if you recognize a word's root (like *effect*), it may be necessary to consult a dictionary to understand related words. Though the adjective *effective* can describe a drug, it can't describe an earthquake, because *effective* is used for good things.

2.3.3 Avoiding word form mistakes To avoid word form problems, remember four things. First, word form choices may depend on what category of word (what part of speech) is needed (a-d). Second, they may depend on the similarity of parts that are joined (e-i). Third, they may depend on an element earlier in the sentence which determines the form(s) that must follow (j-r). Finally, think about the meaning (s, t).

Choose the right category of word (part of speech).	
a. *What is the **difference** between weather and climate?*	A noun is required: *difference*
b. *How do weather and climate **differ**?*	A verb is required: *differ*.
c. *How is weather **different** from climate?*	An adjective is required: *different*.
d. *The words are used **differently**.*	An adverb is required: *differently*. (2.20)
Make joined parts similar.	
e. *This library is open to everyone, it doesn't cost anything, and it has convenient hours.*	The elements are independent clauses.
f. *This phone is **faster** but **more expensive**.*	The elements are comparative.
g. *She **has an M.B.A.** and **speaks Arabic**.*	The elements are predicates.
h. ***Exercising**, **eating well**, and **getting enough sleep** are the keys to physical health.*	The elements are gerund phrases. (Ch. 6).
i. *He loves to sleep late and have breakfast in bed.*	The phrases are infinitives (*to* does not have to be repeated).
Pay attention to how **earlier words** (underlined) **determine forms of later words** (in boldface).	
j. *How does this drug **work**?*	Only a base form can follow DO, a modal auxiliary (4.4), the infinitive marker *to* (Ch. 6), and sequences like *made them* and *let me* (6.12).
k. *This drug might **work**.*	
l. *They made me **work** overtime.*	
m. *They let me **work** at my own pace.*	
n. *She has **published** five papers.*	Only a past participle can follow the auxiliary HAVE (4.12) or the passive auxiliary BE (Ch. 5).
o. *She has **written** two books of poetry.*	
p. *Most popular books **are written** in a simple style.*	
q. *The company is **publishing** two new books next week.*	Only an *–ing* form can follow BE as in a continuous verb phrase (4.7).
r. *…in addition to **reading**… get used to **reading**…. …after **reading**… …by **reading**…. …for **reading**…*	After a preposition (including the preposition *to*), a verb must be transformed into a gerund (6.5).
Think of the meaning.	
s. *He told me to sit down and **explain** what I wanted.*	He told me to explain.
t. *He told me to sit down and **explained** what he wanted.*	He explained.

Exercise 6 Using the hints before the sentence, complete each sentence with an appropriate form of the word. To check your work, look at the box in 2.3.3. (The sentences are the same.)

1. ans.....	Please _____ the question. What's your _____ to question 3?
2. foc...	Keep your _____ on the future. You should _____ on the future.
3. analy...	What's your _____ ? How do you _____ the situation? You need to be more _____ Try to think _____ .
4. arg...	You need to support your _____ . You need to _____ effectively. It's an _____ essay. That's an _____ point. Read the chapter about _____ .
5. -ffect	What are the _____ of this drug? It _____ appetite by suppressing it. It's very _____ .

Exercise 7 Complete the sentences with the words provided. In each numbered item, use one pair of words. Think carefully about which word goes in which blank. The first word in each pair is a noun. The other word is an adjective or a verb.

accuracy, accurate   emphasis, emphasize   response, respond   success, succeed
bias, biased   evaluation, evaluate   summary, summarize   validity, valid

1. In a paragraph, you can __ your main point by putting it in a topic sentence at the beginning. Sometimes a concluding sentence adds __.

2. Most students want grades that show they have learned a lot. In other words, they aim for academic __ . In order to __ academically, you need to be a critical reader.

3. Critical readers try to judge a writer's work as they read it. In other words, they __ it. Their __ depends partly on their expectations.

4. Students are often asked to write a short __ of something they have read. When you __ something, you rewrite it in a short way, eliminating details.

5. A summary has to correctly represent the material that it summarizes. In other words, it must be __. __ is a fundamental requirement of summarizing.

6. Most writing teachers ask students to do more than just summarize. They want students to share their own thinking after they read something – in other words, to __ to it. A common assignment asks students to write a summary and a __.

7. Argumentation is the art of persuading readers that you have a __ point. The __ of your argument depends on factors like how carefully you have assessed causes and effects.

8. Writers are supposed to be fair, avoiding __. If you think a writer is not presenting facts fairly, you might say the writer is __.

2.4 Completing the meaning of a verb: Object or prepositional phrase?

2.4.1 Verbs with objects

- We can complete the meaning of a verb in different ways.
- **Transitive** verbs allow an **object**. An object is a noun (*children*), a noun phrase (*the marshmallow on the table*), a noun clause (*what I want*), or an object pronoun (*you, me, him, her, it, us, them*) that **directly follows** the verb and completes its meaning.
- You can often identify an object by asking a question like "Who or what does [the subject] [verb]?"
- We can also complete the meaning of a verb by adding a prepositional phrase (a preposition plus a noun or noun phrase; 2.4.4) Though these phrases complete the meaning of a verb, they are not considered objects.
- In certain structures, especially questions and relative clauses, the object of a verb appears at the beginning instead of immediately after the verb (e, f).
- We do not normally put any words between a verb and its object (g), except when the object is long and/or complex.

a.	*You will get **a tasty marshmallow**.*	What will you get? *A tasty marshmallow.*
b.	*The researchers interviewed **us**.*	Who did they interview? *Us.*
c.	*The experiment provides **evidence that self-control is important**.*	What does the experiment provide? *Evidence that self-control is important.*
d.	*This photo shows **how I used to look**.*	What does it show? *How I used to look.*
e.	***What** does this photo show?*	*What*, at the beginning of the question, is the object of *show*. See 2.14.2
f.	*The photo **that** I took won a prize.*	*That* (= *the photo*), at the beginning of the underlined relative clause, is the object of *took*. See 8.4.
g.	*I understand ~~very well~~ French.*	The object should be at the end: *I understand French very well.* See also 2.20 (p) and (q).
h.	*I understand very well most of the French on menus and airport signs.*	When it is long, the object may come between the verb and its object.

■ **Exercise 8** Which underlined verbs have an object? Underline the objects. Remember that in a phrase like *It happened to me*, there is no object; *to me* is a prepositional phrase.

Art was always important to Sarah Palmer, and so was nature. Wild animals fascinated her. Hats, too: she never went out without a hat. So when Sara died at the age of 101 in 2015, the residents of the small town where she lived honored her in a suitable way. They commissioned a statue by Evo Ard, a local sculptor. He finished the statue in 2016 and it now stands in the town square. At first glance, it appears to be a woman wearing a dress and a hat. When you look more closely, you see that in fact it is a chimpanzee, and the hat is just like one that Sarah often wore. People remember Sarah for her sense of humor, so the statue would no doubt appeal to her. The old men who use the square every day as their own private front yard appreciate it too. As one remarked, "It's the best thing that ever happened to this town!"

2.4.2 Necessary objects Some verbs, such as *eat, practice,* and *read*, may have implied objects. In other words, the object may not be mentioned, but the listener or reader can imagine it.

a. *We usually **eat** around 1:00 p.m. After that I **read** for a while.* (We eat lunch. I read a book.)

However, if an actual object has been mentioned earlier, an implied object is usually not enough. In such a context, an actual object — often a pronoun — is generally necessary. Some verbs, like *enjoy, find, like,* and *put*, almost always require an object.

b. *~ Where's that last cookie? ~ I'm sorry. I ate it.* (~~I ate.~~)
c. *Squirrels are common in the city. You can find them everywhere.* (~~You can find everywhere.~~)
d. *We took a vacation, but we didn't enjoy it / enjoy ourselves.* (~~We didn't enjoy.~~)

To know whether an object is required, you need to know about the individual verb (lexical grammar). With some verbs, like *finish* and *understand*, objects are often optional (i, j), but if you don't omit pronoun objects, you will usually be correct.

e. *Writing this paper was easy. I finished in a day. / I finished it in a day.*
f. *Would you repeat the question? I didn't understand. / I didn't understand it.*

Lexical grammar: the grammar of an individual word

■ **Exercise 9** Add an object pronoun after each verb that needs one. In each item look for just one place where an object is needed. If you are in doubt about a verb, assume that it requires an object. (For object pronouns, see 2.16.2)

1. ~ There was an interesting article on animal rights in today's paper. Did you read it? ~ I noticed, but I wasn't planning to read it till later.

2. Public telephones used to be a common feature of the urban landscape, but today you can hardly find anywhere.

3. Chili is a kind of stew that is famous in lots of places, but people have different ideas about how to make. Usually it includes beef, onions, tomatoes, chili peppers, and beans, but in Texas they make it without beans.

4. Be sure to proofread your paper before you submit. If there are obvious mistakes, you can find at least some of them. Showing your paper to a friend is also a good idea.

5. If you miss a test for a good reason — such as an illness or an emergency — most teachers will let you take at a later date.

6. If you want to benefit from reading for pleasure, it's important to choose books that are appropriate for your level. If you choose a book that's too hard for you, you won't enjoy.

7. Relationships with neighbors are a key factor in making a neighborhood a good place to live. Your next-door neighbors can make your life more secure by keeping an eye on your house when you're not there. If you don't already know, I suggest that you make friends with them as soon as you can.

8. In the animal world, one common form of self-defense is camouflage. An insect, for example, might change its color to match its background so that its enemies can't easily see.

2.4.3 Verbs without objects

Intransitive verbs may be complete all by themselves, with nothing after the verb (a) except optional adverbial elements (b, c). Intransitive verbs may also be completed by a prepositional phrase (d, e, f).

a. *Nothing* **happened**.	Many intransitive verbs are complete by themselves, though adverbial elements, like phrases of time and place, may follow them.
b. *Mt. Vesuvius* **erupted** *in 1944*.	
c. *Memories* **fade** *(over the years)*.	
d. *Everyone* **participates** *(in class)*.	Many intransitive verbs can or must be completed by a prepositional phrase.
e. *Water* **consists of** *hydrogen and oxygen*.	
f. *Success* **depends on** *many factors*.	

2.4.4 Common intransitive verbs with typical prepositional phrases

If you sometimes forget the preposition after a verb, this list may help you. Some of these verbs work with other prepositions as well, and some have transitive uses (that is, with no preposition). For example, we can *adapt a recipe* and *register a complaint*. Consult a dictionary.

belong to

listen to

participate in

adapt to a new culture	**cope with** challenges	**participate in** class
adjust to living alone	**deal with** a problem	**register for** a class
agree with someone / an idea	**depend on** your friends	**reply to** your request
agree to/on a plan	**enroll in** a class	**respond to** a message
apply to a university	**focus on** the future	**search for** evidence
apply for admission	**go to** the dentist	**stay at** your desk
arrive at a conclusion	**insist on** privacy	**stay in** your room
arrive in the U.S.	**laugh at** a joke	**talk about** sports
belong to a club	**live in** an apartment	**talk to/with** your advisor
care about nutrition	**listen to** music	**think about** the future
care for sick patients	**look at** your phone	**think of** a solution
come to class	**look for** a job	**travel in/to** outer space
complain about the weather	**major in** economics	**wait for** a bus
consist of two parts	**object to** corporal punishment	**work on** a project

• These verbs, if they have noun forms, generally require the same preposition for the noun and the verb: *apply **to** a university*, *submit **an application to** a university*, etc.

With verbs like these, the preposition is necessary even when the object of the preposition is earlier in the sentence, as it sometimes is in questions (a) and relative clauses (b; see Ch. 8).

a. **What kind of music** do you listen **to**?	*To* is required even though its object, *What kind of music*, appears at the beginning.
b. *A taboo topic is a topic <u>that people don't like to talk **about**</u>.*	*About* is required even though its object — *that* in the underlined relative clause) is earlier in the sentence. (See also 8.5.)

■ **Exercise 10** Test yourself by adding a preposition. Check your work by looking at 2.4.4.

depend _____ your friends	stay _____ your desk	register _____ a class
talk _____ your advisor	enroll _____ a class	stay _____ your room
adapt _____ a new culture	respond _____ a message	agree _____ someone / an idea
apply _____ a university	talk _____ sports	listen _____ music
apply _____ job	complain _____ the weather	travel _____ outer space
wait _____ a bus	object _____ corporal punishment	adjust _____ a new culture
arrive _____ the U.S.	agree _____ a plan	care _____ nutrition
care _____ sick patients	laugh _____ a joke	look _____ your phone
work _____ a project	look _____ a job	go _____ the dentist
consist _____ two parts	participate _____ class	belong _____ a club
live _____ an apartment	think _____ the future	stay _____ your room
search _____ evidence	deal _____ a problem	

Chapter 2 — Sentence structure

■ **Exercise 11** The verbs on the right can fill the blanks – but which ones require a preposition? Using 2.4.4 – and maybe a dictionary – decide where and which prepositions are needed. If a verb does not appear in 2.4.4, assume that in the context below it does not require a preposition.

1. One difficult thing about __ a new culture is learning the rules of politeness. For example, how should you __ a stranger politely? And if you're __ your neighbors and you want to __ their noisy music, how you can you do it politely?
   adapting, address, talking, complain

2. After you __ information online, you may find that your paper still __ some evidence that you really need. It may be a good idea to __ the library and __ an expert for help.
   search, lacks, go, ask

3. We need to __ your social life! Instead of __ your room all weekend, why don't you __ a friend? Even if you can't __ anything to do, maybe your friend can.
   talk, staying, call, think

4. Should children __ family decision-making? Many American parents __ their children in family decisions. Of course, it __ the topic and the age of the child. No parent would __ a two-year-old for her opinion about how to spend money.
   participate, include, depends, ask

5. In high school, my goal was to __ Carleton College. To do that, I had to __ a scholarship and write an essay about activities that I was __ and clubs that I __.
   attend, apply, participating, belonged

6. Yesterday's class __ two parts. First we __ an article about gender differences and then we __ it. Some of the students were skeptical. They didn't __ the author's claim that men and women __ different things.
   consisted, read, discussed, agree, laugh

7. Mobile phones have changed how people __ punctuality. Why should you __ being on time for an appointment if you know you can always __ the person you are meeting and __ them that you're going to be late?
   think, worry, text, tell

8. People who __ places like Alaska or Norway in the winter have to __ an environment in which there is very little daylight. If you __ Oslo in December, for example, you will __ only about six hours of daylight.
   visit, adjust, travel, experience

9. Last semester I __ courses in art and music even though I'm __ mechanical engineering. Soon I'll be __ a job, and I've heard that employers often __ employees who have varied interests.
   registered, majoring, looking, value

10. If you __ students at an American university just before class, what do you see? Usually, some students are __ music, and some are reading or __ a text message. Some might be __ an assignment that is due in one minute.
    observe, listening, responding, working

11. How long should you __ a professor who doesn't __ class on time? If you __ professors and students this question, they might __ you different answers.
    wait, come, ask, give

12. It has been one year since Marie and Franco __ New York, and they've decided that the apartment they're __ is too expensive. They've got to __ a plan to economize. Maybe one of them can __ another job.
    arrived, live, agree, look

13. When they are preparing for an exam, some students __ silence. Noise __ them. Others don't __ noise and may even prefer to __ music.
    insist, distracts, care, listen

14. If you __ paying the service fee, you can __ the manager. She always __ complaints and does her best to __ the customer.
    object, talk, listens, satisfy

2.4.5 Sometimes transitive, sometimes intransitive

Many verbs may have an object or not, depending on the meaning. The examples below, along with a dictionary, can help you understand the differences.

Transitive verbs (with objects)	Intransitive verbs + prepositions and objects
a. *Do you **know** a good joke?* (Can you tell one?)	b. *I would have taken that class, but I didn't **know about** it.* (I didn't realize I could take it.)
c. *How long does it take **to learn** a language?* (When you learn something, it becomes yours.)	d. *It's interesting to **learn about** other religions.* (When you learn **about** something, you just learn facts about it.)
e. *I **pay** my bills every month.* (We pay bills, fees, tuition, etc.)	f. *My parents **paid for** my education.* (~~paid my~~...) (We pay **for** goods and services.)
g. *The children were **playing** soccer.* (We play games, musical instruments, roles, etc.)	h. *They were playing **with** their phones.* (We play **with** something to amuse ourselves.)
i. *The teacher is preparing a test.* (She is making it.)	j. *The students are preparing **for** a test.* (~~preparing a test~~) (They are studying.)
k. *We **read** five articles.*	l. *We read **about** twins.* (The topic was twins.)
m. *The police searched the house.* (We search a place.)	n. *They searched for evidence.* (We search **for** the thing we hope to find.)
o. *Laura is **studying** physics.* (That's her major.)	p. *She's **studying for** a degree in physics.* (~~studying a degree~~) That's her goal. She's **studying at** a university. (~~studying~~ a university)
q. *Have you ever **told a joke** that no one laughed at?*	r. *In application essays, you usually have to tell **about** your goals.*
s. *The students **wrote** essays.*	t. *They wrote **about** different topics.*

■ **Exercise 12** Add a preposition if one is needed or add Ø if no preposition is needed. Omit prepositions that are not needed. In **two or three** sentences, no change is needed.

1. Most students spend a lot of time preparing _____ exams.
2. Did you pay _____ your college education by yourself, or did your parents help you?
3. Ben is studying _____ business because he considers it a practical choice. If he had chosen what he really loved, he would be studying _____ a degree in music.
4. When teachers prepare _____ tests, they have to think carefully _____ what they have taught.
5. My brother is studying _____ an MBA at the Wharton school in Pennsylvania.
6. If you pay _____ the student services fee, you have the right to use the Recreation Center.
7. Last weekend, my roommate and I both had to write _____ argumentative essays.
8. We wrote _____ the same topic, but our papers were very different.
9. Young children are able to learn _____ languages without studying them.
10. What are the benefits of learning _____ other religions?

2.5 Prepositions after nouns but not verbs

Contact or contact with?

Answer or answer to?

With many nouns — *contact* and *access*, for example — it is important to remember a preposition: *contact **with**, access **to**.* However, you need a preposition only when these words are used as nouns, not when they are used as verbs. As verbs, they are transitive. Below are typical phrases with verbs and related nouns or adjectives. (Sometimes the forms are different.) Notice that the verbs have no prepositions after them. In a dictionary, you can find additional patterns for the words.

Verbs + objects (no prepositions)	Nouns or adjectives + prepositional phrases
access the internet	have **access to** the internet
admire a film	express **admiration for** a film
advise the president (Note the spelling.)	give **advice to** the president (Note the spelling.)
affect my grade (Note the spelling.)	have an **effect on** my grade (Note the spelling.)
answer the question	give **an answer to** the question
benefit society	provide **a benefit** to society
call someone on the phone	make **a call to** someone
compare Coke with/and Pepsi	make **a comparison between** Coke and Pepsi
contact an old friend	make **contact with** an old friend
damage property	do **damage to** property
discuss politics	have **a discussion about** politics
emphasize education	place **an emphasis on** education
equal 10 percent	be **equal to** 10 percent (*Equal* is an adjective.)
harm children	be **harmful to** children (*Harmful* is an adjective.)
influence people	have **an influence on** people
lack confidence	suffer **from a lack of** confidence
marry a doctor	be **married** to a doctor (*Married* is an adjective.)
research the history of fashion	do **research on** the history of fashion
respect tradition	show **respect for** tradition
respect elders	be **respectful to** elders (*Respectful* is an adjective.)
value privacy	place **a high value on** privacy
visit a friend	make a **visit to** a friend
welcome visitors	extend a **welcome to** visitors

Exercise 13 Test yourself by adding a preposition if one is needed. Write X in the blank if no preposition is needed. Check your answers by looking at 2.5.

emphasize _____ education	call _____ someone on the phone
place an emphasis _____ education	make a call _____ someone
contact _____ an old friend	discuss _____ politics
make contact _____ an old friend	have a discussion _____ politics
access _____ the internet	affect _____ my grade
have access _____ the internet	have an effect _____ my grade
value _____ privacy	research _____ the history of fashion
place a high value _____ privacy	do research _____ the history of fashion
benefit _____ society	respect _____ tradition
provide a _____ society	show respect _____ tradition
answer _____ the question	compare Coke _____ Pepsi
give an answer _____ the question	make a comparison _____ Coke and Pepsi
advise _____ the president	admire _____ a film
give advice _____ the president	express admiration _____ a film
influence _____ people	
have an influence _____ people	

■ **Exercise 14** In each item below, you need a verb in one blank and a noun in the other. Sometimes the verb and noun are the same; for example, *contact* is both a verb and a noun. Sometimes they are different; for example, *emphasize* (a verb) and *emphasis* (a noun) are different. Choose words for each blank, and remember that after a noun you may need a preposition, as in the example. The verbs do not require prepositions, since they are all transitive. Use 2.5 as a resource.

Example: *affect* In the last century, scientists studied the __effect of__ cigarette smoking and determined that it __affects__ the body in very negative ways.

1. *access* In rural parts of the country, people often have less __ information. Libraries and educational facilities are limited, and people may need to travel far from home just to __ the internet.

2. *emphasize* In countries where English is not the native language, teachers often __ grammar more than anything else. In English-speaking countries, there is usually more __ listening and speaking.

3. *compare* It's hard to __ two teaching methods because teaching involves so many variables. To be useful, you need to eliminate variables when you make a __ two things.

4. *contact* Since I started my new job, I haven't had much __ my old work friends. We weren't really close, so I have no reason to __ them.

5. *respect* It's important for soldiers to __ their leaders. If soldiers have a healthy __ their leaders, they are more likely to follow them.

6. *harm* Parents try to protect their children from things that may __ them, but they don't always know what is __ a child.

7. *answer* What's the __ question 4? Were you able to __ that one?

8. *affect* The same medication may have a different __ different patients. For example, a medication may __ a young person differently from an old person.

9. *lack* If you __ confidence, you are less likely to do well. The __ confidence can hurt your performance by making you hesitant and indecisive.

10. *research* Tree rings show the growth of a tree over time. __ tree rings can help us understand climate change, because the rings are wider or narrower depending on how much rain occurred during a growing season. Scientists who __ tree rings to learn about climate change are called dendrochronologists.

11. *influence* In many ways, parents obviously __ their children a lot. However, a child's peers may have an even greater __ the child's language development.

12. *discuss* In my journalism class, we had a heated __ social media and public opinion. The next day, we __ voting behavior, and some students fell asleep.

give me something

give something to me

2.6 Two-object verbs

2.6.1 Verbs like *give* and *tell* can have two objects: an **indirect object** and a **direct object**. We use such verbs, sometimes called ditransitive verbs, in two patterns. When the indirect object is a pronoun (2.16), we use only one pattern (e - h). Verbs in this group include *give, lend, offer, read, sell, show, teach,* and *tell*. Below, S = subject; V = verb; IO = indirect object; DO = direct object.

S V IO DO			S V DO *to* IO		
Subj. + verb	Indirect object	Direct object		Direct object	Indirect object
a. *They gave*	*the children*	*cookies.*	b. *They gave*	*cookies*	*to the children.*
c. *He tells*	*everyone*	*that story.*	d. *He tells*	*that story*	*to everyone.*
e. *We told / gave / showed* ~~*the children it*~~.			f. *We told / gave / showed* **it to the children.**		
g. *We told / gave / showed* ~~*them it*~~.			h. *We told / gave / showed it to them.*		

2.6.2 Use *for*, not *to*, with *buy, find,* and *make*.

S V IO DO			S V DO *for* IO		
Subj. + verb	Indirect object	Direct object	Subj. + verb	Direct object	Indirect object
i. *We bought*	*Ben*	*a present.*	j. *We bought*	*a present*	*for Ben.*
k. *She found*	*him*	*a job.*	l. *She found*	*a job*	*for him.*
m. *I made*	*you*	*dinner.*	n. *I made*	*dinner*	*for you.*

2.6.3 Typical patterns for *ask* are shown below. For other patterns, see 6.10 and 7.7.3.

o. *We asked each candidate two questions.*	There is no difference in meaning.
p. *We asked two questions of each candidate.*	
q. *We asked each candidate for comments. We asked each candidate to say a few words.*	

2.6.4 *Cost, save,* and *take* (*take an hour, take a long time,* etc.) often have an indirect object after the verb.

r. Buying a cheap product may **save (you) money**, but it may also **cost (you) more money** in the long run.

s. *If I walk, it **takes (me) 20 minutes** to get home. **How much time** does it **take you** to get home?*

Exercise 15

a. Using the words below, complete the sentences. Include a pronoun: *me, you, her, him, it, us,* or *them.* If you need explanation about how to choose pronouns, see section 2.16.

Example: I have no idea what the answer is. Can you ___? → *give me a hint*

buy some souvenirs	give some advice	give more time	show your license
find a new job	give a dollar	lend a dollar	tell a story
give a few weeks	√ give a hint	make a pirate costume	

1. If you can't finish a long test, you might ask the teacher, "Can you ___?"
2. I can't decide what to major in. Can you ___?
3. I don't have enough money for the fare. Can you ___ until tomorrow?
4. Jared will get used to his new job. Just ___.
5. If the children can't sleep, why don't you ___?
6. I want my children to learn how to handle money, so I plan to ___ every week.
7. If those police officers stop you, be sure to ___.
8. When my family goes on a trip, the children always say, "Mom, will you ___?"
9. My daughter loves pirates. For Halloween, she asked me to ___.
10. Don't worry. If you get fired, I can ___.

b. Using the words below, complete each sentence. You will need four words. There may be more than one way. In the sentence with *someone,* you can use *them.* If you need explanation about how to choose pronouns, see 2.16.

Example I'm hungry. If you're not going to eat that banana, why not ___? → *give it to me*

give   lend   to   me   you   her   him   it   them   us

1. My daughter needs a bike. I have one I never use, so I plan to ___.
2. If the man at the desk asks for your passport, just smile and ___.
3. If someone asks you for your password, don't ___.
4. If your neighbors need a lawnmower and you have an extra one, you could ___.
5. When she asked for your receipt, why didn't you ___?
6. We didn't ask for his opinion, but he decided to ___ anyway.
7. I like this book, and I know you'll love it. As soon as I'm done with it, I'll ___.
8. I need to borrow a dictionary, and I see that you have one. Can you ___?
9. Maria's laptop is being repaired. I don't need my laptop this weekend, so I can ___.
10. Alicia is so generous! If you admire a piece of jewelry she's wearing, she'll take it off and ___!

HIGH PRIORITY

■ **Exercise 16** Look for a mistake in **two or three** of the items below. Most of the items have no mistakes. In the sentences below, find verbs that appear in 2.6. Look for a mistake related to the patterns for these verbs in **two or three** of the sentences. Most of the sentences have no mistakes.

1. Today my teacher gave us a copy of an article about elephants. He gave the same article to us last week! Unlike an elephant, he's very forgetful.

2. This is a strange story. If you tell it to four different people, they are likely to interpret it in four different ways. If you ask them to tell it back to you, you will hear four very different versions.

3. If you tell someone something personal, you had better be prepared for what might happen if they tell to someone else.

4. Elementary school teachers often tell their students stories. If the children then tell those same stories for their parents, they might change them in interesting ways.

5. A famous saying goes like this: *If you give a man a fish, he eats for one day. If you teach a man to fish, he eats for a lifetime.* If I had a fish, I'd be glad to give someone. I hate the taste of fish!

6. The Riveras rented a car for their vacation. It cost a lot to them, but driving to Quebec took them less than a day, so it saved them some time.

2.7 Avoiding verb completion mistakes

You can avoid many mistakes if you know whether a verb is transitive or intransitive. If it is transitive, use an object directly after it, with no preposition. If it is intransitive, use nothing after it or use a prepositional phrase. Most dictionaries indicate whether a verb is transitive. For the word *consist*, for example, Dictionary.com says "used without object" and "usually used with *of*." It also provides an example.

a. *Zero degrees Celsius equals to 32 Fahrenheit.* b. *How does pop culture influence on fashion?*	Use an **object** after a transitive verb. Don't use a preposition.
c. *They listen to music when they study.* (*listen music*) d. *When I watch a horror movie, sometimes I can't look at the screen.* (*look the screen*)	Don't use an object after an intransitive verb. Use a preposition before the noun or noun phrase.

■ **Exercise 17** Read each item and look for problems in **verb completion** with the verbs *equal, influence, listen, look, focus* and *marry* (see section 2.4). In most of the items, there are no mistakes. Look for only **one or two** mistakes in the whole exercise.

1. Experts say that the first year of a dog's life equals about 15 human years, while the second equals about nine years and each year after that equals about five years. So in terms of development, the common idea that a "dog year" is equal to about seven human years is not really accurate.

2. To what extent do your friends' opinions influence your own opinions? It is generally believed that adolescence is when friends' opinions have the greatest influence, but peers' opinions influence younger children as well. Peers have an influence on adults too, even though most adults think of themselves as independent thinkers.

3. When you look at another person's face, exactly what do you look at? According to some studies, people from East Asian cultures look at the center of a face, while people from Westerners look alternately at the eyes and the mouth.

4. The way we listen to music has evolved significantly in the last 50 years. For most of the last century, people listened to music on records. Cassette tapes came later, followed by CDs. Today, when you listen your favorite performers, you are probably listening to a digital file.

5. Many history books focus on the actions of leaders like kings, presidents, and generals. In recent decades, however, more and more historians have focused on the lives of ordinary people. Some popular history books focus on commodities like oil, salt, or silver, while others focus on products of human ingenuity like clothing and houses.

6. Parents usually want their son or daughter to marry someone who has a good future and is compatible with the family. Sometimes parents actually make the choice: In an arranged marriage, a young person marries someone chosen by his or her parents. If you marry to someone whose economic future is not promising, the parents might argue, you will regret it.

2.8 Linking verbs

2.8.1 Linking verbs can be followed by adjectives (as well as other structures). The most important linking verb is BE. Others appear below, followed by typical structures. These patterns are a matter of lexical grammar — that is, the grammar of the individual word. Sometimes the use of a pattern is limited. For example, we use *turn green* and *turn red* but not usually ~~*turn old*~~. Consult a dictionary.

Linking verbs with typical structures			
If a box is empty, it means that structure is not common after the linking verb, though it may occur.			
+ adjective	+ noun phrase or *like* + a noun phrase	+ infinitive (*to* + verb) or gerund (verb + *ing*)	+ prepositional phrase
be studious	*be a scholar*		*be at school*
appear confident		*appear to know*	*appear in court*
become famous	*become a star*	**come** to believe (~~become~~ *to*)	
end up rich	*end up a rich man*	*end up winning*	*end up on top*
feel foolish	*feel **like** a fool*	*feel **like** quitting*	
get ready		*get to see* (have the opportunity to see)	
grow old		*grow to appreciate it*	
keep quiet		*keep going*	*keep in shape*
look young	*look **like** an athlete*		
prove difficult		*prove to be difficult*	
remain silent	*remain friends*		*remain at home*
seem fair	*seem **like** a good deal*	*seem to be fair*	
smell good	*smell **like** a rose*		
sound great	*sound **like** thunder*		
taste fresh	*taste **like** chicken*		
turn green	*turn into a monster*		
stay awake			*stay in bed*

2.8.2 After a verb or at the end of a clause, we sometimes add an adjective (a), an adjective phrase (b), or a participial phrase (c, d), even if the verb is not usually used as a linking verb.

a. *Mozart died young.*	He was young.
b. *The team arrived at the field ready to win.*	They were ready.
c. *We ended the day satisfied with our efforts.*	We were satisfied.
d. *Justin came to class wearing a gorilla suit.*	He was wearing a gorilla suit.

2.8.3 We use BE *like* with the meaning "be similar to." To express the idea that A is like B and B is like A, we use BE ***alike***.

e. *Have you ever watched a rugby game? It's **like** football but even rougher.* (It ~~likes~~ football.)
f. *Football and rugby are **alike**.*

2.9 Look like, seem like, sound like

The examples show how we use *look* and *look like* differently. We use similar patterns with *seem, sound, feel, taste,* and *smell*. We can also use these verbs with an empty *it* subject (2.11) and a clause (d). To say that A looks like B and B looks like A, we use *look alike* (e).

Patterns for *look, seem, sound, feel, taste,* and *smell*	
a. *This looks interesting.* (~~like~~)	*look* + adjective
b. *This looks like an interesting film.*	*look like* + noun phrase
c. *This looks **like** it could be an interesting film.*	*look like* + clause
d. *It looks like the person who lives here has a dog.*	empty *it* + *look like* + clause (2.11)
e. *My brother and I look **alike**.* (~~each other~~)	I look like him and he looks like me. (We look like each other.)

See also 9.23, "Lexical grammar: Verbs + *like*, as *if*, and *as though*."

■ **Exercise 18** Choose the best answer(s). More than one may be correct.

1. Henry Fonda was a famous actor. Two of his children __ actors as well.
   a. became   b. became like   c. became to be   d. were become

2. Our new neighbors ___ . Let's invite them over for coffee.
   a. seem friendly people   b. seem friendly
   c. seem like friendly people   d. seem to friendly

3. If you don't start paying more attention to your relationships with other people, you're going to __ with no friends at all!
   a. end being   b. end to be   c. end up   d. end it

4. Don't let anyone interrupt you. No matter what happens, just ___ working.
   a. keep to be   b. keep up   c. keep to   d. keep

5. In the novel I'm reading, one of the characters ____ a werewolf when the moon is full.
   a. turns into   b. turns to   c. becomes to be   d. becomes

6. The new movie by Ang Lee __ an interesting film. Would you like to see it?
   a. looks   b. looks like   c. sounds   d. sounds like

7. The new office manager seems __ .
   a. like a competent person   b. competent
   c. as a competent person   d. being competent

8. Do you and your brother __ ?
   a. look like each other   b. look alike each other   c. look alike   d. look like

9. Scarlett doesn't look ___ her mother, but they sound alike.
   a. alike to   b. alike   c. like   d. like to

10. I started going to concerts as a child, but I didn't really ___ appreciate music until I started studying it seriously.
    a. become to   b. come to   c. end up   d. feel like

call off

run out of

2.10 Phrasal verbs

A **phrasal verb** is a verb + particle (adverb or preposition) like *put down, call off, go on, get along,* or *run out,* sometimes with an added preposition (*get along with, run out of*). A phrasal verb usually needs to be learned as a unit because the meaning is often not understandable from the parts.

a.	The test is over; **put down** your pencils.	The meaning comes from *put* and *down*.
b.	They **called off** the game. = They canceled it.	
c.	What's **going on**? = What's happening?	The meaning is not understandable from the parts.
d.	Do you **get along with** your boss? = Do you have a friendly relationship?	
e.	We've **run out of** time. = We have no more time.	

Most phrasal verbs are transitive (2.4). That is, they may be followed by an object (a noun, a noun phrase, or a pronoun). They may be **separable** or **inseparable**. With separable verbs, the object may come at the end or between the parts (f, h). If the object is a pronoun, it **must** come between the parts (g, i). With inseparable verbs, the parts are never separated (j – m).

	Separable verbs with a noun object		With a pronoun object
f.	Put down **your pencils**. Put **your pencils** down.	g.	Put them down. (*Put down them*)
h.	They called off **the game**. They called **the game** off.	i.	They called it off. (*They called off it*.)
	Inseparable verbs		
j.	The teacher **called on** Sara. (chose her to answer)	k.	The teacher **called on** her.
l.	Jo **takes after** her father in every way. (is similar to)	m.	Jo **takes after** him in every way.

Phrasal verbs are based on easy words, but these words may be part of many phrasal verbs (*get across, get along, get away, get back, get by,* etc.), and a single phrasal verb may have more than one meaning. Most dictionaries list phrasal verbs, often with examples, after the main word.

■ **Exercise 19** Using a dictionary if you need one, identify the phrasal verbs in the sentences below. Which ones have objects? Which ones appear to be separable? How do you know?

1. If you miss a test, ask your professor if you can make it up.
2. Sophie is a fast learner. If you try to teach her something, she catches on immediately.
3. Does your teacher usually go over the homework in class after you hand it in?
4. Please look over Chapter 1 tonight. If you have questions, bring them up in class tomorrow.
5. When Mary Kate introduces herself, she never leaves out her middle name.
6. Are you a procrastinator? In other words, when you have something to do, do you put it off?
7. We waited almost an hour, but the bus never showed up.
8. Sometimes twins look so much alike that you can't tell them apart.
9. We have to follow the rule. There's no way to get around it.
10. If you can't figure out the meaning of a word from the context, look it up.
11. When you take on an important project, it's important to see it through.
12. In one of the labs, a fire broke out, and it took the firefighters an hour to put it out.
13. On weekends, I like to sleep in, because on weekdays my alarm goes off at 5.
14. When he was 90, the founder of the company passed away and his daughter took over.
15. When Donald Trump started his run for the presidency, most experts didn't believe he could pull it off.

It's obvious that people make mistakes.

2.11 Empty *it* subjects

- Some sentences have what we call an **empty** *it* subject.
- *It* occupies the subject position, but in terms of meaning, the subject is later in the sentence.
- The delayed subjects can be noun clauses (a, c) or infinitives (e).
- We can paraphrase these sentences with noun clauses (b, d) or infinitives (f) in subject position, but we often prefer the version with empty *it* because it allows us to put the important information at the end of the sentence. See also 6.7, 6.8, and 7.5.

a. *It is obvious that people make mistakes.*	What is obvious? *That people make mistakes.* b. *That people make mistakes is obvious.* (See also 7.5)
c. *It doesn't matter what other people think.*	What doesn't matter? *What other people think.* d. *What other people think doesn't matter.* (See also 7.5)
e. *It is almost impossible to find parking.*	What is almost impossible? To find parking. f. *To find parking is almost impossible.* (See also 6.7 and 6.8)

These structures can appear inside subordinate clauses.

g. *I apologized **because it was** obvious that I was wrong.*	(An adverbial clause; Ch. 9.)
h. *I know **that it** doesn't matter what other people think.*	(A noun clause; Ch. 7.)
i. *I want to live in a city **where it's** not so hard to find parking.*	(A relative clause; Ch. 8)

We also use empty *it* in sentences about time and weather.

k. When *it's* noon in New York, *it's* 6:00 a.m. in Hawaii.
l. *It's* cloudy now, but they say *it* will be sunny tomorrow.

■ **Exercise 20**   Complete each sentence by filling the blank.

1. Children should start learning a foreign language as soon as possible because __ obvious that language learning is easier at an early age.

2. At noon this cafeteria is really crowded. __ almost impossible to find a place to sit.

3. It's noon in New York, but in Chicago __ only 11:00 a.m.

4. These days many people dress casually all the time. They think __ doesn't matter how they dress as long as they are neat and clean.

5. It's hot right now, but by evening __ will be cool enough to take a run.

6. I want to live in a place where __ sunny almost all the time.

2.12 There is (existential *there*)

There is a difference.

There are differences.

- We use *there* — called existential or expletive *there* — as an **empty** subject with a BE verb to say that something exists or does not exist (a, b) or to describe what something includes (c).
- To make a negative sentence we use *there is/are no* or *there isn't/aren't* (b).
- Although *there* is the grammatical subject, the **logical** subject (the subject in terms of meaning) is after the verb, and it determines whether the verb is singular or plural (c): *There **is a difference**, There **are differences**.*
- For inversion (2.13), we put the BE verb before there (d).

a. *There is a mistake in this sentenc.*
b. *There is no E at the end. There isn't any E.*
c. *There are 26 bones in the human foot. There are 10 syllables in Parangaricutirimícuaro.*
d. *Is there anything good in the refrigerator? Are there any cupcakes?*

Existential *there* can appear inside subordinate clauses.
e. *We're taking our vacation at a park **where there is** no WIFI.* (A relative clause; Ch. 8.7.)
f. *We chose the park **because there was** no WIFI.* (An adverbial clause; Ch. 9)
g. *I don't care **whether there is** a TV.* (A noun clause; Ch. 7.)

Sentences with *there* can sometimes be paraphrased using HAVE.

h. *There are a lot of cafés in this neighborhood. = This neighborhood has lots of cafés.*

Avoid mistakes like these:

i. WRONG: *In Japan are many volcanoes.*	→ *In Japan there are many volcanoes.* OR *Japan has many volcanoes.*	
j. WRONG: *In Japan there have many volcanoes.*		
k. WRONG: *In this state there are two factories make tools.* → *... two factories **that** make ...*	The revised sentence uses a relative clause. See Ch. 8.3.	
l. WRONG: *There is a family of birds live outside my window.* → *There is a family of birds **living** ...*	The revised sentence uses a reduced relative clause. See 8.12.	
m. WRONG: *There was an earthquake destroyed the town.* → *An earthquake destroyed the town.*	**There was** is not needed.	

■ **Exercise 21**   Find and fix an error involving existential *there* in **three or four** of the sentences below. Most of the sentences have no mistakes.

1. There are about 218 bones in the human body.
2. On the British channel island of Sark there are no cars. They aren't allowed.
3. There is not *w* sound in *answer*.
4. In New Orleans there have many great restaurants.
5. I want to work in a city where lots of cultural amenities like educational institutions, museums, and theaters.
6. In Japan there are many famous hot springs where people go to enjoy the health-giving waters.
7. Before 1959, there were 48 states in the U.S. During that year, Alaska and Hawaii became states, so now they are 50 states.
8. There are many ways to spell some common names. For example, *Lori, Laurie,* and *Lorrie* are all common spellings of the same name.

2.13 Inversion

it is → is it

2.13.1 Reversing the order of a subject and auxiliary
- Inversion, used mainly for questions (2.14), means reversing the order of a subject and verb. The auxiliary verb (or BE) goes before the subject.
- For simple present we use *do* or *does* (d) and for simple past, we use *did* (e). When we use *do, does,* or *did,* the main verb is always in the simple form (for example, *write* or *invent* but not *writes* or *wrote* or *invents* or *invented*).

	Normal order (statement order)		Inverted order (question order)	
	Subject	Verb	Auxiliary or BE	Subject
a.	*It*	*is ...*	*Is*	*it ...?*
b.	*The problem*	*has become ...*	*Has*	*the problem become ...?*
c.	*Studying a language*	*can be ...*	*Can*	*studying a language be ...?*
d.	*The government*	*spends ...*	*Does*	*the government spend ...?* (spends)
e.	*Thomas Edison*	*invented ...*	*Did*	*Thomas Edison invent ...* (invented)

- We usually do not use inversion when the *wh* word or phrase is (or includes) the subject (f).
- We do not use inversion in a noun clause (g). See section 7.4 in Chapter 7.

f.	**What causes** climate change? (does cause) **Who invented** the light bulb? (did invent)
g.	I don't know **what he wants**. (does he want)

■ **Exercise 22** Form a question based on the content of the first sentence.

Example. Hotels are expensive. How about camping? → *Is camping expensive?*

1. Riding a bike is easy. How about riding a motorcycle?
2. Walking is a safe way to exercise. How about running?
3. The LG company makes refrigerators. How about SONY?
4. Children like cartoons. How about adults?
5. Jane Austen wrote novels. How about Shakespeare?
6. Mozart died young. How about Beethoven?
7. Elephants can swim. How about lions?
8. Most birds can fly. How about penguins?
9. It rains a lot in Seattle. How about in Los Angeles?
10. Paris has great restaurants. How about London?

2.13.2 Inversion with a fronted negative element
We use inversion when we move a negative element to the beginning of a sentence.

Negative-initial order with inversion	Usual word order
a. **Only if** you try it **will you know** how hard it is. (Notice that there is no comma.)	b. You will know how hard it is **only if...**
c. **Never have I seen** such destruction!	d. I have **never** seen such destruction!
e. **Not only did he lose** his job, but his wife left him.	f. He **not only** lost his job, but his wife...

See also 2.17.3 (e) for the use of *nor* at the beginning of a clause.

■ **Exercise 23** Complete the paraphrase of each sentence, with the negative element at the beginning. Remember to use inverted word order. For simple present or simple past of verbs other than BE, use a form of DO.

0. Wait until you're married. You will understand <u>only then</u>. ➞ Only then *will you understand.*
1. You will understand <u>only when you are older</u>. ➞ Only when ...
2. I did not meet my grandfather <u>until I was 20</u>. ➞ Not until ...
3. Women did not get the right to vote <u>until 1920</u>. ➞ Not until ...
4. You will be able to play well <u>only after years of practice</u>. ➞ Only ...
5. A few years ago, a well-known financier cheated thousands of people out of their life's savings. So many people have <u>never</u> been deceived so thoroughly! ➞ Never ...
6. He <u>not only speaks French</u>, but he's a great dancer. ➞ Not only ...

Does it snow in Florida?

2.14 Questions

2.14.1 Yes/no questions usually have inverted word order (2.13) and end with a question mark.

a. *Is Shanghai the largest city in the world? Are dogs colorblind? Was Confucius married?*
b. *Do women live longer than men? Does it snow in Florida? Did Shakespeare write novels?*
c. *Is the Internet making us smarter? Have you been sleeping well lately? Can gorillas swim?*

2.14.2 Wh questions begin with a *wh* word (*what, who, whom, whose, when, where, why, how*) or phrase. We use inversion (d), except when the *wh* phrase is (or is part of) the subject (e).

d. *What kind of films do you like? How long has Apple been in business? When should we meet?*
e. *What makes you happy?* (~~does make~~) *Who has already finished? Which team is winning?*

2.14.3 We do not use inversion when the question is inside another sentence. (The *wh* clause is a noun clause, not a true question. See 7.4.)

f. *I want to know* **what kind of films you like**. (~~do you like~~)
g. *We couldn't agree on* **when we should meet**. (~~should we~~)
h. *Do you think* **this paper is** *well-written? Do you think* **it is** *interesting?* (~~is this paper, is it~~)

■ **Exercise 24** Imagine questions you might ask for each situation. Try to include some *yes*/no questions and some *wh* questions.

Example: You will have a test in your grammar class in a couple of days, but you don't know anything more about it. ⟶ *What will the test be about? How long will it be? How should I prepare for it? Will it be open-book? Will we have any review before the test?*

1. You are a parent. It is 3:00 in the morning. Your 15-year-old son has just come home. His clothes are dirty and he smells like smoke.

2. Your spouse (husband or wife) is out of town and promised to call you, but you have been home all day and have received no calls. It is now 9:00 p.m. and finally you get a call.

3. You are the president of a small import company, and you are interviewing a person who wants a job in your company. This person will have to talk with people from all over the world.

4. You are the person in the situation above who wants to be hired.

5. You are the parent of seven children under the age of ten. You are trying to find a babysitter for this coming Saturday night. You are talking to a person who might do it.

6. You are the person who might babysit in the situation above.

7. You are at a big shopping mall, just about to get into your car. You see a small boy in your car!

8. On the first day, your teacher says, "Writing will be very important in this class!"

9. You want to rent an apartment and you are talking on the phone with the manager.

10. You want to rent an apartment, and you have a chance to ask questions of a person who lives in the same building.

2.14.4 *What is it like / How is it?*

To ask for a general description, we use *What is someone / something like?* (a, b). To ask about the temporary condition of someone or something (c) or to get an evaluation (d), we usually use *How is...?*

a. *What is your brother like?*	What kind of person is he?
b. *What is your literature class like?*	What kinds of things do you do in the class?
c. *How is your brother?* (*How is he like?*)	Is he well?
d. *How is your literature class?*	Do you like it?

2.14.5 Problems with questions

Problem sentences	Revisions	
a. Why we can't agree? →	*Why can't we agree?*	Subj.+ auxiliary → Aux. + subj.
b. What means ASAP? →	*What does ASAP mean?*	Don't omit the auxiliary DO.
c. When did it happened? →	*When did it happen?*	Use a base form verb after DO.
d. How does it works? →	*How does it work?*	
The following items relate to specific uses of *what* and *how*.		
e. How is this called? →	*What is this called?*	Use *what*, not *how*.
f. How do you call this? →	*What do you call this?*	
g. How many percent(age) of bikers wear helmets? →	*What percentage of people are left-handed?*	
h. How should I do? I don't know how to do. →	*What should I do? I don't know what to do.*	Use *what*, not *how*, unless you add an object after DO: *I don't know how to do this problem.*
i. How do you think of jazz? →	*What do you think of jazz? How do you feel about jazz?*	**What** do you **think of** OR **How** do you **feel about**

Chapter 2 — Sentence structure

■ **Exercise 25** If you want to get to know someone deeply, what kinds of questions might you ask? The questions below (based on questions suggested by a radio project called "Story Corps") cover a variety of topics.

   Step 1: Read the questions and think about the content. At the same time, look for **two or three** mistakes and correct them. The mistakes are related to question formation as described in section 2.13. Remember: Most of the sentences are correct. Only two or three have a mistake.

1. Who is the most important person in your life? Can you tell me about him or her?
2. Who has been the biggest influence on your life? How have they influenced you?
3. What is one important lesson you've learned in life?
4. What is your earliest memory?
5. Where did you grow up? What kind of place was it?
6. What was your childhood like?
7. As a child, what did you like to do?
8. What are / were your parents like?
9. How did your parents motivated you to do well in school?
10. How is / was your relationship with your parents now?
11. Did you / do you have a big family?
12. When you think of your family, who do you think mostly of?
13. What are / were your grandparents like?
14. What do you remember about your first day of school?
15. Did you ever get into trouble as a child? What was the worst thing you did?
16. What is your best memory of childhood?
17. Who were your best friends? What were they like?
18. As a child, did you have a nickname? How did you get it?
19. Can you remember something you didn't like as a child? Why you didn't like it?
20. When you began to study English? What do you remember about it?
21. What is one thing you are proud of?
22. What is one thing that you care deeply about?
23. Looking back on your life so far, do you have any regrets?
24. What challenges are you facing right now?
25. What are you looking forward to right now?
26. What do you think will you be doing ten years from now?
27. If I really want to know you well, is there anything else I should ask?

   Step 2: Choose some questions to ask classmates. When you get an answer, ask follow-up questions. That is, keep asking about the same topic, to get more information. Then move on to new topics.

2.15 Commands, requests, and exclamatory sentences

2.15.1 Three sentence types We use sentences to give information (statements, a), to ask for information (questions, b; see 2.14), and to get people to do things (commands and requests, c).

a. *Memories fade. We easily forget things.*	Statements (declarative sentences)
b. *Do you remember? What makes us forget?*	Questions (interrogative sentences)
c. *Try to remember. Please don't forget!*	Commands and requests (imperative sentences)

2.15.2 Commands and requests A command (an imperative) is expressed with a base form verb, sometimes with *don't* or *do not* or an adverb (*always, never, just, please*) before it (d). The implied subject is "you," but there is no overt subject. We can add a subordinate clause or phrase before a command (e), but when we **report** a command (7.12), we transform it into an infinitive (f) or we report it directly, as a quotation (g).

  d. *Please pay with a check or credit card. Do not mail cash. Never share your passwords.*
  e. *When in Rome, do as the Romans do. If you're getting a cup of coffee, get me one too.*
  f. *They advised us to do as the Romans do. (They ~~advised us do~~ ...)*
  g. *They said, "Do as the Romans do."*

2.15.3 Exclamatory sentences We can think of exclamatory sentences as transformations of statements, with more emotion. They begin with *How* or *What* or *What a* and usually end with an exclamation point. Although these sentences begin with *wh* words, they do not have inversion (2.14). The subject and verb in an exclamatory sentence is sometimes implied, not overt (d).

	Statements	Exclamatory sentences	
a.	*We had fun.*	***What fun** we had!*	*What* + uncountable noun + S V
b.	*It was **a great party**.*	***What** a great party it was!*	*What a* + countable noun + S V
b.	*It is **good** to remember.*	***How good** it is to remember!*	*How* + adjective + S V
c.	*We **laughed**.*	***How** we laughed!*	*How* + SV
d.	*It was a great day.*	***What** a great day!*	The subject and verb are implied.

The three sentence types described above are based on the speaker's or writer's purpose: to give information, ask for information, or tell someone what to do. For another way of classifying sentences, based on grammatical structure, see 2.23.1, "Traditional sentence types."

2.16 Pronouns and reference

2.16.1 Pronouns usually refer to earlier nouns, noun phrases, or noun clauses. The noun that a pronoun refers to is the **referent** (also called the antecedent). The referent is often the noun closest to the pronoun (a), but sometimes we rely on context to make the reference clear (b). When the reference is not clear (c), it's better not to use a pronoun.

a. *The boy spoke to the old man, but he just turned away.*	*He = the old man.*
b. *The boy looked for the old man, but he didn't find him.*	*He = the boy. Him = the old man.*
c. *The boy sat next to the old man. He looked tired.*	*He = ? Change He to The boy or The man, or rethink the sentence.*

Sometimes the referent of a pronoun is later in the sentence (d).

| d. *When he wants to go out, my dog sits by the door.* | *He = my dog.* |

2.16.2 Pronouns take different forms, depending on how they are used.

Subjects	Objects (after a verb or preposition)	Possessives before a noun	Possessives not before a noun
I have...	Remember *me*.	*my* name	This is *mine*.
You can...	Good for *you*!	*your* name	This is *yours*.
She will...	Listen to *her*.	*her* name	This is *hers*.
He should...	Help *him*.	*his* name	This is *his*.
It works.	Try *it*.	*its* name	This is *ours*.
We know.	I like *them*.	*our* name	This is *theirs*.
They are....		*their* name	

2.16.3 Pronouns agree with their referents in number (e) and gender (f) We can also use *it* for referents that are noun clauses, to talk about actions (g), facts (h), and ideas (i).

e. *Your paper should include details, but it doesn't need them in every paragraph.*	*It = your paper* (singular). *Them = details* (plural).
f. *The king loved the queen but she didn't love him.*	*She = the queen. He = the king.*
g. *Taking a taxi is convenient, but it costs a lot.*	*It = taking a taxi.*
h. *Sylvia is talented, but she doesn't seem to realize it.*	*It = the fact that she is talented.*
i. *He said he had been ill, but it wasn't true.*	*It = that he was ill.*

2.16.4 Don't use a pronoun that has no clear referent. Use a noun or noun phrase instead.

Unclear	Clear
j. *This is a strict school.* **They** *have to follow lots of rules.*	**The teachers** *have to follow lots of rules.* OR **The students** *have to follow lots of rules.* OR **Everyone** *has to follow lots of rules.*

2.16.5 Use a pronoun to avoid needlessly repeating a noun or noun phrase.

Repetitive	Improved
k. *They didn't like the film because the film was confusing.*	*They didn't like the film because it was confusing.*

For a chart that shows all the pronouns, see **pronouns** in the glossary at the end of the book. See 2.24, "Avoiding gender bias in pronoun choice," and 2.25, "Avoiding shifting points of view."

■ **Exercise 26**

a. Complete the sentence below with appropriate pronouns, starting with *I*.

When __ was young, __ parents always helped __ with __ homework.

Now create five more sentences with *she, he, we, you,* and *they*. The content will be the same except for the pronouns. Change *was* to *were* when it's required.

b. Complete the sentences by adding pronouns. To choose the right pronoun, look carefully at the rest of the sentence. There may be more than one way.

1. How can parents give ___ children a clear understanding of right and wrong? One of the most important things ___ can do is set an example through ___ own behavior. We all know that's the best way, but sometimes ___ have a hard time doing ___.

2. A message on a neighborhood website said, "My husband and I are looking for a babysitter for ___ two-year-old daughter. ___ is a very active child, and ___ need a break from watching ___ 24 hours a day. If ___ can help ___ out, please call ___ at the number listed below."

3. The title of an article said, "Broke your left arm? Exercise your left. ___ might help." According to the article, exercising the muscles on one side of your body can keep the muscles on the other side strong, even if ___ do not move ___.

4. To help ___ babies learn to fly, a mother bird doesn't push ___ out of the nest, but ___ might put food for ___ on a branch at some distance from the nest. Trying to get the food, a baby bird might fall to the ground. As ___ falls, ___ flaps ___ wings and begins to learn how to fly.

5. My niece always wanted a big family. ___ said ___ didn't mind if ___ had boys or girls. Now ___ and ___ husband have five boys, and ___ are expecting another baby soon. ___ will love ___ all equally, but if the new baby is a girl, ___ will have a special place in ___ hearts.

6. A woman named Sylvia Bloom was a legal secretary for 67 years in New York. ___ salary was modest, but ___ saved as much as ___ could. ___ wanted ___ money, after ___ death, to be used for college scholarships. That money amounted to more than eight million dollars. Today ___ helps students from low-income families achieve ___ dreams.

2.17 Sentences and clauses

2.17.1 Two kinds of clauses: Independent and subordinate

A **clause** consists of a subject, a verb or verb phrase, and associated parts such as objects and adverbials. An **independent clause** (also called a main clause) can stand alone as a sentence. A **subordinate clause** (also called a dependent clause) is **part** of a sentence. It cannot stand alone as a sentence.

Independent clauses (main clauses)	Subordinate clauses (dependent clauses)	Sentences
I will call you	*when we arrive*	*I will call you.* *I will call you when we arrive.* *When we arrive, I will call you.* NOT a sentence: ~~*When we arrive.*~~
there was no school	*because it was Sunday*	*There was no school.* *There was no school because it was Sunday.* *Because it was Sunday, there was no school.* NOT a sentence: ~~*Because it was Sunday.*~~
is this the town	*where you grew up*	*Is this the town?* *Is this the town where you grew up?* NOT a sentence: ~~*Where you grew up.*~~
we have everything	*that we need* *we need*	*We have everything.* *We have everything that we need.* *We have everything we need.* NOT sentences: ~~*We need.*~~ ~~*That we need.*~~

2.17.2 Building sentences with subordination

Subordination refers to the ways we construct sentences with subordinate clauses. Other chapters of this text deal with subordinate clauses and the subordinating conjunctions that introduce them.

Types of subordinate clauses	
Noun clauses, using *that* or a *wh* word (*what, when,* etc.)	Chapter 7
Relative clauses, using *that, which, who, whose,* etc.	Chapter 8
Adverbial clauses, using *when, because, although,* etc.	Chapter 9
Conditional clauses, using *if, unless,* etc.	Chapter 10

2.17.3 Building sentences with coordination

Coordination refers to the use of coordinating conjunctions (coordinators). The most important are *and* (for addition), *but* and *yet* (for contrast), *or* (for alternatives), and *so* (for a result.) We also use *nor*, meaning "and…not," after a negative clause and *for*, which is similar to *because*. To remember these words, students sometimes use the mnemonic *FANBOYS*, from the first letters of the words.

a.	*We all want to contribute to society, **and** our daily work is one way we do that.*	*And* introduces additional information.
b.	*People seek a sense of purpose from their work, **but** /**yet** many jobs don't really provide that.*	*But* and *yet* introduce contrasting information. Sometimes we use *and yet*: *People seek a sense of purpose from their work, and yet many jobs …*
c.	*Machines are capable of doing many types of work, **so** some companies are replacing humans with machines.*	*So* introduces a result. Sometimes we use *and so*: *Machines are capable of doing many kinds of work, and so …*
d.	*Factory owners often face a difficult choice. They can continue to employ a human work force, **or** they can replace human workers with machines.*	*Or* introduces an alternative.
e.	*Machines do not complain about working conditions, **nor do they** miss work because of illness or childcare problems.* = *… **and they do not** miss …*	We can use *nor* (usually after a negative clause) to mean "and … not." Note the structure: *nor **do they** …* (*nor they*) See 2.13.2.
d.	*Machines tend to be more reliable than human workers, **for** even the best-trained workers make mistakes.*	*For* is like *because*, but it is rather formal. It may sound too formal in some writing.

In the examples above, coordinating conjunctions join independent clauses, and commas separate the parts; the coordinating conjunction does not begin a new sentence. The same is true in (e) below. However, we *can* begin a sentence with a coordinating conjunction, especially if the part before the conjunction is long and complex (f, g).

When can you begin a sentence with *and* or *but*?

e.	*Email is a convenient way to communicate, **but** it can be a burden for employees.*	After short, simple information, the part with a coordinating conjunction is added after a comma.
f.	*According to one study, office workers spend 28 percent of their time dealing with email. They check for messages constantly, interrupting other tasks. **And** a lot of that checking happens at home.*	After long, complex information, especially if it is expressed in more than one sentence, a coordinating conjunction often begins a new sentence.
g.	*Many important ideas in education — like having students do group projects and emphasizing active learning instead of lectures — have been implemented in grade schools and high schools. **But** in many colleges and universities, lecture-style education persists.*	

For information about using coordinating conjunctions with other sentence parts (besides independent clauses), see 2.18.4.

■ **Exercise 27** Choose one of the three coordinating conjunctions for each blank. (If you think another coordinating conjunction could be used, prepare to discuss that option.)

The end of work?

"The end of work" is a phrase that some writers have used to describe the way machines are doing more of the work that used to be done by people. This trend is also referred to as automation. We can welcome automation, __ we can view it with skepticism.   *or, so, nor*

People who welcome automation point out an unfortunate fact: Most work is not very interesting, __ does it provide the worker with a sense of purpose. If automation frees people to do more interesting things, that's a good result.   *so, but, nor*

Of course, unemployed people still need an income, __ no one is going to pay them for learning to paint or play the guitar, no matter how rewarding those activities are. Skeptics also argue that Americans tend to view work as a good thing in itself, regardless of benefits. The idea is that all work is honorable, __ even the lowliest ditch digger contributes to the welfare of society.   *so, and, or*

for, or, but

Whether we view automation with joy or fear, it is not going to go away. It is true that certain jobs may seem to require a human touch, __ machines are already doing some of those jobs. You may think that only a person can write a news article, __ some news organizations are already publishing articles generated by machines. The content of some types of articles is predictable and repetitive, __ machines can produce them quite easily.   *but, and, for*

so, and, yet

yet, or, so

Is automation something to look forward to, __ is it something to fear? Maybe both.   *and, or, but*

2.18 Parallelism with independent clauses and other structures

2.18.1 *And*

- The coordinating conjunction *and* can join independent clauses (a), verbs or predicates (b), objects (c), adverbials (d), subjects (e), prepositions (f), and subordinate clauses of various types (g-i).
- Elements joined by *and* may be inside phrases and clauses of all types.
- We use the term **parallelism** or **parallel structure** for structures involving *and*. The parts we join with *and* have the same grammatical role and usually the same or similar forms.
- We sometimes use a comma between **independent clauses** joined by *and* (a). With other elements, we do not usually use a comma.
- We can also join more than two elements of any type (j), using commas and *and*: A, B, C, *and* D. (The comma before *and* is optional.)

a. *I drink coffee, and you drink tea.*	Independent clause + independent clause (See also section 2.17.3.)
b. *I drink coffee and watch the news.*	Predicate + predicate
c. *I drink coffee and tea.*	Object + object
d. *I drink coffee in the morning and after dinner.*	Adverbial + adverbial
e. *My mom and my sister drink green tea.* (~~drinks~~)	Subject + subject (+ a plural verb)
f. *There are cafés in and around my neighborhood.*	Preposition + preposition
g. *I find that wine gives me a headache and (that) coffee keeps me awake.*	Object noun clause + object noun clause (Ch. 7)
h. *What you do and where you go is up to you.*	Subject noun clause + subject noun clause (Ch. 7) Note that the verb (is) is singular.
i. *A widow is a woman whose husband has died and who has not remarried.*	Relative clause + relative clause (Ch. 8)
j. *Teaching assistants grade papers, hold office hours, and help professors in other ways.*	Predicate + predicate + predicate

2.18.2 Avoiding faulty parallelism

Elements joined by *and* should have the same grammatical function: subjects, objects, predicates, etc. Usually they have the same form: nouns and nouns, verbs and verbs, etc. In (a)-(j), *and* joins elements with the same function and the same form. Sometimes the forms can be different if the functions are the same. In particular, parallel predicates (k) and modifiers (l) often have different forms. To avoid the mistake of faulty parallelism, do not join elements with different functions (m).

k. *I have worked here for 10 years and hope to continue.*	Parallel predicates of different forms
l. *Are you experienced and able to work well with others?*	Parallel modifiers (adjective phrases) of different forms
m. Wrong: *Are you experienced and can work well with others?* → *Are you experienced and able to work well ...?* OR *Are you experienced, and can you work well ...?*	Faulty parallelism: A modifier (an adjective) + a predicate (*can* ...). Use parallel modifiers or parallel clauses.

2.18.3 The algebra of coordination

One way to understand coordination is to think of it as shown below.

$d(a + b) = da + db$	The first element, d, is "distributed" to the conjoined elements. D goes with both a and b.
WRONG: *For this assignment, our professor asked us to choose a major news event from the year of our birth ~~and did a little research about it~~.*	... asked us to choose ... and do ... The "distributor" is ... *asked us to*. *Asked us to choose* (da) is correct, but *asked us to did* (db) is not.

2.18.4 *But* and *or* with a variety of structures

We also use the coordinating conjunctions *but* and *or* to join a variety of types of structures, as long as the functions are the same.

n. *I like **oysters**, but **oysters don't like me**.*	Independent clause + independent clause
o. *She is **qualified** but **unable to start right away**.*	Modifier + modifier
p. *With breakfast I drink **coffee** or **tea**.*	Object + object
q. *We need an employee who **knows this software** or **can learn it quickly**.*	Predicate + predicate

■ **Exercise 28** Compare the structures of the sentences below, focusing on the two things in each one that are joined with *and*. In the blanks, copy one word from the part before *and* which is "distributed" (2.28.3) to the words after *and*. The first item is done for you. The answers follow.

Notice that only the last one has a comma before *and*. Why?

1. She asked us to read several books and poems.	*several* poems
2. She asked us to read several books and one poem.	_____ one poem
3. She asked us to read several books and prepare for a quiz.	_____ prepare for a quiz
4. She asked us to read several books and gave us only three days to do it.	_____ gave us three days
5. She asked us to read several books, and I thought "There goes the weekend!"	Nothing is "distributed," since the part after *and* is complete by itself.

Fix the problem in the sentence below. It is a problem because the part that is "distributed" does not go well with the part after *and*.

6. She asked us to read several books and poems, summarize them, and prepared for a quiz.

Answers: (2) <u>read</u> one poem, (3) <u>to</u> prepare for a quiz, (4) <u>She</u> gave. In (5) there is a comma before and (optionally) because the joined parts are both sentences (independent clauses). In (6), change *prepared* to *prepare* because *to* is the part that needs to be "distributed": *She asked us to prepare*. (See also 2.2.3.)

■ **Exercise 29** In the passage, underline the coordinating conjunctions (*and, or,* and *but*) and notice the parallelism. What kind of elements are joined? (For example, in the first paragraph, *and* joins subjects, and *but* joins independent clauses.) Look for **two or three** faulty parallelism problems. These problems are also word form problems (2.3). Fix each one by changing a word to make it parallel to an earlier word.

What kind of exercise is best? Running, playing a sport, and lifting weights all have their attractions, but what about walking?

Walking provides good exercise and doesn't cost a dime. You don't have to pay for a health club membership or special equipment. You can walk in your neighborhood, near your work place, or in a park. If you walk in your neighborhood, you'll notice what's going on — like a garage sale or remodeling project — and you might run into neighbors you don't often see. If you walk near your place of work, you might ask a coworker to join you. It's an easy way to socialize with a co-worker and develop a relationship without the bother of inviting the person to an event or have a party. If your neighborhood or work place isn't convenient for walking, a public park is probably just a short drive or bus ride away. There you can not only exercise your limbs but enjoy a calm atmosphere, away from traffic.

And yes, traffic can be a hazard. So if you walk where traffic is heavy, keep alert and resist the temptation to listen to music as you walk. Listening to a favorite song, you might not notice a careless driver or an obstacle in your path.

If you're worried about being bored while walking, think of it as an opportunity to reflect and maybe even solving problems. Doing nothing (or nearly nothing) is a platform for creativity. When your mind is free of distractions, you might be surprised to find that ideas bubble up, invite you to inspect them, and strengthen themselves, just as you strengthen your legs, your heart, and your lungs.

■ **Exercise 30** Correct the faulty parallelism mistakes, one in each item. In different items, you may need to change a word form (see 2.2), omit words, reorder words, or add words. There may be more than one way.

1. Everyone wants to be successful, healthy, and happiness.

2. When I think about being happy, healthy, and success, I think first of my family.

3. This new product costs less, lasts longer, and it works better.

4. This new product lasts longer, works better, and less cost.

5. Seeking input from experts, weighing alternatives wisely, considering consequences carefully, and learn from mistakes are all things we expect of a good leader.

6. A good leader seeks input from experts, weighs alternatives wisely, considers consequences carefully, and learning from mistakes.

7. Careful driving reduces energy consumption and less dangerous.

8. If you drive more carefully, you can reduce your energy consumption and lowering your risk of an accident.

9. We need applicants who communicate well, know the local market, and good teamwork skills.

10. If you have good teamwork skills, knowledge of the local market, and experienced in sales, you might be the person we need.

11. As a job seeker, you need to identify companies you'd like to work for, find out what those companies value, and different versions of your resume that match each company's needs.

12. When you prepare different versions of your resume, you can highlight the experience and skillful that the company needs.

13. In your writing class, you will read articles, write and revise papers, keep a journal, and weekly quizzes.

14. Teachers teach, grade homework, prepare quizzes, and faculty meetings every week.

15. Diligence, obedience to authority, and respect for elders are admirable qualities, but we also want students to be creative, tolerant, and they should be resilient.

2.19 Fragments, run-ons, and comma splices

- Independent clauses (sentences) must be separated by a period. When you fail to separate sentences with a period, you create an error known as a **run-on** (a, b).
- If you separate independent clauses (sentences) with a comma instead of a period, you create an error known as a **comma splice** (c).
- If you punctuate a sentence part as a sentence, you create a **fragment** (d, e).

Some books use the term *run-on* for both run-ons and comma splices. See also Appendix B, "Basic punctuation for joining clauses," at the end of the book.

Problem	How to fix it	Revision
Run-on: a. WRONG: *Humans use tools we are not the only animals that do that.*	Add a conjunction between the parts, usually with a comma before it.	*Humans use tools, but we are not the only animals that do that.*
Run-on: b. WRONG: *Apes are smart they even use twigs as tools.* **Comma splice:** c. WRONG: *Apes are smart, they even use twigs as tools.*	Separate the parts with a period.	*Apes are smart. They even use twigs as tools.*
Fragments: d. WRONG: *Twigs are useful to apes. Because they can serve as tools.*	Join the fragment to the sentence before it (sometimes with a comma).	*Twigs are useful to apes because they can serve as tools.* OR: *Twigs are useful to apes, because ...* OR *Because they can serve as tools, twigs are useful to apes.*
	Omit the subordinating conjunction, creating two sentences.	*Twigs are useful to apes. They can serve as tools.*
e. WRONG: *When an animal uses an object in its environment to accomplish some goal. We can say that the animal is using a tool.*	Join the fragment to the sentence after it. Omit the subordinating conjunction and use different words to create two sentences.	*When an animal uses an object in its environment to accomplish some goal, we can say that the animal is using a tool.* **Sometimes** *an animal uses an object in its environment to accomplish some* **goal.** **Then** *we can say that the animal is using a tool.*

2.20 Adverbs

Adverbs are a large class of words and phrases that serve various functions, usually optional, in sentences. The term *adverbial* is also used, especially for adverbs that consist of more than one word. (For adverbial clauses, see Ch. 9. Transition expressions are also a kind of adverb; see Ch. 3.) Adverbs can appear in various places in a sentence. The examples below show typical patterns, but there are often other options.

Adverbs **modify verbs** or **predicates** to express time, place, manner, frequency, reason, purpose, and intensity:

a.	Time (when):	do it **now**	leave **tomorrow**	start **as soon as possible**
b.	Place (where):	come **here**	move **forward**	interact **in cyberspace**
c.	Manner (how):	say it **clearly**	work **slowly**	answer **with a smile**
d.	Frequency (how often):	**often** makes mistakes	**always** asks questions	**never** happens
e.	Reason (why):	thank him **for helping**	quit **out of frustration**	resign **because of a scandal**
f.	Purpose (what for):	travel **for fun**	stop **to rest**	stand up **in order to see**
g.	Intensity (how much):	talk **a lot**	**really** like sports	agree **to some extent**

Adverbs **modify adjectives** (h) or other **adverbs** (i) to express intensity (how much, to what degree):

h.	Turtles are **somewhat / quite / pretty / rather / very** slow.	(*Pretty* is informal.)
i.	Turtles move **somewhat / quite / pretty / rather / very** slowly.	

We do not usually use the adverbs in (h) and (i) to modify verbs or predicates.

j.	Most children ~~very~~ like animals. → **really** like animals / like animals **a lot**

We use adverbs that **modify sentences** to express our characterization of the message (k) or our degree of certainty (l) or to limit a generalization (m).

k.	**Frankly**, I don't care.	**Unfortunately**, the dog ate my homework.
l.	**Maybe** I'm wrong.	**No doubt** you've heard the news.
m.	**In general**, we agree.	**For the most part**, people are cooperative.

We can often form an adverb by adding *-ly* to an adjective (n). However, we use *hard*, *late*, and *fast* as adverbs without *-ly* (o). Some words with *-ly* (*friendly*, *ugly*) are adjectives, not adverbs. With these words, we can form an adverb phrase: *She smiled in a friendly way* (NOT ~~smiled friendly~~).

	Sentences with adjectives	Sentences with adverbs
n.	Her explanation was **slow** and **clear**.	She explained **slowly** and **clearly**. (~~slow, clear~~)
o.	He's a **hard** worker. He's a **fast** worker. His work is never **late**.	He works **hard**. He works **fast**. He never hands his work in **late**. (~~hardly, fastly, lately~~)

• *Hardly* and *lately* have other uses not related to the examples above. Check a dictionary.

We don't usually put an adverb (or other words) between a verb and its object (p). Note, however, that a particle in a phrasal verb (*on, in, off, away*, etc.; see 2.10) is considered part of the verb (q).

p.	She ~~speaks fluently~~ French.	She speaks French **fluently**.
q.	You should put on ~~first~~ your glasses.	You should put on your glasses **first**. You should **first** put on your glasses. **First**, you should put on your glasses.

2.21 Time expressions in the form of noun phrases

Expressions with time words like *time, day,* and *year* can be used a subjects or objects (a, b) and as adverbials (c, d) without any preposition.

Time expressions as subjects	Time expressions as adverbials
a. **The day after tomorrow** is my birthday.	c. I'll see you (on) **the day after tomorrow**.
b. Can you recall **the first time you heard a foreign language**?	d. **The first time I heard a foreign language**, I was about six years old.

Days of the week (e) and phrases based on them (f) can be used as adverbials alone or after *on*.

e. Do you work **(on) Sunday**?	f. Our class meets **(on) Tuesday evening**.

We don't use a preposition before expressions like *this year* (*week, morning, season,* etc.), no matter where they are in a sentence. The same is true for expressions with *last* and *next* when they are followed by nouns like *week, month, season, semester, term,* and *year*.

f. I took 20 credits last semester. This semester I have 21. (~~in last / in this~~)	Expressions like *this semester, last week,* and *next year* do not require a preposition.

Time expressions with *this, last,* and *next* are usually oriented to the moment of speaking or writing, just like *tomorrow* and *yesterday*. That is, *this week* means now, and *next week* means the week after now (f). When such expressions are not oriented to the moment of speaking, we add *the* (h).

g. *Classes begin next week. I registered last week.*	The reference point for *next* and *last* is now, the moment of speaking.
h. *We arrived on a Friday. Classes began **the** next week.*	*The next week* is not related to now.

■ **Exercise 31** Look for two kinds of mistakes: (1) Find words that come between a verb and the object of the verb. Change the word order so that each object comes directly after its verb. (2) Look for time expressions like those in 2.2.1 and revise them if they are incorrect. Every item has one mistake.

1. I usually drink coffee with my breakfast, but I have sometimes tea. This morning I had tea.
2. If you speak fluently Chinese or English, you can form relationships with millions of people you might otherwise never be able to communicate with.
3. The Language Center provides labs for classes. They have also a lab for independent work.
4. Last semester I took Professor Allen's rhetoric class. In most of her classes, the students give every Friday oral presentations.
5. I took in high school Latin, but since then I haven't taken any foreign language classes. Next term I might take Greek.
6. Haiku is a very short form of poetry in Japanese. A haiku has three lines. It includes often a theme from nature.
7. I couldn't finish my paper last night. I was too busy. I'll try to do it in this evening.

USAGE GUIDE

2.22 Beginning and ending sentences

2.22.1 Beginning with an adverbial The most basic sentences begin with a subject, but we often begin with adverbial elements (2.21), especially to avoid confusing a reader or listener (a-c).

a.	*We read an article about a single mother who raised 12 children last week.* → *Last week, we read an article ...*	She didn't raise 12 children *last week!*
b.	*The author writes about problems his family had when he was growing up in the first chapter.* → *In the first chapter, the author writes about...*	Beginning with the adverbial *in the first chapter* puts it closer to the word it modifies, *writes*.
c.	*In small towns, all high school students study the same things. Students can choose from lots of different courses in large urban schools.* → *In large urban schools, students can choose ...*	Starting with information about the place (*in large urban schools*) makes the sentence easier to process.

2.22.2 Old before new We often begin with **old** information that echoes something from the preceding sentence, making the connection clear for the reader or listener (d, e). In general, we end a sentence with the most important information — **new** information that we are going to develop in the following sentence. See also Appendix D, "Principles for ordering information in sentences."

d.	*Our goal is to increase production by 20%.* **To meet this goal**, *we need to hire more staff and upgrade our equipment.*	*To meet this goal* (an adverbial of purpose; see 9.12) echoes old information (*Our goal*) from the preceding sentence.
e.	*In high school, I became interested in other languages and countries.* **That interest** *was nurtured by a history teacher who encouraged me to take a "gap" year for travel after graduation.* **During that year**, *I traveled to South America, where I immersed myself in another language and learned things I could never have learned from books.* **Now, as I look ahead to my college years**, *I am drawn to universities with strong international ties.*	*That interest* (the subject) echoes old information (*I became interested in ...*) from the preceding sentence. *During that year* (an adverbial of time) echoes old information (*a "gap" year*) in the preceding sentence. *Now, as I look ahead ...* (an initial adverbial of time) clearly marks a shift in the topic.

USAGE GUIDE

2.22.3 Beginning with a noun phrase If you begin with a noun or noun phrase that is not a time adverbial (2.22), use it as a subject — that is, with a verb after it. Avoid the mistake of starting a sentence with a noun phrase that is neither a subject nor part of an adverbial (f - i).

f. *In suburban areas, people rely on cars.* ~~Large cities, people can use public transportation.~~	→ **In** *large cities, people can ...* *Large cities* is changed to an adverbial. OR **Large cities have** *better public transportation.* *Large cities* is the subject, with predicate that matches it.
g. ~~*Recent years*~~, *more and more young people have been deciding to delay or even forgo marriage.*	→ **Recently,** *more and more young people ...* OR **In recent years,** *more and more young people ...* *Recent years* can become an adverbial with *–ly* or with *in* before it.
h. ~~*My long term goal*~~, *I want to get a job in the financial sector.*	→ *My long term goal is to get a job ...* (See 6.7)
i. ~~*Our main problem*~~, *we didn't have enough time.*	→ *Our main problem was that we didn't ...* (See 7.6.)

Days of the week are used as adverbials with no preposition or with *on*, no matter where they appear in the sentence (j).

j. *Sundays we are open from 10 to 6.*	*Sundays* by itself can be an adverbial. Also correct: *On Sundays*.

2.22.4 Beginning with *For* We sometimes use a phrase starting with *For* at the beginning of a sentence to clarify the thing of person we are talking about (k). We usually don't begin with *For X* if we can instead begin with *X* as the subject (l, m).

k. *For older people in the U.S., November 22, 1963, is a memorable date.*	*For older people* at the beginning makes it clear whose memories we are talking about.
l. ~~*For older people in the U.S., they will*~~ *never forget November 22, 1963.* → *Older people in the U.S. will never ...*	*For* is not needed because *Older people* can be the subject of the sentence.
m. *Mexican people tend to value family and tradition.* ~~*For Americans, they seem to be more individualistic and less concerned about the past.*~~ *Americans seem ...*	*For* is not needed because *Americans* can be the subject of the sentence. Another option: *As for Americans, they seem ...*

2.22.5 Beginning with an *–ing* word An *–ing* word or phrase at the beginning may be a subject (n; see also 6.4). It may also be an adverbial, usually with a comma after it (o). If it is an adverbial, you need a subject after it. Avoid mixing these two types of structures (p). See also 2.2.4.

n. *Kendra is bilingual.* <u>*Knowing a second language*</u> *is a great advantage.*   [Subject]   [Predicate]
o. *Knowing a second language,*   <u>*she*</u>   <u>*has*</u> <u>*a*</u> <u>*great*</u> <u>*advantage*</u>.   [Adverbial]   [Subject]   [Predicate]
p. ~~*Knowing a second language has a great advantage.*~~

USAGE GUIDE

2.23 Sentence variety in your writing

2.23.1 Traditional sentence types Traditional grammar classifies sentences as shown below. When writing teachers advise students to add sentence variety to their writing, they are often thinking of this classification.

Simple:	*I will call you.*	There is just one clause.
Compound:	*I will call you, and you can pick us up.*	Two or more clauses are joined by coordination (2.17.3).
Complex:	*I will call you when we arrive.* *When we arrive, I will call you.*	There are two or more clauses with at least one subordinate clause (*when we arrive*).
Compound-complex:	*I will call you when we arrive, and you can pick us up.* *I will call you when we arrive, and you can pick us up if you're not too busy.*	There are two or more independent clauses (*I will call you, you can pick us up*) with at least one subordinate clause (*when we arrive, if you're not too busy*).

2.23.2 Avoiding choppiness We use the term **choppy** to describe writing in which sentences are short and simple, mostly following the same pattern (usually with the subject first). You can avoid choppiness by combining sentence parts using coordination (2.17.3) and subordination (2.17.2 and Ch. 9) and by omitting unnecessary parts.

	Choppy style	Improved style	
a.	*My name is J. M. I am 23 years old. I am a social worker. I got my degree in social work because I love to help people. I have worked as a social worker for one year.*	b. *My name is J.M., and I am 23 years old. Because I love to help people, I got my degree in social work and have worked in the field for one year.*	• Two short sentences are joined by *and* (2.17.3); the third is omitted. • The part with *Because* ... is moved to the beginning. • The last sentence is reduced to a predicate that is parallel to *got my degree in social work* (2.18).
c.	I'm going to Florida during winter break. There are many tourist attractions in Florida. It's hard to choose among them. We plan to spent 10 days there. I don't know whether it is enough or not.	d. I'm going to Florida during winter break. There are so many tourist attractions in Florida that it's hard to choose among them. Though we plan to spend ten days there, I don't know whether it is enough.	• Two simple sentences are joined by subordination with *so...that* (9.11). • Two simple sentences are joined by subordination using *though* (9.19.2) and the unnecessary words or *not* are omitted (7.4.2).

Usage Guide

2.24 Avoiding gender bias in pronoun choice

Choosing between male and female pronouns can be difficult. Should you say *Everyone has his own opinion? Everyone has his or her own opinion? Everyone has their own opinion?* Should you avoid the choice by saying *Everyone has an opinion?* Traditionally, male pronouns were often used to refer to words like *everyone* and *someone* and phrases like *a student* or *an applicant*. Today, to avoid gender bias, we use other options. Options (d) and (e) below can help you avoid problems.

a. *For this job, we need an applicant who knows how to use **his** time efficiently.*	The sentence may suggest that only men can be hired. To avoid gender bias, this style is avoided today.
b. *For this job, we need an applicant who knows how to use **his or her** time efficiently.*	We can use *his* or *her* — and *he or she*, *he/she*, and *s/he* — but this style is becoming less common today.
c. *For this job, we need an applicant who knows how to use **their** time efficiently.*	This style is sometimes recommended today, even though *their* traditionally refers only to a plural noun.
d. *For this job, we need **applicants** who know how to use **their** time efficiently.*	This revision uses a plural noun as the referent of *their*.
e. *For this job, we need an applicant **with good time management skills**.*	This revision avoids problems of pronoun choice by using a different expression.

2.25 Impersonal *you* and *one* in generalizations

We can use the pronouns *one* and *you* (impersonal *you*) in generalizations. *One* is formal.

a. In this painting, one can see the artist's mastery of color.	The sentence is a generalization, in formal style, about what anyone can see.
b. When you reach a certain point in life, ask yourself, "How do I want to be remembered?"	The sentence is a generalization about what happens to everyone.

2.26 Avoiding shifting points of view

Avoid the problem shown below, sometimes referred to as **shifting points of view**. Below, each sentence on the left begins well, but the pronoun that follows doesn't work well with the beginning. This problem often occurs in generalizations. When you use *you* or *people* in making a generalization, be consistent throughout the sentence.

Avoid this:	Use a consistent point of view:
a. *When people are motivated, you can do almost anything.*	*When you are motivated, you can do almost anything.* *When people are motivated, they can do almost anything.*
b. *The library employees help me a lot. When you need help, they are always there.*	*The library employees help me a lot. When I need help, they are always there.* *The library employees are very helpful. When you need help, they are always there.*

2.27 Problems with sentence structure (see also 2.14.5)

Problem sentences	Revisions	
1. In my country has a centralized education system.	- <u>My country</u> <u>has</u> ... - In my country, <u>we</u> <u>have</u> ... - In my country, <u>there</u> <u>is</u> ...	A sentence or clause needs a <u>subject</u> and a <u>complete verb</u>. See 2.2. (There are some exceptions.*)
2. We returned the product because didn't work properly.	We returned the product because <u>it</u> <u>didn't work</u> properly.	
3. The Wall Street Journal one of the most influential news organizations in the country.	<u>The Wall Street Journal</u> <u>is</u> one of the most ...	
4. People that you have never met, they have different experiences.	<u>People that you have never</u> met <u>have</u> different experiences.	Don't use an extra subject. (2.2.2)
5. Recent years, the world has experienced many serious natural disasters.	In recent years, the <u>world</u> <u>has</u> ... OR <u>Recent years</u> <u>have been marked</u> by a number of serious natural disasters.	Every noun phrase needs to have a grammatical role — usually as subject, the object of a verb, or the object of a preposition. (2.2)
6. A lot of food are wasted.	<u>A lot of **food**</u> <u>is</u> ...	
7. Problems related to global warming is especially serious for low-lying countries.	**<u>Problems</u>** <u>related to global warming</u> <u>are</u> ...	Verbs must agree with subjects. (2.2.5)
8. I went to a party but I didn't enjoy.	I went to a party, but I didn't enjoy it. OR I didn't enjoy myself.	Some verbs require an object. (2.4.2)
9. By the time we arrived our apartment, we were exhausted.	By the time we arrived, we were ... OR By the time we arrived at our apartment, we were ...	Don't use an object after an intransitive verb. (2.4.4)
10. I don't need my laptop today, so I can lend you.	... lend it to you ...	For two-object verbs, follow the rules in section 2.6.
11. The committee gives scholarships for needy students.	... gives scholarships to needy students / gives needy students scholarships.	
12. There are five parts each one has four pages. (This type of error is called a run-on.)	There are five parts. Each one has ... OR There are five parts, and each one ...	Make separate sentences or use a conjunction between the parts. (2.19 and Appendix B)
13. There are five parts, each one has four pages. (This type of error is called a comma splice.)		

14. Spellchecking programs are not completely reliable. Because they miss some mistakes and they point out some things that are not mistakes.	Spellchecking programs are not completely reliable (,) because they miss … OR … not completely reliable. They miss …	This type of error is called a fragment. Join the fragment to another sentence OR omit the conjunction, creating two sentences. (2.19 and Appendix B)
15. We live on a bus line. But, we never take the bus.	We live on a bus line, but we never take the bus. OR We live on a bus line. However, we never take the bus.	We don't normally use a comma after *but*. The comma goes before *but*. (2.19 and Appendix B)
16. Many performers who are known primarily for their acting can also sing and dancing.	Many performers who are known primarily for their acting can also <u>sing</u> and <u>dance</u>. (<u>Performers can sing</u> and <u>performers can dance</u>.)	Elements joined by a coordinating conjunction (usually *and*) should be in the similar forms: noun phrase and noun phrase, predicate and predicate, etc. The first part (A) must work well with both of the other parts, B and C: A (B and C) = AB and AC.
17. Texting while driving will distract you and might have an accident.	Texting while driving will distract you and you might have an accident. (Parallel independent clauses) OR Texting while driving will distract you and might cause an accident. (Parallel predicates: <u>will distract you</u> and <u>might cause</u> …)	
18. If you exercise regularly will make you feel stronger.	If you exercise regularly, <u>you will feel</u> stronger. OR <u>Exercising regularly</u> <u>will make</u> you feel …	
19. One of the sports I like best is playing tennis.	One of the **sports** I like best is **tennis**. OR One of the **things/ activities** I like best is **playing tennis**.	The beginning of the sentence must fit the end. Avoid mismatches. (2.2.4)
20. Driving a car instead of taking the bus spends too much money.	**Driving** a car instead of taking the bus costs too much money. OR If you drive instead of take the bus, you spend too much money.	
21. I very like it.	I really like it / like it very much / I like it a lot.	(2.20 h and i)

*Some exceptions to the rule that every sentence needs a subject and a verb:
- In imperative sentences (commands), there is an implied subject *you* but there is no overt subject. An imperative sentence usually begins with a verb: Be careful. (= YOU should be careful). Don't go so fast. (= YOU should not go so fast.)
- Some special sentence patterns do not always require a subject and a verb: *The sooner, the better*.
- We often shorten sentences, especially in conversation, omitting subjects and parts of verb phrases: *Seen any good movies lately?* (= *Have you seen…?*) *Want some more coffee?* (= *Do you want…?*) *Having a good time?* (= *Are you having…?*) In writing as well as in speaking, we often answer a question without using a complete sentence. (*What accounts for academic success? A combination of ability and effort.*)

Chapter 3

Transition expressions and sentence flow

IN THIS CHAPTER
Linking sentences by using transition expressions and other techniques for smooth sentence flow

Chapter 3
Transition expressions and sentence flow

This chapter is about **transition expressions** – like *however*, *in addition*, and *as a result* – as well as the larger topic of **sentence flow:** the ways in which we help readers or listeners follow our thinking, sometimes with words like *however* and sometimes with other techniques, like parallel construction and placing old before new information.

Other names for transition expressions are *conjunctive adverbs, linking adverbials,* and *transitions.*

Chapter 3: Transition expressions and sentence flow		...65
3.1	Transition expressions in context	67
3.2	What are transition expressions?	67
3.3	Transition expressions listed alphabetically	68
3.4	Expanded transition expressions.	69
3.5	Placement and punctuation of transition expressions	70
3.6	Transition expressions and conjunctions.	71
3.7	Meanings that transition expressions express	72
3.8	Addition, examples, details, and restatement	74
3.9	Result, time, and text structure	76
3.10	Contrast	77
3.11	Correcting a misconception	78
3.12	Concession	79
3.13	Condition	80
3.14 Usage guide	Punctuation with *so* and *yet*	81
3.15 Usage guide	Placing *however* and *for example* between sentence parts	81
3.16 Usage guide	Using expanded transition expressions for conciseness	82
3.17 Usage guide	Old before new information	82
3.18 Usage guide	Parallel structure and repetition	83
3.19 Usage guide	Review: Five ways of achieving good sentence flow	83
3.20	Problems with transition expressions	87

Chapter 3 — Transition expressions and sentence flow

3.1 Transition expressions in context

■ **Exercise 1** In the passage below, underline the transition expressions. (If you wish, look first at 3.2 and 3.3) How do you think these expressions help the reader understand the paragraph? Do you know other expressions that function like these?

> It is common knowledge that modern humans originated in Africa. Most textbooks say that modern humans left Africa about 60,000 years ago. Recently, however, archaeologists discovered stone tools in the Arabian Peninsula, suggesting that the migration of humans out of Africa may have happened earlier. In fact, the dating of these tools indicates that humans were present in the area more than 100,000 years ago. Other discoveries have shown that Arabia at that time was cooler, had a wetter climate and was much more fertile. As a result, there would have been more plants, grassland, and animals to provide food for a human population.

KEY
Ch. 6 = Chapter 6
Ex. 23 = Exercise 23
5.2 = Chapter 5, section 2
2.14.3 = Chapter 2, section 14, subsection 3
(a) = an example

3.2 What are transition expressions?

Transition expressions are words and phrases that show how the ideas in sentences are related. They indicate addition (a), contrast (b), result (c), and other relationships.

a. *The house is too small.* **In addition**, *the neighbors are noisy and there's no garage.*
b. *He says they've never met.* **However**, *I've seen photos of them together.*
c. *The man was born in Texas.* **Therefore**, *he's an American citizen.*

- We often put transition expressions at the beginning of the sentence, followed by a comma (d).
- We also put transition expressions at the end (e) or inside the sentence, separated by commas (f).
- We don't usually put transition expressions between a verb and its object (g) or after a pronoun subject (h).
- We can use a transition expression after a pronoun subject if the pronoun itself is contrasting information (i).

d. *Lucy has a degree in art.* **However**, *she doesn't see herself as an artist.*	*However, ...*
e. *She can play the piano. She has not studied music formally,* ***however***.	*, however.*
f. *She enjoys art. Her real love,* ***however***, *is music.*	[Subject], *however*, [verb]
g. *She likes classical music. Her friends prefer,* ~~however~~, *pop music. However, her friends prefer / Her friends, however, prefer...*	Don't put the transition expression between a verb and its object. (See Ch. 2.3.3.)
h. *She likes jazz.* ~~She, however, does not usually play it.~~ *However, she does not usually play it.*	*She* and *she* refer to the same person.
i. *I like pop music. She, however, prefers jazz and classical.* (*She* contrasts with I.)	*She* contrasts with *I*.

HIGH PRIORITY

■ **Exercise 2** Without looking at Exercise 1, choose three of the transition expressions to complete the text. Write them in the blanks at the right. Include the punctuation that is required (including a period before the transition expression if it is needed.) One of the connectors will not be used.

as a result   *for example*   *however*   *in fact*

Most school textbooks say that modern humans left Africa about 60,000 years ago. Recently __ archaeologists have discovered stone tools in the Arabian Peninsula, suggesting that the migration of humans out of Africa may have happened earlier. __ the dating of these tools indicates that humans were present in the area more than 100,000 years ago. Other discoveries have shown that Arabia at that time was cooler, had a wetter climate and was much more fertile __ there would have been more plants, grassland, and animals to provide food for a human population.

Recently _____

... earlier _____ the dating ...

fertile _____ there...

3.3 Transition expressions listed alphabetically

In the list of common transition expressions below, which do you recognize? Which do you use? Which are new to you? (The numbers refer to sections in this chapter.)

8	above all		fortunately, unfortunately*	9	next
8, 10	actually	8	for instance	10	nevertheless
	after all*	8	furthermore	10	nonetheless
9	after that	12	granted	12	of course
9	afterward(s)	10	however	11	on the contrary
10	all the same	13	if not	10	on the other hand
8	also	13	if so	13	otherwise
8	among other things	8	in addition	8	similarly
9	as a consequence		in comparison	9, 14	so
8	as a matter of fact	9	in conclusion	8	specifically
9	as a result	10	in contrast	10	still
	at last*	8	in fact	9	subsequently
10	at the same time	8	in other words	8	that is (to say)
8	besides	8	in particular	9, 13	then
8	beyond that	10	instead	9	therefore
9	consequently	9	in sum	9	thus
10	even so	13	in that case	9	to begin with
9	first(ly)	8	in the same way	12	to be sure
9	finally	8	likewise	9	to sum up
9	for a start	9	meanwhile	12	true
8	for example	9	moreover	10, 14	yet
		8	more / most important(ly)		

* See Appendix C for *after all, at last, fortunately,* and other transition expressions.

Chapter 3 — Transition expressions and sentence flow

■ **Exercise 3** Put a mark (√ = correct, X = incorrect) by each transition expression. Some are correct, some have incorrect forms, and some are misspelled. To check your answers, see 3.3.

__ to begin with	__ another word	__ for examples	__ after all
__ for example	__ in addition	__ in other words	__ infact
__ for instance	__ on the contrary	__ in contrast	__ therefore
__ moreover	__ above all	__ to sum up	__ at the same time
__ as the result	__ furthermore	__ meanwhile	__ on the other hand
__ however	__ in particular	__ in the other hand	__ granted

■ **Exercise 4** Based on what you already know about transition expressions, identify the one that is least similar to the others in the row, in terms of meaning. The rest are not synonymous, but they are similar.

1. therefore, above all, as a result, consequently
2. after that, afterward, after all, finally
3. moreover, furthermore, in addition, thus
4. meanwhile, however, nonetheless, nevertheless
5. in fact, in sum, in conclusion, to begin with

3.4 Expanded transition expressions

as a result of X

in addition to X

Some transition expressions can be expanded to form prepositional phrases (see also 3.16). If you want to use verb after a preposition, you must transform it into a gerund (g, h). See also 6.5.

a. As a consequence of the new law …	b. In comparison to/with earlier studies …
c. As a result of your efforts …	d. In contrast to other countries …
e. In addition to these problems …	f. Instead of our usual routine -…
g. In addition to working part-time … (work)	h. Instead of complaining … (complain)

■ **Exercise 5** Complete the sentences using the words provided to create transition expressions. One word cannot be used. Some words will be used more than once. There may be more than one way.

a   the   as   of   to   in   from   addition   contrast   instead   result

1. Our team had a difficult season. __ injuries, we even had to forfeit one game.

2. We're giving you a full scholarship. In __, we're buying you a new house and a new car.

3. I'm starting a business. __ a boring job with some company, I want a job of my own creation.

4. I grew up in Mexico. __ Mexico City, Minneapolis feels like a small town.

5. I want to attend a school with a good recreation center. __ studying, I want to enjoy myself.

3.5 Placement and punctuation of transition expressions

Most transition expressions can be used at the beginning of a sentence, between sentence parts, or, less commonly, at the end. The examples below show correct and incorrect ways for a typical transition expression.

1 *Running is good exercise. However, no exercise is right for everyone.*

2 *Running is good exercise; however, no exercise is right for everyone.*

3 *Running is good exercise. No exercise, however, is right for everyone.*

4 *Running is good exercise. No exercise is right for everyone, however.*

5 ~~*Running is good exercise, however(,) no exercise is right for everyone.*~~

6 ~~*Running is good exercise however no exercise is right for everyone.*~~

An error like (5) is called a *comma splice*. An error like (6) is a *run-on* sentence. Avoid comma splices and run-ons with transition expressions. See also 2.19 and Appendix B, "Basic punctuation for joining clauses."

Not all transition expressions follow exactly the same punctuation patterns, but for most transition expressions the safest pattern is this one:

. However,   . As a result,   . In addition,

After *so, then,* and *yet,* we usually do not use a comma (see 3.14). But if you use the pattern above for most transition expressions, you will usually avoid a mistake.

■ **Exercise 6** Connect the sentences in (1) below with *however* in four ways. Punctuate carefully. Then do the same with the sentences in (2), using *for example*.

1. Running exercises your heart and legs. Swimming exercises your arms too.

2. For most sports you need equipment. Running requires good shoes.

Chapter 3 — Transition expressions and sentence flow

3.6 Transition expressions and conjunctions

however, but, although

therefore, so, because

Some transition expressions are used with meanings similar to conjunctions, but with different punctuation. Below are examples for contrast (a - c), result (d – f), addition (g, h), and condition (i, j). For more about subordinating conjunctions, see Ch. 9.

a.	*He made a lot of money.* ***However,*** *he wasn't happy.*	A transition expression
b.	*He made a lot of money,* ***but*** *he wasn't happy.*	A coordinating conjunction
c.	***Although*** *he made a lot of money, he wasn't happy.*	A subordinating conjunction
d.	*He was born in Texas.* ***Therefore,*** *he is an American citizen.*	A transition expression
e.	*He was born in Texas,* ***so*** *he is an American citizen.*	A coordinating conjunction
f.	***Because*** *he was born in Texas, he is an American citizen.*	A subordinating conjunction
g.	*Current interest rates discourage saving.* ***Moreover,*** *they limit investment.*	A transition expression
h.	*Current interest rates discourage saving,* ***and*** *they limit investment.*	A coordinating conjunction (The comma is optional.)
i.	*You must include payment.* ***Otherwise,*** *your application won't be processed.*	A transition expression
j.	*You must include payment,* ***or*** *your application won't be processed.*	A coordinating conjunction (The comma is optional.)

Sometimes we use a conjunction and a transition expression together. We can put *and* before *so, then, therefore* (k), *thus, still* (l) and *yet* as part of the second clause.

k. *He was convicted of a serious crime,* ***and therefore*** *he was sentenced to prison.*

l. *I bought them a new television,* ***and still*** *they complained.*

If we omit *and* from (k) and (l), we change the comma to a period or semicolon.

■ **Exercise 7**   For 1 and 2, connect the sentences in three ways (write three sentences for each item): use a transition expression, a coordinating conjunction, and a subordinating conjunction. For 3, write two sentences each: one with a transition expression and one with a coordinating conjunction. Choose among the words that are provided. There is more than one way.

HIGH PRIORITY

although   because   and   but   however   in addition   so   therefore

1. Dogs and cats are both popular pets. Cats are better suited to city living.

2. He's 21 and he's a citizen. He can vote.

3. Her new job pays better than her last job. She finds the work more interesting.

■ **Exercise 8**   Rewrite the sentences using the conjunctions *and, because, but,* and *so* instead of the transition expressions. The sentences are correct; your task is to paraphrase them. There is more than one way.

1. The earthquake survivors will need food and water first. In addition, they'll need blankets and tents or material they can use for shelter.

2. I tried to get an appointment for Monday. However, it's a national holiday and the office will be closed.

3. Raising animals requires vast resources. As a result, a diet that is heavy on meat will be more expensive than a vegetarian diet.

4. There isn't enough money for every service. Consequently, non-essential services must be cut.

3.7   Meanings that transition expressions express

Transition expressions express a variety of meanings. In the examples below, the transition expressions alert listeners or readers to the type of information that is coming: an example, an additional point, a contrasting idea, a result, or a restatement.

1   *You have good people skills.* **For example,** *you're a great listener.*

2   *You have good people skills.* **In addition**, *you work really hard.*

3   *You have good people skills.* **However**, *that's not all you need.*

4   *You have good people skills.* **As a result**, *we've chosen you to head the social committee.*

5   *You have good people skills.* **In other words**, *you communicate well, you understand how to work with others, and you know how to motivate people and inspire trust.*

In the sections that follow, transition expressions are divided into six groups, according to meaning.

3.8   Addition, examples, details, and restatement: *in addition, for example, in other words,* etc.

3.9   Result, time, and text structure: *as a result, afterwards, to begin with,* etc.

3.10   Contrast: *however, in contrast,* etc.

3.11   Correcting a misconception: *on the contrary*

3.12   Concession: *granted, of course, to be sure, true, yes*

3.13   Condition: *if, if so, if not, in that case, otherwise*

Some of the areas of meaning are broad and not clearly defined, and some transition expressions are in more than one group. The best way to learn how to use transition expressions is to learn them as individual items, by studying them in well-written paragraphs. With a few exceptions (like *for example* and *for instance*), there are no truly synonymous expressions among them. See also Appendix C.

■ **Exercise 9** Below is the beginning of an essay arguing that good teachers and classmates are the key to a good education. There is one point in the writing where a reader might become confused. At that point, the addition of one of the transition expressions in 3.7 would help readers follow the writer's thinking. Where should a transition expression be added, and which transition expression would be a good choice?

I got a good high school education. I took a wide variety of courses, I liked my teachers, and I benefited from friendly competition with my peers. I was well-prepared for the university. My old school has declined in quality since I was there. If I have children someday, I'm sorry to say I don't want them to go to the same school I went to.

■ **Exercise 10** In 3.7, the same sentence (*You have good people skills*) is used in combination with five different transition expressions. Using the same transition expressions, create five pairs of sentences based on one or more of the items below (five pairs in which the first sentence is the same for each).

1. You've done well in all your courses.
2. Jacob has money problems.
3. This is a great neighborhood.
4. Some animals have remarkable abilities.
5. English grammar rules often have exceptions.
6. The internet is full of news about celebrities.

in addition

for example

3.8 Addition, examples, details, and restatement

Addition		Examples and details		Restatement
actually *also* *as a matter of fact* *besides* *beyond that* *in addition* *in fact* *not only that, but...*	*above all* *in the same way* *furthermore* *more / most important(ly)* *moreover* *likewise* *similarly*	*for example* *for instance* *among other things*	*for one thing* *in particular*	*specifically* *in other words* *that is (to say)*

Also is the most common transition expressions for adding information. We can put it at the beginning (a) or inside the sentence (b). Especially when the two sentences have the same subject (c), we tend to put *also* inside the second sentence after the subject, the first auxiliary verb (c), or BE (b).

   a. *Intensive farming methods have depleted the soil in many areas.* **Also,** *the excessive use of fertilizer is creating toxic blooms of algae in rivers.*
   b. *There are* **also** *problems caused by diverting more water for irrigation.*
   c. *Using too much fertilizer has negative environmental effects. It may* **also** *waste the farmer's money.* (More idiomatic than *Also, it may waste...*)

We can use a transition expression such as *in addition* in front position to emphasize that there is more information (d). We can use *besides* to introduce another reason or argument to support a previous idea (e).

   d. *Food production costs rise as more fertilizer is used.* **In addition**, *the cost of producing chemical fertilizers is only going to increase.*
   e. *Improving crop yields will have to be accomplished by other means. More fertilizer is no longer the key to higher yields.* **Besides**, *the focus now is on quality, not quantity.*

Informally, we can use *Not only that* or *Not only that, but* to introduce additional information (f).

   f. *Coal is a dirty fuel.* **Not only that, but** *it's dangerous and costly to extract.* (*But* is optional.)

We can use transition expressionss to elaborate on a previous idea by introducing an example (g) or a similar idea (h) or restating the idea in another way (i).

   g. *Climate change affects the rhythm of the seasons.* **For example**, *winter arrives later and rainy seasons become shorter.*
   h. *Everything depends on seasonal change. Warmer weather stimulates plant growth.* **In the same way**, *insects proliferate and birds start building nests.*
   i. *Citizens are concerned about unemployment, inflation, and the power of business interests.* **In other words**, *the economy is their number one concern.*

Such as is not a transition expression. It cannot introduce a clause (j). We use *such as* to introduce an example in the form of a noun or noun phrase. To introduce a clause, use a transition expression like *for example*.

j. *This company has great benefits,* ~~*such as they have free day care.*~~	*This company has great benefits, such as free day care.* *This company has great benefits. For example, they have free day care.*

Chapter 3 — Transition expressions and sentence flow — Grammar Advantage **75**

■ **Exercise 11** Choose four of the transition expressions to complete the text. Write them on the right.

also   for example   in other words   in particular   moreover

The world's population is steadily expanding. __, an increasing proportion of that population is living in cities. City-dwellers are richer and eat more. __, they eat more food that has been processed. They are __ more likely to eat meat, which is the most expensive type of food to produce. In the past twenty years, population growth has slowed to about one and a half percent. The growth in rice harvests has declined by about fifty percent. __, we may not have as many new mouths to feed, but we won't have as many new supplies of food to share among them.

_____

_____

_____

_____

as a result

afterwards

to begin with

3.9 Result, time, and text structure

Result		Time		Text structure	
as a consequence as a result consequently	hence so therefore thus	after that afterwards eventually later	meanwhile next subsequently then	finally first for a start in conclusion	in sum next to begin with to sum up

- The transition expression *after all* is not related to time. See Appendix C.

So is the most common word for marking a result. We can begin a sentence with *so* (a) or use it to join clauses in the same sentence (b). (*So* is also a coordinating conjunction; see 3.14 and 2.17.3.)

a. *In poor countries, there are limited facilities for storage and refrigeration.* **So** *a lot of food is wasted at or near the source.*	Punctuation: refrigeration. So a ...
b. *Many insects are now immune to pesticides,* **so** *damage to crops will increase.*	... pesticides, so damage ...

We also mark a result with transition expressions like *as a result* (c). We often use *therefore* to emphasize a logical result (d).

c. *In parts of Africa, the rainy season now begins much later.* **As a result**, *crops have to be started later and the growing season is shorter.*

d. *Waste will be reduced by at least 3% per year.* **Therefore**, *over a seven-year period, the reduction in waste should be significant.*

We can use *then* (usually with no comma after it) to introduce something that is a logical result (e) or is simply later in time (f). We can use other time-related transition expressions such as *meanwhile* to introduce another idea to be considered at the same time (g).

e. *More food can be produced at a lower cost.* **Then** *everyone benefits.*

f. *There was dry weather early in the season.* **Then** *there was only a little rain.*

g. *Bad weather creates transportation delays.* **Meanwhile**, *harvested crops are rotting on the ground.*

We can use *first, second*, etc. to present a list of ideas (h). We use some infinitive phrases such as *to begin with* to mark how the text is structured (i). We use *finally* to end a list (j).

h. *Waste can be reduced in many ways.* **First,** *we need better storage facilities.*

i. *There are ways to help.* **To begin with**, *farmers need access to better seeds.*

j. **Finally**, *consumers must use food more efficiently.*

■ **Exercise 12** Choose four of these transition expressions to complete the text. Write them on the right. Add punctuation if it is needed.

as a result   first   in conclusion   second   so

Wheat is physically different from corn in two main ways. __ its genes are arranged in pairs of three, not single pairs. __ the wheat genome is much larger than that for corn. __ unlike corn, the reproductive parts of the wheat plant are close together __ wheat tends to self-pollinate.

_____
_____
_____
_____

3.10 Contrast

however all the same at the same time	nevertheless nonetheless	in contrast on the other hand	still yet	instead even so

however

in contrast

- For *fortunately* and *unfortunately,* see Appendix C.

However is the most common transition expression to show contrast. We use it at the beginning (a) and often between sentence parts (b). Less often, we place it at the end (b).

a. *Rich countries waste about the same amount of food as poor countries.* **However,** *they do it in different ways.*

b. *They do it,* **however,** *in different ways. They do it in different ways,* **however.**

Do not use *although* like *however* (c). For ways to use *although,* see 9.19.2.

c. *Junk food is not nutritious.* ~~Although~~*, it can be very tasty.* ➤ *However, it can be …*

We can use *yet* as a transition expression joining sentences in contrast, usually with no comma after it (d), or as a coordinating conjunction joining clauses (e).

d. *Rich countries waste a lot of food.* **Yet** *people in poor countries are starving.*

e. *It's all a matter of better distribution,* **yet** *no one is seriously trying to improve it.*

We use *in contrast* with two different ideas (f). We use *on the contrary* to say the opposite is true, usually after a negative claim (g). See also 3.11.

f. *At that time Arabia was lush and green.* **In contrast,** *it's a desert now.*

g. *At that time Arabia wasn't a desert.* **On the contrary,** *it was lush and green.*

On the other hand is useful for weighing contrasting points. Sometimes we introduce the first point with *on (the) one hand* (h).

h. *Our decision to emigrate was not easy.* **On the one hand,** *we knew it would improve our economic prospects.* **On the other hand,** *it meant leaving behind all our friends.*

Instead marks an alternative or substitute.

i. *We no longer take a summer vacation.* **Instead,** *we make short weekend trips.*

■ **Exercise 13** Choose four of these transition expressions to complete the text. Add them on the right. Add punctuation if it is needed.

HIGH PRIORITY

 also however in fact instead yet

The main reason for famine in many poor countries is not a shortage of basic food. It is political divisions and patronage. __, during the Bengal famine of 1943, government agencies continued to export the results of a successful harvest from some areas. In other areas with bad harvests, __, people were starving to death. This type of problem could be solved by better distribution systems, __ there is often no political will to create such systems. Politicians in power tend not to devote resources to areas where there is opposition. __, they are more likely to feed their own supporters.

on the contrary

3.11 Correcting a misconception

We usually use *on the contrary* after a negative sentence or a question in order to correct a mistaken idea. These examples are from newspapers:

a. *He was not brought up to be a slave.* **On the contrary**, *he was brought up to be a leader.*

b. *He* (a soccer star) *has not requested time off.* **On the contrary**, *he wants to play in every game.*

c. *I was not intimidated.* **On the contrary**, *I felt inspired.*

d. *Decentralization is not something that lies in the past;* **on the contrary**, *it is a goal to which politicians are only now beginning to aspire.*

e. *…and the United States did nothing positive.* **On the contrary**, *they did everything in their power to dissolve …* (= *to destroy …*)

We sometimes use *in fact* and *actually* in a similar way.

We also use *contrary to* (without *on the*) followed by a noun or noun phrase to introduce an opposite idea (f). *Contrary to popular belief* (g) and *contrary to conventional wisdom* mean "in contrast to what most people think."

f. *I moved to Minnesota in June, looking forward to a cool summer.* **Contrary to** *my expectations, it was really hot and humid.*

g. **Contrary to** *popular belief, northern summers are not always cool and pleasant.*

■ **Exercise 14** Use the words to create expressions for the blanks. Write them on the right. Add punctuation if it is needed.

    on   in   to   the   contrary   contrast

1. Women are generally happier living alone than men are, but it's not because they are more inclined to solitude. ___, women are likely to have strong social networks, which enable them to live alone without being lonely. ___, men generally have fewer friends and close family members, so they are more at risk of withdrawing into isolation.

2. There is no evidence that a positive attitude prevents cancer or helps recovery. ___, one study in which people were followed for almost 30 years found no significant association between any personality traits and the chance of developing or surviving cancer.

3. Who were the first European visitors to North America? ___ what is taught in many schools around the world, the Spanish, led by Christopher Columbus, were not the first. Vikings from Scandinavia reached what is now Canada about 500 years earlier.

4. Conventional business leaders look to their customers to find out what they want. ___, a visionary leader can create products that customers never knew they wanted.

3.12 Concession

| Admittedly, | Of course, | True, | It is true that… | + concession + **contrast** |
| Granted, | To be sure, | Yes, | There is no doubt that … | |

granted

of course

to be sure

We use transition expressions like *granted* and *of course* and expressions like *It is true that* and *There is no doubt* that to concede a point (to make a concession). That is, we state an idea that expresses the opposite side of the point we are making. Then we use a contrasting transition expression or *but* to reduce the importance of the information in the concession — so that we end with the point we really want to make.

> Some experts encourage the use of corn as a biofuel. **Of course**, this reduces the amount of corn going into the food supply. **However**, biofuel production continues to have widespread support in some states.

We use transition expressions of concession in a common text structure – **yes, but** arguing. We present an idea, introduce a thought that might weaken that idea (a concession), and dismiss that thought by returning to the first idea.

Yes, but arguing	
Classes should be small.	← Main idea
Of course, there are times when large classes are necessary for practical reasons.	← Concession (a possible reason to doubt the main idea)
However, learning is rarely effective in large classes.	← Return to the main idea (dismissing the concession)

■ **Exercise 15** Choose concession markers and contrast markers to complete the text. Pay attention to the punctuation. There is more than one way.

granted   it is true that   of course   but (x2)   however

1. Punishing children physically is not effective in the long run. ___ hitting a child will get his attention and stop him from misbehaving, ___ the main message is that violence is OK and that the strong have a right to make the weak suffer.

2. Most people would probably agree that soccer is the world's most popular sport. ___, many other sports — including rugby, cricket, and basketball — are played all over the world. ___, by most measures, soccer is far more popular as a sport to watch and to participate in than any other.

3. It is sometimes said that spices were introduced to Europe as a way of disguising the bad flavor of rotting meat. This is a myth. ___, spices might have had the power to overcome the smell of rotting meat, ___ spices were very expensive. Anyone who could afford spices could afford fresh meat.

then

in that case

otherwise

3.13 Condition

in that case   if not   if so   otherwise   then

We can use *if so* or *in that case* or *then* to show that something follows from a previous condition (a) and *if not* or *otherwise* to describe what happens if it doesn't (b). *Then* is similar to *in that case*, but we don't usually use a comma after it (c).

a. *The jet stream may change course again.* **If so / In that case**, *catastrophic floods will recur.*
b. *Global food production must continue to increase.* **If not / Otherwise**, *there will be wa fought over access to food supplies.*
c. *The jet stream may change course again. Then there will be catastrophic floods.*

A common mistake (d) involves using a transition expression that shows result when a better choice is *then* (e), expressing the condition "if that happens" or a subordinator like *so that*, expressing purpose (f). For transition expressions of result, see 3.9. For subordinators of purpose, see 9.12.

| d. *I hope to transfer to Cornell. As a result, I can major in hotel administration.* | → e. *... to Cornell. Then I can major in ...* OR f. *... to Cornell so that I can major in ...* |

See also Chapter 10, Conditionals.

■ **Exercise 16** Choose four of the transition expressions to complete the text. Write them on the right.

all the same   granted   in addition   in that case   otherwise

Relatively cheap food in western countries has led to increased waste. __, some of this waste is perishable food that can't be saved or redistributed. __ , it is clear that the way people treat food is directly tied to its cost. People must become better educated about food efficiency. __, the current abundance of food will not last. It may only take one disastrous wheat harvest in China to change everything. __, market forces would push the cost of wheat beyond reach for many poorer countries.

_____

_____

_____

_____

USAGE GUIDE

3.14 Punctuation with *so, yet, but,* & *and*

So and *yet* are coordinating conjunctions (see 2.16.3) as well as transition expressions. That affects punctuation.

a. *There were no seats in front, **so** we sat in back.*	With short, simple clauses, we usually put *so* and *yet* after a comma. No comma follows.
b. *The seats in back were far from the stage, **yet** the sound was good.*	
c. *There were no seats in front, except for separate seats, and we wanted to sit together. **So** we sat in the back.*	When the part before *so* or *yet* is long and complex, we often start a new sentence with *So* or *Yet*. Usually no comma follows.
d. *The seats were far from the stage, and the performers looked so tiny we could hardly see them. **Yet** the sound was good.*	

In the same situation — when the part before is long and complex — we often start a new sentence with *And* or *But*. There is no comma (e).

e. *This book makes a great contribution to the field. As a reference, it should prove invaluable to students and researchers alike. It's well-written and well-researched. **But** that does not mean it is above criticism.*

3.15 Placing *however* and *for example* between sentence parts

Some transition expressions, especially *however* and *for example*, are often placed after the first part of the sentence — for example, after the subject (a) or an introductory phrase (b) or clause (c). To make your writing more idiomatic, consider placing these transition expressions inside sentences occasionally.

a. *It has often been claimed that coffee is unhealthy. New research, **however**, questions that.*
b. *These used to be expensive. In recent years, **however**, the price has fallen dramatically.*
c. *Sam isn't as strong as he was. When he hikes, **for example**, he has to stop and rest often.*

We place the transition expression inside the sentence only if the part before it presents the contrasting part or the example.

d. *I don't like hip-hop. My husband, however, listens to it all the time.*	The subject is the contrasting part (*My husband* contrasts with *I*), so we can place *however* after it.
e. *I don't like hip-hop. I, ~~however~~, listen to it sometimes with my husband.*	→ *However, I ...* The subject is not the contrasting part, so we do not place *however* after it.

Usage Guide

3.16 Using expanded transition expressions for conciseness

Using an expanded transition expression (*as a result of X, in addition to X, in contrast to X,* etc.) plus a noun phrase (a) or pronoun (b) or a gerund (c) can help you make connections more concise (3.4).

a. *She has an M.B.A. so she could have had a career in business. Instead she went into teaching.* ➝ **She has an M.B.A.** but instead of a career in business, she went into teaching.
b. *I was given a really difficult task. In contrast, his task seemed easy.* ➝ **In contrast to mine**, *his task seemed easy.*
c. *I graduated in 2010, but I didn't look for a job immediately. Instead, I did some traveling.* ➝ *I graduated in 2010.* **Instead of looking** *for a job immediately, I did some traveling.*

■ **Exercise 17** Complete the sentence to create a paraphrase, using the information in italics. Use expanded transition expressions (3.4).

1. *There is industrial pollution. As a result, the atmosphere has changed.* As a result ...
2. *There are small changes, such as butterflies moving north, and there are large changes, such as glaciers melting and flowing into the ocean.* In addition ...
3. *There will be some countries with much higher temperatures. In contrast, a few areas will experience substantially lower winter temperatures.* In contrast ...

3.17 Old before new information

Good writers generally follow this principle for good **sentence flow**: At or near the beginning of the sentence, use words that show how your sentence is linked with what comes before. See also 2.22 in Chapter 2 and Appendix D at the end of the book.

Transition expressions are one technique for doing this. Equally important is the technique of putting **old information before new information**. Phrases with old information are phrases that refer to things already mentioned or repeat information already implied.

a. *When I was a high school student, I was active in the student senate.* **As a member of the senate**, *I played a key role in getting several rules changed.*

As a member of the senate is old information because the previous sentence says, *I was active in the student senate.*

We use pronouns and definite noun phrases (beginning with *the, these* ... or *this* ... at the beginnings of sentences to connect to preceding ideas. We use them by themselves as well as with transition expressions:

b. *Our goal is to increase output by 20%.* **To meet this goal**, *we need to hire more staff and upgrade our equipment.*
c. *The French won the Battle of Hastings in 1066.* **As a result of their victory**, *French became the language of the ruling class in England.*

Usage Guide

3.18 Parallel structure and repetition

One of the most useful ways to achieve good sentence flow is through repetition. That means using the same type of structure repeatedly. You can see it in these paragraphs.

a. If you are an American city dweller and find yourself walking down the street in Tuxtla Gutierrez, Mexico, you will be struck by signs of a way of life that is very different from what you are used to. **In the Parque Central, you will see** whole families strolling, arm in arm, at a leisurely pace. **In the square near the cathedral, you will see** Indian vendors selling textiles with intricate designs and trinkets of all kinds. **In the market, you will find** colorful fruits and vegetables fresher than any you can get in most U.S. supermarkets. **On many street corners, you can buy** soda pop in the kind of bottles that went out of use in the U.S. decades ago.

b. The concept of role is central to sociology. To understand it, consider the different ways in which you relate to others — your ways of behaving and the expectations others have of you — in the course of a week or even a day. **As a sister, brother, husband, or wife, you have** certain responsibilities and obligations to your family. **As a student, you have** academic responsibilities. **As a friend you are expected to** be a good companion and a good listener. **If you have a job, you are expected to** show up, do your work, and behave in certain ways. Each of these aspects of your life is a different role.

In this paragraph from William Zinsser's "College Pressures," there is repetition and old-before-new connecting. Zinsser tells about advice that he gives students as they think about their future.

c. **I tell students that** there is no one "right" way to get ahead – that each of them is a different person, starting from a different point and bound for a different destination. **I tell them that** change is a tonic and that all the slots are not codified nor the frontiers closed. **One of my ways of telling them** is to invite men and women who have achieved success outside the academic world to come and talk informally with my students during the year …

You may have learned that repetition is boring and should be avoided. Yes, sometimes. But the best writers in English use parallel structure and repetition. The writer of the passage above, for example, is a well-known writing teacher and author of books on writing.

3.19 Review: Five ways of achieving good sentence flow

Transition expressions are an important means of connecting, but they are just one technique. See also Appendix D.

Transition expressions are important. **However**, they are not the only tool we use to connect ideas. There are other tools. **One of these** is the technique of old-before-new information. And what about repetition? **You may** have the idea that repetition is to be avoided. **You may** have heard it's bad style. **You may** even think it's a mistake. It's not! Lists and rules help you learn about connecting ideas, **but** it's even more important to learn from examples you find in things that you read. **Although** there is a lot to learn, you can do it!	← A transition expression ← Old before new information (3.17) ← Repetition and parallel structure (3.18) ← A coordinating conjunction (2.17.3) ← A subordinating conjunction (Ch. 9)

Exercise 18 Choose transition expressions that fit the context. In most cases, two choices, not just one, are correct. In three or four cases, only one is a good choice. Consult Appendix C as needed.

1. *For example   However   In addition   Nevertheless   On the contrary*
   Americans often complain about the U.S. Congress. ___, they tend to have a positive attitude toward their own representatives in Congress.

2. *In fact   Besides   In other words   Moreover   However*
   History books traditionally name Christopher Columbus as the first European to visit the New World. ___, people from Scandinavia visited North American nearly 500 years earlier.

3. *For one thing   Such as   In sum   For example   As a result*
   A number of stereotypes are associated with people from Minnesota. ___, they are said to be reluctant to express strong opinions.

4. *After all,   In addition,   Then   In that case,   After that,*
   You need to talk to your advisor, register for classes, and buy your books. ___, you are ready to attend class.

5. *After all   Consequently   However   In other words*
   It's not surprising that one of the most popular boys' names in the U.S. is José, a Spanish name. ___, Spanish-speaking people are the fastest-growing minority in the U.S.

6. *For instance   In other words   Beyond that   On the other hand   That is to say*
   Citizens are concerned about unemployment, inflation, and the power of business interests. ___, they care a lot about the economy.

7. *Consequently   Otherwise   Then   On the other hand   As a result*
   Credit cards make it very easy to spend money you don't have. ___, many consumers are in debt.

8. *On the other hand   On the contrary   As a result   Moreover   In addition*
   The Vikings are likely to do well in Sunday's game against the Rams. They have a great record so far. ___, the Rams have been doing well lately too, so the Vikings could lose.

9. *Meanwhile   In fact   On the other hand   On the contrary   However*
   Presidential candidates don't always need government experience to attract voters. ___, it is often an advantage to have no government experience. Many voters like "outsiders."

10. *In fact   Granted   As a result   For one thing   At the same time*
    In the 19th century, northerners and southerners in the U.S. had opposite ideas about the morality of slavery. ___, they had very different economies: the South was primarily agricultural and the North was increasingly industrial.

11. *Meanwhile   In fact   At the same time   As a result   Therefore*
    For many years, labor-saving devices have resulted in reduced physical activity. ___, the variety and availability of junk food have increased.

12. *Meanwhile   However   After all   Thus   As a result*
    People are spending more and more time in sedentary activities, and junk food has become an increasing part of our diet. ___, we are in some ways less healthy than our ancestors.

13. *Among other things   In sum   For one thing   On the other hand   Otherwise*
    The public is often very critical of the media. ___, they sometimes accuse media companies of bias.

14. *As a consequence   Nonetheless   After all   Among other things   Therefore*
    In some communities, a high proportion of high school students drive to school. ___, some schools have had to spend money to add parking space.

15. *In contrast   Similarly   On the contrary   Among other things   Then*
    People in North America tend to eat a lot of meat and fat. ___, the traditional Japanese diet includes more fish and vegetables.

16. *However   Granted   At the same time   True   In contrast*
    I do not think discipline is the main problem in schools today. ___, discipline problems are important and contribute greatly to "teacher burnout." But the more serious problems in education come from other sources.

17. *In that case   Therefore   Thus   Then   As a result*
    What happens if you can't remember your password? ___ you can usually just click a link and you'll be instructed to create a new one.

18. *Then   As a result   On the other hand   However   Meanwhile*
    I plan to take five classes, but I'm going to register for six. ___ I can drop one of them during the first week.

19. *In that case   For instance   Otherwise   Therefore   Moreover*
    You need to save some money. ___ you won't be ready for a financial emergency.

20. *As a result   Then   In that case   After all   In sum*
    – I think I might not be able to submit my application on time.
    – ___, you can ask for an extension.

■ **Exercise 19**   Write the transition expression in the blank on the right. Include punctuation.

also   as a result of   in contrast   in fact   on the contrary   still

1. Agricultural productivity has increased a lot in recent years ___ there are food shortages.   _____

2. The most successful producers are now the BRIC countries ___ Brazil, Russia, India and China have all become major food exporters.   _____

3. People in the United States might ask, "What should I have for dinner tonight?" ___ people in other parts of the world are asking, "Will there be anything for dinner tonight?"   _____

4. The abundance of cheap food is clearly linked to obesity. It may ___ be behind the increase in other health problems such as diabetes.   _____

5. Farming in China has increased substantially ___ increases in livestock farming, meat consumption has more than doubled in the last ten years.   _____

6. People may think that China and India, with such huge populations, are not able to feed themselves. ___ neither of these countries currently imports much food.   _____

86 Grammar Advantage — Transition expressions and sentence flow — Chapter 3

HIGH PRIORITY

■ **Exercise 20** Create a paraphrase of each item by completing the sentence.

1 Some countries have increased their agricultural output. However, they continue to import a lot of food. Although…

2 We are always reacting to emergency food shortages. Instead, we should be working harder to prevent them. Instead…

3 The cost of chemical fertilizers is tied to the price of oil. Consequently, rising oil prices now mean that fertilizers will cost more later. Because…

4 The US is not very efficient in biofuel production. In comparison, Brazil is a model of efficiency in biofuel production. In comparison…

HIGH PRIORITY

■ **Exercise 21** Correct one mistake in each sentence. Two transition expressions are in the wrong form (with wrong or missing parts). One is in the wrong place. One is not needed at all.

1. There have been calls to reduce carbon emissions. Some countries don't want, however, these kinds of limitations on their productivity.

2. The cost of food is at the mercy of market forces. An example, the spike in food prices in 2007 was caused not by a shortage but by panic buying.

3. There are some reasons for optimism. To begin, certain major food crops are becoming more resistant to disease.

4. India and China have joined the group already. Besides, Brazil is expected join the group next year.

■ **Exercise 22** Choose words from the ones provided to fill each blank.

1	(a) This	(b) In addition, this	(c) Therefore, this	(d) However,
2	(a) For the result	(b) As the result	(c) As a result	(d) The result
3	(a) moreover	(b) however	(c) for example	(d) on the contrary
4	(a) First	(b) of course	(c) for instance	(d) moreover
5	(a) on the other hand	(b) instead	(c) therefore	(d) in addition

It is now possible to sequence a human genome in about eight days, at a cost of about $10,000. Researchers are working on ways to reduce both the time and cost of this process. The most promising way to develop faster, cheaper ways of sequencing is described as "nanopore sequencing." _1_ involves pulling individual strands of DNA through tiny nanoscopic pores. Nanopores are holes about one thousand millionth of a meter wide.

How does nanopore sequencing improve on existing sequencing techniques? All current techniques have to label the DNA chemically and copy it in order to have enough to read it. _2_, the current state of the art technology requires between five and ten days just preparing the DNA. With nanopores, _3_, virtually no chemical pre-processing is required and no amplification. Instead, a single strand of DNA can be read, one base pair at a time, and without the need for labeling. _4_, existing sequencing techniques involve breaking DNA into small chunks of less than 100 base pairs. These chunks then have to be sequenced many times to find identifiable overlaps so that they can be pieced together. Nanopore sequencing, _5_ , can cope with much longer strands, which should help speed up the process.

3.20 Problems with transition expressions

See also Appendix C.

	Problems	Revisions	Comments
1.	Most birds can fly however penguins are an exception.	Most birds can fly. However, penguins are an exception.	Avoid comma splices and run-ons. Use correct punctuation. (3.5 and Appendix B)
2.	Most birds can fly, however penguins are an exception.		
3.	Running is good exercise. It, however, is not for everyone.	Running is good exercise. However, it is not for everyone. / No exercise, however, is ...	Do not put *however* inside the sentence if the part before it does not show the contrast. (3.5)
4.	Robin has two dogs. She has also a cat.	Robin has two dogs. She also has a cat.	We usually don't put a transition expression (or anything else) between a verb and its object.
5.	In contrast to swim, jogging causes a lot of impact.	In contrast to swimming, jogging causes a lot of impact.	After a preposition, use a gerund or other noun. (3.4, 3.16, 6.5)
6.	Unemployment is high. In addition to, government benefits have been cut.	Unemployment is high. In addition, government benefits have been cut.	Don't use a preposition without an object after it (exception: *To begin with*). (3.4)
7.	Fossil fuels dominate the world's energy supply, such as oil provides 35%...	Fossil fuels dominate the world's energy supply. For example, oil provides 35% ... / Fossil fuels, such as oil, dominate the world's ...	Don't use *such as* to introduce a clause. Use *For example*. After *such as*, use a noun phrase. (3.8)
8.	She can't eat certain foods. For example, garlic.	She can't eat certain foods, for example(,) garlic. / ... foods. For example, she gets a rash if she eats garlic.	When you begin with a transition expression, make a complete sentence. (3.8)
9.	I like my new phone. Although it has one big disadvantage. (Although, it...)	I like my new phone, although it has one big disadvantage. / I like my new phone. However, it has one big disadvantage.	Use a conjunction like *although* to join clauses, not sentences. Use a transition expression like *however* to join sentences. (3.10)
10.	The report was well-written. Even though, it contained errors.	The report was well-written. Even so, it contained factual errors. / The report was well written even though it contained errors.	*Even though*, like *although*, is a conjunction. It joins clauses, not sentences. Use *even so* as a transition expression to join sentences. (3.10)
11.	It wasn't hard. In contrast, it was very easy.	It wasn't hard. On the contrary, it was very easy.	Use *on the contrary* to correct a mistaken idea. (3.11)
12.	The speaker will talk for 30 minutes. After, there will be time for questions.	After that, there will be time for questions. / Afterward, there will ... / Then there ...	Don't use *after* as a transition expression. (Appendix C)

Chapter 4

Tenses

Chapter 4
Tenses

IN THIS CHAPTER

Past, present, and future

used to and *would*

tense choice and verb choice

tenses in discourse

Chapter 4: Tenses		.91
4.1	Tenses in context	.93
4.2	Tense chart	.94
4.3	Tenses in passive verb phrases	.94
4.4	Modal auxiliaries and semi-modals	.95
	4.4.1 Modal auxiliaries	.95
	4.4.2 Semi-modals	.95
	4.4.3 Avoiding errors with modals	.95
4.5	Verbs with no tense: infinitives, gerunds, and participles	.96
	Tense chart with negative sentences and questions (Exercise 5)	.98
4.6	Simple present	.99
4.7	Present continuous	.100
4.8	Simple present and present continuous in contrast	.101
4.9	Simple past	.104
4.10	Past continuous	.106
4.11	*Used* to and *would* for past actions	.107
4.12	Present perfect	.108
4.13	Present perfect and simple past in contrast	.113
4.14	Present perfect continuous	.115
4.15	Past perfect	.116
4.16	Past perfect continuous	.117
4.17	Past tenses in contrast	.117
4.18	Future with *will* and BE *going to*	.117
4.19	Present tenses for future time	.118
4.20	Present tense for future time in subordinate clauses	.119
4.21	Future continuous	.120
4.22	Future perfect	.120
4.23	Future perfect continuous	.120
4.24	Future in the past	.121
4.25	Tense choice and verb choice	.122
4.26	Usage guide Simple present for reporting what an author says	.124
4.27	Usage guide Simple present with performative verbs	.124
4.28	Usage guide Avoiding unanchored past tenses	.124
4.29	Usage guide Past forms in unreal conditionals and after *wish*	.124
4.30	Usage guide Continuous tenses with stative verbs	.125
4.31	Usage guide Continuous tenses for change over time	.125
4.32	Usage guide Continuous tenses with verbs that describe momentary actions	.125
4.33	Usage guide Continuous tenses with *always* to express emotion	.125
4.34	Usage guide Place adverbials and *–ing* phrases indicating "at the same time"	.126
4.35	Usage guide Using future-oriented verbs	.126
4.36	Usage guide Understanding time reference in reduced clauses	.126
4.37	Usage guide Tenses in generalizations	.127
4.38	Usage guide Marking tense shifts	.128
	Test yourself	.128
4.39	Problems with tenses	.130

Chapter 4

4.1 Tenses in context

Verb tenses express present, past, and future time (*calls, called, will call*) as well as notions like action in progress (*is calling, was calling, will be calling*) and completed action (*has called, had called, will have called*).

We often use the term **verb phrase**, even for a one-word verb like *calls*. A verb phrase consists of a **main verb** and often one or more **auxiliary verbs** (auxiliaries) before it. The auxiliaries are forms of DO, BE, and HAVE and, for the future, *will*. We place *not* and sometimes other adverbs, such as *just*, after the first (or only) auxiliary verb: *is not calling, has just been calling*, etc.

KEY
Ch. 6 = Chapter 6
Ex. 23 = Exercise 23
5.2 = Chapter 5, section 2
2.14.3 = Chapter 2, section 14, subsection 3
(a) = an example

■ **Exercise 1** Based on what you already know about tenses, find the verb phrases that have a tense, and tell what the tense is. (Look at 4.2 first if you wish.) Paragraph 1 is done for you.

Is 7 a.m. too early?

In recent years, high schools in some U.S. communities have changed their schedules so that the school day now starts later. Other schools are considering making the same change. They are responding to research into the sleep needs of adolescents.

Researchers at the University of Minnesota studied eight high schools before and after they moved to later start times. They found that later start times had benefits related to mental health, safety, and attendance. In some schools, later times correlated with better grades.

Research has also led to a better understanding of what kind of sleep schedule is most natural for a teenager. Through the release of the hormone melatonin, the human brain makes a person feel sleepy late in the day. But what does "late" mean? It means different things for people of different ages. The typical adult starts to feel sleepy around 10:00 pm, but teenagers generally don't feel sleepy until around 11:00. An early start the next morning — high schools typically start before 8:00 — deprives them of the sleep they need. And, as a *New York Times* article about sleep research noted, the blue light of electronic devices sometimes "tricks the brain into sensing wakeful daylight, slowing the release of melatonin and the onset of sleep." Since electronic devices have become such an important part of kids' lives, many have them close at hand, in their bedrooms.

In spite of the possible benefits, the change to a later starting time is controversial. Many parents object because the current schedule fits better with their work schedules and with after-school activities like sports and part-time jobs.

There is also a deep-seated belief that sleep deprivation is somehow admirable. According to one sleep expert, "It's still a badge of honor to get five hours of sleep. It supposedly means you're working harder." And, of course, society values hard work.

Still, the arguments in favor of a later start have convinced many skeptics, and the movement is gaining momentum in many communities. Whether it will catch on in a big way depends on practical factors like parents' schedules as well as cultural attitudes about sleep and work.

Based on "To Keep Teenagers Alert, Schools Let Them Sleep in," Jan Hoffman, *New York Times*, Mar 13, 2014

Answers for paragraph 1: *Have changed:* present perfect. *Starts:* simple present. *Are considering* and *are responding:* present continuous.

4.2 Tense chart

The chart shows the forms for a regular verb in 12 tenses. It does not include passive voice (4.3). For a chart that includes passive voice, see Appendix A.

	Simple VERB + s / VERB	**Continuous** BE + VERBing	**Perfect** HAVE + past participle	**Perfect continuous** HAVE **been** + VERBing
Present	Simple present *calls / call* He **calls** *his parents Mom and Pop.* Negative: *does / do not call* Question: *Does ... call? / Do ... call?* Emphatic: *does call / do call*	Present continuous *is / are / am calling* *Sara* **is calling** *all her friends with the news.* *Experts* **are calling** *this the worst storm in ten years.* **I'm calling** *restaurants to find out about job opportunities.*	Present perfect *has / have called* *Ben has my number but he* **has** *never* **called** *me.* *I* **have called** *him lots of times.*	Present perfect continuous *has / have been calling* *Lee* **has been calling** *hotels to ask about their rates.* *Farmers* **have been calling** *this the driest summer of the century.*
Past	Simple past *called* *I* **called** *yesterday, but no one answered.* Negative: *did not call* Question: *Did ... call?* Emphatic: *did call*	Past continuous *was / were calling* *I* **was calling** *your number when I realized I couldn't remember why.* *Advertisers* **were calling** *me constantly, so I changed my number.*	Past perfect *had called* *Last night an emergency vehicle drove up next door. Our neighbor* **had called** *911.*	Past perfect continuous *had been calling* *I finally reached my lawyer. I* **had been calling** *all afternoon.*
Future	Simple future *will call* *I* **will call** *you right back.*	Future continuous *will be calling* *We* **will be calling** *you "Grandpa" soon.*	Future perfect *will have called* *By the end of the day, I* **will have called** *every number on this list.*	Future perfect continuous *will have been calling* *By the end of the day I* **will have been calling** *potential customers for 10 hours straight.*

is called

was called

will be called

4.3 Tenses in passive verb phrases

When you study tenses, keep in mind that verb phrases with transitive verbs (2.4) can be active or passive. The tenses in the chart in 4.2 are all in active voice. In other words, they have a subject that performs the action (*He calls them ...*) not a subject that receives the action (*They are called ...*). Below are passive voice forms for the most common tenses. (See also Ch. 5 and Appendix A.)

	Simple passive	Continuous passive	Perfect passive
Present	*is / are / am called*	*is / are / am being called*	*has / have been called*
Past	*was / were called*	*was / were being called*	*had been called*
Future	*will be called*	(Rarely used.)	*will have been called*

4.4 Modal auxiliaries and semi-modals

4.4.1. Modal auxiliaries, below in phrases, can occupy the same place in a verb phrase as *will*.

can swim	*may* rain	*Shall* we go?	*ought* to know	*will* help
could swim	*might* snow	*should* eat well	*must* work hard	*would* help

- Modals are followed by a base form verb (except for *ought*, followed by *to*).
- Modals never have *–s, –ed, –ing*, or any other ending.
- Only one modal can appear in a verb phrase, and it is always first.
- To negate a modal, we usually add *not* after it – for example, *may not understand*.
- We never use the auxiliary DO with a modal: *might not go* (~~might don't go~~), *Can you go?* (~~Do you can go?~~)

We do not usually apply traditional names of tenses to verb phrases with modals (except for *will*). Some modals have present or future reference (a-e). *Could* and *would* sometimes have past reference (f, g). Also with past reference, we can use most modals with *have* and the past participle of the main verb (h-j). A good dictionary can help you understand the modals.

a. Lily **can** speak three languages.	She **has** the ability.
b. You **must** be Thomas.	I assume you **are** Thomas.
c. I **may / might** be wrong.	Maybe I **am** wrong.
d. I **can / could** leave tomorrow.	It **is** possible for me to leave **tomorrow**.
e. We **may / might** leave tomorrow.	Maybe we **will leave** tomorrow.
f. Yesterday I **couldn't** go to school.	It **was** not possible.
g. I asked, but no one **would** help me.	They **refused**.
h. I **may / might** have been wrong.	Maybe I **was** wrong.
i. You **must have been** a cute baby.	No doubt you **were**.
j. I **should have taken** physics.	It **was** the right thing to do but I **didn't do** it.

4.4.2. Semi-modals have meanings related to modals: BE *able to* (like *can* and *could*), BE *willing to* (like *will*), BE *supposed to* (like *should*, sometimes *must*), and HAVE *to* (like *must*).

4.4.3. Avoiding errors with modals

k. ~~Do you can~~ swim? → Can you swim? Don't can → cannot, ~~might doesn't~~ → might not, ~~must don't~~ → must not, etc.	Questions (2.14) and negative sentences with a modal do not require DO.
l. You ~~must can~~ → **must be able to** work well both individually and with a team.	After a modal, never use another modal. Instead, use a semi-modal like BE *able to*.
m. Last week I ~~could find~~ → **I was able to find / I found** a used bike for only $50.	Use *was/were able to*, not *could*, for an action successfully achieved at a moment in the past.
n. Yesterday, ~~I must~~ → **I had to** take the bus.	Use *had to*, not *must*, for a necessary past action.
o. In academic writing, you have to use sources carefully. For example, you ~~don't have to use~~ → **must not use / cannot use** a source without citing it.	Don't use *not have to* for an action that is not permitted. Use *not have to* when an action is not necessary (but permitted). *You don't have to write 20 pages; 15 is enough.*
p. In my lab, ~~we should~~ → **we have to [must / are supposed to]** write weekly reports.	Avoid *should* for an action that is **required**.

infinitives, gerunds, and participles

4.5 Verbs with no tense

Nonfinite verbs are verbs in contexts that do not allow tense variation — for example, they are used as nouns or modifiers. They have no tense. (See also Chapter 6.)
- An imperative verb functions as a command or request: **Relax! Don't worry.** (See also 2.15.2)
- An infinitive is *to* plus a base form: *The new drug was found to **affect** appetite.*
- A bare infinitive is a base form verb: *We didn't let our disagreement **affect** our friendship.*
- A gerund is a verb with *–ing* used as a noun: **Writing** *is difficult.*
- Present participles, also with *–ing*, can be used as modifiers: *a **falling** star.*
- Past participles are often used as modifiers: *a **written** response, a **divided** country.*

■ **Exercise 2** Read the passage and identify the tenses, referring to the chart in 4.2. Underline each main verb and the auxiliaries that precede it. (The first few are already underlined.) In addition to simple present and simple past, there is at least one example for seven other tenses. Some of the verbs are irregular. A few are passive (4.3). Don't underline nonfinite verbs (verbs with no tense; see 4.5).

Sleep well?

> *Last night I* <u>went</u> *to bed at 10:30,* <u>fell</u> *asleep right away and then* <u>woke up</u> *after midnight. I was unable to get back to sleep, so I* <u>got up</u> *and opened a document I* <u>had been working</u> *on. I* <u>started</u> *adding to it. It seemed like I was getting a lot done, so I kept it up for a couple of hours before going back to bed. But I feel bad when I do that. Healthy people don't follow that type of schedule! Today I have plenty of energy and I'm working productively, but all day I've been telling myself, "Don't do that again!"*
> – Anne H., 26

Does it sound familiar? Many people today worry about their sleeping habits. And don't we all know that everyone requires eight hours of continuous sleep between 10 p.m. and 7 a.m.?

In fact, if we look at history, we find that people have not always followed the sleeping customs that most people in industrialized societies believe in today. For much of human history, people went to bed when it got dark. After four or five hours of sleep — their "first sleep" — they woke up and were active, by candlelight, for another few hours. Then they went back to bed for their "second sleep" and rose with the sun. The time between the two "sleeps" was valued as a productive period.

In an experiment conducted by Thomas A. Wehr in the 1990s, people were deprived of artificial light for long periods. In the beginning, Dr. Wehr observed that the subjects slept through the night, but eventually they began waking up after midnight. They lay awake for a couple of hours and then drifted back to sleep. It seemed that their bodies had adapted to prefer a two-part sleep schedule just like that of their ancestors. Though it isn't considered normal to sleep in two phases today, this research suggests that is in fact natural.

The problem, of course, is that sleeping in two phases does not work well on a regular basis if a person doesn't go to bed with the sun. If you go to bed at 10 and get up at 6, with an active period in between, you will not get enough sleep — and most people do need close to eight hours, whether they are continuous or not.

Based on "Rethinking Sleep," David K. Randall, *New York Times*, Sept. 20, 22, 2012

Chapter 4 — Tenses

■ **Exercise 3** Review the content of Ex. 2. Then complete the text below with appropriate forms. In some cases you will be supplying the complete verb and in some cases just part of a verb phrase. For some blanks, various answers are possible. Think about the meaning. When you're finished, check exercise 2.

> Last night I went to bed at 10:30, __ asleep right away and then woke up after midnight. I __ unable to get back to sleep, so I got up and __ a document that I had been __ on. I __ adding to it. It seemed like I was __ a lot done, so I kept it up for a couple of hours before going back to bed. (But I __ bad when I do that.) But I feel bad when I __ that. Healthy people __ follow that type of schedule! Today I __ plenty of energy and am __ productively, but all day I have been __ myself, "Don't do that again!"
> – Anne H., 26

Does it __ familiar? Many people today worry about their sleeping habits. And don't we all __ that everyone __ eight hours of continuous sleep between 10 p.m. and 7 a.m.?

In fact, if we look at history, we find that people __ not always followed the sleeping customs that most people in industrialized societies believe in today. For much of human history, people __ to bed when it got dark. After four or five hours of sleep — their "first sleep" — they __ up and were active, by candlelight, for another few hours. Then they went back to bed for their "second sleep" and __ with the sun. The time between the two "sleeps" __ as a productive period.

In an experiment conducted by Thomas A. Wehr in the 1990s, people __ deprived of artificial light for long periods. In the beginning, Dr. Wehr observed that the subjects __ through the night, but eventually they __ waking up after midnight. They __ awake for a couple of hours and then __ back to sleep. It seemed that their bodies had adapted to prefer a two-part sleep schedule just like that of their ancestors. Though it __ not normal to sleep in two phases today, this research suggests that it __ in fact natural.

The problem, of course, is that sleeping in two phases __ not work well on a regular basis if a person __ not __ to bed with the sun. If you go to bed at 10 and __ at 6, with an active period in between, you __ not __ enough sleep. And most people __ need close to eight hours, whether they __ continuous or not.

■ **Exercise 4** Fix **one or two** form mistakes. Most of the sentences have no mistakes.

1. He calls his parents Mom and Pop. He doesn't call them Mother and Dad.
2. Sara is calling all her friends with the good news, but she isn't calling everyone today.
3. Ben has my number, but he has never called me. Why hasn't he called?
4. Lea has been calling hotels to ask about their rates. Has she been calling all day?
5. I called yesterday, but no one answered. Why didn't you answered?
6. I was calling your number when I realized I couldn't remember why. I wasn't thinking clearly at the time.
7. Last night an emergency vehicle drove up next door. Our neighbor had called 911.
8. I finally reached my lawyer. I had been calling all afternoon.
9. I will call you right back. You won't need to wait more then five minutes.
10. We will be calling you "Grandpa" soon. You'll be babysitting and changing diapers.
11. By the end of the day, I will have call every number on this list.
12. By the end of the day, I will have been calling potential customers for 10 hours straight.

Exercise 5: Tense chart with negative sentences and questions

Complete the chart by writing the negative form and the question form of each verb phrase, as in the shaded boxes.

	Simple VERB + s / VERB	**Continuous** BE + VERBing	**Perfect** HAVE + past participle	**Perfect continuous** HAVE been + VERBing
Present	*He **calls** his parents Mom and Pop.* Negative: *does not call* Question: *Does he call?*	*Sara **is calling** all her friends with the news.* Negative: Question:	*Ben has my number but he **has** never **called** me.* Negative: Question:	*Lee **has been calling** hotels to ask about their rates.* Negative: Question:
Past	*I **called** yesterday, but no one answered.* Negative: Question:	*I **was calling** your number when I realized I couldn't remember why.* Negative: Question:	*Last night an emergency vehicle drove up next door. Our neighbor **had called** 911.* Negative: Question:	*I finally reached my lawyer. I **had been calling** all afternoon.* Negative: *had not been calling* Question: *Had you been calling...?*
Future	*I **will call** you right back.* Negative: Question:	*We **will be calling** you "Grandpa" soon.* Negative: Question:	*By the end of the day, I **will have called** every number on this list.* Negative: *will not have called* Question: *Will you have called...?*	*By the end of the day I **will have been calling** potential customers for 10 hours straight.* Negative: *will not have been calling* Question: *Will you have been calling?*

4.6 Simple present

calls
call

does not call
do not call

VERB + S / VERB	*does not / do not* + VERB	*Does / do* ... VERB
It works. They work.	It does not work. They do not work.	Does it work? Do they work?

- We use the simple present for general truths (a) and present states (b).
- We use *it* for repeated actions, customs, habits, and routines and for generalizations based on previous actions and probable future actions (c, d).
- We use it to describe what usually happens (e), in contrast to the situation right now (f).
- We use *do/does* (with a base form verb) in questions and negative sentences and sometimes for emphasis (g). For rules of subject-verb agreement, see 2.2.5.

a.	The earth **revolves** around the sun, but it **doesn't move** in a circular orbit. How fast **does** it **move**?	These are facts of nature or circumstance.
b.	This book **belongs** to the library. It **doesn't belong** to me. Which section **does** it **belong** in?	
c.	Prof. Brown **gives** a quiz every Tuesday. She **doesn't give** make-up quizzes. **Why doesn't** she **give** make-up quizzes?	It has happened repeatedly in the past and will probably continue (a generalization).
d.	When I **don't sleep** well, I **feel** irritable all day.	
e.	This key **works** on all the doors in the building.	*Is not working* is present continuous. (4.7)
f.	Compare: This key *isn't working*. Did I damage it?	
g.	My job isn't perfect, but it **does pay** well and I **do like** it.	*Do* and *does* are stressed: **does** pay, **do** like.

We sometimes use simple present for a planned future event.

f. ~ **Do** classes **start** next week? ~ No, they **don't begin** until the following week.

Avoid using past tense for a generalization that is true at the present time. (See also 4.37.)

g. I am a careful shopper. When I ~~bought~~ something, I always ~~compared~~ prices first. → When I **buy**...I always **compare**...

We usually use simple present (not *will*) in a time clause referring to the future. (See also 9.7.1.)

h. I will call you after I finish my work. (after ~~I finished~~, after ~~I will finish~~)
i. When you are a little older, you will understand. (when you ~~will be older~~)

■ **Exercise 6** Use the verbs in appropriate tenses. There may be more than one way.

When an American [say] "Thank you," the other person [reply] "You're welcome." That is what I learned in my first English class. But now I [live] in the U.S., and I [not hear] "You're welcome" very often. When I [thank] my roommate for something, she usually [answer] "No problem." Sometimes she [say] "No worries." Many people [say] "You bet." From older people, sometimes I [hear] "My pleasure." My experience [show] that language in real life [not always match] the language that a student [learn] in class.

HIGH PRIORITY

■ **Exercise 7** Fill the blanks with verbs in the appropriate tenses. Use *do* or *does* for negatives and questions.

not believe	*not depend, depend*	*eat*	*gain, gain*
not happen, take place	*live*	*make, make*	*put off, not understand*
represent	*wash, not know*		

1. They say that everyone __ mistakes but only a fool __ the same mistake twice.
2. Are you a vegetarian, or __ you __ meat?
3. A person who __ in God is called an *atheist*.
4. Many students __ weight during their first year. How much __ the typical student __?
5. An ambassador __ his or her national government in another country.
6. A discussion that __ in real time is called *asynchronous*. Asynchronous discussions __ online.
7. The writer Stephen King always __ his hands before going to bed. He __ why.
8. A careless student __ required reading, so he __ what's going on in class.
9. __ women __ longer than men?
10. Your grade __ only on how hard you try. It __ on the quality of your work.

am working

is working

are working

4.7 Present continuous

am/is/are + VERB + *ing*	*am/is/are* not VERB + *ing*	*am/is/are* … VERB + *ing*
I am working.	I am not working.	Am I working effectively?
It is working.	It is not working.	Is it working?
They are working.	They are not working.	Are they working?

- We use the present continuous (present progressive) for actions in progress now (a) and temporary or recently begun actions (b, c).
- Sometimes an adverb or adverbial phrase separates the BE verb and the *–ing* verb (d, e; see 4.34).
- We sometimes use present continuous, often with a time adverbial, for a planned future event (f).
- We don't usually use the present continuous with verbs **stative** verbs (g) – that is, verbs that name a state or a relationship rather than an action.

a. The earth's climate is **growing** warmer.	The action is in progress now.
b. Hannah **is living** with her parents again.	It's a recent or temporary arrangement.
c. The copy machine **isn't working**.	
d. Sandy **is** downtown **shopping** for shoes.	She is downtown and she is shopping.
e. My company **is** gradually **replacing** full-time workers with part-timers.	The company is replacing full-time workers and it is happening gradually.
f. ~ Are you **leaving** tomorrow? ~ I'm not **going** till Friday. I'm **working** all day tomorrow.	The actions are planned.
g. Olivia just bought her grandfather's car. It's ~~belonging~~ to her now. ➔ belongs	

■ **Exercise 8** Find and fix **two or three** mistakes. The simple present verb phrases are all correct and most of the present continuous verb phrases are correct.

It's midnight where I am at this moment, which means that it's 7 in the morning in my hometown. Though they're far away, I can easily imagine what my family is doing at this moment. My mother is drive to work. She almost always leaves just before 7. My father is drinking his tea. He's reading the paper and listening to the news on the radio. He works at home, so usually he doesn't start until later. My brother is getting ready for school, but he's stopping every few minutes to text a friend: *What are you wearing? Are we having a math quiz today?* He doesn't like school, but he loves fashion. My four-year-old sister still sleeping. Simba, the cat, is lying on her bed, where he always sleeps.

■ **Exercise 9** Imagine the activities of some people you know well who are far away at this moment: family (as in the exercise above) or friends. Write a description using present continuous verb phrases and verbs in other tenses as needed.

■ **Exercise 10** Imagine that the paragraphs below are a message from a friend. Fill the blanks with appropriate forms of the verbs. Do not use present continuous if the verb is stative.

backpack   belong   go   not have   learn   live   still look

I started my new job last week, and so far things __ well. Everything is new to me, but I __ a lot every day, and my coworkers are helpful. I __ for an apartment; I __ my own place yet. For now, I __ in an apartment that __ to a friend of my boss who __ around Europe this summer.

not come   happen   make   take   not work   want

Unfortunately, my car __ very well. The engine __ a strange noise. I __ it to a mechanic this weekend. But how are you? Get back to me soon. I __ home for a visit until next month, and I __ to know what __ in your life.

4.8 Simple present and present continuous in contrast

Smiles or is smiling?

Simple present	Present continuous
a. *Newborns* **sleep** *16 or more hours a day.* (That is their habit.)	b. *Shhh! The children* **are sleeping.** (That's their activity at this moment.)
c. *Economists* **study** *decision-making.* (That is their job.)	d. *Ryan* **is studying** *economics at UCLA.* (That is his current activity.)
e. *Prof. Brown* **gives** *quizzes on Tuesdays.* (That is her routine.)	f. *This semester she's* **giving** *shorter quizzes.* (That is her current way.)
g. *Muslims* **don't eat** *pork.* (That is their custom.)	h. *I'm not eating pizza until I lose 5 lbs.* (That's my current diet.)
i. *Every time I look at her, she* **smiles**. (She begins to smile when she sees me looking at her.)	j. *Every time I look at her, she's* **smiling**. (She has a smile on her face even before I look at her.)

■ **Exercise 11** Without looking at Exercise 8, fill the blanks with verbs in the appropriate forms. Then check Exercise 8.

do	*drive*	*drink*	*get*	*not like*	*leave*	*lie*	*listen*	*love*
mean	*read*	*still sleep*	*sleep*	*not start*	*stop*	*wear*	*work*	

It's midnight where I am at this moment, which __ that it's 7 in the morning in my hometown. Though they're far away, I can imagine what my family __ at this moment. My mother __ to work. She almost always __ just before 7. My father __ his tea. He __ the paper and __ to the news on the radio. He __ at home, so usually he __ start until later. My brother __ ready for school, but he __ every few minutes to text a friend: What __? *Are we having a math quiz today?* He __ school, but he __ fashion. My little sister, who is only four, __. Simba, the cat, __ on her bed, where he always __.

■ **Exercise 12** Complete each sentence with one pair of verbs using simple present or present continuous. In some of them, the verbs have the same tense.

assist, value	*live, visit*	*not work, use*	*prefer, not read*
study, study	*teach, teach*	*wait, spend*	*write, never talk*

1. Like most people, Ted __ near his work place, but this week he __ a friend two hours away.
2. This week a substitute teacher __ the lab class that Professor Allen normally __.
3. All of our representatives __ other callers. Please stay on the line. We __ your business.
4. Meg __ TV to books, so generally she __ much.
5. Hurry up! Everyone __ for you. Why __ you __ so much time on your hair?
6. Paleontologists are scientists who __ fossils, but what kind of fossils __ they __?
7. We have a copy machine, but it __ today. When that happens, most of us __ the copy center in the library.
8. My history professor __ a book, but she __ about it in class.

belong, not belong	*increase, mean*	*look, hire*	*not understand, laugh*
see, begin	*seem, work*	*sound like, hit*	*work, never complain*

9. Did Matt find a job, or __ he still __? My cousin's company __ new employees this month.
10. Someone left this key in the reception area. __ it __ to you? It __ to anyone I've asked so far.
11. This isn't funny. I __ why you __.
12. What's that noise? It __ someone __ a metal sheet with a hammer.
13. ~ What's wrong with Sarah? She __ irritable.
    ~ She's just nervous about a big project she __ on.
14. Most historians __ the 1950s as a time of relative stability, but now scholars __ to question that view.
15. Because so many people are out of work these days, petty crime __. *Petty* __ "not serious," but people are still concerned about it.
16. Martha has great work habits. She __ hard and she __.

■ **Exercise 13** Using the phrases, create a sentence like the examples, using an adverbial expression like *usually* and simple present in one clause and present continuous with a phrase like *this week* in the other clause. You don't need to imagine any words, but remember to add *–s* when you need it, and remember that each verb phrase needs a subject.

Dan needs lots of sleep.   usually / sleep 10 hours / but this week / get up really early
➤ *He usually sleeps late, but this week he's getting up really early.*

I tend to dress informally.   today / wear dress shoes / but usually / wear sneakers
➤ *Today I'm wearing dress shoes, but usually I wear sneakers.*

Adverbials often used with simple present: *usually, generally, typically, normally*
Adverbials often used with present continuous: *now, today, this week, this semester*

There is often more than one option for the position of the adverbial: *She usually works / Usually she works, Now he's working / he's now working / he's working now,* etc.

1. Helen loves to read.   usually / prefer science fiction / but this summer / read romance novels
2. Linda looks different today.   generally / wear a dress / but today / wear jeans
3. Hi. I'm on the bus.   usually / run on time / but today run late
4. I'm surprised at how active Gregory is.   usually / not talk in class / but this afternoon / participate a lot
5. The Browns are staying home this summer.   often / take a vacation / but this year / not go anywhere
6. Marisa needs a break from the violin.   typically / practice three hour a day / but today take it easy
7. Jane loves science.   this semester / take French / but usually / take only science classes
8. The traffic is worse than usual today.   normally / move quickly / but today / not move at all
9. My cat and dog usually / not do anything / but right now / run around like crazy
10. What's wrong with Carl?   usually / ask lots of questions / but today / not say anything
11. My commute is usually quick.   generally / take me 15 minutes / but today / take forever
12. I'm usually careful with my money.   this week / buy a lot / but usually / not spend so much
13. Something's wrong with this machine.   usually / work fine / but now / make a strange noise
14. We will answer your call soon.   at the moment / experience high call volume / but typically / answer within five minutes
15. Josh is learning how to use a new program.   generally / learn fast / but today / not do very well

worked

didn't work

4.9 Simple past

VERB + ed	did not + VERB	did ... VERB
It worked. They worked.	It did not work. They did not work.	Did it work? Did they work?

We use the simple past for a completed action viewed as a whole (a) and for habitual past actions (b). We use *did* (before a base form verb) in questions and negative sentences and sometimes (stressing *did*) for emphasis (c). For the use of past tenses in unreal conditional sentences, see Ch. 10.

a. *I **studied** economics in college, but **I didn't major** in it. What **did** you **major** in?*
b. *A hundred years ago, most women **worked** in the home. They **didn't have** paid jobs.*
c. *Jake **did** **make** progress last term; he just didn't make enough progress.*

We use *could* as the past tense of *can* when it expresses possibility or ability (d). We can use *would* as the past of *will* when it expresses willingness or, with *not*, refusal (e).

d. Some dinosaurs could run very fast.	They had that ability.
e. I tried to pay in cash, but they wouldn't take it.	They refused to take cash.

■ **Exercise 14** Complete the texts with the appropriate forms of the verbs. Some are irregular.

close   get   not have   land   look   need   realize   run   surprise   throw

One glove, two gloves

One January day, I was waiting for the subway. When the F train arrived I __ on and then watched as a young woman __ up and jumped on just before the doors __. Unfortunately, when she __ out the window, she __ that she had dropped one of her gloves on the platform. What she did next __ me. With a sorry look on her face, she stepped up to the door and __ the other glove out. It __ just a few inches from its mate. She __ any use for a single glove, but maybe someone else __ a pair.

be   begin   end   enter   not get   give (x2)   not have   impress   include   not look   say (x2)   start

Generosity

Before Christmas a year ago, I was in New York City on the subway. At West Fourth Street, a young man __ the train with a boombox. He __ loudly, "I'm trying to stay out of trouble tonight, so I'm offering you a dance, like we do it in the Bronx." Most of the passengers __ at him.

Then he plugged his iPhone into the boombox and __ to dance his heart out. His performance __ back flips and body spins on the floor with just one hand. By this time everyone was watching in amazement. When the performance __, several passengers __ the young dancer dollar bills, five-dollar bills, and even ten-dollar bills. Their generosity __ me.

Just then, at the other end of the car, an older man got on and __ asking for money. He __ dirty and poorly dressed and __ any dance routine or musical act to offer. All he had was a wish for kindness, but he __ a dime. Then just before the next stop, the dancer went up to the old man and __ him all those dollar bills, fives, and tens. "Merry Christmas, man," he __.

The stories were adapted from the New York Times Metropolitan Diary feature.

Chapter 4 — Tenses — Grammar Advantage 105

■ **Exercise 15** ***Then and now*** Read the past description ("Then") and the present description ("Now"). Write a description of events to link "then" and "now," as in the example. Use past tenses and any other tenses that seem appropriate.

Then: There was a small, shabby house at 2000 Emerson Avenue with a well-kept vegetable garden in the back. An old woman lived there alone. *Now:* The house at 2000 Emerson Avenue is large and beautiful. A family of five lives there. There is no garden. What happened?

Example answer: The old woman started selling vegetables from her garden and she was so successful that she sold the house and moved to Hawaii. A young couple bought the house and remodeled it. They were expecting a child at the time, but they had quadruplets. They were too busy to keep the garden up.

Write as if you know exactly what happened (or use the adverb *maybe*).

1. *Then:* Henry was unemployed. He spent most of his time playing video games and watching old Star Trek programs. *Now:* Henry is rich. He spends most of his time working. *What happened?*

2. *Then:* Jacob wore a beard and was overweight. He drove an SUV to work every day. *Now:* He is clean-shaven and fit. He rides a bike to work every day. *What happened?*

3. *Then:* Star Prairie was a town of 600 people near a large lake. *Now:* The town has a different name. The population is 30,000 and growing. *What happened?*

4. *Then:* A factory stood by the Willow River for 30 years. The river was polluted. *Now:* The factory is closed and the river is clean. *What happened?*

5. *Then:* A statue of Beethoven stood in the public square of a small city for many years. *Now:* The statue is gone. In its place is a huge sculpture of a guitar. *What happened?*

6. *Then:* In college, Jared majored in education and never took a business course. *Now:* He runs a profitable business. *What happened?*

7. *Then:* In college, Tara majored in business and never took an art course. *Now:* She teaches art at an elementary school. *What happened?*

■ **Exercise 16** Write your own "Then" and "now" descriptions like the ones above, ending with the same question, *What happened?* Ask a classmate. Be sure that your "then" description uses past tenses and your "now" description uses present tenses.

■ **Exercise 17** Without looking at Ex. 6, fix **two or three** mistakes in the use of simple past and/or simple present. Most of the verbs are correct.   **HIGH PRIORITY**

When an American says "Thank you," the other person replies "You're welcome." That is what I learn in my first English class. But now I live in the U.S., and I don't hear "You're welcome" very often. When I thank my roommate for something, she usually answers "No problem." Once last week she said "No worries." Many people said "You bet." Sometimes I hear "No problem." What I studied in high school was useful, but I don't learn how Americans really talk in daily life.

was working

was not working

were working

were not working

4.10 Past continuous

was/were + VERB + ing	was/were not + VERB + ing	was/were ... VERB + ing
It was working.	It was not working.	Was it working?
They were working.	They were not working.	Were they working?

We use the past continuous (past progressive) to focus on part of a past action (not the action as a whole), in progress (a). We often use past continuous as the background for another action, expressed with the simple past (b). We use it for an action that was in progress at a particular moment in the past (c) and to show that a past action was temporary (d). We don't normally use stative verbs (4.7) in continuous tenses (e).

a. In 1990, Barack Obama **was studying** at Harvard. He began in 1988 and graduated in 1991.
b. We **were talking** about Liam when he showed up at the door.
c. When he stopped us, the officer asked, "Why **were** you **driving** so fast?"
d. When I was 20, I **was working** as a waiter and **struggling** to pay my bills.
e. When she said "I'll think about it," she **meant** "No way!" (was meaning)

■ **Exercise 18** Complete each sentence using one pair of verbs in the appropriate tenses.

drive, see   look for, work   not hear, make   not notice, look at   sit, get back   try, call

1 We __ to Chicago on highway 94 when we __ four-car accident. We were lucky to avoid it.

2 Tess was at the library. She __ some material she needed for a class, but then the copy machine __, so she had to go back the next day.

3 I saw a young couple with a little girl at the mall. The little girl walked into the men's restroom, but her parents __ because they __ at their phones.

4 Two men were picked up by the police. They __ to break into a car, but a witness __ 911.

5 There was an announcement on the PA system, but Janet __ it because the people around her __ too much noise.

6 At the theater last week, I went to the lobby to get a drink during intermission. Someone else __ in my seat when I __. She apologized and moved.

■ **Exercise 19** Use the verbs in brackets in the appropriate forms: simple past, past progressive, or simple present.

When "off" means "on"

I was teaching a class one morning when the fire alarm sounded. My students and I immediately left the building. After a few minutes, the alarm [stop] and we went back inside. To get back on track, I [ask] my students, "OK, what were we doing when the alarm went off?" I thought someone would say "We [talk] about verbs" or "We [look] at page 165." Instead, someone said, "We [wait] outside." For a moment I was confused, but then I [understand] the problem. They didn't understand the meaning of "go off." To them, "off" [mean] "not operating," as when we say "The lights went off." But in fact when we say an alarm "goes off" it [mean] the alarm starts. In other words, when it "goes off" it really goes on!

4.11 Used to and would for past actions

used to call

would call

- We use the past auxiliary **used to** for past states (a) and repeated past actions (b).
- *Used to* is especially useful when we don't want to specify a particular past time.
- For the negative, we use *didn't use to* (c).
- The auxiliary *used to* has no present tense. For present time, we use the simple present, sometimes with *usually* (d).

   a. *Alaska **used to** belong to Russia. Now it is part of the U.S.*
   b. *People **used to go** to bed at sundown.*
   c. *People **didn't use to** stay up so late.*
   d. *Today people (usually) remain active for several hours after sundown. (Today people use to remain active)*

We sometimes use *would* for repeated past actions (e). For conditional uses of *would*, see Ch. 10.

   e. *The toddlers played a game they called Beauty and the Beast. One of them, the beast, **would roar** loudly and the other, the beauty, **would run** away. Then they **would change** parts.*

Do not confuse the past expression *used to* with the expression BE *used to*, which can have any tense. *I am (was) used to X = X is (was) familiar (not new) to me*. After BE *used to* we use a noun or gerund (not a base form): *I was born in Tokyo, so **I am used to city life**. I am used to living (live) in a big city.*

■ **Exercise 20** Use each pair of verbs in one sentence. Use *used to* with one of the verbs. Think carefully about the content and notice context clues (like *today*).

| be, be | be, end | ✓ get, watch | dress, not see | go, go |
| spend, take | have, depend | watch, have | not write, be | |

Example: *Most people today **get** their news online. Everyone **used to watch** news on TV.*

1. People __ to bed with the sun. Now almost no one __ to bed that early.
2. Families __ about a fourth of their income on housing. Now they __ about a third.
3. Almost everyone __ a mobile phone these days. People __ on landlines.
4. In the U.S. most people __ informally. You __ a lot of men in suits and neckties.
5. In industrialized societies today, families __ smaller than they __.
6. Divorce __ rare. Now about a third of marriages in the U.S. __ in divorce.
7. Families __ TV together. Nowadays in many families everyone __ a different schedule.
8. Most people __ letters very often. Letters __ an important way of keeping in touch.

■ **Exercise 21** Fix **one or two** mistakes in the use of past tenses, *used to*, and *would*.

HIGH PRIORITY

The one-room schoolhouse used to be a common feature of American life. The population of communities was often so small that children of all ages would attend school in the same room. Children would do different activities depending on their age, and older children would sometimes taught younger children. Today children use to attend schools large enough to allow kids to be separated by age, but their great-grandparents may still be nostalgic for the one-room schoolhouse.

has stopped

has not stopped

have decided

have not decided

4.12 Present perfect: has/have + past participle

has/have + PAST PARTICIPLE	has/have not + PAST PARTICIPLE	has/have ... PAST PARTICIPLE
It has arrived.	*It has not arrived.*	*Has it arrived?*
They have arrived.	*They have not arrived.*	*Have they arrived?*

We use present perfect for completed actions to show the relevance of the action to the present. The action may be recent (a, b) continuing (c, d), or just potential (e). It may have occurred at an indefinite past time (f).

	Present relevance:
a. *Adrian **has found** a job.*	He now has a job.
b. *The rain **has stopped** and the sun **has come out**.*	Now the weather is fine.
c. ***Have** you **worked** here very long?*	You work here now.
d. *Antibiotics **have saved** millions of lives.*	They still save lives.
e. *~What's your major? ~I **haven't decided**.*	There is still a chance to decide.
f. *Research **has shown** that smoking is unhealthy.*	It is still believed to be unhealthy.

We can include a clause beginning with *since* to specify the present period during which the action took place, but the time of the action itself is not mentioned (g).

g. *Adrian **has found** a job since you saw him last.*	The *since* clause, with simple past, does not say exactly when he got the job. It only specifies a period of time.

We often include *ever* ("at any time") in a question but not usually a statement (h).

h. *Have you ever eaten frogs' legs? I ~~have ever eaten~~ frogs' legs.* → *I have eaten*

With the present perfect we often use adverbials of frequency (i) or other expressions that indicate how much or how many (j).

i. *We have competed at the national level five times.*
j. *We have won three national championships.*

We use simple past (4.9), not present perfect, with adverbials referring to a specific past time, like *yesterday, a year ago, at that time, last week, in 2018, after I left,* and *in ancient Rome* (k).

k. *I ~~have written~~ several papers last semester.*	*I wrote several papers last semester.* OR *I've written several papers.* (The time is not specified.)

- We use present perfect with a duration phrase, often beginning with *for* or *since* (sometimes *ever since*), to express or ask about the duration of an action (how long) from the past until now (l). We do not use present or past (m).
- With *for* we specify a **period of time** (*two years, a long time*). With *since* we specify a **point in time** (*2011, last year, yesterday, 10 years ago*). *Since* often introduces a clause with a simple past verb (n).

l. *Dan **has worked** here <u>since 2011</u>. He **hasn't had** a vacation <u>for two years</u>. <u>How long</u> **have** you **worked** here?*	The underlined phrases combine with the present perfect to express or ask *how long* (duration).
m. *~~I'm working~~ (~~work~~, ~~worked~~) here since last year / since a year ago.*	→ *I have worked here since last year.* OR *I have been working here ...*
n. *I've worked here since I finished college.*	The clause with *since* tells when I began working here.

■ **Exercise 22** Underline the present perfect verb phrases. Note also that we usually use the simple present tense in writing about published ideas — *the author says*, for example.

Has the world become less violent?

Steven Pinker, a professor at Harvard, is the author of *The Better Angels of our Nature*, in which he argues that the world has become less violent over the course of history. He writes:

> This book is about what may be the most important thing that has ever happened in human history. Believe it or not — and I know that most people do not — violence has declined over long stretches of time, and today we may be living in the most peaceable era in our species' existence. The decline, to be sure, has not been smooth; it has not brought violence down to zero; and it is not guaranteed to continue. But it is an unmistakable development, visible on scales from millennia to years, from the waging of wars to the spanking of children.
> – Steven Pinker, preface to *The Better Angels of our Nature*

Pinker acknowledges that traditions of family and religion have grown weaker with the advance of individualism and science, but he argues that the changes have resulted in a less violent world.

To support his thesis, he examines numerical evidence related to violence: wars, crime, and even physical punishment of children by parents. For example, he notes that between the Middle Ages and the 20th century, European counties experienced "a tenfold to fiftyfold decline in rates of homicide." In the home, increased respect for women's rights has contributed to an overall decline in domestic violence. Worldwide, more and more people have come to regard corporal punishment of children as unacceptable.

Of course, it is easy to point to find examples of terrible violence in today's world, but Pinker's point is that, overall, violence in all areas of life has declined.

Pinker's book is optimistic. As he puts it, "The belief that violence has increased suggests that the world we made has contaminated us, perhaps irretrievably. The belief that it has decreased suggests that we started off nasty and that the artifices of civilization have moved us in a noble direction, one in which we can hope to continue."

■ **Exercise 23** Fill the blanks with verbs in the appropriate tense. You may refer to the passage above. There may be more than one way.

become (x2)   *contribute*   *decrease*   *grow*   *result*   *take place*

__ the world __ less violent throughout the course of human history? Stephen Pinker argues that in fact violence __. Though traditions of family and religion __ weaker, this __ in a more peaceful world, according to Pinker. He notes that violent practices such as executions and the beating of children __ less widespread and that no wars between major nations __ since the middle of the 20th century. Pinker argues that changes in many aspects of life — politics, economic life, technology, and communications, and more — __ to this change.

■ **Exercise 24** Complete each sentence with appropriate forms of the verbs (including auxiliaries in some blanks). In some of the sentences, you also need to add *since* or *for*. These items involve actions that have continued throughout the time marked by the duration phrase.

| be (x3) | believe | belong | encourage | √have | know (x2) | live |
| not have | √not rain | not see | not talk | use | not win | not work |

0. It usually <u>doesn't rain</u> at this time of year, but this month <u>we've had</u> rain twice already.
1. Dogs serve people in many ways. __ thousands of years, people __ dogs for hunting.
2. Scientists __ about the greenhouse effect __ the 19th Century.
3. Toyota __ the world's number 1 producer of automobiles __ several years.
4. __ you __ at your current address __ more than two years?
5. I really miss my cousins. I __ them ____ five years. We __ on the phone __ a year.
6. Alaska __ to the U.S. __ more than 150 years.
7. This is a dry year. We __ any rain __ a month. The fields __ dry __ June.
8. I tend to see the good side of people. I __ always __ that human nature is basically good.
9. Mia is a confident person. Her teachers __ always __ her to believe in herself.
10. It's time for me to quit this job. I __ always __ that it wouldn't last forever.
11. I have an interesting job. In my ten years here, I __ never __ bored.
12. My boss never takes time off. He __ a vacation __ he started at this company.
13. The basketball team at this school is famous for losing. They __ every game __ 1999.
14. Something's wrong with the copy machine. It __ properly __ last week.

■ **Exercise 25** Complete each sentence with the verbs that are provided. These items involve actions at unspecified past times within the period described by the duration phrase.

become (x2) *change* *fall* *have* *improve* *join* *lose* (x2) *spend* *win*

1. Brazil is a soccer powerhouse. How many times __ the Brazilians __ the World Cup?
2. My chemistry teacher likes to give quizzes. Since the start of the semester, we __ five.
3. You look thin. __ you __ weight since the last time I saw you?
4. The two countries get along well. Since the free trade agreement, relations between them __.
5. Since the 1950s, more and more women __ the labor force.
6. Textbooks are expensive. I __ $300 so far and I still have more books to buy.
7. Since they stopped using bagpipes, the Hipsters __ the most popular band in town.
8. Henry went to school here a decade ago. The campus __ a lot since then.
9. Todd is writing a song titled "Since we met, I __ in love (with someone else)."

Chapter 4 — Tenses

■ **Exercise 26** Match the parts to create questions with *Have you ever* using the present perfect.

Example: *Have you ever rented a car?*

√ rent	a Disney park
visit	horsemeat
taste	a boxing match
watch	√ a car

talk	at a youth hostel
stay	chess
play	with a celebrity

compete	a dog or cat
want to	in a tournament
own	quit school

apply for	a garden
drop	a job you didn't want
plant	a class

work on	a poem
argue	homework all night
memorize	with your parents

play	ten miles
hike	a meal for some friends
prepare	ping-pong

perform	to a musical group
belong	about being famous
dream	in a play

live	in a national election
vote	on TV
appear	in a high-rise apartment

borrow	an organization
start	your age
lie about	someone's car

work	awake all night
stay	in your sleep
walk	in a restaurant

■ **Exercise 27** Follow the instructions for Ex. 26. The verbs in this exercise are irregular.

get sick	some money
find	a horse
ride	at school

fall asleep	a lottery ticket
lose	your keys
buy	in class

win	in the ocean
break	a prize
swim	an arm or leg

know	a bike
do	a person older than 100
fall off	a crossword puzzle

take	a cake
sleep	a four-hour exam
make	in a tent

wear	in an unfamiliar city
write	a cowboy hat
get lost	a research paper

speak	without any money
sleep	all day
go shopping	in front of a large group

go to a movie	a novel in English
read	at a famous restaurant
eat	alone

tell	a bear
hold	a lie
see	a newborn baby

leave home	in a hot-air balloon
fly	popcorn
make	without your keys

■ **Exercise 28** Match the three parts to create a sentence like the one in the example. Note: Though we do not usually use *ever* in an affirmative sentence (*I have ~~ever~~ been to Europe*), sentences with superlatives (*best, most interesting*) are an exception.

Example: *This is the best sushi **I have ever tasted**.*

√ This is the best	car		drive
1 "Titanic" is the most romantic	√ sushi	I … ever	have
2 Prof. Simpson is the most helpful	movie		√ taste
3 This is the most dependable	teacher		see

4 How long was the longest	musician		meet	
5 How old was the oldest	test	you … ever	take	?
6 Who is the most talented	person		hear	

7 This is the most delicious	winter		take
8 This is the coldest	class	I … ever	eat
9 This is the most difficult	pizza		experience

10 This is the longest	person		take
11 This is the most crowded	flight	I … ever	live in
12 You are the tallest	city		dance with

13 You're the most generous	hotel		see
14 That dog is the ugliest	person	I … ever	stay in
15 This is the nicest	animal		know

4.13 Present perfect and simple past in contrast

Has called or called?

When we use present perfect, we do not include past time expressions (*yesterday, a year ago, last week, when I was young, in Roman times,* etc.). The implied time is "up to now." When we include past time expressions we usually use simple past, not present perfect.

	Present perfect		Simple past
a.	*I've studied three languages.* The implied time period is my life so far.	b.	*I **studied** French **when I was in high school**.* (*have studied*) My high school days are past.
c.	*We haven't missed any games.* The implied time period is present — for example, "this season."	d.	*We **didn't miss** any games **last season**.* (*haven't missed*) Last season is past.
e.	*Have you finished your paper?* The implied time period is present. You still have a chance to finish the paper.	f.	***Did** you **finish** your paper **by the due date**?* (*Have you finished*) The due date is past.
g.	*How long has Zack worked here? I have worked here for two years.* The duration continues to the present time.	h.	*How long **did** Zack **work** there? I **worked** there for five years.* The duration is past.
i.	*I have lived in this house since graduation / since I graduated / for a long time.* The duration includes the present time.	j.	*I lived in an apartment before I graduated / from 2013-2018 / for four years.* The duration is past.

We can use present perfect for actions that are still possible (k), actions that could happen again (l), and actions that continue (m). If an action is not still possible or could never happen again, we use simple past, not present perfect (n).

k.	*Has your country ever won the World Cup?*	It could happen in the future.
l.	*Brazil has won the World Cup several times.*	It could happen again.
m.	*My teachers have influenced me a lot.*	They still influence me, either through their actions or through my memories of them.
n.	*My first-grade teacher made me love learning.* (*has made*)	The action happened in the past and will not happen again.

When we include a duration adverbial referring to a time that continues until now, we use present perfect. These adverbials often start with *since* (o) or *ever since* (q). If the duration adverbial refers to a duration that is completely past, we use past tense (p, r). In American English, present perfect and simple past are sometimes used interchangeably for recent past actions, even if they are relevant to the present (s).

o.	*This school **has been** co-ed **since 1980 / for many years**.*	p.	*This **was** a girls' school **from 1950 to 1980 / for 30 years**.*
q.	*Sharon **has lived** alone **ever since her husband died / for years**.*	r.	*Sharon and Tom **lived** on a farm **from the time they were married until he died / for four decades**.*
s.	*I've bought a car. / I bought a car. Now I don't have to ask my friends for ride.*		

■ **Exercise 29** Use either simple past or present perfect for each verb.

1 The astronaut Neil Armstrong [land] on the moon in 1969. Eleven others [walk] on the moon since then.
2 I [take] the most advanced French course last term, so now I [take] everything I can.
3 Noah [work] for some great companies. He [work] for Apple before it became famous.
4 The city's population [increase] dramatically. From 2000 to 2010 it [double].
5 Ever since I was 15, I [want] to go to this school, and last fall I [start] my first year.

■ **Exercise 30** Using words from the boxes in Exercises 26 and 27, create question-and-answer pairs like the ones below. The answer uses past tense and a past time adverbial.

~ **Have** you ever **tried** kimchi? (present perfect)
  ~ Sure. In fact, I **ate** kimchi **last night**! (past tense with a past time adverbial)

~ **Have** you ever **gotten** sick at school? (present perfect)
  ~ Yes, I **got** sick at school when I **was about six**. (past tense with a past time adverbial)

Chapter 4 — Tenses — Grammar Advantage 115

4.14 Present perfect continuous

has been working

has not been working

has/have been + VERB + ing	Has/have not been + VERB + ing	Has/have ... + been VERB + ing
It has been working. They have been working.	It has not been working. They have not been working.	Has it been working? Have they been working?

- We use present perfect continuous with a duration phrase to express or ask about the duration of an action from the past until now (a).
- With actions that do not have a natural end point, present perfect continuous and present perfect are more or less the same when they are used with a duration phrase (a). With actions that have a natural end point (like writing a paper or solving a problem), we use present perfect continuous but not present perfect to indicate duration (b).
- We use present perfect progressive with no adverbial for an action that is in progress now, after some time (c), or that has just finished (d).

a. *People have been farming / have farmed this land for centuries.*	They are still farming (they still farm) this land.
b. *I have been writing (have written) this paper all week.*	I'm still writing.
c. *Nora has been looking for a job.*	She is looking now and started a while ago.
d. *Have you been sleeping?*	You look like you just woke up.

■ **Exercise 31** Underline the present perfect continuous verb phrases.

My aunt has had an interesting life and she has always loved writing, so she's been writing a book of anecdotes about her experiences. She's been working on it for a month, and she recently told me this story that she plans to include. She found herself in an elevator with Mike Wallace, a TV journalist who had a very famous program, *Sixty Minutes*. They were alone and stood in silence as the elevator went higher and higher. As she was getting out on her floor, she said, "Mr. Wallace, I've been watching you for 20 years, and you're terrific!" He smiled and said, "I've been watching you for two minutes, and you're terrific too!"

■ **Exercise 32** Fill the blanks with verbs in the present perfect continuous. In some cases another tense is possible.

buy   do (x2)   *decline   die out   happen* (x2)
live   play (x2)   *recover   not work*

1. Lara has become quite good at chess. She __ a lot with her father.
2. This is an old village. People __ in this valley for thousands of years.
3. I can't figure out this new software. Strange things __ with my laptop since I installed it.
4. What's new? What __ you __ lately?
5. Salvador is still not back at work. He __ from a serious illness.
6. Clothing sales have been good lately. People __ more now that the weather is better.
7. Cars and highways are safer now. As a result, traffic fatalities __.
8. I need to get my phone checked. It __ well.
9. Many species of mammals are nearly extinct. They __ as a result of environmental devastation.
10. The extinction of mammals isn't a new phenomenon. It __ for centuries.
11. Terry's favorite sport is rugby. He __ rugby since he was in middle school.
12. Dr. Keane is in the middle of a big project. She __ research on the effects of advertising.

had arrived

had not arrived

4.15 Past perfect

had + PAST PARTICIPLE	*had not* + PAST PARTICIPLE	*had* ... PAST PARTICIPLE
It had arrived.	*It had not arrived.*	*Had it arrived?*
They had arrived.	*They had not arrived.*	*Had they arrived?*

- The past participle of a regular verb is the same as the past tense form (*worked, studied*). Irregular verbs have special forms (*taken, spoken*); consult a dictionary.

- We use past perfect to show that a past action occurred before another past action.
- Usually a verb in the past tense appears first and then a verb in the past perfect appears, referring to an earlier action (a, b). Often the earlier verb is a reporting verb such as *said* or *told* (c; see also Ch. 7.9).
- We also use past perfect with a duration phrase to show that a past action continued before another past time (d).

a. *Abby was home alone. Her parents **had gone** out.*	They went out and then she was alone.
b. *We called 911. Our neighbor **had had** a heart attack.*	It happened and then we called.
c. *Sonia told us that she **had been** sick.*	She was sick and then she told us.
d. *I quit my job in 2000. I **had worked** there 10 years.*	I worked there 10 years and then quit.

■ **Exercise 33** Fill the blanks with verbs in appropriate tenses. There may be more than one way.

| arrive, leave | be, do | came, study | decide, spend | find, close |
| get, be | look, disappear | reply, forget | see, fall | want, sell |

1. By the time the police __, one of the drivers __ the scene of the accident.
2. At the mall we __ a little boy who was crying. He __ down some stairs.
3. When I first __ to this country, I didn't speak the language well, even though I __ it in high school.
4. Lisa said "Hi, Marcus," and he __, "Hi yourself!" He __ her name.
5. I __ to buy a used bike, but by the time I contacted the seller, he __ it.
6. We __ home at midnight after driving 600 miles. It __ a long day. I __ very tired because I __ most of the driving.
7. My dog was nowhere to be found. I __ for him everywhere, but he __ . I finally __ him in my garage! I __ the door without realizing he was inside.
8. The Hansens __ to cut their vacation short because they __ most of their money at a casino near the airport.

■ **Exercise 34** In some sentences below, two verbs are underlined. In one sentence, change one of the underlined verbs to past perfect to show that the action took place before the action of the other verb. Change only one verb in one sentence, not one verb in each sentence.

I was sitting on a park bench near a bus stop when a young man approached me. He said, "Can you spare fifty cents? That's all I need to get a bus pass." I said I didn't have any change. He thanked me politely and walked away. Then I had a change of heart. I called him back and gave him a dollar. He thanked me again and disappeared into a nearby tobacco shop. I thought, "Oh, great! I gave him money for cigarettes!" A minute later he came out and held out two quarters for me to take. At first I was confused, but then I saw that he bought a bus pass. He gave me my change and got on the next bus.

Chapter 4 — Tenses — Grammar Advantage 117

4.16 Past perfect continuous

had been calling

had not been calling

We use past perfect continuous to express or ask about the duration of an action until a point in the past. With actions that have no natural end point, we can use past perfect in the same way.

The bus came at 9:00. We **had been waiting (had waited) for an hour / since 8:00.**

4.17 Past tenses in contrast

a.	When I arrived, Mickey had (already) left.	He left before I arrived.
b.	When I arrived, Minnie was leaving.	She started leaving before I arrived.
c.	When I arrived, Donald left.	I arrived and then he left.

Left?

Was leaving?

Had left?

HIGH PRIORITY

■ **Exercise 35** Use simple past, past continuous, or past perfect for each of the verbs in brackets. Almost all of them should be simple past. One should be past continuous. Two should be past perfect.

> A few years ago I was invited to a wedding, and though the couple and most of the guests had a good time, for me it was a disaster. About an hour before the event, I called a taxi. With my gift for the bride and groom in a shopping bag by my side, I [sit down] on the curb outside my apartment and [wait]. When the cab arrived, the driver [talk] on his phone in an angry voice. His arguing really [annoy] me, but I [get into] the cab. I [hand] him a slip of paper with the address on it and we [drive] off. Within 20 minutes I was at the wedding hall, admiring a table full of gifts. Then it hit me: I [forget] my gift on the curb outside my apartment. Another guest [drive] me back to my apartment, but where the gift [be] we [find] nothing but the empty shopping bag. I blamed the distraction of the cab driver's arguing for the loss. On the way back to the hall, we [have] car trouble, so we [miss] the ceremony.

4.18 Future with *will* and BE *going to*

will call

is going to call

We can use *will* and a base form verb for future actions and situations. We often use the contractions *'ll* (after a pronoun, not usually a noun) and *won't*. *Will* is common in offers (a), promises (b), and warnings (c), often with an *if* clause (Ch. 10) that has a present tense verb (c).

a.	~Is someone at the door? ~**I'll check**.	I'm offering to check.
b.	**You'll have** a job here as long as you want it.	I promise you.
c.	If you park here, your car **will be** gone when you get back.	I'm warning you.

We often use BE *going to* for planned actions and events we see as already coming.

d.	Jenny and Chris have both been accepted to Yale. They**'re going to share** an apartment.	That's their plan.
e.	Melanie **is going to have** a baby.	She's pregnant.

Will and BE *going to* are often interchangeable, but sometimes there is a difference in meaning.

f.	How old **will** you **be** in 2050?	The sentences are interchangeable.
g.	How old **are** you **going to be** in 2050?	
h.	You don't need any money. I**'ll pay** for everything.	I'm offering to pay.
i.	You don't need any money. I**'m going to pay** for everything.	I've decided. It's my plan.

In a time clause referring to the future, we usually use present tense (j), not *will* or BE *going to*.

j. When the weather **warms** up, we're going to go camping. (when the weather ~~will warm up~~)

■ **Exercise 36** Fill the blanks with will or BE *going to* and one of the verbs. There may be more than one correct way.

adopt   get married   give   let   look   take

1 - Do you have any vacation plans? - You bet. We __ a bike trip along the Mississippi.
2 My fiancé and I aren't religious. We __ at City Hall instead of in a church.
3 You forgot your office key? Don't worry. I __ you in.
4 The Millers don't have any children, but they __ a foster child who is living with them.
5 If you lose your job, where __ you __ for another one?
6 Prof. Mansour doesn't have to plan a lecture for tomorrow. He __ a test.

4.19 Present tenses for future time

Classes begin next week.

We sometimes use simple present (a) or present continuous (b), often with time adverbials, for a planned future event. (These examples are from 4.6 and 7.)

a. **Do** classes **start** next week? - They **don't begin** till the following week. We **start** next Tuesday.
b. **Are** you **leaving** tomorrow? - I'm not **going** till Friday. I'm **working** all day tomorrow.

■ **Exercise 37** Change **two** of the underlined verb phrases to more appropriate forms.

- What are your plans for the weekend?
  - I'm going to do some yard work. Then Sunday I'm going to the mall. I need to buy something to wear to my sister's wedding. She will get married in two weeks.
- Why don't we go together? I'll pick you up.
  - Actually, my brother is picking me up, but you can join us. We're going to pick you up after lunch.
- Sounds good. I'll be ready.

Chapter 4 — Tenses — Grammar Advantage

4.20 Present tense for future time in subordinate clauses

when I see you tomorrow

In subordinate clauses that refer to the future, we usually use present tenses. These clauses are introduced by subordinating conjunctions such as *after, as soon as, before, if, once, until,* and *when*. See also 4.6 and 9.7.1.

*We expect to plant a garden when (as soon as / after / if) it **gets** warmer. (will get / got)*

■ **Exercise 38** Fill the blanks with appropriate forms of the verbs. There may be more than one correct way.

arrive, get	not be, graduate	be, take	buy, get	come in, let
do, retire	go, leave	learn, feel	let, show	spend, do

1. We've run out of this model, but when the next shipment __, we __ you know.
2. Quinn needs a new tablet. He __ one as soon as he __ his next paycheck.
3. I expect to like this job after I __ a little more about office politics. Then I __ more at ease.
4. I have a headache, but I __ fine after I __ an aspirin.
5. My parents __ happy until the last of their children __ from college.
6. We'll see you tomorrow. Our flight __ at 8:00 p.m. Can you pick us up after we __ our luggage?
7. This building has tight security. The doorman __ you in only after you __ him your ID.
8. Before we __ any money on new equipment, we __ some research.
9. Seth believes in keeping active as he gets older. He __ some volunteer work after he __.
10. There's no need to turn off the lights. They __ off automatically when we __ the room.

■ **Exercise 39** Complete the passage using the verbs that are provided. Most of them require *will*. **One or two** should be in present tense (4.6).

    be (x2)   believe   choose   continue   have   take

The economist Alvin Roth of Stanford University recently offered predictions about what the world __ like in the 21st century. Roth __ that worldwide economic growth __. This means that people __ more choices about "whether and how hard to compete." Many people, he says, __ to pursue a slower pace of life. Young people __ more time to seek new experiences and retirement __ a longer phase of life.

    allow   be   enhance   continue   make

Roth also predicts a bigger role for performance-enhancing drugs—drugs that __ concentration, memory, or even intelligence. In the same way that drugs __ us to improve our performance, he says, our increasing understanding of genetics __ it possible for parents to select characteristics of a baby before it __ born. Ethical considerations related to this __ to be a concern.

    become   occupy   regard   remain

Roth believes that many family arrangements that most people now __ as "alternative" – such as same-sex marriage and polygamy – __ more usual. Families __ important, but childrearing __ a smaller proportion of people's lives.

Source: *Financial Times*, Feb. 15-16, 2014, p. 7

will (not) be calling

4.21 Future continuous

We can use future continuous — *will be* plus a verb with *-ing* — for a future action in progress (a) or for a planned or expected action (b).

a. *Please don't call between 7 and 8. We'll be eating.*	Our dinner will be in progress then.
b. *Can you join us for dinner tomorrow? We'll be eating around 7.*	We will start around 7.

will (not) have called

4.22 Future perfect

We can use future perfect — *will have* plus a past participle — to show the completion of an action before a future time. We often use an adverbial expression such as *by then* (a) or a clause beginning with *by the time* (b).

a. *You can visit me in June. I **will have graduated** by then.*
b. *My internship **will have ended** by the time you come.*

will (not) have been calling

4.23 Future perfect continuous

We can use future perfect — *will have been* plus a verb with *-ing* — continuous to express the duration of an action from an earlier point up to a future time.

*We're planning to move at the end of this year. We **will have been living** here for 10 years.*

■ **Exercise 40** Fill the blanks verb phrases in appropriate forms, using the verbs that are provided.

| get, arrive | have, call | not live | look for | make | see |
| sleep | spend, live | start | start, lie | watch, go | work |

1 If Joel doesn't improve his performance at work, he __ a new job soon.
2 Please don't call between midnight and 7 a.m. I __.
3 Adam's daughter __ a baby. We __ Adam "Grandpa" soon.
4 My vacation __ next week. While you're at work, I __ on the beach in Cancún.
5 By the time I retire, I __ for this company for 32 years.
6 Thank you for your order. You __ a confirmation email soon, and your order __ within five days.
7 I'm late. By the time I get to class, the lecture __.
8 ~ Have a good week. ~ You too. I __ you soon.
9 Next year Kelly __ a semester in Japan. She __ with a family.
10 Security in this building is tight. The security staff __ every move you make as soon as you __ past the front desk.
11 The orchestra __ its tenth appearance on this stage next month.
12 I __ here much longer. I'm looking for a new apartment.

4.24 Future in the past — *I knew I would*

We use *would* and *was/were going to* for actions that were, at a point in the past, still ahead (a). We use *could* in a similar way, meaning "would be able" or "would have the capacity" (b). We often use both *would* and *could* in this way in purpose clauses (9.12) introduced by *so that* (c).

a. *When I started this job, I knew I **would like** it. I didn't know it **was going to be** so hard.* (will, ~~is going~~ to)

b. *Fortunately, I was confident that I **could do** a good job, and so far I have.* (~~can~~)

c. *We posted a sign on the office door so that students **would** know that we **would be** closed the next day and **could plan** accordingly.* (~~will~~, ~~can~~)

■ **Exercise 41** Fill the blanks with verb phrases in the appropriate forms: past tenses or *would* or *was/were going to* for "future in the past."

be, predict, end   begin, be, last   conduct, know   think, work   use, not know, be

1   When the First World War __ in 1914, many people thought it __ over in a few months. They had no idea that it __ for more than four years.

2   In 2012, Warren Jeffs, a religious leader who __ in prison at the time, made a prediction: He __ that the world __ before the year 2013.

3   In the 1950s, elementary schools __ civil defense drills from time to time so that children __ what to do in the case of a nuclear attack.

4   When the telephone was introduced in the late 19th century, its inventor thought that people __ it primarily for business purposes. He __ that it __ important for social reasons as well.

5   In the late 1990s, as the year 2000 approached, there was a lot of media attention to the "Y2K problem." Many people __ that computers __ properly at the turn of the millennium.

know, be   not forget, forget   use, not confuse   start, like   want, misunderstand

6   Steve Jobs, the co-founder of Apple, quit the company in 1985. No one __ that he __ back as the company's CEO in 15 years.

7   Yesterday I set an alarm on my phone so that I __ to call my mom. Unfortunately, I __ anyway.

8   When you __ high school, did you have any idea which subject you __ best?

9   My father had the same name as my grandfather, but he always __ a nickname so that people __ him with his dad.

10 The teacher explained everything carefully. She __ to be sure that no one __ .

■ **Exercise 42** Change **one or two verbs** so that they have future-in-the-past forms.

When Jasmine began at the university, she thought she would graduate in four years, but that turned out to be harder than she expected. When she was in her sophomore year, her father became sick and she dropped out for a semester to take care of him. She thought she can catch up by attending classes in the summer, but then she realized that she will need to work in the summer in order to pay her tuition. Last December she finally graduated after four years and one semester.

Get or **have**?

Be or **become**?

4.25 Tense choice and verb choice

Often we can describe something as an **action** — for example, *catch a cold* — or as a **result** of that action — *have a cold*. Actions are **punctual**: they take place at a point in time. Results are **durative**: they have duration. Confusion about punctual and durative expressions may lead to mistakes (a) that can be corrected in two ways: by keeping the same tense and changing the verb (b) or by keeping the same verb and changing the tense and the time adverbial (c).

a. I ~~have caught~~ a cold for two days. →	b. I **have had** a cold for two days.	The tense (present perfect) and the adverbial (a duration phrase) remain the same, but a durative verb is used. *Having a cold* has duration. *Catching a cold* does not.
OR →	c. I **caught** a cold **two days ago**.	The verb (*catch*) remains the same, but the tense is simple past and the adverbial (*two days ago*) describes a past point in time.

Punctual and durative expressions include not just verbs but objects, prepositions, and other words and structures: *get a job / have a job, get married / be married, die / be dead, leave / be gone, start doing something* (verb + gerund object) / *be doing something* (present continuous). They are not limited to one-to-one associations, since actions and results can often be described in more than one way. For example, *get a job* and *find a job* are similar punctual expressions that may be associated with the durative expressions *have a job* and *be employed*.

Examples of punctual expressions	Examples of durative expressions
arrive in/at a place Ming arrived in Dubai a month ago.	*be in a place* Ming is in Dubai now.
become friends We became friends in grade school.	*be friends* We are friends.
die Elvis died in 1977.	*be dead* Elvis is dead.
fall asleep The baby fell asleep an hour ago.	*be asleep / be sleeping* The baby is asleep / sleeping.
join an organization I joined the chess club last year.	*belong to an organization* I belong to the chess club.
leave / go out Celia left / went out this morning.	*be gone* Celia is gone / is out / is away.
get used to something I got used to the weather long ago.	*be used to something* I'm used to the weather now.
marry / be married / get married We married / were married / got married in 2013.	*be married* We are married.
find a job Chad found a job last summer.	*have a job* Chad has a job.
learn how to do something I learned as a child.	*know how to do something* I know how to play the piano.
meet someone We met a long time ago.	*know someone* We know each other.
start school She started law school in August.	*be in school / be studying* She's in law school / is studying law now.
start wearing glasses Tim started wearing / got glasses when he was 7.	*wear glasses* Tim wears / has glasses.

Chapter 4 — Tenses — Grammar Advantage 123

■ **Exercise 43** Referring to 4.25 if you need to, complete the chart with examples of durative and punctual expressions.

Punctual expressions	Durative expressions
Ming _____ in Dubai a month ago.	Ming is in Dubai now.
We _____ friends in grade school.	We are friends.
Elvis died in 1977.	Elvis _____.
The baby _____ an hour ago.	The baby is asleep / sleeping.
I joined the chess club last year.	I _____ the chess club.
Celia left / went out this morning.	Celia _____.
I _____ the weather long ago.	I'm used to the weather now.
We married / were married / got married in 2010.	We _____ married.
Chad _____ a job last week.	Chad has a job.
I learned how to play piano as a child.	I _____ how to play the piano.
We _____ a long time ago.	We know each other.
She _____ law school in August.	She's in law school / is studying law now.
Tim started wearing / got glasses when he was 7.	Tim _____ glasses.

■ **Exercise 44** Choose the best answer(s). Most of the expressions are in 4.25. Think carefully about the meanings of the verbs.

1. Harvey is here. He arrived an hour ago. He __ here for an hour.
   has arrived / has been
2. The baby is sleeping. He __ for an hour.
   has fallen asleep / has been asleep
3. I caught a cold two days ago. I __ this cold for two days.
   have caught / have had
4. Cindy and I have known each other a long time. I __ on Christmas day 1999.
   met / knew
5. Jeremy wears glasses. He __ glasses when he was ten.
   started wearing / has been wearing
6. Marge and Homer are happily married. They __ for more than 20 years.
   have gotten married / have been married
7. My goldfish died a week ago. He __ for a week.
   has died / has been dead
8. Pepe learned Spanish as a child. He knows it perfectly. He __ Spanish since he was a child.
   has learned / has known
9. I belong to a book club. I joined two years ago. I __ the club for two years.
   have joined / have belonged to
10. I heard the news from Joe last night, so I __ all about it.
    have already known / already know

Usage Guide

4.26 Simple present to report what an author says

We usually use simple present to report authors' ideas in current publications (a, b) and opinions that are widely accepted (c). (See also 4.6.)

a. Paul Theroux **argues** that the best travel books are about places where life is difficult.
b. The authors of this article **compare** political campaigns to the marketing of products.
c. Doctors **say** that having an active lifestyle prolongs life.

4.27 Simple present with performative verbs

We use simple present when we use verbs *performatively*, with the subject *I*.

a. I apologize for making you wait.	
b. I admit that I've made mistakes.	By saying the words, the speaker performs the action.
c. I insist that you let me pay.	

4.28 Avoiding unanchored past tenses

When we use the simple past, we usually specify or imply a past time. This **anchors** the event in the past. Events can be anchored in the past with past time adverbials like *yesterday, a week ago*, and *when I was younger* or through reference to something commonly known to have existed in the past, like dinosaurs or Shakespeare. See also 4.9.

A common mistake involves using an unanchored past tense: a past tense without a specified or implied past time (a). You can avoid such mistakes by using present tense, if you are generalizing (b), or by anchoring the past tense with an adverbial (c).

a. I try to be very punctual with all my work. When I missed a deadline, I felt terrible.	→ b. When I miss a deadline, I feel terrible.
	→ c. Last semester, when I missed a deadline in my math class, I felt terrible.

One way to mention a past event without anchoring it to a specific past time is to use *once*, which means "at an unspecified past time" (d). Another way is to use present perfect, with no time specified (e). Verb phrases with *used to* (f) are very often unanchored.

d. I once worked as a waiter, so I know what it's like.	
e. I've worked as a waiter, so I know what it's like.	At an unspecified past time, I worked as a waiter.
f. I used to work as a waiter, so I know what it's like.	

4.29 Past forms in unreal conditionals and after *wish*

In **unreal conditionals** (10.4) and clauses after *wish* (7.7.4), we use past tenses in special ways. In these structures, the past tenses do not indicate past time. They indicate that the situation is imaginary, not true.

a. If I **were** a bird, I would fly home. I **wish I were** a bird.	In fact, I **am not** a bird.
b. If I **had** wings, I would fly home. I **wish I had** wings.	In fact, I **do not have** wings.
c. If I **could fly**, I would fly home. I **wish I could** fly.	In fact, I **cannot** fly.

Usage Guide

4.30 Continuous tenses with stative verbs

We don't normally use stative verbs in continuous tenses (*I am having two sisters*). However, with some stative verbs, including BE and HAVE, we can use continuous tenses to describe a temporary or special behavior or situation.

~ *Why is Michael **being** so selfish?*
~ *He's **not being** selfish. He's just **having** money problems this month.*

4.31 Continuous tenses for change over time

We use continuous tenses, especially present continuous, with verbs that have *change* as part of their meaning, with the change extending over a period of time. These verbs include *become, change, decrease, develop, expand, get, grow, increase,* and *learn*.

   a. *Your child is **developing** normally.* (*develops*)
   b. *The planet **is getting** warmer.* (*gets*)
   c. *Researchers **are learning** more about the link between achievement and practice.* (*learn*)

A common mistake involves using these verbs in simple present tense or simple past when present continuous or present perfect is more appropriate.

| d. *The economy is better now, and unemployment starts / started to decrease.* | → *Unemployment is starting to decrease.* OR *Unemployment has started to decrease.* |

4.32 Continuous tenses with verbs that describe momentary actions

With momentary actions — actions that take place instantly — we can use the continuous tenses to describe repeated actions (a) or to describe a change as incomplete (b, c).

a. *The warning light is / was flashing.*	*There are / were repeated flashes.*
b. *The old tree is / was dying.*	*It is / was approaching death.*
c. *I am / was beginning to understand.*	*I am / was coming closer to understanding.*

4.33 Continuous tenses with *always* to express emotion

Though **simple** tenses are usual for repeated actions (4.6), we sometimes use **continuous** tenses with *always* to express annoyance at repeated actions (a) or to indicate that we are impressed (b).

   a. *It's hard to get things done in this office. Someone **is always interrupting** me.*
   b. *Harry is kind person. He's **always offering** to help.*

Usage Guide

4.34 Place adverbials and –ing phrases indicating "at the same time"

Between BE and the *–ing* form in a continuous verb phrase, we often use a place adverbial — a word or phrase that indicates location.

  a. *The children **are /were outside playing**. Their dad **is /was in the kitchen making** lunch.*
  b. *If you need me, I'll **be in my office counting** paper clips.*

We can add an *–ing* phrase at the end of a clause (without *and* or any other conjunction before it) to indicate an action going on at the same time (c). We sometimes do this with stative verbs (d).

c. *Everyone just stood (there) watching.*	While they stood, they were watching.
d. *I came in not knowing what to expect.*	When I came in, I did not know what to expect.

4.35 Using future-oriented verbs

We often use future-oriented verbs like *plan*, usually in simple present or present continuous tense, in describing likely future events. A few of these verbs, in typical phrases, are below. Most of them are followed by an infinitive (Ch. 6). You can sometimes use such verbs as an alternative for verb phrases with *will*. Each verb adds meaning of its own, so check a dictionary.

anticipate going   **expect** to attend   **hope** to leave   **intend** to register   **plan** to work

We can use the verb *promise*, usually for something good that we foresee (a), or *threaten*, for something bad that may happen (b), in describing future actions. When we use these verbs this way, we use them with inanimate subjects (things, not people). After *promise* and *threaten*, we use an infinitive. See also 6.9.

a. *This project **promises** to be very rewarding.*	It will probably be very rewarding.
b. *This conflict **threatens** to destroy the country.*	It may destroy the country.

4.36 Time reference in reduced clauses

In **reduced** clauses, verb phrases are shortened. These reduced verbs have no tense. The main verb of the sentence helps us understand their time reference as present (a, b, d) or past (c, e). See also 4.5, 8.12, 9.7.3.

Reduced relative clauses (8.12)	
a. *A sonnet is a poem **consisting** of 14 lines.*	= a poem that **consists** of 14 lines.
b. *Do you know any students **looking** for jobs?*	= students who **are** looking for jobs.
c. *A student **looking** for a job came to see you.*	= A student who **was** or **is** looking…
d. *Crops **planted** early are harvested early.*	= Plants that **are** planted early are….
e. *I took a picture of a tree **planted** when I was born.*	= that **was** planted when I was born.
Reduced adverbial clauses (9.7.7)	
f. *After living abroad, you will never be the same.*	= after you **live** (present or future)
g. *After living abroad, I was never the same.*	= after I **lived / had lived** abroad…

Usage Guide

4.37 Tenses in generalizations

Generalizations are usually expressed with present tenses (4.6), even though a generalization is a belief based on past actions (a).

| a. *My brother sleeps late on weekends.* | He slept late last weekend and most weekends before that. He will probably sleep late on future weekends. |

In writing about research findings, we may choose **present tense** if we are confident that the findings can be accepted as true in general (b) and **past tense** if we want to make a more limited claim (b).

| b. *Later start times in high school **have** benefits related to mental health, safety, and attendance, according to a study done at the University of Minnesota.* | With present tense, the sentence implies that the results apply generally. |
| c. *Later start times in high school **had** benefits related to mental health, safety, and attendance, according to a study done at the University of Minnesota.* | With past tense, the sentence is about the students **in the study**; it does not necessarily apply to others. |

Though **simple** present is the most common tense in generalizations, we use present **continuous** (4.7) when we wish to focus on action in progress (d, e) and present **perfect** (4.12) to show that an action extends back in time (f) or to focus on a completed action (g).

d. *Vicki seems to be enjoying herself. Every time I look at her, she's **smiling**.*

e. *The clerks at this store are very attentive. Someone is always **waiting** to serve you.*

f. *Men and women **have** always **misunderstood** each other.*

g. *A widower is a man whose wife **has died**.*

When we generalize about the past, we use past (h, j), past continuous (i) and past perfect (j) in similar ways.

h. *Before the industrial revolution, most people **lived** in rural areas.*

i. *My first-grade teacher smiled all the time. Whenever I saw her she **was smiling**.*

j. *My seventh-grade English class always started class the same way. The teacher asked, "What's new?" She didn't start the lesson until one or two students **had answered**.*

Usage Guide

4.38 Marking tense shifts

Tenses do not need to agree like subjects and verbs, but in writing we tend to avoid shifts in tense that may confuse a reader. To do this, we often put time adverbials at the beginning of a sentence rather than at the end.

Avoid this style:	Improved:
a. *In my teens, I loved playing video games. **I think** video games **are** a waste of time now.*	*Now I think video games are a waste of time.*

We can avoid sudden tense shifts (b) by consistently using past (c) or present (d) or by marking the shift with an adverbial at the beginning of the sentence that introduces a different tense (e).

Avoid this style: b. *The school I went to **was** very competitive. It **is** a tough school to get into, and getting in **is** only the start. Most students **worked** hard. They **arrived** at 7 and most of them **don't leave** until 5.*	The time frame shifts suddenly from past to present to past to present again. This is confusing.
Acceptable: c. *The school I went to **was** very competitive. It **was** a tough school to get into, and getting in **was** only the start. The students **worked** hard. They **arrived** at 7 and most of them **didn't leave** until 5.*	Past tenses are used consistently. The writer's generalizations apply to the past.
Acceptable: d. *The school I went to **is** very competitive. It **is** a very tough school to get into, and getting in **is** only the start. The students **work** hard. They **arrive** at 7 and most of them **don't leave** until 5.*	Present tenses are used consistently. The generalizations apply to both past and present.
Acceptable: e. *The school I went to **is** very competitive. It **is** a tough school to get into, and getting in **is** only the start. The students **work** hard. When **I was there**, they **arrived** at 7 and most of them **didn't leave** until 5.*	Present tense is used in the beginning; an adverbial introduces a shift to past time.

Test yourself

■ **Exercise 45** (4.2)   Find and fix **one or two** mistakes in the formation of tenses.

The sun's heat causes air masses to form and circulate in our atmosphere. When a warm air mass circulates, it rises and cools. Eventually that cool air sinks back to Earth. In places where the air sinking, an area of low pressure will develop, but where the air is rising, high pressure is the result. Since the atmosphere constantly works to restore equilibrium, air moves from areas of high pressure to areas of low pressure.

■ **Exercise 46** (4.6, 7, 8, 27)   Use the verbs in the appropriate tenses.

be (x2)   *not depend*   *discover*   *not have to*   *involve*   *play*   *say*   *study*

Researchers __ more and more evidence that high achievement __ only on innate ability. Intelligence certainly __ a big role in achievement, but many experts __ that practice __ equally or even more important. The most effective practice __ setting specific goals, getting immediate feedback, and concentrating as much on technique as on results. This __ good news for a student who __ a foreign language. You __ be a grammar genius to succeed.

Chapter 4   Tenses   Grammar Advantage 129

■ **Exercise 47** (4.6, 9, 12)   Find and fix **two or three** mistakes. Focus on the underlined parts.

Over the last few decades, grades at most U.S. colleges and universities have risen. The case of Brown University is typical. During the 2012-2013 academic year, 53.4 percent of grades at Brown <u>were</u> As. In the 1992-1993 school year, only 9.1 percent <u>have been</u> As. Since the early 90s, the proportion of Cs at Brown <u>has decreased</u>, falling from about 8 percent to about 4 percent. In the same period, the proportion of Bs <u>has fallen</u> from about 29 percent to about 24 percent. Educators <u>called</u> this type of change grade inflation, and it is very controversial, because no one <u>knows</u> for sure what <u>has caused</u> the change. Some say that today's students <u>are</u> better prepared or that they <u>work</u> harder. Others worry that academic standards <u>fell</u>.

■ **Exercise 48** (4.6 – 8, 9, 12, 16, 17)   Put the verbs into the most appropriate tenses. Most should be simple present or simple past. One or two should be past perfect. One should be future. One should be present continuous. For some, there may be more than one way.

My daily walk to work [take] half an hour, and on the way I sometimes I [stop] at a restroom in a park. I [stop] there one day recently and [notice] that someone [remove] the mirrors above the sinks. A few days later, I [stop] again. Above the sinks someone [write] in big red letters "You look great!" Later I [read] in the paper that they [remodel] the restrooms in the park, so the mirrors [be] back soon. Too bad. For me the "You look great" sign [work] a lot better.

■ **Exercise 49** (4.9, 12, 17)   Fix **two or three** tense mistakes.

Rowan is starting at the university next semester. He didn't decide on a major, but he's thinking about majoring in philosophy. He once watched a movie about great philosophers and thought he would like philosophy. At the same time, he has heard that philosophy classes are difficult, and he knows that philosophy is not as practical as some majors. Before he will register, he plans to discuss it with his advisor and talk to a professor or two. The university doesn't require students to choose a major until after a few semesters, so he doesn't feel that he has to decide right away.

■ **Exercise 50**   Fix **one** mistake in each item. Focus on the underlined parts.

1. Careful drivers <u>don't text</u> while they are driving. They <u>keep</u> their eyes on the road and <u>avoiding</u> distractions.

2. In most states, *daylight saving time* <u>begins</u> on the second Sunday in March. Everyone <u>sets</u> their clocks ahead on that date. When daylight time <u>ended</u> on the first Sunday in November, we <u>move</u> the clocks back one hour.

3. My college <u>has changed</u> from a quarter system to a semester system last fall. They <u>had followed</u> the quarter system for four decades. Now that classes are 15 weeks, students <u>will be</u> able to study subjects in more depth.

4. In our discussion, someone said, "I <u>understand</u> what you<u>'re saying</u>, but I <u>don't agree</u> with it." He<u>'s trying</u> to be polite.

5. At the beginning of the movie, I <u>thought</u> the main character <u>will fall</u> in love with his neighbor and they <u>would</u> get married, but instead he <u>fell</u> in love with her brother.

6. When you <u>will be</u> 80 years old, <u>do you think</u> you <u>will still enjoy</u> the music you <u>listen</u> to today?

7. Brazil <u>used to be</u> a Portuguese colony, so most Brazilians <u>are speaking</u> Portuguese. The language <u>has changed</u>, but people from Portugal <u>don't have</u> trouble understanding Brazilians.

8. As a consequence of global warming, glaciers around the world <u>are shrinking</u>. One hundred years ago, there <u>were</u> more than 150 glaciers in Glacier National Park. Since then, the number <u>is decreasing</u> to fewer than 25. A few decades from now, it is likely that all of the glaciers <u>will have disappeared</u>.

9. The teachers at this school <u>value</u> active learning. They <u>don't do</u> a lot of lecturing. They <u>say</u> that most students <u>didn't learn</u> effectively that way.

10. In old movies, you often <u>see</u> people smoking. Now smoking in movies <u>become</u> less common. The producers of movies <u>don't want</u> to offend viewers who <u>object</u> to smoking.

11. The famous writer Oscar Wilde <u>once</u> said that a writer is someone who <u>has taught</u> his mind to misbehave. Wilde <u>understood</u> that creativity <u>is</u> not always come from an orderly mind.

12. When Spanish explorers <u>came</u> to the western hemisphere in the late 19th Century, they <u>had brought</u> horses. The native people <u>had never seen</u> horses, but they soon <u>became</u> an important part of life in the Americas.

13. Most Americans who were at least 12 years old in 1963 <u>remembered</u> what they <u>were doing</u> when they <u>heard</u> the news that President John Kennedy <u>had been</u> assassinated.

14. Jessie <u>has been looking</u> for work <u>since</u> the first of the year. As soon as he <u>found</u> a job, he<u>'s going to look</u> for an apartment.

15. We bought this house <u>when</u> we moved here from L.A. three years <u>ago</u>. <u>For</u> two years, we kept everything as it was, but <u>from</u> then we have made lots of improvements.

4.39 Problems with tenses (see also 4.4.3)

Form problems: Form tenses correctly, with auxiliaries and the main verb in the correct forms. See 4.2 and 4.4 and T – W below.

Usage problems: See the examples below. Can you predict the revisions by looking only at the problem sentences? If it confuses you to look at problem sentences, just study the revisions column and the rules.

Problem sentences	Revisions	Rules
1. I'm a slow writer. When I wrote a paper, it always took me a long time.	I'm a slow writer. When I **write** a paper, it always **takes** me a long time.	Use present tense for generalizations about present situations. (4.6)
2. Thanks for the explaining. Now I understood.	Thanks for the explanation. Now I **understand**.	Make sure tenses work well with time adverbials.
3. When I graduate in 2010, my family is living in the countryside. We don't have much money. I have never dreamed of going abroad.	When I **graduated** in 2010, my family was living in the countryside. We **didn't have** much money. I **had never dreamed** of going abroad.	Use past tenses for past situations. (4.9)
4. Can you call back later? We eat dinner.	Can you call back later? We **are eating** dinner.	Use continuous tenses to show that an action is or was in progress. (4.7, 4.10)
5. Last night the power went off when I slept.	Last night the power went off when I **was sleeping**.	
6. I sold my car. Now I use(d) to take the bus.	I sold my car. Now I **take** the bus. (Now I **usually take**...)	The past-tense auxiliary *used to* (4.11) has no present tense. Use simple present.

Problem sentences	Revisions	Rules
7. I've seen that movie last week.	I **have seen** that movie. I **saw** that movie last week.	Don't use a past time adverbial with a present perfect verb. (4.12, 4.13)
8. Lu loves this apartment. She lived here since 2016.	Lu loves this apartment. She **has lived** here since 2016.	With a *since* clause or another adverbial that names a time continuing until now, use present perfect or present perfect continuous. (4.12)
9. I'm working here for 25 years.	I **have been working / have worked** here for 25 years.	
10. We know each other for a long time.	We **have known** each other for a long time.	
11. I had a happy childhood. We had lived in a small town with friendly people.	I had a happy childhood. We **lived** in a small town with friendly people.	Don't use past perfect unless it is needed. (4.15, 4.17)
12. The machine stopped. Someone pulled the plug.	The machine stopped. Someone **had pulled** the plug.	Use past perfect to show that an action happened before a previously mentioned past action. (4.15)
13. You forgot your key? I let you in.	You forgot your key? I **will let** you in.	Use *will* for an offer. (4.18)
14. ~ Do you have plans for the weekend? ~ I will visit my some friends.	~ Do you have plans for the weekend? ~ **I'm going to visit / I'm visiting** some friends.	Use *BE going* to or present continuous for planned actions. (4.18)
15. We can leave as soon as it will stop raining / as soon as it stopped raining.	We can leave as soon as it **stops / has stopped** raining.	Use a present tense for a future action in an adverbial clause. (4.20)
16. I know / knew / met / have met her since we in college together.	I **have known** her **since** we were in college together. I **met** her **when** we were in college together.	Make sure your tense choices are appropriate for your verb choices. (4.25)
17. I've arrived since Monday.	I **arrived on** Monday. I've **been here** since Monday.	
18. This job was hard for me at the beginning, but now I start to do better.	Now I **am starting** to do better. Now I **have started** to do better.	Use present continuous (4.7) or present prefect 4.12). With an action verb, simple present refers to recurring actions.
19. When I was a child, I would like to go to the beach.	When I was a child, I liked to go to the beach.	*Would like to* does not usually express past time. We usually use *would like* for something we want now: *I would like to talk to you.*
20. I'm belong to the chess club.	I **belong** to a jazz band.	Don't use an unnecessary BE verb. Use BE for continuous tenses (e.g. *is calling, were looking*) and passive voice (e.g. *are called, have been seen*). See also 5.8.
21. It's depend on the cost.	It **depends** on the cost.	
22. The program was consist(ed) of three parts.	The program **consisted** of three parts.	
23. I've never been thought about that.	I've never **thought** about that.	

Chapter 5

Passive and active voice

IN THIS CHAPTER

Formation of passive and active voice

by phrases

uses of passive voice

tricky words like *bore*, *bored*, and *boring*

stative passives and prepositions

Chapter 5
Passive and active voice

Chapter 5: Passive and active voice 135

- 5.1 Passive and active voice in context 137
- 5.2 Comparing active and passive 137
- 5.3 Passive voice in different tenses and with modal auxiliaries 138
- 5.4 Indicating the agent with a *by* phrase 139
- 5.5 Visualizing the relationship between active and passive 140
- 5.6 Which verbs can be passive? 142
- 5.7 Verbs that are never passive 143
  - 5.7.1 Intransitive verbs to avoid using in the passive voice 143
  - 5.7.2 Verb + preposition combinations that allow passive voice 143
- 5.8 Avoiding the extra BE problem 144
- 5.9 Ergative verbs 145
- 5.10 Uses of the passive voice 145
- 5.11 Stative passives 147
- 5.12 Words like *bore*, *bored*, and *boring* 149
  - 5.13 Usage guide Passive voice and the dictionary 151
  - 5.14 Usage guide Choosing passive or active 152
  - 5.15 Usage guide Phrases like *is said to be* 153
- 5.16 Problems with passive and active voice 154

Chapter 5 — Passive and active voice — Grammar Advantage **137**

5.1 Passive and active voice in context

■ **Exercise 1** Based on what you already know about passive and active voice, underline the passive verb phrases in the passage below. What helps you identify them as passive? The first passive verb phrase is already underlined. (If you prefer, read 5.2 first.)

The blue eyes / brown eyes lesson

In 1968, in an elementary school in Iowa, a class of third graders experienced an unusual lesson. The students <u>were divided</u> into two groups: blue-eyed students and brown-eyed students. The brown-eyed students were told they were the "superior" group. They were told that they were smarter, cleaner, and more civilized. They were given five extra minutes of recess and allowed to take seconds at lunch. The "inferior" group wasn't allowed to take seconds at lunch, play with kids in the "superior" group, or use the playground equipment.

The next day, the groups were reversed. Now the blue-eyed children were the "superior" group and the brown-eyed children were "inferior."

This unusual lesson was designed as a way of teaching the students what it is like to experience discrimination.

KEY
Ch. 6 = Chapter 6
Ex. 23 = Exercise 23
5.2 = Chapter 5, section 2
2.14.3 = Chapter 2, section 14, subsection 3
(a) = an example

5.2 Comparing active and passive

We use the terms **passive voice** and **active voice** (or just passive and active) to describe a grammatical difference that involves word order and verb forms.

Active:	***The teacher** evaluated **the students**.* 1 2 3	• The object in the active sentence is the subject in the passive sentence.
Passive:	***The students** were evaluated (by **the teacher**).* 3 2 1 *The Students **are not evaluated** every day.* *They **are usually evaluated** once a week.*	• The passive verb phrase consists of a form of the auxiliary BE and a main verb in the past participle form (*taken, evaluated, written*). • The tense of the active verb becomes the tense of auxiliary BE. • The verb is plural because *students* is plural. Compare: *The student* (just one) *was evaluated* … • The doer of the action — the agent — may be expressed in a prepositional phrase beginning with *by*. • *Not* and other adverbs often appear after the auxiliary BE.

■ **Exercise 2** The same information is expressed below in a version with all active sentences (a) and a version with some passive sentences (b). Underline the subject-verb-object sequences in (a) and their passive paraphrases in (b). The first pair is already underlined.

| a. In 1968, in a small town in Iowa, <u>Jane Elliott taught an unusual lesson</u> in her third-grade class. She divided the students into two groups: blue-eyed students and brown-eyed students. She told the brown-eyed students they were the "superior" group. She told them they were smarter, cleaner, and more civilized. She gave them five extra minutes of recess and allowed them to take seconds at lunch. She didn't allow the "inferior" group to take seconds at lunch, play with kids in the "superior" group, or use the playground equipment.

The next day, Elliott reversed the groups. Now the blue-eyed children were the "superior" group and the brown-eyed children were "inferior."

Why did Jane Elliott design such an unusual lesson? Her goal was to teach the students what it is like to experience discrimination. | b. <u>In 1968, in a small town in Iowa, an unusual lesson was taught to</u> a third-grade class. The students were divided into two groups: blue-eyed students and brown-eyed students. The brown-eyed students were told they were the "superior" group. They were told that they were smarter, cleaner, and more civilized. They were given five extra minutes of recess and allowed to take seconds at lunch. The "inferior" group wasn't allowed to take seconds at lunch, play with kids in the "superior" group, or use the playground equipment.

The next day, the groups were reversed. Now the blue-eyed children were the "superior" group and the brown-eyed children were "inferior."

Why was such an usual lesson designed? The goal was to teach the students what it is like to experience discrimination. |

5.3 Passive voice in different tenses and with modal auxiliaries

The BE verb in a passive verb phrase may have any tense, and the usual tense rules apply (Ch. 4).

	Simple passive	Continuous passive	Perfect passive
Present	*is / are / am called*	*is / are / am being called*	*has / have been called*
Past	*was / were called*	*was / were being called*	*had been called*
Future	*will be called*	(Rarely used.)	*will have been called*

A verb phrase beginning with a modal auxiliary — *can, could, may, might, must, shall, should, will,* or *would* — can be passive, using BE and a past participle after the modal (a). A modal can be followed by *have* in sentences about the past, in both active and passive voice (b).

Active	Passive	
*Someone **might follow** you.*	a. *You **might be followed**.*	Maybe it will happen.
*Someone **might have followed** you.*	b. *You **might have been followed**.*	Maybe it happened.

Chapter 5 Passive and active voice Grammar Advantage 139

5.4 Indicating the agent with a *by* phrase

We can mention the agent — the doer of the action — in a phrase with *by* (a). The agent is not necessarily a person, especially with verbs that refer to the cause of a feeling, like *bore* and *confuse* (b) see also 5.12.

Passive with a *by* phrase	Active
a. *The blue eyes / brown eyes lesson was designed by* **Jane Elliott**.	*Jane Elliott designed the blue-eyes / brown-eyes lesson.*
b. *Students are often confused by English spelling.*	*English spelling often confuses students.*

■ **Exercise 3**   Use the verbs in the correct forms, active or passive. Pay attention to the tenses (for example, *were* instead of *are*) as well.

1. *divide, tell, give*   In the blue eyes / brown eyes lesson, the children in an elementary classroom _____ into two groups according to eye color — blue or brown. The children in the blue-eyed group _____ that they were superior. They _____ special privileges.

2. *reverse, tell, give, allow*   The next day the groups _____. The brown eyed children _____ that they were superior, and they _____ privileges. They _____ to take seconds at lunch, for example.

3. *design, want, treat*   This unusual lesson _____ by Jane Elliot, the students' teacher. She _____ to teach the children how it feels when you _____ unfairly.

4. *gather, learn, describe*   Many years later, Jane Elliott _____ her former students together for a discussion of the experience. Some said they _____ a useful lesson. Others _____ the experience as traumatic.

■ **Exercise 4**   Choose the right form of the verb, active or passive, in the designated tense.

affect – simple present tense
1. Diet, exercise, and sleep all ___ a person's health.
2. When a disaster strikes, everyone ___ .
3. Natural disasters like floods and earthquakes ___ everyone.

spend – simple present tense
4. In a typical month, how much money ___ you ___ on entertainment?
5. Every year, millions of dollars ___ on luxury goods like fine watches and handbags.
6. Many citizens criticize the government because it ___ so much on defense.

invent – simple past
7. When ___ the safety belt that we use in cars ___ ?
8. Before the electric light bulb ___, people tended to go to bed earlier.
9. Pasteurization makes it safe to drink milk. The process ___ in the 19th century.
10. No one knows who ___ the first mechanical clock.

write – simple past tense
11. Before the invention of the printing press, everything ___ by hand.
12. Some of the greatest English novels ___ by women writers.
13. Jane Austen ___ Pride and Prejudice, one of the most famous English novels.

5.5 Visualizing the relationship between active and passive sentences

One way to understand the formation of active and passive voice is to visualize the transformation of an active sentence to a passive sentence. Below are examples for one-object verbs (a) and two-object verbs in two variations (b, c). Only simple tenses are shown (present in a, past in b and c), but similar representations are possible for other tenses.

a. Sentences with one-object verbs (*affect, include, spend*, etc. – 2.4.1)

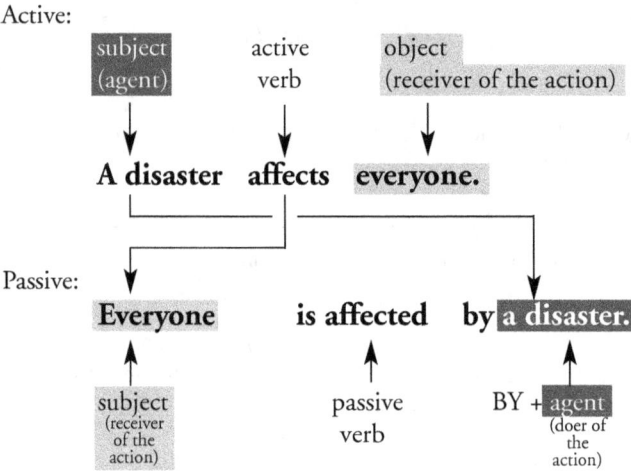

b. Sentences with two-object verbs (*give, show, tell*, etc. – 2.6)

b.1. Active, with the **verb + indirect object + object** pattern:

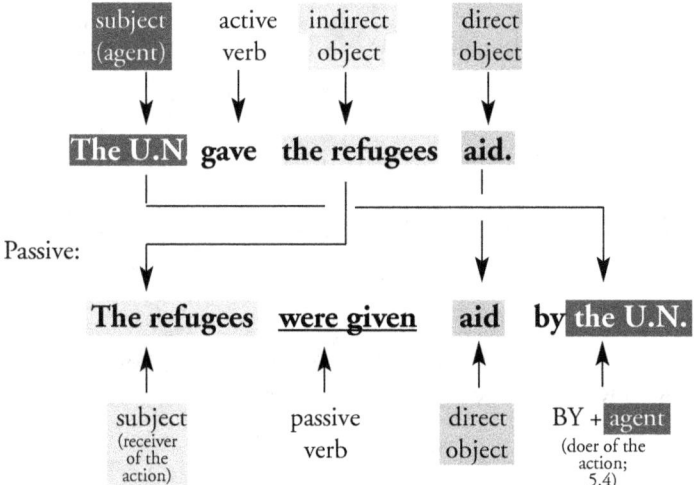

b.2. Active, with the **verb + direct object + preposition + indirect object** pattern:

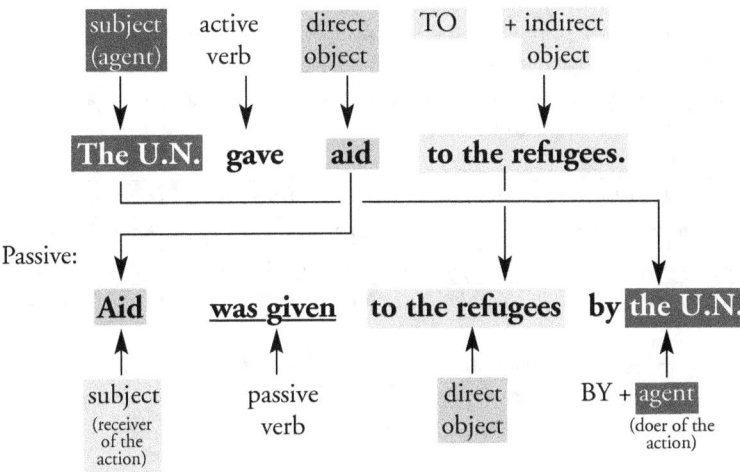

■ **Exercise 5** Change each active sentence to passive. Change each passive sentence to active. Keep the tenses the same. (For reference, see Appendix A, which includes examples of active and passive in all tenses.) Don't include the agent unless it expresses useful information.

1. A fire destroyed their home.
2. Vandals broke the school windows.
3. They planted some trees.
4. They organized a contest to come up with a new name.
5. How do you spell your last name?
6. When do they serve lunch?
7. How do they organize their schedules?
8. Where do they keep the cleaning supplies?
9. They awarded the winner a one-hundred dollar bill. (There are two ways; choose one.)
10. They gave me a prize. (There are two ways; choose one.)
11. They always show an orientation video to new students. (There are two ways; choose one.)
12. They assigned everyone a task. (There are two ways; choose one.)
13. They didn't invite us to the party.
14. In my dorm, they don't serve breakfast on weekends.
15. They didn't allow me to cross the border.
16. At this school, they don't require uniforms.
17. The Mets were defeated by the Yankees.
18. The *Mona Lisa* was painted by Leonardo.
19. Many casinos are operated by American Indians.
20. Most of the citizens of this town are employed by Walmart.
21. The most successful websites are designed by professionals.
22. A lot of accidents are caused by distracted drivers.

5.6 Which verbs can be passive?

A transitive verb is a verb that can have an object — that is, a noun (a), noun phrase (b), noun clause (c), or pronoun (d) that immediately follows the verb. Because transitive verbs allow objects, they usually have passive paraphrases in which the object becomes the subject of a passive verb (e, f, g, h). Only a transitive verb can be passive.

a. *At this company, we value* **innovation.**	e. *At this company,* **innovation is valued.**
b. *We have just hired* **a new vice-president.**	f. ***A new vice-president has just been hired.***
c. *Everyone understands* **what we need.**	g. ***What we need is understood*** *(by everyone).*
d. *We chose* **her** *for her innovative thinking.*	h. ***She was chosen*** *for her innovative thinking.*

Verbs that never have an object — such as *happen* and *seem* — are called *intransitive*. Intransitive verbs are always active, never passive (g). Even if the subject does not come first in the sentence, the verb is in active form, with the subject before it (h).

g. *Nothing important* **happened** *at our last meeting.* (~~was happened~~)
h. *At our last meeting, nothing important happened.* (~~was happened~~)

For more about transitive and intransitive verbs, see 2.4.

■ **Exercise 6** (5.3) Which underlined verbs have an object? In this paragraph from Ch. 2, underline the objects.

Art was always important to Sarah Palmer, and so was nature. Wild animals <u>fascinated</u> her. Hats, too: she never <u>went</u> out without a hat. So when Sara <u>died</u> at the age of 101 in 2014, the residents of the small town where she <u>lived</u> <u>honored</u> her in a suitable way. They <u>commissioned</u> a sculpture by Evo Ard, a local artist. He <u>finished</u> the statue in 2015 and it now <u>stands</u> in the town square. At first glance, it appears to be a woman wearing a dress and a hat. When you <u>look</u> more closely, you see that in fact it is a chimpanzee, and the hat is just like one that Sara often wore. People <u>remember</u> Sarah for her sense of humor, so the statue would no doubt appeal to her. The old men who use the square every day as their own private front yard <u>appreciate</u> it too. As one remarked, "It's the best thing that ever <u>happened</u> to this town!"

■ **Exercise 7** (5.1, 5.2, 5.3) Create a passive paraphrase of each sentence that has a transitive verb and an object. Do not do anything with the other sentences. In the passive sentences, don't include a phrase with *by* unless it gives important information. Do not change the tenses.

Examples: Sarah lived in a small town. ➤ *No change is possible.* People called Sarah *Sally.* ➤ *Sarah was called "Sally."* (Passive with no *by* phrase.) A friend told this story to me. ➤ *This story was told to me by a friend.* (Passive with a *by* phrase.)

1. Wild animals fascinated her.
2. She never went out bareheaded.
3. In 2014, she died at the age of 101.
4. She lived in a small town.
5. The town's residents honored her in a suitable way.
6. They commissioned a sculpture.
7. The sculptor finished the statue in 2015.
8. They installed it in 2015.
9. It now stands in the town square.
10. People remember Sarah for her sense of humor.
11. The statue would appeal to her.
12. The old men use the park.

5.7 Verbs that are never passive

5.7.1 Intransitive verbs to avoid using in the passive voice

The verbs below, with sample sentences, are not normally used in passive voice because they are intransitive. (See also 2.4.)

agree *Do you agree? I don't agree.*	happen *What happens when you die?*
appear *Halley's comet will appear 2061.*	last *The U.S. Civil War lasted four years.*
arrive *I arrived in this country last fall.*	live *Do dogs live as long as cats?*
become *When did you become fluent?*	matter *It doesn't matter if you're late.*
belong *Have you ever belonged to a club?*	occur *More violent crimes occur in hot weather.*
consist of *The chapter consists of two parts.*	participate *Have you ever participated in an auction?*
cost *Early computers cost a lot.*	remain *The question remains.*
depend on *Your success depends on you.*	rise *Prices usually rise when supply falls.*
die *Thousands die in traffic accidents.*	seem *Do Americans seem friendly to you?*
disappear *Dinosaurs disappeared 65 million years ago.*	sleep *How long do you usually sleep?*
exist *Do you believe that ghosts exist?*	stay *I stayed with friends instead of at a hotel.*
fall *Prices usually fall when supply rises.*	wait *How long do you usually wait for the bus?*

- We sometimes use *agree* in a stative passive phrase (5.11): *It was agreed that both sides would compromise.*

5.7.2 Verb + preposition combinations that allow passive voice

We can use some verb + preposition combinations (including *depend on*, in the list above) in passive voice. That is, we use the verb + preposition combination just as we use a transitive verb (b, d). These are exceptions to the rule that intransitive verbs cannot be passive (5.6).

Active voice	Passive voice
a. *People listen to K-pop all over Asia.*	b. *K-pop is listened to all over Asia.*
c. *Do employers discriminate against older workers in hiring?*	d. *Are older workers discriminated against in hiring?*
e. *Someone has slept in this bed.*	f. *This bed has been slept in.*
g. *None has ever lived in this house.*	h. *This house has never been lived in.*

This type of passive is quite common with certain verb + preposition combinations in infinitive phrases (i), bare infinitive phrases (j) and gerund phrases (k).

i. *No one wants to be discriminated against.* (No one wants others to discriminate against them.)
j. *This problem can be dealt with later.* (Someone can deal with this problem …)
k. *I hate being talked about behind my back.* (I hate it when people talk about me …)

Impossible verb phrases

5.8 Avoiding the extra BE problem

A common mistake is to use a BE verb before an intransitive verb (5.7, 2.4.3, 2.4.4). If the verb is in the past participle form (a), this mistake looks like a passive verb phrase, which is impossible with an intransitive verb. If the verb is in the base form (b), this mistake looks like a misformation of simple past or past continuous (c), simple present (d), or present continuous (e).

a. *The accident was happened at noon.* →	An intransitive verb cannot be used in the passive.
b. *This watch was belong to my father.* →	This watch belonged to ... (simple past tense)
c. *The children were stay at home.* →	The children stayed / were staying at home. (simple past or past continuous)
d. *This custom is no longer exist(ed).* →	This custom no longer exists. (simple present)
e. *What's happen in your life these days?* →	What is happening ...? (present continuous)

With transitive verbs, remember not to use BE except in a properly formed passive sentence (f) or in a sentence with a continuous verb phrase (h, i).

f. *The accident was seen by two bystanders.*	A BE verb is used correctly in a passive sentence.
g. *Leonardo was painted the Mona Lisa.*	BE is not needed in the active sentence. *Leonardo painted* the Mona Lisa. (Passive: *The Mona Lisa was painted by Leonardo.*)
h. *The children were playing soccer.*	Forms of BE are used correctly in continuous verb phrases.
i. *The population is no longer growing.*	

■ **Exercise 8** In the sentences below, use the right forms of the verbs that are provided. Avoid the extra BE problem. Pay attention to your choice of tenses.

agree   become   belong   consist   not cost   not depend

1. I suggest we split the cost 50-50. __ you __?
2. I can't afford this. Let's find one that __ so much.
3. The U.S. congress __ of two bodies: the House of Representatives and the Senate.
4. Do you own anything that __ to your great grandparents?
5. We have so many ants they __ a problem.
6. Your pay is based on your performance. It __ on how long you have worked here.

die   disappear   not exist   happen   last   live

7. As their habitat shrinks, many species of wildlife __.
8. I heard you were in an accident. When __ it __?
9. The poems of Emily Dickinson were not published until after she __.
10. When you live abroad, you have to get used to customs that __ in your native culture.
11. The American Civil War __ from 1861 to 1865.
12. When you were born, where __ your family __?

not matter   not occur   remain   sleep   stay   wait

13. You should reserve your ticket now. Only five seats __.
14. We can go out to eat or we can eat at home. It __ to me.
15. When the plane landed, I __. I didn't wake up till the cabin was almost empty.
16. ~ Is this your hotel? ~ No. I __ at a friend's house to avoid the cost of a hotel.
17. With some diseases, symptoms __ until it is too late for effective treatment.
18. If people are standing at a bus stop, it's likely that they __ for a bus.

5.9 Ergative verbs

The weather changed.

Ergative verbs — *break, change, close, develop, move, shake* and many others — can appear not only in active and passive sentences but in a third type of sentence, sometimes called middle voice (a-c). Many of these verbs describe a change of state (*boil, burn, cook*). Most verbs are not ergative and cannot be used this way (d).

Active voice	Passive voice	Middle voice: The subject is the same as in the passive sentences, but the verb is not passive.
a. They changed the law before I got my driver's license.	The law was changed.	**The law changed** before I got my driver's license.
b. The storm shook the house.	The house was shaken.	**The house shook.**
c. We close the office at six.	The office is closed at six.	**The office closes** at six.
d. The storm destroyed the house.	The house was destroyed.	~~The house destroyed~~. *Destroy* (like most verbs) *is not an ergative verb.*

5.10 Uses of the passive voice

When do we use passive voice?

We can use the passive voice when we prefer not to mention the doer of the action (a), when we don't know who did it (b), when we want to focus on the action itself or its result (c, d), and when we want to focus on the receiver of the action (e).

a. *Mistakes were made.*	Passive voice allows us to avoid saying who made the mistakes. (We can do the same by saying "Someone made mistakes," but that calls attention to the question of *who* did it.)
b. *Several books were left in the classroom.*	Passive voice is useful because we don't know who left the books. It's awkward to say "Some student or students left …"
c. *This tree has been damaged.*	Passive voice allows us to avoid the awkward sentence "Someone or something has damaged this tree."
d. *Paper is made from wood pulp.*	Passive voice allows us to focus on the action and the result of the action, not the people who do it.
e. *A suspect in the crime was arrested.*	Passive voice allows us to focus on the receiver of the action. It is not necessary to mention the agent (*the police*), since it is obvious that police performed the action.

We often like to keep the same noun phrase (or other words that refer to it) in the subject position in a series of sentences. This may result in several passive verbs in successive sentences (f). We can make sentences more concise by combining clauses, omitting repeated subjects, and using the auxiliary BE only in the first passive verb phrase (g).

f. Not concise: **The men** *who were arrested were taken to the police station. Then* **the men** *were photographed,* **they** *were fingerprinted, and* **they** *were questioned.*	The second sentence has needless repetition.
g. More concise: *The men who were arrested* ***were taken*** *to the police station,* ***photographed, fingerprinted,*** *and* ***questioned.***	We don't need to repeat the auxiliary verb *were* before *photographed, fingerprinted,* and *questioned*. Those words must, however, be in the past participle form, just like *taken*.

■ **Exercise 9**   Rewrite the sentences so that the focus is on the object and the actions, as in the example. Do not include the agent (that is, don't say *by us* or *by someone*).

Someone opened the letter, modified it, resealed it, and gave it to the principal. ⟶ *The letter was opened, modified, resealed, and given to the principal.*

1. They wash all the cars, wax them, and polish them.
2. The police apprehended the suspects, took them to the station, and questioned them.
3. We have hired new workers, gave them uniforms, trained them, and put them to work.
4. The museum has purchased five new paintings, catalogued them, and put them on display.
5. Someone stole my purse, emptied it out on the sidewalk, and threw it in the trash.
6. They remodeled the house, painted it, and sold it for a good profit.
7. They closed the store, restocked it, and reopened it in two weeks.
8. A committee reviewed the rules, rewrote them, and expanded them.
9. Someone has washed the clothes, folded them, and put them on shelves.
10. We have greeted the new students, given them a tour of the campus, and introduced them to their host families.

5.11 Stative passives

My dog is lost.

Stative passives look like passive verb phrases (with BE and a past participle), but they are not true passives, because they do not have active paraphrases. The same verb may be used in both and stative passives and true passives. In stative passives, it becomes an adjective with *–ed*.

Stative passive	True passive
a. *Portuguese is related to Spanish.* *Is related to* expresses a state, not an action. There is no active paraphrase.	b. *Portuguese is spoken in Brazil as well as in Portugal.* Active paraphrase: *They speak Portuguese …* Speaking is an action.
c. *Are the classroom walls painted?* The question is about the **state** of the rooms. There is no active paraphrase.	d. *Are the classrooms painted every year?* The question asks about an action. Active paraphrase: *Do they (Does someone) paint the classrooms …?*
e. *They are married.* *Are married* expresses a state.	f. *Most couples are married in religious ceremonies.* (A religious official marries them.)
g. *My dog is lost.* *Is lost* expresses a state.	To express the action, we can use *get lost*: *My dog got lost*. (See 4.25)

The distinction between stative passive and true passive is not always clear-cut, but it's good to be aware of stative passives, because they are common. It's helpful to think of them as phrases including typical prepositions, like *be related to*. In some cases, more than one preposition is possible.

be accustomed to	*Are you accustomed to being addressed as "Sir"?*
be associated with	*Smoking is associated with heart disease.*
be based on	*Our number system is based on 10.*
be composed of	*The government is composed of three parts.*
be concerned about	*Are you concerned about the future?*
be equipped with	*Most classrooms are equipped with a projection system.*
be exposed to	*Children of smokers risk being exposed to secondhand smoke.*
be interested in	*Lots of men are interested in cooking.*
be involved in	*Have you ever been involved in student government?*
be located in	*The sign says, "You are located in Kolthoff Hall."*
be lost	*My dog is lost.*
be made from	*Paper is made from wood pulp.*
be made of	*Is this plate made of plastic?*
be married to	*Prince Harry of Britain is married to an American.*
be opposed to	*Are you opposed to capital punishment?*
be prepared for	*It's impossible to be prepared for everything.*
be qualified for	*Are you qualified for this job?*
be related to	*The Persian language is distantly related to English.*
be used to	*People who live in Minnesota are used to cold winters.*
be worried about	*If you're worried about the time, let's leave now.*

Exercise 10 Complete each sentence with a form of BE, an adjective from the first group of words, and a preposition from the second group (for example, *is opposed to*, *are equipped with*, *be concerned about*). Note that sometimes a gerund follows the preposition (6.5), as in *I am used to getting up* early and *We are interested in launching* a start-up. Think about the meaning. If you are not sure about the meaning of a word, check a dictionary.

based   equipped   exposed   related   on   to (x2)   with

1   It's important to seek medical attention if you ... radiation.
2   In the late 18th century it was discovered that some languages of India ... English.
3   In the interest of safety, every classroom ... a first aid kit.
4   Lots of movies ... historical events.

concerned   opposed   prepared   used   about   for   to (x2)

5   I bought a warm jacket, so now I ... cold weather.
6   Liam made an appointment with his teacher because he ... his grade.
7   We sometimes use the term *doves* for leaders who ... military action.
8   Everyone pays attention to Anne. She ... being the center of attention.

accustomed   interested   married   qualified   for   in   to (x2)

9   If you have a teaching degree, you ... a teaching job.
10 Some companies won't hire you if you ... an employee of the company.
11 This campus has lots of clubs for students who ... meeting other students.
12 It's hard to live independently if you ... relying on your parents.

5.12 Words like *bore*, *bored*, and *boring*

bored workers

boring jobs

Words like *bore* — which relates to a state of mind — are used in a variety of ways. We can use the verb *bore* in active sentences with an object (a) and in passive sentences (b). We can use related adjectives (participial adjectives) with *–ing* (c) and *–ed* (d). When there is no agent phrase (with *by*), a verb phrase like *is bored* can be viewed either as a verb and adjective or as a passive verb. We can use participial adjectives after linking verbs (c, d) and before nouns (e, f).

a. *Repetitive tasks bore me.*	b. *I am bored by repetitive tasks.*
c. *Repetitive tasks are boring.*	d. *If you're bored with your job, just quit!*
e. *Bored workers aren't productive.* (~~boring~~)	f. *There are lots of boring jobs.* (~~bored~~)

Words that work this way include *confuse/confused/confusing*, *interest/interested/interesting* and many others. Understanding how to use these verbs can help you avoid mistakes.

g. WRONG: *I confuse about prepositions.*	→ *I am confused about/by prepositions. Prepositions confuse me. Prepositions are confusing.*
h. WRONG: *We didn't satisfy the service.*	→ *We weren't satisfied with the service. The service didn't satisfy us. The service wasn't satisfactory.*
i. WRONG: *The results were disappointed me.*	→ *The results disappointed me. I was disappointed with/by the results. The results were disappointing.*

As the examples show, there is variation in the patterns. We use different prepositions: *confused **about**, disappointed **in**,* etc. Even with the same word we can use different prepositions: *disappointed **in/with/by**.* (There may be meaning differences; consult a dictionary.) We may use other words in place of some of the forms, like *satisfactory* instead of *satisfying*.

It may help to keep in mind that these sentences involve three elements (though sometimes only two are expressed): a cause, a feeling, and a person. We can start with the cause or the person.

Put the **cause** first:			Put the **person** first:		
Cause	Feeling	Person	Person	Feeling	Cause
Prepositions	*are confusing.*	------	*I'm*	*confused.*	------
Prepositions	*confuse*	*me.*	*I'm*	*confused about / by*	*prepositions.*

If you notice how the words are used when you find them in context, you can learn the prepositions and the variations in patterns. Below are some typical phrases.

be bored with	*Are you bored with your job?*
be confused about	*We were confused about the requirements of the assignment.*
be disappointed with/in	*Sometimes I'm disappointed in my test results.*
be embarrassed about	*The boy was embarrassed about his poor grades.*
be excited about	*Are you excited about your new job?*
be fascinated with	*Children are often fascinated with animals.*
be frustrated by	*We were frustrated by our supervisor's unreasonable demands.*
be interested in	*Are you interested in other religions?*
be satisfied with	*We were satisfied with our progress.*
be worried about	*I'm worried about you.*

■ **Exercise 11** Create three simple sentences that give more or less the same information, following the examples.

bore – TV ⟶ TV is boring.   (a form of BE and an -*ing* adjective.)
              TV bores me.   (subject + verb + object.)
              I'm bored by TV.   (passive sentence or a linking verb + an -*ed* adjective)

confuse – prepositions (often) ⟶ Prepositions are often confusing.
                                    Prepositions often confuse me.
                                    I'm often confused about prepositions.

If you wish, change the content to fit your situation. For example, you might change *politics* to something else or you might add *not* or *sometimes*.

1   disappoint – the election results
2   embarrass – mistakes (sometimes)
3   excite – the future
4   fascinate – politics
5   frustrate – software problems
6   interest – history
7   satisfy – my breakfast (use past tense)
8   worry – climate change
9   bore – some books
10 confuse – English spelling

To learn about passive infinitives (*to be injured*) and gerunds (*being injured*), see 6.20.

Usage Guide

5.13 Passive voice and the dictionary

Lexical grammar: the grammar of individual words

Dictionaries can help you with passive voice. If you look up the verb *fund*, for example, you will find that it can be used with an object, which means it can also be passive. If you look up *thrive*, you will find that it is intransitive and thus can never have an object or be passive. Dictionaries mark transitive and intransitive verbs in different ways. This is part of lexical grammar.

	Transitive verbs	Intransitive verbs
Marking:	v.t. or T or "With object"	v.i. or I or "Without object"
Active:	*The state funds thousands of programs.*	*In a loving home, children thrive.*
Passive:	*This program is funded by the state.*	--

Many mistakes involving passive voice come from not understanding the true meaning of a verb. For example, compare the four boldface verbs below, which share the idea of **decreasing**. If you don't know the verbs, try to understand from the context.

*The soldiers faced a crisis. Their food supplies were rapidly **diminishing**. Central command had **reduced** their access to water. By the end of the winter, their numbers had **dwindled** from 40 to 25. Finally, when the army's budget for medical supplies was **slashed**, they couldn't go on.*

Based on the passage, how would you describe the meaning of *diminish*? Is it like "get smaller" or "make (something) smaller"? The same question can be asked about the other three verbs.

In fact, *diminish* and *dwindle* mean something like "get smaller." Accordingly, they are active, not passive. *Reduce* means something like "make (something) smaller." So does *slash*. Since they are transitive, these verbs can be either active (*Central Command had reduced their access to water*) or passive (*The budget was slashed*).

Many verbs can be both transitive and intransitive. Some of these, like *revise* and *eat*, are basically transitive but sometimes don't need an object. Others, like *change*, are ergative (5.9). A good dictionary includes many examples that can help you understand a verb's use and meaning.

	Transitive uses	Intransitive uses
Active:	*Good writers revise their work.*	*Good writers always revise.*
Passive:	*This book has been revised twice.*	
Active:	*They changed the law in 2019.*	*The law changed in 2019.* (See also 5.9.)
Passive:	*The law was changed in 2019.*	

When should you use passive voice?

USAGE GUIDE

5.14 Choosing passive or active

Is passive voice a good choice? It depends on what you want to emphasize and what verbs you want to use. (See also 5.10.)

a.	**YES:** *This song **was downloaded** by a million people last week.*	Passive is fine. The topic is the song, so *this song* is the subject. With that subject, the verb *download* must be passive.
b.	**NO:** *Our team was very successful. Every game **was won**.*	The focus is on our team. There is no need to hide that by not using *we*. Better: *We won every game.*
c.	**YES:** *A child **is kidnapped, held** for ransom, and finally **rescued** in the heart-stopping final scene of this riveting new movie.*	Passive is preferable. The focus is on what happened to the child. The identity of the criminals and rescuers is not important to the sentence. With *the child* as the subject, those verbs must be passive.
d.	**NO:** *When the child is finally rescued, **she asks the police** to be gentle with the kidnappers.*	Active voice is best, keeping the focus on the child. Passive (*the police are asked*) would be a bad choice if the child is the asker.
e.	**YES:** *The noun advice is spelled differently from the verb advise.*	The topic is the word *advice*, so that is the subject. Of course it is people who spell the word, but it's not important to mention people.
f.	**NO:** *This lab has all the equipment you need. If anything more is needed, please let us know.*	Active voice is better. The focus is on what **you** need, so it makes sense to say *If you need anything more.*

The important thing to remember is that neither active nor passive is **always** better. You need to look carefully at the context and the content. Consider what your topic is; it will usually be the subject of the sentence(s). After that subject, use active voice if the subject is the performer of the action: *She asks the police*. Otherwise, use passive voice: *The child is rescued*.

Native speakers are sometimes advised to avoid passive voice. The grammar checking feature of Microsoft Word, for example, consistently identifies passive sentences and suggests changing them. However, this advice is mainly for native speakers who use passive voice when it is not needed (as in *Everything I needed to do was accomplished*). Non-native speakers don't usually have this problem. Grammar checking programs can be helpful, but with regard to passive voice, don't depend on their advice.

Usage Guide

■ **Exercise 12**

1. In the passage below, underline the verbs — both active and passive.

    Some people drive other people crazy with their phones in public. They speak loudly and don't notice others around them. Moreover, when they talk, sometimes very personal information is revealed. Don't they realize how annoying this is?

    All the clauses except one use active voice. Find the one clause with passive voice. How should it be changed?

2. In the passage below, underline the verb phrases — both active and passive.

    Unlike English, Arabic is written from right to left. The letters are connected in complicated ways, and usually vowels are not written at all. When vowels are included, people mark them above the line. These features make Arabic difficult for speakers of other languages.

    All the clauses except two use passive voice. Find the two clauses with active voice. One s should be changed. Which one, and how can you change it?

5.15 Phrases like *is said to be*

are believed to

We use passive phrases like *is said, are considered, was found,* and *were thought* — plus an infinitive — as shown below. Sometimes the infinitive itself is passive (f) or perfect (g) or both passive and perfect (h). For passive and perfect infinitives, see 6.20 and 6.21.

was found to

a.	Laughter **is said to be** the best medicine.	People say it is.
b.	The value if x **is determined to be** 3.5.	The calculation is that *x* equals 3.5.
c.	The company **was estimated to have** assets worth more than a billion.	It was estimated that the company has or had assets worth more than a billion.
d.	Paintings in museums **are** generally **assumed to be** genuine.	People don't question the idea that they are genuine.
e.	The water **was found to be** unsafe.	Someone discovered that it is or was unsafe.
f.	These diseases **are believed to be caused** by vitamin deficiencies.	The belief is that they are caused by vitamin deficiencies.
g.	Human activity **is known to have played** a major role in climate change.	We know it has played a major role. It's not just a belief.
h.	The Great Pyramid **is thought to have been built** around 2560 B.C.E.	Experts think it was built then.

5.16 Problems with passive and active voice

	Problem sentences	Revisions	Rules
1.	The students evaluated (by their treachers)	The students were evaluated. The students are evaluated. The students have been evaluated. The students will be evaluated.	Include a BE verb in a passive verb phrase.
2.	An experiment was conduct. English is speaking all over the world.	An experiment was conducted. English is spoken...	Use the past participle of the main verb: *conducted, spoken, taken, written,* etc
3.	Michelangelo was painted the Sistine Chapel.	Michelangelo painted the Sistine Chapel.	Don't use a passive verb when the sentence starts with an agent (the doer of the action).
4.	The Sistine Chapel was painted Michelangelo.	The Sistine Chapel was painted by Michelangelo.	When you express the agent in a passive sentence, *use by*.
5.	The Sistine Chapel was painted for Michelangelo.		
6.	Accidents are usually happened because of carelessness.	Accidents usually happen because of carelessness.	Don't use an intransitive verb in passive form. (5.7.1)
7.	The accident was happened because of carelessness.	The accident happened because of carelessness.	
8.	This watch was belong to my father.	This watch belonged to my grandfather.	Avoid the "extra BE problem" (5.8). Use BE for the passive voice and continuous tenses (4.7, 4.10), but don't use it when it's not needed.
9.	The children were stay home.	The children stayed / were staying home.	
10.	I'm agree with you.	I agree with you.	
11.	I confused what to do next.	I am (was) confused about what to do next.	Follow the rules of stative passives, with correct prepositions. (5.11, 5.12)

Chapter 6
Gerunds and infinitives

IN THIS CHAPTER

Gerunds and infinitives after verbs, in special sentence patterns, as complements of nouns and adjectives, and more

Chapter 6
Gerunds and infinitives

Chapter 6: Gerunds and infinitives 157

6.1	Gerunds and infinitives in context	159
6.2	What are gerunds and infinitives?	159
6.3	Gerunds and infinitives in sentences	160
6.4	Gerund subjects	161
6.5	Gerunds after prepositions	162
6.6	Gerunds after verbs: *enjoy doing something*	163
6.7	Infinitive subjects, delayed infinitive subjects, and infinitives after BE	165
6.8	Common expressions with empty *it*	165
6.9	Empty it as an object	165
6.10	Verb (+ object) + infinitive: *tend to do something, allow someone to*	168
6.11	Verbs + gerund OR infinitive: *remember, try, like,* etc.	171
6.12	Verb + object + bare infinitive	171
6.13	Causative HAVE	172
	6.13.1 *Have someone do something*: active complements	172
	6.13.2 *Have something done*: passive complements	172
	6.13.3 *Get someone to do something, get something done*	172
6.14	Perception verbs + object + bare infinitive	174
6.15	*Too* and *enough* + infinitive	178
6.16	Adjectives like *easy* + infinitive	179
6.17	*Wh* words + infinitives	179
6.18	Relative clause type infinitives	180
6.19	Implied subjects and phrases like *for someone to do something*	180
6.20	Passive gerunds and infinitives	183
6.21	Perfect gerunds and infinitives	183
6.22	Noun + *of* + gerund: *The process of learning*	185
6.23	Nouns and adjectives with infinitive complements	185
6.24	Usage guide Expressing probability: *be likely to* and *be sure to*	186
6.25	Usage guide *Prevent someone from doing* something, *look forward to doing something*	188
6.26	Usage guide Three patterns: *Have difficulty walking, go shopping, stand waiting*	188
6.27	Usage guide Implied subjects of gerunds: *I appreciate your asking*	188
6.28	Usage guide Gerunds and infinitives and lexical grammar	190
6.29	Problems with gerunds and infinitives	191

Chapter 6 — Gerunds and infinitives

6.1 Gerunds and infinitives in context

KEY
Ch. 6 = Chapter 6
Ex. 23 = Exercise 23
5.2 = Chapter 5, section 2
2.14.3 = Chapter 2, section 14, subsection 3
(a) = an example

■ **Exercise 1** Based on what you already know, identify gerunds (verbs with *–ing* that function similarly to nouns) and infinitives (*to* + a base form verb) in the sentences below. If you wish, read 6.2 first. The first infinitive and the first gerund are already underlined.

a. More and more people these days are living alone. Do you think most of these people choose <u>to live</u> alone or is it something they have to do? Does <u>living</u> alone have some advantages?

b. Who tends to have stronger social networks — women or men? What makes you think so?

c. Do you generally prefer to spend your time with others or on your own?

d. Do you think you could live alone without being lonely?

e. How does staying in touch electronically affect long-distance relationships? How do you think it compares with seeing people face to face?

f. Who is more likely to be happy alone — men or women? Why do you think so?

6.2 What are gerunds and infinitives?

- A gerund is a base form verb followed by *–ing*: *seeing, working, living, being*, etc.

- An infinitive consists of *to* and a base form: *to wait, to see, to live, to be*, etc. When verbs are joined with *and*, only one form of *to* is needed: *to wait and see*.

- Gerunds and infinitives are nonfinite forms, which means they do not have *-s* forms or past tense forms (4.5).

- Gerunds and infinitives are often expanded to phrases. Like verbs, they can be negative (b), modified by adverbials (c), followed by objects and other structures (d), and passive (e). They can have perfect aspect in both active voice (f) and passive voice (g).

- The dictionary form of a verb (*see*) is called the **bare infinitive** or **base form**. (British books may use the term *infinitive*.)

		Gerunds	Infinitives
a.	Basic forms:	seeing	to see
b.	Negative forms:	not seeing	not to see
c.	With adverbials:	seeing clearly	to see clearly
d.	With objects:	seeing something	to see something
e.	Passive forms:	being seen	to be seen
f.	Perfect aspect – active:	having seen	to have seen
g.	Perfect aspect – passive:	having been seen	to have been seen

6.3 Gerunds and infinitives in sentences

- Like nouns, gerunds and infinitives can be subjects (a). They can also be delayed subjects (6.7 and 6.8) after empty *it* (b).

- Gerunds and infinitives can come after BE (c) and other verbs (d). For example, *avoid, enjoy,* and *finish* are often followed by gerunds (but not infinitives), and *expect, tend,* and *want* are often followed by infinitives (but not gerunds).

- We can use a gerund (but not an infinitive or bare infinitive) after a preposition (e), including the preposition *to*, which looks the same as the infinitive marker *to*.

- Infinitives can be used adverbially, sometimes after *in order* (f, g), to express purpose (Ch. 9.12).

a. **Laughing** *is good for you.* **To laugh** *at yourself is not easy.*
b. *It's hard* **to laugh** *at yourself.* (Less common: *It's hard laughing at yourself.*)
c. *My biggest problem is* **wasting** *time. My goal is* **to manage** *my time better.*
d. *I avoid* **walking** *alone at night. I don't want* **to take** *any risks.*
e. *In addition* **to taking** *classes, I work on my English* **by listening** *to podcasts.*
f. *Gauguin went to Tahiti (in order)* **to paint**.
g. **To stay** *fit, you need to exercise, eat well, and get enough sleep.*

■ **Exercise 2** In the passage, find two gerund subjects (as in [a] above), an infinitive as a delayed subject (b), a gerund after BE (c), three gerunds after verbs and three infinitives after verbs (d), and three gerunds after prepositions (e).

Are women better than men at living alone? Some evidence suggests that they are.
  Women tend to have stronger social networks, so they can live alone without being lonely. Men who live alone have a greater risk of withdrawing socially. The typical woman who lives alone does not dread coming home to an empty apartment after work. On the contrary, she looks forward to interacting with friends. She enjoys going out or just staying in touch electronically.
  Sociologists expect to see the number of single-person households continue to rise. In view of this trend, it's important to remember that maintaining a strong social network contributes significantly to happiness. Being alone is not a problem. The problem, if there is one, is being lonely.

6.4 Gerund subjects

Like nouns, gerunds can be subjects (a). Do not use a verb as a subject (b). You must first transform it into a gerund by adding *-ing*. Do not use *it* after a gerund subject (c, d).

a. ***Writing*** is hard work, but ***keeping a journal*** can help you find something to say. Is ***finding ideas*** hard for you?	Gerunds and gerund phrases can be subjects.
b. ~~Discuss~~ your topic can help you clarify your ideas. → ***Discussing your topic*** can help you clarify your ideas.	In order to use *discuss* as a subject, you must change it into a noun by adding *-ing*.
c. ***Explaining your ideas to others*** ~~it~~ helps you refine them.	The gerund phrase (boldface) is the subject. Adding *it* creates an unnecessary extra subject (2.2.2).
d. ***Sharing ideas*** ~~it's~~ (→ *is*) helpful.	

Sometimes a gerund or gerund phrase at the beginning of a sentence is an adverbial, not the subject (e). In that case, a subject follows the gerund or gerund phrase. See also 2.2.4, 2.22.5, and Ch. 9.

e. *Living on campus, I can visit the library any time.* = *Now that I live / Because I live on campus, I…*	The gerund phrase is an adverbial (Ch. 9).

Gerunds can be used after BE (as subject complements, f), and they can be used after *as, than,* and *like* (g). With some common expressions, we use a gerund as a delayed subject after empty *it* (h). For more about empty it, see 6.7.

f. *My favorite weekend activity is **taking** naps.*	A gerund is used after BE.
g. *Walking is better **than not exercising** at all, but it isn't as good **as swimming**. Nothing exercises all your muscles **like swimming**.*	Gerunds follow *than, as,* and *like*.
h. *It was nice **meeting you**.*	*Meeting you* is a delayed subject. More commonly we use an infinitive as a delayed subject (6.7).

■ **Exercise 3** Transform the words on the left into gerund subjects and create sentences by matching them with the words on the right.

1. Breathe deeply
2. Get used to a different culture
3. Worry about unimportant things

4. Read in bad light
5. Wear a seatbelt
6. Speak two languages

7. Eat at McDonalds every day
8. Open an umbrella indoors
9. Live in a foreign country

is a waste of time.
helps you relax.
requires flexibility.

can help you get a job.
can be hard on your eyes.
might save your life.

exposes you to new ways of life.
is not healthy.
is bad luck.

■ **Exercise 4** Using the words on the right in Exercise 3, create sentences with new topics. What else, for example, *is a waste of time?* What else *helps you relax?* What else *requires flexibility?* Use gerund subjects if you need them. (A simple noun or noun phrase might be enough.)

6.5 Gerunds after prepositions

We use gerunds after prepositions, including prepositions that are also conjunctions, such as *before* and *after*. (See also Ch. 9.7.3.)

a. ***By telling*** *friends about products they like, consumers help companies advertise.*

b. *How accurately can you type **without looking** at the keys?*

c. ***Before starting*** *an assignment, make sure you know what is required.*

d. *What are you doing in addition **to taking** classes?*

e. *I look forward **to seeing** you soon.*

f. *We succeeded **in creating** a stress-free workplace.*

■ **Exercise 5** Complete the sentences — advice for young people planning to marry — with gerund forms of the verbs that are provided.

be (x2)　*contribute*　*complain*　*deal*　*not do*　*go*　*ignore*　*stay*　*talk* (x2)

1. Marriage requires compatibility. __ in love is not the same thing as __ compatible.
2. You are both equally responsible for __ to the success of the marriage.
3. __ to bed angry after an argument is never a good idea. Settle your differences first.
4. Instead of __ about what you don't like in your spouse, praise what you like.
5. __ problems doesn't solve anything. __ with a disagreement is better than __ anything at all.
6. Build trust by __ openly about your fears and insecurities.
7. If you are truly committed to __ together, be willing to compromise.

6.6 Gerunds after verbs

enjoy doing something

We use gerunds after certain verbs, shown below in typical phrases. Many verbs have more than one pattern. With some verbs, like *dream, insist,* and *succeed,* we use a preposition and a gerund.

*I avoided **spending** money. She enjoys **being** alone. When did you finish **eating**? Stop **laughing**!*

advise *registering early*	**dream of** *visiting Hawaii*	**prefer** *working alone*
advocate *changing the law*	**enjoy** *visiting museums*	**put off** *leaving*
anticipate *winning*	**finish** *getting dressed*	**quit** *procrastinating*
allow *texting*	**give up** *smoking*	**risk** *getting hurt*
appreciate *having time*	**hate** *being late*	**recommend** *taking the bus*
avoid *overeating*	**imagine** *living to be 100*	**recall** *being teased*
begin *working*	**insist on** *paying*	**regret** *not studying*
can't help *wondering*	**like** *playing soccer*	**remember** *learning to read*
consider *buying a car*	**love** *learning*	**start** *worrying*
continue *growing*	**don't mind** *waiting*	**stop** *making noise*
dislike *being alone*	**miss** *seeing my family*	**succeed in** *reaching a compromise*
dread *being alone*	**practice** *shooting baskets*	**suggest** *taking notes*
		think of *quitting*

- Some of these verbs are also followed by an infinitive (6.10) or a noun clause (7.7).
- *Stop* can be followed by an infinitive of purpose: *On my way through town, I stopped to see a friend.*
- We can sometimes add a possessive before a gerund: *I hope you don't mind my using your computer.* See 6.27.

Gerund-taking verbs can appear in any form. They can be gerunds or infinitives themselves. The form of the gerund-taking verb does not affect the gerund that follows it.

a.	*Are you **considering getting** a job?*	The gerund-taking verb has *-ing*, but a gerund still follows.
b.	***To quit smoking,** you need willpower.*	The gerund-taking verb is an infinitive, but a gerund still follows.

■ **Exercise 6** Complete each sentence with a preposition followed by a gerund, using the words provided. Consult a dictionary if necessary.

about, grow up   *after, live*   *before, write*   *by, buy, sell*
for, find   *for, store*   *to, serve*   *without, change*

1 *Boomerang kids* are grown children who return to live with their parents __ __ for a while on their own.
2 A *scalper* is a person who makes money __ __ tickets and __ them at a higher price.
3 When you *paraphrase,* you rewrite something in different words __ __ the meaning.
4 *Coming of age novels* are stories __ __ .
5 A *flash drive* is a device __ __ data.
6 *Invention techniques* are strategies __ __ ideas. They help you explore ideas __ __ a first draft.
7 A *monastery* is a community of men who devote their lives __ __ God.

164 Grammar Advantage — Gerunds and infinitives — Chapter 6

■ **Exercise 7** Paraphrase each sentence by replacing the italicized words with a word on the right (choose the one that fits the content). Sometimes you will need to change the form of the word that follows. In some cases, more than one answer might work.

1. Do you *expect to* graduate in four years?   consider
2. I *never* argue with my friends.   anticipate
3. Have you ever *thought about* getting a tattoo?   give up
4. You'll save money if you *no longer* shop online all the time.   avoid

5. I *have a terrible feeling about* going to work tomorrow.   dislike
6. I *like* to meet people.   keep
7. I *don't like* shopping.   enjoy
8. Why do you *continue to* ask questions?   dread

9. Most students don't *object to* sharing their notes.   put off
10. You shouldn't *delay* making appointments.   mind
11. I *am sorry about* wasting my money.   regret
12. If you don't slow down, you *could* get stopped by the police.   risk

■ **Exercise 8** Fill the blanks using the verbs that are provided, in the same order. Use them in the appropriate forms. Sometimes you need a form of DO before *not*. Choose the tense that best fits the context.

- *keep +work, finish + analyze, not anticipate + need, miss, imagine + finish*
- *regret + not spend, enjoy + remember*
- *consider + start, put off + have, avoid +go*
- *wash, stop + worry, risk +get*
- *like + live, hate + be*

- *dislike + give, imagine + give, not mind +talk, avoid + participate*
- *give up + smoke, smoke, quit + go*
- *come, miss + see, visit*
- *improve, suggest + take*
- *begin + study, love +play*

1. I've finished my experiment. If I __ __ , I can __ __ the results within a week. I ___ __ more time. Far from __ my deadline, for once I can __ __ a project well in advance.
2. As I look back on my childhood, I __ __ more time with my grandparents. Now that they are gone, I __ __ the good times we had.
3. Lee and Chris __ __ a family soon after they got married, but they finally decided to __ __ kids until they were financially secure. They wanted to __ __ into debt.
4. Angelina is obsessive about __ her hands. She can't __ __ about germs. She says she doesn't want to __ __ sick.
5. Even people who __ in the country sometimes __ so far from the attractions of the city.
6. Lots of people __ __ presentations, but my case is extreme. I really can't __ __ a speech to a room full of people. I __ __ in one-to-one conversations, but I __ __ in discussions if there are more than three or four in the group.
7. __ __ is not easy, because it might require other changes in your life. If you are accustomed to __ with friends over drinks, for example, you might need to __ __ to bars.
8. Since __ to the US, I __ __ my family every day. I look forward to __ them as soon as I can.
9. If you're interested in __ your flexibility, I __ a yoga class.
10. Jonah __ __ piano when he was five. He no longer takes lessons, but he still __ __.

Chapter 6 — Gerunds and infinitives — Grammar Advantage **165**

6.7 Infinitive subjects, delayed infinitive subjects, and infinitives after BE

It's difficult to apologize.

- We use infinitives as delayed subjects after expressions with empty *it* (2.11), such as *It's difficult* and *It takes time* (a). We can also begin with an infinitive subject (c), but it is more common to use a delayed infinitive subject (a) or to use a gerund subject at the beginning (b).
- We can use an infinitive after BE (a subject complement), especially with certain nouns (*plan, goal*) as the main noun in the subject (d).
- Infinitives can follow *as* and *than* (e), but after comparative *like* we usually use a gerund (e).
- When infinitives are joined with *and*, *than*, or *as*, we often omit the second *to* (d, e).

a. *It's difficult **to apologize**.*	← More common.
b. ***Apologizing** is difficult.*	
c. ***To apologize** is difficult.*	← Less common.
d. *Our **plan** is **to reorganize** the staff and (to) **streamline** production. Our main **goal** is **to cut** costs.*	Typical nouns: *aim, advice, dream, function, goal, hope, idea, job, motive, plan, point, purpose, role, step, strategy, suggestion, way.*
e. *It's better to stay with relatives than (to) **spend** money on a hotel. It's like **staying** in your own home. (~~like stay~~, ~~like to stay~~)*	

Though gerunds are sometimes used as delayed subjects (*It was nice meeting you*), a delayed infinitive subject is usually the best choice (f).

f. *Is it impolite to refuse (~~refusing~~) an offer of food or drink?*

6.8 Common expressions with empty *it*

The expressions are presented in groups with related meanings. As the examples show, the BE verb that follows empty *it* may be in various forms.

a. *It is **important / necessary / possible** to prevent disease.*
b. *It's **wise / a good idea / better / best** to avoid traveling today.*
c. *It **makes sense** to plan your meals before buying groceries.*
d. *It was **fun / interesting / relaxing / rewarding** to spend time with friends.*
e. *It used to be **common / customary / typical / usual** to use titles like "Mr."*
f. *It will be **challenging / easy / difficult / hard** to meet the deadline.*
g. *It would be **foolish / unwise / a waste of time** to worry about what we can't change.*
h. *It is **dangerous / risky / unhealthy** to drink too much.*
i. *It is **against the law / illegal / unethical / wrong** to cheat on your taxes.*
j. *It **took a long time / all day / energy / effort / courage** to accomplish our goal.*

6.9 Empty *it* as an object

make it possible to

We use empty *it* as an object in expressions like *make it possible, consider it important*, and *find it interesting* — that is, with *make, consider*, or *find* plus an expression like those in 6.8 above (*important, necessary, possible*, etc.). An infinitive follows. We use empty *it* as both subject an object with the adjective *worth* (n).

k. *Medical tests **make it possible to** prevent some diseases. (~~make possible to prevent~~)*
l. *Most parents **consider it important to** teach their children manners. (~~consider it's important~~)*
m. *I always **find it interesting to** ask people about their names.*
n. *It's **not worth it to** repair a bicycle you never use. (= Repairing … is not worth it.) See also 6.23.)*

166 Grammar Advantage — Gerunds and infinitives — Chapter 6

■ **Exercise 9** **Three** of the underlined parts are wrong. The others have no mistakes. Find and fix the mistakes.

<u>Is it</u> wrong <u>to eat</u> meat? Animal rights advocates sometimes express views like these: <u>It's</u> unethical <u>eating</u> meat because it takes the lives of creatures that can feel pain. Moreover, <u>it takes</u> enormous amounts of energy <u>to raise</u> animals for meat on factory farms, and <u>it would be</u> more efficient <u>to use</u> those resources for <u>growing</u> crops. Finally, they point out <u>that is</u> unnecessary <u>to eat</u> meat because in most developed countries there are other sources of protein. <u>Eating</u> meat is something most of us take for granted, but for many of us <u>it's</u> difficult <u>to dismiss</u> arguments against it. Moderate animal rights advocates generally realize <u>it is</u> impossible <u>they expect</u> everyone to give up meat. Their goal is <u>to reduce</u> the consumption of meat and <u>to ensure</u> that animals are raised and treated as humanely as possible.

■ **Exercise 10** Complete each sentence using a phrase with empty *it* and an infinitive and using one pair of words. Use *is* or *was* after empty *it*.

difficult + drive	easy + communicate	important + find out
√ impossible + travel	interesting + ask	necessary + win
possible + control	unnecessary + launch	useful + make

1. *During the flood, ... on foot.* → *During the flood,* **it was impossible to travel** *on foot.*
2. *If you have a cell phone, ... with friends at any time.*
3. *The enemy surrendered, so ... another attack.*
4. *Our company believes ... what our customers want.*
5. *If you like history, ... people about their ancestors.*
6. *Good parents don't think that ... every argument with their teenage kids.*
7. *When you have to write an essay, ... an outline first.*
8. *With some thermostats, ... your home's temperature remotely.*
9. *During rush hour, ... downtown.*

■ **Exercise 11** Transform the main clauses from the exercise above (the parts beginning with *it*) into phrases, to create expressions like *make it possible to* and *find it important to*.

Example: *These days cell phones* **make it possible to communicate** *with friends at any time.*

1. *The flood made ...*
2. *Cell phones make ...*
3. *The enemy's surrender made ...*
4. *At our company, we consider ...*
5. *As a history major, I consider ...*
6. *Good parents don't consider ...*
7. *When you write an essay, do you find ...*
8. *Some thermostats make ...*
9. *During rush hour, I find ...*

Chapter 6 — Gerunds and infinitives

Exercise 12 Create a sentence (or a sentence sequence) by matching three parts, as in the example, adding a BE verb, and using an infinitive.

*When I started looking for work, my primary aim **was to earn enough** to repay my loans.*

√ When I started looking for work	her dream	√ earn enough to repay my loans
1. When I write something	√ my primary aim	become an Olympic athlete
2. When Jenna was a child	our goal	review the assignment guidelines
3. At this company	my first step	make innovative ideas practical

4. We hired a new employee.	Its purpose	oversee international marketing
5. Think about what you did wrong.	The idea	clarify everyone's responsibilities
6. We have a new guidebook.	Her job	learn from your mistakes

7. Try practicing at the same time every day.	Their strategy	make it a routine
8. How can you improve your listening?	The point	listen to podcasts
9. The lawyers questioned me for hours.	One good way	tire me out

Exercise 13 Create a sentence by matching items from the left with items from the right, using *it* and a delayed infinitive subject. Then create a paraphrase with a gerund subject.

Examples: *It takes time to learn a language. Learning a language takes time.*
It's fun to look at old family pictures. Looking at old family pictures is fun.

√ take time	chew with your mouth open
√ fun	maintain a positive attitude
1. impolite	√ learn a language
2. cost a lot	go to a private school
3. important	√ look at old family pictures

4. difficult	do nothing all day
5. boring	eat a lot of fried foods
6. unhealthy	work and study at the same time

7. take planning	submit someone else's work as your own
8. dangerous	manage your money
9. dishonest	drive and text at the same time

Exercise 14 Create sentences. Add *it*, *is*, *to*, *-s*, and *-ing* as needed. There is more than one way.

1. in some cultures / impolite / not make eye contact
2. take 20 credits / make / hard / have a social life
3. consider / you / do / important / stay in touch with old friends?
4. make / sense / plan your meals / buy groceries / before
5. you / find / difficult / do / save money?
6. make / the Internet / possible / publish information / without / pay for printing

tend to do something

allow someone to do something

6.10 Verb (+ object) + infinitive

We use infinitives after certain verbs (a) and after certain verb + object combinations (b). Some verbs — especially *expect, get,* and *want* — allow both patterns (c). *Arrange, plan,* and *wait* often include *for* and an object before the infinitive (d). *Not* may precede the *to* (e).

a. *Sophie **tends to be** forgetful, but she always **manages to remember** my birthday.*
b. *We **require the students to wear** uniforms, but we **allow them to choose** between two styles.*
c. *We **expect to work** hard, and we **expect you to work** hard, too.*
d. *We **arranged for them to stay** at a hotel, but they had to **wait for the room to be** cleaned.*
e. *We agreed **not to talk** about work. (don't talk) They asked us **not to say** anything. (don't say)*

Most verbs that can be followed by an object and an infinitive (b) can be passive. The infinitive then follows the past participle directly (f).

f. *They **were required to wear** uniforms, but they **were allowed to choose** between two styles.*

In the box below, the verbs appear in typical phrases. If a verb in the box is followed by an object without parenthesis, it means that an object is most often required; that is, we don't usually use the infinitive by itself. Some verbs that are not shown with objects may sometimes have an object.

advise *him to register early*	**get** *(them) to choose a topic*	**promise** *(me) to come back*
can't **afford** *to lose*	**happen** *to be in town*	**refuse** *to accept defeat*
agree *to help*	**hate** *to be late*	**remember** *to proofread*
allow *us to participate*	**help** *us (to) do our best*	**remind** *them to proofread*
appear *to be angry*	**hesitate** *to speak up*	**request** *to see a lawyer*
arrange *(for them) to meet*	**induce** *them to buy*	**require** *us to work hard*
ask *(her) to speak*	**influence** *him to study art*	**seek** *to understand*
attempt *to answer*	**intend** *(it) to be helpful*	**seem** *to be listening*
begin *to work*	**invite** *them to stay*	**start** *to worry*
cause *them to quit*	**lead** *us to conclude*	**stimulate** *them to grow*
choose *(him) to represent us*	**learn** *to use a dictionary*	**teach** *them to read*
claim *to be right*	**like** *to play soccer*	**tell** *him to relax*
come *to believe*	**love** *to learn*	**tempt** *him to be lazy*
continue *to rise*	**manage** *to find a job*	**tend** *to make mistakes*
convince *them to change*	**mean** *to be helpful*	**threaten** *to make trouble*
dare *to try* (also **dare** *try*)	**motivate** *her to study*	**trust** *them to be on time*
decide *not to quit*	**need** *(you) to answer*	**try** *not to laugh*
demand *to see evidence*	**neglect** *to lock the door*	**turn** *out to be true*
deserve *to be rewarded*	**offer** *to pay*	**urge** *her not to give up*
enable *us to thrive*	**order** *them to leave*	**volunteer** *to help*
encourage *them to think*	**permit** *me to leave early*	**wait** *(for me) to respond*
expect *(them) to do well*	**persuade** *her to sing*	**want** *(them) to succeed*
fail *to meet the deadline*	**plan** *(for her) to attend*	**warn** *him not to interfere*
forbid *them to enter*	**prefer** *to work alone*	**wish** *to comment*
force *him to quit*	**prepare** *(them) to compete*	**would like** *(them) to know*
forget *to say good-bye*	**pretend** *to understand*	

• We also use infinitives after the modal *ought* (*I ought to try*) and after *have* (*He has to go.*); see 4.4.
• Some of the verbs above may also be followed by a gerund; see 6.11.

■ **Exercise 15** For each blank, choose one verb from the lefthand group (an infinitive-taking verb) and one from the righthand group, in the infinitive form — for example, *attempt to explain*. For some items, there may be more than one way.

attempt   intend   pretend   tend   +   *be   explain   hire   understand*

1. Does the management __ any interns next summer?
2. They say that highly successful people __ taller than average.
3. She never listens. Whenever I __, she turns away.
4. Ask questions. Don't just __.

afford   deserve   fail   manage   +   *delay   get   know   meet*

5. Students __ how they will be evaluated.
6. If you somehow __ an extra ticket, let me know.
7. I would like to take more courses, but I can't __ my graduation.
8. If you __ the deadline, your application will not be considered.

dare   hesitate   neglect   refuse   +   *answer   ask   believe   offer*

9. Jason is an honest person. I __ that he cheated.
10. Sara doesn't seem to want advice, so I __ any.
11. You did well on the test, but unfortunately you __ the last question.
12. They have very strict rules. I don't __ for an exception.

appear   get   offer   threaten   +   *go   lend   need   take*

13. If the bus drivers __ on strike, we need to make plans for alternative transportation.
14. A man by the side of the road tried to get us to stop. He __ help.
15. I'm exhausted. When do we __ a break?
16. If you don't have a pen, a classmate will usually __ you one.

arrange   demand   happen   promise   +   *have   inspect   meet   obey*

17. In traditional weddings many years ago, the bride used to __ her future husband.
18. When you cross an international border, officials may __ your bags.
19. If the meeting rooms are all reserved, we can __ in one of the larger offices.
20. I didn't have a ticket, but luckily my friends __ an extra one.

agree   claim   mean   prefer   +   *be   offend   not talk   participate*

21. No one is ever forced to take part in opinion polls. People __.
22. Most people __ about private matters.
23. I'm sorry. I didn't __ you.
24. Many products __ "organic," but what does that really mean?

■ **Exercise 16** Complete each sentence using one pair of verbs, with the second one in infinitive form. Remember to include an object pronoun (*them, him,* etc.).

convince + change   get + stop   need + be   require + raise

1. Please don't make noise while I'm on the phone. I __ as quiet as you can.
2. Don't even try to argue with him. You can't __ his mind.
3. The hotel's owners feel that adding a pool would __ their prices too much.
4. My computer was making an odd noise, and I couldn't __ .

encourage + be   forbid + go   invite + address   stimulate + buy

5. My friends always __ more assertive.
6. They're very strict with their daughter. They __ out on weekends.
7. He's an inspiring speaker. We should __ our annual meeting.
8. A marketer's job is to attract customers and __ more.

enable + survive   help + understand   ordered + lie down   persuade + give

9. The robbers took our money and __ on the floor.
10. The deep roots of this tree __ for long periods without rain.
11. My boss is a reasonable woman. I think I can __ me a day off.
12. If you want children to develop good manners, you should __ why manners are important.

cause + wear out   remind + log off   tempt + break   warn + not say

13. When students are getting ready to leave the computer lab, we always __ .
14. I promised not to tell anyone. Please don't __ my promise!
15. You should have listened to me and kept quiet. I __ anything.
16. People who sell vacuum cleaners say that dirt in a carpet will __ sooner.

■ **Exercise 17** Complete the sentence using the words provided. Include an object pronoun. Then complete the short paraphrase of the sentence in passive voice. Use present tense except if otherwise indicated. Example: *expect + recover* My brother is in the hospital, but he is doing well. We <u>expect him to</u> recover. ~ <u>He is expected</u> to recover.

not allow + use   expect + improve   require + take
teach + wash   tempted + try   warned not + travel

1. The weather is bad, but we __ within a few days. ~ It __ within a few days.
2. Our teachers say we can use calculators in class, but they __ them on tests. ~ We __ calculators on tests.
3. It was against the rules, but her friends __ it anyway. ~ She __ it.
4. When students are in their first year, we __ math. ~ They __ math.
5. The police told me I should travel with a group. They __ alone. ~ I __ alone.
6. To help children stay healthy, we __ their hands before eating. ~ They __ their hands.

6.11 Verbs + gerund OR infinitive: *remember, try, like,* etc.

After some verbs, gerunds and infinitives express different meanings.

- *Remember* **to do** *it* = remember and then do it (a).
- *Remember* **doing** *it* = have a memory of something you did earlier (b).
- After *try*, an infinitive expresses a goal (c). We use a gerund after *try* when something else is the goal (d).
- After *begin, start, continue, like, love, prefer,* and *hate*, we can use a gerund or an infinitive, usually with little difference in meaning (e).
- After *stop*, we use a gerund for the end of an activity (f). An infinitive after *stop* indicates the purpose of stopping (g). (See also 9.12.)

Remember to do it or remember doing it?

Stop to ask or stop asking?

a. *I always remember to lock my door.*	I remember and then I lock it.
b. *Do you remember learning to read?*	Is the memory still in your mind?
c. *I tried to open the file.*	My goal was to open the file.
d. *I tried opening a window, but it was still too hot.*	My goal was to make it cooler.
e. *Everyone likes listening / to listen to music.*	There is no difference in meaning.
f. *No one answered my questions, so I stopped asking.*	I didn't ask anymore.
g. *When I got lost, I stopped to ask for directions.*	I stopped and then asked.

- A gerund may contrast with an infinitive with some verbs, such as *like* and *hate*, as shown below.

h. *Lana hates smoking / to smoke alone.*	She smokes, but not alone.
i. *Liam hates smoking (to smoke), so he favors strict anti-smoking regulations.*	He doesn't smoke. He hates it when other people smoke.

6.12 Verb + object + base form

- After *let*, we use an object + a base form, not an infinitive (a).
- After *make*, we use an object + a base form, not an infinitive (b).
- We usually omit *be* after *make*, leaving only an adjective after the object (c).
- After *help*, we use an object + a base form or an infinitive (d).
- We do not use a past tense form after *let, help,* or *make* (e).

let them leave

make them wait

help students understand

a. *When they finish, we will* **let them leave**. (to)	let them do something
b. *Talk to them now. Don't* **make them wait**. (to)	make them do something
c. *Waiting* **makes me nervous**. (be)	make + object + adjective
d. *Examples* **help students (to) understand**.	help them (to) do something
e. *The teacher helped / let / made them* **finish**.	*Let, made,* and *helped* are past, but *finish* is not.

- When *make* is passive (Ch. 5), we use an infinitive after it: *The visitors were made to feel unwelcome.*

have someone do something

have something done

get someone to do something

get something done

6.13 Causative HAVE

6.13.1 *Have someone do something*: active complements

- A phrase like *have someone do something* is similar to *make someone do something* but without the idea of coercion (forcing) that *make* often indicates.
- If you *have someone do something*, you might ask him or her to do it or you might arrange it. He or she does it because of your influence or authority.
- We use HAVE + an object + a **base form** verb, not an *–s* form (b, c) or a past tense form (e).

a. When I visit my grandparents, they always **have me sleep** in my father's old bedroom.	They invite me to sleep there.
b. When a student asks a question, some teachers **have another student answer it**.	They encourage other students to answer it.
c. Prof. Jax doesn't like collecting test papers. She always **has her assistant collect them**.	She assigns her assistant the job of collecting them.
d. Teachers sometimes **have students give** oral reports.	They assign oral reports.
e. During the strike last week, some parents had their children **stay** home from school. (stayed)	*Had* is past, but *stay* is not.

6.13.2 *Have something done*: passive complements

- In a passive complement after HAVE, we use an object and a past participle, sometimes with a *by* phrase: HAVE *something done (by someone)*.

HAVE with an active complement	HAVE with a passive complement
f. The judge **had the officers take the defendant** away.	g. The judge **had the defendant taken** away (by the officers).
h. My neighbor had **his kids paint his garage**. He was too busy to do it himself.	i. My neighbors **had their house painted** while they were on vacation.

- We use a passive complement for the same reasons we choose passive voice in other sentences: We want to focus on the action or we can't (or don't want to) identify the doer of the action (5.10).

6.13.3 *Get someone to do something, get something done*

- We use GET in a similar way, but in an active complement, we use *to*.

Causative GET with an active complement	Causative GET with a passive complement
j. We finally got the **landlord to fix our sink**.	k. We finally **got the sink fixed**.

- With causative GET, there is often an idea of skill, effort, or persuasion.

l. A good manager gets everyone to perform at a high level.	The manager's skills and efforts lead to high performance.
m. Good leaders know how to get things done.	As a result of their skills and efforts, things are done.

Chapter 6 — Gerunds and infinitives

■ **Exercise 18:** *Make* or *let*? Imagine that the statements below describe your childhood — several things that your parents **let you do** or **made you do**. For each one, make a sentence beginning with *They made me* or *They let me*. The choice depends on whether the action is something a child usually wants to do. Discuss your choices.

Example 1: I helped with housecleaning every Saturday. ⟶ *They made me help with housecleaning. They made me help* is a more likely choice because children don't usually want to help with housecleaning.

Example 2: I stayed home from school when I was sick. ⟶ *They let me stay home* ... A child often wants to stay home from school, so this is a likely choice. OR *They made me stay home* ... Some children like to go to school even when they are sick, so *They made me stay home* is also possible.

1. I went to bed early on school nights.
2. I did my homework right after dinner.
3. I stayed up late on Friday and Saturday night.
4. I slept late on Saturday mornings.
5. I visited my grandmother every week.
6. I played outside when the weather was nice.
7. I apologized whenever I said something mean to my brother.
8. I ate vegetables that I didn't like.
9. I chose the dinner menu on my birthday.
10. I spent a lot of time with my friends.
11. I wore a helmet when I rode my bike.
12. I wrote thank-you notes for every gift I received.
13. I rode my bike whenever I wanted to.
14. I had a dog when I was eight.

see someone do something

see someone doing something

6.14 Perception verbs + object + bare infinitive

After *feel, hear, see,* and *watch,* we often use an object and a bare infinitive (a, b). To express the perception of action in progress, we can use a gerund after the object (c, d). Like causative *have* (6.13), perception verbs can also have passive complements (e). After *find* (f), we can also use an object and a gerund (for an active complement) or a past participle (for a passive complement).

a. Our team hasn't been doing well. I've **seen them win** only one game this season.
b. Rick is in charge. When you **hear him snap** his fingers, pay attention.
c. I felt **the earth shaking** and I **heard people shouting**.
d. My neighbors are painting their house. I've **watched them working** on it all week.
e. I've never **seen them lose**. (Active complement) I've never **seen them defeated**. (Passive complement)
f. I **found my cap lying** on the ground. (Active complement) **I found my shirt stuffed** into my backpack. (Passive complement)

HIGH PRIORITY

■ **Exercise 19** Choose the correct forms.

1. If you can't sleep, try __ around for a while.
   (a) to get up and walking   (b) getting up and walking
   (c) getting up and walk   (d) to get up and walk

2. We welcomed our guests and tried ___ at home.
   (a) make them feeling   (b) making them feel
   (c) to make them to feel   (d) to make them feel

3. Do you always remember __ your name at the top of your papers before handing them in?
   (a) put   (b) to put   (c) putting   (d) you put

4. People generally don't remember __. It happens too early in life.
   (a) to learn to walk   (b) to learn walking   (c) learning to walk   (d) learning walking

5. Do most professors assign topics to their students, or do they let __ their own topics?
   (a) they choose   (b) them to choose   (c) them choose   (d) them choosing

6. Our victory in the tournament made us __ unbeatable.
   (a) feel   (b) to feel   (c) felt   (d) feeling

7. You have a responsibility to your employees. Your job is __ the best employees they can be.
   (a) help them be   (b) helping to them be   (c) help them being   (d) to help them be

8. At the Great Wall, my friends and I had our guide __ a picture of us.
   (a) take   (b) to take   (c) taken   (d) taking

9. When I visited Washington, I had __ in front of the Washington Monument.
   (a) taken my picture   (b) my picture taken
   (c) someone took my picture   (d) my picture to take

10. What should you do if you see someone __ something in a shop?
    (a) stole   (b) steal   (c) stolen   (d) to steal

11. You asked Paul a question, and I heard __ "Beats me!" What does it mean?
    (a) he said   (b) him to say   (c) him say   (d) he say

Chapter 6 — Gerunds and infinitives — Grammar Advantage 175

■ **Exercise 20** Paraphrase each sentence using one of the verbs below. Use each one twice. In your paraphrase, use pronouns – e.g. *them*, not *the children*.

let   help   make   have (causative - 6.13)

1 They didn't permit my friends to attend. *They didn't …*
2 Because of your encouragement, I felt better. *Your encouragement …*
3 I was late because of a detour. *The detour …*
4 Ms. Song asked the students to work in groups. *She …*
5 After rereading the passage, I understood. *Rereading the passage …*
6 We allowed the children to stay up late. *We …*
7 I write things down because then I can usually remember. *Writing things down …*
8 On orders from the CEO, the delivery man was fired. *The CEO …*

■ **Exercise 21** Reorder the words to create a sentence with causative HAVE (6.13) and an active complement. Sometimes there is more than one way, with different meanings.

Example: usually have / the Smiths / wash their car / a neighbor boy ⟶ *The Smiths usually have a neighbor boy wash their car.*

1 had / Jeremy / a friend / critique his paper
2 are having / a professional designer / Celia and Lana / their house / remodel
3 have / can / you / a volunteer / type up the notes from our meeting?
4 had / my parents / the Post Office / forward their mail / during their vacation
5 is going to have / my company / an outside consultant / redesign our payroll system

■ **Exercise 22** In the sentences in Exercise 21, change the active complements to passive complements.

Example: *The Smiths usually have their car washed by a neighbor boy.*

■ **Exercise 23** Fill the blanks with the words that are provided, using the right forms.

accept   have   help   let   made (3)   pay   play   clean   take

One weekend when I was in high school my parents had me __ care of my two brothers while they were out of town for the weekend. I was only 16, but they were __ the house repainted at the time, so there were adults nearby all day, and I guess that __ it safe enough. The boys __ it easy for me by __ quietly the whole weekend. They even __ me __ the house before mom and dad got back. It was such an easy weekend I didn't want to __ my parents __ me, but my dad insisted. He __ me __ $20!

■ **Exercise 24** Fill the blanks with the words that are provided, using the right forms. There is more than one way.

be   create   get   learn   listen   made   stay   study   want   work (x2)

I remember __ a lot from all of my old teachers, but one of them, Ms. Lund, was especially skilled at __ a good atmosphere for learning. She often had us __ in groups. __ together gave us a break from __ to lectures and __ independently and it helped us __ to know each other. That turned out __ one of the most important benefits. My friendships with classmates __ me __ to come to class even on days when I would have preferred __ home.

appreciate   let   keep   learn (x2)   made   participate   summarize   take   work (x2)

Sometimes she __ us __ with anyone we wanted __ with, but usually she arranged the groups. She had each person in the group __ a particular role. For example, one person's responsibility was __, while another was in charge of __ track of the time. So in addition to __ the content of the lesson, we learned __ effectively in discussions. Her technique really __ me __ the value of __ from classmates.

Chapter 6 — Gerunds and infinitives

■ **Exercise 25** The box below includes most of the verbs from the preceding sections. Test yourself by marking each one with the type(s) of complement it takes, using the appropriate letter. Some will require more than one letter. As you mark them, practice saying phrases — e.g. *advise registering early* and *advise them to register early*. Don't forget to include objects (*advise them to register early*) when they are required. See Chapter 7 for more patterns for some verbs.

a. verb + gerund: *enjoy* **doing something**   (6.6)
b. verb + infinitive: *expect* **to do something**   (6.10)
c. verb + object + infinitive: *expect* **them to do something**   (6.10)
d. verb + *for* object + infinitive: *arrange* **for them to do something**   (6.10)
e. verb + object + bare form: *let* **them do something**   (6.12)
f. verb + object + gerund: *watch* **them doing something**   (6.14)

a, c *advise + register early*	*give up + smoke*	*prepare + compete*
b *can't afford + lose*	*get + choose a topic*	*pretend + understand*
agree + help	*happen + be in town*	*promise + come back*
allow + participate	*hate + be late*	*put off + leave*
anticipate + win	*hear + snap his fingers*	*refuse + accept defeat*
allow + text	*help + do our best*	*regret + not study*
appear + be angry	*hesitate + speak up*	*remember + proofread*
appreciate + have time	*imagine + live to be 100*	*remind + proofread*
arrange + meet	*induce + buy*	*request + see a lawyer*
ask + speak	*influence + study art*	*require + work hard*
attempt + answer	*intend + take charge*	*quit + procrastinate*
avoid + overeat	*invite + stay*	*report + make progress*
begin + move	*involve + collect data*	*risk + get hurt*
cause + quit	*keep + talk*	*see + win*
choose + to marry	*lead + conclude*	*seem + be listening*
claim + be right	*learn + use a dictionary*	*start + worry*
come + believe	*let + watch TV*	*stimulate + grow*
consider + buy a car	*like + play soccer*	*stop + make noise*
continue + grow	*love + learn*	*suggest + take notes*
convince + change	*make + wait*	*teach + read*
dare + try	*manage + find a job*	*tempt + be lazy*
decide + not quit	*mean + be helpful*	*tend + make mistakes*
demand + see evidence	*don't mind + wait*	*threaten + make trouble*
deserve + be rewarded	*motivate + study*	*trust + be honest*
dislike + be alone	*need + answer*	*try + explain*
enable + thrive	*neglect + lock the door*	*turn out + be true*
encourage + think	*offer + pay*	*urge + not give up*
enjoy + visit museums	*order + leave*	*volunteer + help*
expect + do well	*permit + leave early*	*wait + respond*
fail + meet the deadline	*persuade + sing*	*want + succeed*
forbid + enter	*plan + attend*	*warn + not interfere*
force + quit	*practice + shoot baskets*	*wish + comment*
forget + say good-bye	*prefer + work alone*	*would like + know*

too old to

old enough to

6.15 Too and enough + infinitive

We can use an infinitive complement after phrases with *too* (*too old, too much,* etc.) and *enough* (*old enough, enough time*). With *too*, the infinitive describes an action that cannot or should not happen. With *enough*, it describes an action that can happen.

a. My nephew is 12. He is **old enough to baby-sit** but **too young to baby-sit** overnight.	A 12-year-old can baby-sit, but he can't baby-sit overnight, because of his age.
b. This is **too much to spend** for dinner.	We should not spend so much.
c. Are you making **enough money to save a little?**	Are you able to save a little?

We also use the preposition *for* after phrases with *too* and *enough*. A noun (never a verb) follows.

d. Is your niece old enough **for** school / **to go to** school? (*for going to school*)

Enough usually precedes a noun, but it follows an adjective or adverb.

e. We had **enough books**, but they weren't **interesting enough** (*enough interesting*) to keep the children occupied.

Use *too*, not *too much*, before an adjective that has no noun after it.

f. Is the language of Shakespeare too difficult for modern audiences? (*too much difficult*)

■ **Exercise 26** Finish the sentence, using *too* or *enough* and the words provided. Include *to*.

1. The body of a camel can store ...   *water / keep it alive for many days*
2. We have to help endangered species before it's ...   *late / save them*
3. Do you know anyone who is ...   *old / remember the 1940s?*
4. Nursing homes are intended for people who are ...   *ill / live independently*
5. When they are born, human babies are ...   *helpless / survive without intensive care*

6.16 Adjectives like *easy* + infinitive

easy to understand

- We use an infinitive after adjectives like *easy, difficult, impossible, fun,* and *interesting*.
- The sentence ends with a transitive verb (a) or a verb and a preposition (b).
- If there is an object after the infinitive or verb and preposition, we don't use this structure (c).
- To test the correctness of a sentence (d), make a phrase using the verb (or verb + preposition) from the end with the subject after it. If the phrase is correct, the sentence is correct.

a. *Pancakes are easy to make.*	≈ *It's easy to make pancakes.* (6.7) *Making pancakes is easy.* (6.4)
b. *This topic is fun to talk about.*	≈ *It's fun to talk about this topic.* (6.7) *Talking about this topic is fun.* (6.4)
c. ~~*Jill is easy to make friends.*~~	→ *Jill makes friends easily.* *It's easy for Jill to make friends.* (6.19) *Making friends is easy for Jill.* (6.4)
d. *Jill is easy to talk to.* ~~*Jill is easy to talk.*~~	*Talk to Jill* (unlike ~~*talk Jill*~~) is a correct phrase, so the sentence is correct.

■ **Exercise 27** Paraphrase the sentence with a structure like the ones in 6.16.
It's hard to change bad habits. ➔ *Bad habits are hard to change.*

1. It's interesting to look at old newspapers.
2. It's hard to remember birthdays.
3. It's impossible to clean a white carpet.
4. It's difficult to resist peer pressure.
5. It's easy to talk with children in a foreign language.
6. It's impossible to argue with a three-year-old.
7. It's challenging to work with oil paint.
8. It's difficult to pay attention to boring lectures.
9. It's not always easy to appreciate modern art.
10. It's comforting to look at family photos.

6.17 *Wh* words + infinitives

- We can use infinitives after *wh* words (a).
- After verbs such as *show, tell* and *teach,* we often include an object before the infinitive (b).
- The infinitive phrase is like a *wh* clause (7.4) with *can, should,* or *will*.
- *Wh* words include *how* (c) as well as words like *what, where,* and *when*.

a. *I didn't know where to go or what to do.*	≈ ... *where I should go or what I should do.*
b. *Can you tell me where to find parking?*	≈ ... *where I can find parking?*
c. *Knowing how to swim is important.*	

papers to sign

6.18 Relative clause type infinitives

We can use an infinitive after a noun (a, b) or an indefinite pronoun (c), in a structure similar to a relative clause (Ch. 8) with *can*, *should*, or *will*. This construction is common after *way*, *time*, and *place*.

a. There is a hidden key to use in emergencies.	≈ ... a key that you can use ...
b. The papers to sign are on your desk.	≈ The papers that you should sign ...
c. Do you have anything to add?	≈ ... anything that you can add?
d. We couldn't think of a way to save money.	≈ ... a way in which we could save ...
e. The time to act is now.	≈ The time when you should act ...
f. We had no place to store our things.	≈ ...no place where we could store ...

That's easy for YOU to say!

6.19 Implied subjects and phrases like *for someone to do something*

- Infinitives do not have overt subjects. They have implied subjects.
- The implied subject may be *anyone* (a) or something else determined by the context (b, c).
- In structures like *want him to go*, the object of the verb (*him*) provides an implied subject for the infinitive (*he goes*).

a. It's easy to learn to ride a bike.	Implied subjects: **Anyone** (can learn and can ride).
b. We want our children to succeed.	**Our children** (will succeed).
c. Do you have anything to say?	**You** (may say something).

- We can provide an implied subject for an infinitive by using *for* and a noun or pronoun.
- For most functions of infinitives (a-e), a *for* phrase is possible.
- We also use a *for* phrase and an infinitive after certain verbs, including *arrange, plan,* and *wait* (f).
- Infinitives that are used adverbially (Ch. 9.12) can also include *for* phrases (g).

a. **For the Giants to lose** now would be awful.	A subject infinitive (6.7)
b. It would be tragic **for them to lose** now.	A delayed subject infinitive (6.7)
c. The film was too **fast for me to follow**.	An infinitive complement after *too* (6.15)
d. Pancakes are easy **for children to make**.	An infinitive after *easy* (6.16)
e. Where is the paper **for my advisor to sign**?	A relative-clause type infinitive phrase (6.18)
f. We waited **for the concert to begin**.	A verb with a *for-to* phrase (6.19)
g. **For the paper to be** accepted, it needs to be reviewed by outside readers.	An infinitive used adverbially (9.12)

Chapter 6 — Gerunds and infinitives

■ **Exercise 28** In the box below is a summary of some important uses of gerunds and infinitives, with sections listed for reference. Below the box are examples. Match each example with a description in the box.

6.4	Gerund subjects	6.13	Causative HAVE + active complement
6.5	Gerunds after prepositions	6.13	Causative HAVE + passive complement
6.6	Gerunds after verbs	6.14	Perception verb + object + base-form
6.7	*It* with delayed-subject infinitives	6.14	Perception verb + object + gerund
6.7	BE + infinitive	6.15	*Too* and *enough* + an infinitive
6.10	Verb + infinitive	6.16	Adjectives like *easy* + an infinitive
6.10	Verb + object + infinitive	6.17	*Wh* words + infinitives
6.10	Passive verb + infinitive	6.18	Relative clause type infinitives
6.12	Verb + object + base form	6.19	*For* phrases before infinitives

0. This topic is hard to talk about.   6.16 – Adjectives like *easy* + infinitives
1. We expect them to do well.
2. They are expected to do well.
3. Laughing is good for you.
4. Our goal is to cut costs.
5. I don't know where to go.
6. I had them replace my hard drive.
7. I saw them win.
8. It's important to log off.
9. In addition to taking classes, I work.
10. He's too young to baby-sit.
11. I had my hard drive replaced.
12. I avoid overeating.
13. The papers to sign are on your desk.
14. They expect to do well.
15. We let them watch TV.
16. I've watched them working all week.

■ **Exercise 29** Match each sentence beginning with one or more of the forms (a) through (e). The first one is already marked.

a. doing it.   b. to do it.   c. them to do it.   d. them do it.   e. them doing it

c. We invited   They don't enjoy   No one saw
   They avoided   We thanked her for   She finished
   You shouldn't risk I'm not used to   Someone suggested
   Don't hesitate   I watched   You will never persuade
   Please let   She made   We were not allowed
   We expect   He didn't remind

■ **Exercise 30** Create sentences from Exercise 29 by replacing *do* with other verbs and more content: *We invited them to participate in our discussion. They avoided eating meat*, etc.

■ **Exercise 31** Reorder the words to create a sentence, using infinitives (add *to* — more than once — if you need it).

1. I'm new to this campus. *can / how / tell / get to / me / you / the library?*
2. We had a new student today. *show / the teacher / me / use the equipment / asked / how / him*
3. We encourage our children to help with meals. *want / cook for themselves / how / them / we / teach*
4. If you're looking for maps, ask the librarian. *look / can / you / where / she / tell*
5. Studying lists of vocabulary is boring. *the most interesting way / students / for / improve their vocabulary / read / is*
6. Newspapers everywhere are reducing their staff. *this / a good time / isn't / a job / look / for / as a newspaper reporter.*
7. The student lounge is inadequate. *we / relax between classes / need / more places / students / for*
8. We are planning a party for the employees next week. *for / will / it / a time / celebrate our accomplishments / be / everyone*
9. The people at my doctor's office are great with kids. *even have / play with / children / for / while they wait / they / toys*
10. The foreign office treats visiting diplomats very well. *translators / they / accompany / everywhere / for / them / arrange*

■ **Exercise 32** Reorder the words to create a sentence with a *for* phrase as an implied subject for an infinitive (add *to*).

1. There's a big game tomorrow. *the Giants / for / would / awful / lose now / be*
2. I've cheered this team all season. *tragic / them / lose now / it / for / be / would*
3. I didn't enjoy the film. *too / it / fast-paced / follow / me / for / was*
4. The children are going to cook breakfast. *are / make / children / for / easy / pancakes*
5. Do you have the papers? *where / the papers / my advisor / for / are / sign?*
6. We got to the auditorium early. *begin / the concert / waited / we / for*

6.20 Passive gerunds and infinitives

We use passive gerunds with *being* (a, b) passive infinitives with *to be* (c), and passive bare infinitives with *be* (d) in the same contexts that allow active ones.

a.	***Being fired*** *is a traumatic experience.*	passive gerund subject
b.	*I'm tired **of being criticized**.*	preposition + passive gerund
c.	*It was unfair for them **to be punished** so severely.*	passive infinitive as delayed subject
d.	*We must not let the rainforests **be destroyed**.*	let + object + bare infinitive

Verbs that can be followed by gerunds and infinitives can be followed by passive gerunds and infinitives as well.

- e. *Somehow the thieves **avoided being seen**.*
- f. *If a newspaper publishes lies, it **risks being sued**.*
- g. *We **expect to be treated** well.*
- h. *Everyone **wanted to be included**.*
- i. *You **deserve to be rewarded**.*
- j. *No one **likes to be called** lazy. / No one **likes being called** lazy.*

We don't use passive infinitives if the infinitive has an implied subject (6.16).

- k. *The stars are easy to see tonight.* (*be seen*) *See* has an implied subject: ***Anyone*** *can see them.*

6.21 Perfect gerunds and infinitives

We sometimes use a perfect gerund, especially formally, after a gerund-taking verb (a). Usually we can use a simple gerund in the same context.

- a. *We regret having caused concern to our shareholders.* ≈ *We regret causing ...*

We can use a perfect gerund when it's necessary to show clearly that an action happened earlier.

| b. | *He talked about losing his job.* | Will he lose his job or has he already lost it? The sentence does not give that information. |
| c. | *He talked about having lost his job.* | The perfect gerund clarifies that he has lost his job. |

We can use a perfect infinitive to indicate an earlier action after verbs like *claim, happen, seem,* and *turn out* and adjectives such as *likely* (6.24). The perfect infinitive may also be passive (d).

d.	*He claims to **have won** an award.*	He claims (now) that he **won** an award (earlier).
e.	*The economy seems **to have improved**.*	It seems that it **has improved**.
f.	*The car turned out to **have been stolen**.*	It was discovered that the car **had been stolen**.

Exercise 33
Complete the sentences using the verbs that are provided and passive infinitives or gerunds.

| appreciate + include | avoid + eat | deserve + treat | need + do |
| like + tell | prefer + call | tend + affect | want + remember |

1. This is a serious problem. Something __ about it.
2. Small fish stay away from open areas to __ by larger fish.
3. Shall I use your last name or do you __ by your first name?
4. Sara never asks for advice. She doesn't __ what to do.
5. Everyone __ with respect.
6. Thank you for inviting me. I __ .
7. Men who have lost their wives __ more seriously than women who have lost their husbands.
8. After you die, how do you __ ?

Exercise 34
Complete the sentences using the verbs that are provided. Some will be passive and some will be active.

elect (x2)   infect (x2)   keep (x2)   kill   reduce (x2)   spend

1. Washing your hands frequently can help you avoid __ .
2. The constitution permits a U.S. president __ only twice.
3. Politicians are often criticized for not __ their promises.
4. Our organization seeks __ more women to congress.
5. My doctor advised me __ the amount of salt in my diet.
6. The patient died after __ alive by machines for 20 hours.
7. Money is scarce. We expect our budget __ by 20% next year.
8. If you're sick, you should try to avoid __ people near you.
9. The hero of the movie risks __ when he tries to escape.
10. Why do you never want do anything that involves __ money?

Exercise 35
Using one of the verbs, complete the sentence with an infinitive or gerund. Use passive (*being taken, to be taken*) or perfect (*having taken, to have taken*) or both passive and perfect (*having been taken, to have been taken*). There may be more than one correct way.

be   escape   know   lose   misuse   relate   steal   tell

1. Kristina can always answer our questions. She seems __ everything.
2. I left my bike outside and now it's not there. It seems __ .
3. A boy showed up at the police station claiming __ from kidnappers.
4. As a child I learned to be cautious. I remember __ never to talk to strangers.
5. The mayor apologized for __ city funds.
6. I met someone with the same last name as me, and we turned out __ .
7. I'm pretty sure I'm right, but if I turn out __ wrong, I'll be the first to admit it.
8. Have you been sick? You seem __ weight.

6.22 Noun + *of* + gerund

the process of learning

After certain nouns, we can use *of* + a gerund (a) or a negative gerund (d). In these structures, the noun specifies what the activity named by the gerund is.

a. He has an annoying habit of interrupting people. (an annoying habit ~~that he interrupts people~~)	Interrupting people is his habit.
b. I like the Asian custom of not wearing shoes indoors. (the Asian custom ~~that they do not wear shoes indoors~~)	Not wearing shoes indoors is a custom.

the **advantage** of being good at math	the **mistake** of using *to* for *too*
the **benefit** of being hired first	the **possibility*** of not graduating
the **crime** of cheating on your taxes	the **practice** of forcing employees to work overtime
the **custom** of not wearing shoes indoors	the **problem** of not remembering things
the **experience** of living alone	the **process** of learning to read
his annoying **habit** of interrupting people	the **thought*** of going all day without coffee
the **idea*** of not eating meat	your **way*** of putting people at ease

*For another type of complement after *idea*, *possibility*, and *thought*, see 7.8.1. For *way* followed by a *that* clause, see 8.7.

6.23 Nouns and adjectives with infinitive complements

the power to influence others

We use infinitive complements after some nouns (a), shown below in typical phrases. Many of the nouns that allow this structure (like *attempt* and *tendency*) are related to infinitive-taking verbs (6.10). We also use infinitive complements after certain adjectives (b).

a. *Young children have an amazing* **ability to learn** *languages.*
b. *Many customers are* **willing to pay** *a little more for "greener" products.*

6.23.1 Nouns + infinitive complements		
the **ability** to adapt	a **failure** to communicate	his **promise** to do better
their **attempt** to escape	her **need** to know the truth	a **proposal** to raise tuition
your **capacity** to love	an **opportunity** to expand	the **right** to remain silent
a **chance** to win	get **permission** to leave	their **refusal** to cooperate
my **decision** to resign	under **pressure** to conform	his **request** to see a lawyer
his **desire** to succeed	their **plan** to cut taxes	her **tendency** to exaggerate
my **effort** to improve	the **power** to influence others	your **willingness** to compromise

6.23.2 Adjectives + infinitive complements		
was **able** to explain	be **glad** to help	was **quick** to volunteer
is **afraid** to ask	am **happy** to be here	were **slow** to respond
were **curious** to find out	were **hesitant** to criticize	am **sorry** to tell you
are **eager** to learn	be **ready** to go	was **surprised** to find
am **excited** to participate	be **reluctant** to say no	are **willing** to pay

USAGE GUIDE

6.24 Expressing probability: BE *likely* to and BE *sure* to

We can use the adjectives *apt, likely, unlikely, certain,* and *sure* followed by an infinitive to express probability. Sentences like these express the expectation of the speaker or writer, not the attitude of the subject of the sentence.

a. *Sea level is likely to rise dramatically within a few years.*	It will probably happen.
b. *This is sure to cause problems for low-lying areas.*	It will certainly cause problems.
c. *Susan is well qualified. She's sure to get a job soon.*	The speaker is sure it will happen. (Susan may also be sure, but the sentence does not say so.)

■ **Exercise 36**   Create a paraphrase by completing the sentence using a noun + *of* + a gerund.

0. I thought I was in control. It was a mistake. *I made a mistake …* ⟶ *I made the mistake of thinking I was in control.*
1. Our team knew the field. That was an advantage for us. *Our team had the …*
2. We exchange gifts on Christmas Eve. It's our custom. *We follow the …*
3. Public schooling introduces children to diversity. That's a benefit. *Public schooling has the …*
4. I object to punishing children physically. It's a barbaric practice. *I object to the …*
5. Jason calls everyone "Dude." It's an annoying habit. *He has an …*

■ **Exercise 37**   Create a paraphrase. Use the noun form of the boldface verb, preceded by a possessive noun or pronoun.

- We **needed** to save money. We were limited by **that**. ⟶ We were limited by **our need** to save money.
- The consultant **proposed** to change the company's name. **That** came as a surprise.
  ⟶ **The consultant's proposal** to change the company's name came as a surprise.

1. David **tends** to exaggerate. **That** makes people mistrust him.
2. They **refused** to cooperate. We were surprised by **that**.
3. The government **decided** to jail the dissidents. **That** led to an international outcry.
4. I **failed** to get into law school. **That** disappointed my parents.
5. Senator Smith **promised** to create jobs. Her supporters were encouraged by **that.**
6. You **attempted** to improve. Everyone admired **that**.

■ **Exercise 38**   Complete the sentence with a pair of words, using either an infinitive or *of* + a gerund.

      advantage + belong   custom + have   effort + catalog   experience + grow up

1. The baby boomer generation was shaped by the __ in an era of unprecedented prosperity.
2. In politics, it's hard to overestimate the __ to a large and powerful family.
3. Polygamy is the __ more than one wife or husband at the same time.
4. The biologist E.O. Wilson thinks scientists should launch a massive __ all the species on the planet.

    failure + adapt   problem + store   tendency + release   way + introduce

5. The development of nuclear power has been hampered by the __ spent fuel.
6. Steve Jobs, the Apple Computer entrepreneur, was known for his dramatic __ new products.
7. American automotive companies have often been criticized for their __ to changing energy needs.
8. The stink bug gets its name from its __ an unpleasant odor when it is disturbed.

Usage Guide

■ **Exercise 39** Write a sentence that is similar in meaning, using one of the adjectives and an infinitive. There may be more than one possibility.

    afraid   eager   √ reluctant   willing

1. Dan **prefers not** to take responsibility. ~ Dan is reluctant to take responsibility.
2. They **didn't mind** changing their plans.
3. We **really wanted** to contribute.
4. They **didn't want** to face the enemy.

    curious   happy   sorry

5. I **felt bad** about losing.
6. It will be **my pleasure** to help you.
7. They **wanted** to know more.

    able   hesitant   surprised

8. Most people **can** cook at least a little.
9. We **did not expect** to see you.
10. Daniel **doesn't usually** criticize others.

    quick   reluctant   slow

11. **It took them a long time** to respond.
12. She admitted her mistake **right away**.
13. They **didn't want** to get involved.

■ **Exercise 40** Sentences with *more* (or *less*) *likely* are often used to compare probability: *Smokers are more likely to develop lung cancer than nonsmokers.* Form sentences in this pattern, using the words provided. For example: *Boys are more likely to skip school than girls.* If you're not sure about the facts, form a question instead of a statement: *Are boys more likely to skip school than girls?*

1. Girls or boys?   skip school, run away from home, speak up in class, do well on tests of verbal ability, do volunteer work

2. Women or men?   live to be 100, be vegetarians, remarry after getting divorced, say they are happy, suffer from depression, keep social media profiles private, be happy living alone

3. Europeans or Americans?   speak a second language, take long vacations, have large families, go to church weekly

4. City people or small town people?   know their neighbors, belong to a health club, have college degrees, take public transportation

5. Old people or young people?   want to live in a big city, smoke, watch TV every day, read newspapers / vote

USAGE GUIDE

I look forward to seeing you.

6.25 Prevent someone from doing something, look forward to trying, etc.

Thank you for not smoking is an example of a common pattern: a verb or adjective, sometimes followed by an object, plus a preposition and a gerund. Some verbs and adjectives that use this pattern are shown below. The adjectives are italicized and appear after forms of BE. See also 9.16.

They **accused** him of lying.	I **look forward to** seeing you.
I am *accustomed* to working alone.	I don't **object to** being questioned.
Were you *afraid* of being hurt?	They **plan**ned to stay. (They stayed.)
We **apologize**d (to them) for laughing.	They **plan**ned for me to stay. (I stayed.)
We **arrange**d to meet. (We met.)	They **prevent**ed me from entering.
We **arrange**d for them to meet. (They met.)	**Stop** the disease from spreading.
I don't **blame** you for not caring.	She **succeed**ed **in** gaining access
You **are** *capable* **of** doing better.	We **suspect** him of cheating
Don't **discourage** her from joining in.	**Thank** you for not smoking.
I **was** *excited* about being promoted.	I'm **think**ing about changing jobs.
Are you *good* **at** fixing things?	I **wait**ed to leave. (I left.)
She **insists** on having her own way.	I **wait**ed for him to leave. (He left.)
Are you *interested* in making money?	I **am** *sorry* **for** being late.
I couldn't **keep** from falling. (I fell.)	He **is** *used to* being alone.
I couldn't **keep** him from falling. (He fell.)	(Also: get used to *-ing*…)

have trouble planning

have fun talking

spend time working

6.26 Three patterns: *Have difficulty walking*, *go shopping*, and *stand waiting*

6.26.1 We often use a gerund after expressions like these:

a. We **had difficulty / trouble / problems** planning our project.
b. They **had fun / a good time** working together.
c. Why did you **spend / waste time (the day, two hours)** doing nothing?

6.26.2 We use *go* and a gerund for common activities like shopping and leisure activities.

d. *We went biking / bowling / camping / dancing / hiking / hunting / shopping / swimming.*

6.26.3 We can describe activity at the same time as another activity by adding a phrase with an *–ing* form. We don't use *with*. (See also Ch. 2.8.2.)

e. *We just stood there waiting.*	≈ We stood and waited.
f. *I left home not knowing if I would ever come back.*	≈ When I left, I did not know.
g. *She looked around (~~with~~) smiling.*	Compare: without smiling (6.5).

I appreciate your asking.

6.27 Implied subjects of gerunds

We sometimes use a possessive pronoun or noun before a gerund as an implied subject (a). This usage is quite formal. We also sometimes use a noun or pronoun in the object form (b, c).

a. *I have no questions, but I appreciate **your** asking.*
b. *Do you remember **me** telling you about this?* (More formal: my telling you.)
c. *The chance of **a person** breaking into your apartment are very small.*

Chapter 6 — Gerunds and infinitives — Grammar Advantage 189

Usage Guide

■ **Exercise 41** Write a sentence that is similar in meaning, using the words that are supplied. Do not use the boldface words.

1. They **said** he **had** cheated. — *accuse*
2. **After** laughing, **I said I was sorry.** — *apologize*
3. They stayed at a hotel. I made arrangements. — *arrange*
4. You criticized me, **but it's OK.** — *I don't blame*
5. My parents **advised** me **not to** study art. — *discourage*
6. He **demanded** to see the manager. — *insist*
7. They interrupted. I couldn't **stop** them. — *couldn't keep*
8. I **will** talk to you next week. **It will be a pleasure.** — *look forward*
9. We were ignored. We **protested.** — *object*
10. He **couldn't** escape. The police **stopped** him. — *prevent*
11. **Thanks to your efforts,** the problem **didn't** get worse. — *You stopped*
12. We met our deadline. — *succeed*
13. **I think that he did** not answer honestly. — *suspect*
14. They **were grateful to** me **when I** paid. — *thank*
15. I'm **considering** buying a bike. — *think*
16. We waited **and finally** the rain stopped. — *wait*

The items below involve adjectives, so you need a form of BE (for example, *am* accustomed).

17. **It no longer bothers me** to get up early. — *used to*
18. I **usually** sleep late. — *accustomed*
19. **My fear is that** I **will** lose my job. — *afraid*
20. She **has the ability to** be a leader. — *capable*
21. I'm starting my new job tomorrow. **I can't wait!** — *excited*
22. Nathan **always** remembers names. — *good*
23. They **want to** start a business. — *interested*
24. I **did** not invite you. I apologize. — *sorry*

■ **Exercise 42** Choose the correct forms. HIGH PRIORITY

1. Children who have __ reading usually struggle with everything else in school too.
   (a) difficult to   (b) difficulty to   (c) difficult   (d) difficulty

2. If you have a hard time __ billboards along the road, you probably need glasses.
   (a) reading   (b) read   (c) to read   (d) for reading

3. On the weekend, I went __ at the mall.
   (a) shopping   (b) to shopping   (c) shopped   (d) for shopping

4. We talked about __ next summer.
   (a) going to camping   (b) to go camping   (c) going camping   (d) go camping

5. I started my new job __ it would be temporary.
   (a) to know   (b) knowing   (c) I knew   (d) know

6. Carlos spent his first week in Miami __ to find a job.
   (a) tried   (b) to try   (c) trying   (d) for trying

Usage Guide

Lexical grammar: the grammar of individual words

6.28 Gerunds and infinitives and lexical grammar

The choice between a gerund and an infinitive is sometimes related to **actual** action expressed with a gerund (a) vs. **potential** action expressed with an infinitive (b).

a. *My cousins like **living** in New York.*	They actually live there.
b. *I would like **to live** in New York someday.*	I could potentially live there.
c. *I like **taking / to take** a short nap after lunch.*	A nap is sometimes possible.

Although the concept of actual or potential action can sometimes help you decide whether to choose a gerund or an infinitive, the decision is largely a matter of lexical grammar. Four points to remember:

First, when you learn a verb (*resent, condescend, coax*), you also have to learn what forms may follow it. Examples in a dictionary or online may help.

d. *Do you **resent paying** for messaging when you don't even use the service?*
e. *Superstars don't usually **condescend to answer** fan mail.*
f. *In Oaxaca, a vendor **coaxed us to try** fried grasshoppers.*

Second, verbs with similar meanings may have different patterns. The choice may seem arbitrary.

g. *When customers ask us, we always advise (~~suggest~~) them to buy the service agreement.*
h. *Most cats like (~~enjoy~~) to be scratched behind the ears.*

Third, remember that the grammar of gerunds and infinitives also involves nouns and pronoun objects (i) and prepositions (j) and that a few verbs (6.12-14) allow a complement with a base form verb (k). In addition, many verbs also take noun clause complements (l). (See 7.7.) Again, which verbs allow which patterns may seem arbitrary.

i. *advise **them** to stay, advise ~~to stay~~, advise ~~them~~ staying*
j. *succeed **in** getting elected, succeed ~~to get~~ elected, insist **on** paying, insist ~~to pay~~*
k. *let (make, have, see) them work together (~~to work~~)*
l. *prefer that I study economics, want ~~that I~~ study economics, want me to study economics*

Finally, complements are not allowed after some verbs that you might expect to allow them.

m. *My parents always ~~supported~~ me to study → supported my studies / encouraged me to study / insisted that I study.*

Because lexical grammar is such a significant aspect of the grammar of gerunds and infinitives, it is important to learn from examples and to use references such as dictionaries effectively.

6.29 Problems with gerunds and infinitives

	Problems	Revisions	
1.	Eat junk food is a bad habit.	Eating junk food is a bad habit.	When you need a verb as a subject, change it to a gerund (6.4) or sometimes an infinitive. (6.7)
2.	I know that maintain a healthy diet is important.	I know that maintaining a healthy diet is important.	
3.	Unfortunately, is hard for me to avoid sweet, salty snacks.	It is hard for me to avoid sweet, salty snacks.	Use empty *it* with a delayed infinitive subject. (6.7)
4.	Avoiding junk food it's not easy	Avoiding junk food is not easy.	Don't add an extra subject. (6.4 and 2.2.2.)
5.	My goal is change my eating habits little by little.	My goal is to change my eating habits little by little.	After nouns like *goal* and *plan* (and a BE verb), use an infinitive. (6.7)
6.	I look forward to see you. I want to thank you for help me by cook a nice dinner for you.	I look forward to seeing you. I want to thank you for helping me by cooking a nice dinner for you.	After a preposition, use a gerund, no other form of verb. (6.5)
7.	Do you enjoy to be alone? Some people don't mind not have company all the time. They don't avoid spend time alone.	I enjoy being alone. I don't mind not having company. I avoid spending time alone.	Use a gerund after the verbs in 6.6.
8.	I consider important to save money. It makes easier to plan for the future.	I consider it important to save money. It makes it easier to plan for the future.	Use empty *it* as an object as described in 6.9.
9.	Let me know if you decide join us. Ask me pick you up.	I hope you decide to join us. Ask me to pick you up.	Use an infinitive after the verbs in 6.10.
10.	Try to don't be so messy!	Try not to be so messy!	Use *not + to ...* for a negative infinitive.
	I like not have to get up early on weekends.	I like not having to get up early on weekends.	Use *not + Ving* for a negative gerund.
11.	We don't require students wearing uniforms, but we want that they look neat.	We require students to wear uniforms. We want them to look neat.	Verb + object + infinitive (6.10)
12.	The teacher had the students worked in groups.	had the students work	
13.	We let them to do whatever they wanted.	let them do	*have / let / make* + object + bare infinitive. (6.11, 6.12)
14.	They let us worked together.	let us work	
15.	I like movies that make me to think.	make me think	
16.	That movie made me thought about my childhood.	make me think	

	Problems	Revisions	
17.	I can help you getting ready.	*help you (to) get*	*help* (someone) (to) do (6.12)
18.	The boy stole a laptop, but no one saw he did it.	*saw him do it*	Rules for verbs of perception: 6.14.
19.	I heard the rain fell on the roof.	*heard the rain falling*	
20.	She's too young for voting.	*too young to vote*	*Too* and *enough*: 6.15
21.	She's not enough old to vote.	*not old enough to vote*	
22.	I'm easy to remember names.	*I remember names easily. It's easy for me to remember names. Names are easy for me to remember.*	Using adjectives like *easy* and *hard*: 6.16.
23.	The instructions were hard to me to understand.	*hard for me to understand*	*For* + object + infinitive: 6.19
24.	It was hard to understand the instructions for me.		
25.	I want to appreciate for all the work I've done.	*want to be appreciated*	Passive infinitives and gerunds: 6.20
26.	Celebrities usually try to avoid recognizing on the street.	*avoid being recognized*	
27.	I went to Mexico for learning Spanish.	*went to Mexico to learn*	To express the purpose of an action, use an infinitive. (9.13)
28.	It's hard to remember for me.	*It's hard for me to remember.*	Use the order *for X to Y*.

Chapter 7

Noun clauses and reporting

IN THIS CHAPTER
Transforming ideas and thoughts into sentence parts

Chapter 7
Noun clauses and reporting

reporting what others say

tenses in reporting

noun clauses and lexical grammar

Chapter 7: Noun clauses and reporting 195		
7.1	Noun clauses in context 197	
7.2	What are noun clauses? 197	
7.3	Noun clauses with *that* or no marker 198	
7.4	Noun clauses beginning with *wh* words 199	
	7.4.1 Embedded questions 199	
	7.4.2 *Whether* and *if* 199	
	7.4.3 Punctuation 199	
	7.4.4 Noun clauses that are like relative clauses 199	
	7.4.5 Grammatical roles of *wh* clauses .199	
	7.4.6 *Wh* words + infinitives 200	
	7.4.7 Verbs that often introduce *wh* clauses 200	
7.5	Noun clauses as subjects and delayed subjects 203	
7.6	*That* clauses after BE 204	
7.7	*That* clauses after verbs 206	
	7.7.1 Verb + *that* clause: *know that you're ready* 206	
	7.7.2 Verb + indirect object + *that* clause: *tell them that you're ready* . .206	
	7.7.2a Verbs with an optional indirect object after *to* 206	
	7.7.2b Verbs with an optional or required indirect object . . .206	
	7.7.3 Verbs followed by a subjunctive *that* clause: *ask that he leave* .208	
	7.7.4 Noun clauses after *wish* and *hope* 208	
7.8	*The fact that* and other nouns and adjectives followed by *that* clauses . . .211	
	7.8.1 Nouns that can be followed by a *that* clause – in typical phrases .211	
	7.8.2 Adjectives that can be followed by a *that* clause 211	
7.9	Reporting with noun clauses and other structures 213	
7.10	Tenses, modals, and adverbials in reporting 215	
7.11	Reporting questions 216	
7.12	Reporting commands and requests 218	
7.13	Verbs that are not followed by a *that* clause 218	
7.14	Usage guide Reporting special types of speech indirectly 220	
7.15	Usage guide *According to* and other phrases for attribution 222	
7.16	Usage guide Directly reporting parts of sentences 222	
7.17	Usage guide When to include *that* 223	
7.18	Usage guide *Feel like, look like, sound like, seem like* 223	
7.19	Usage guide *Like it that…, make it clear that…* etc. 223	
7.20	Usage guide *Consider, find, regard,* and *see* .223	
7.21	Usage guide Recreated or typical speech in academic writing 225	
	7.21.1 Usage guide Direct reporting for recreated speech 225	
	7.21.2 Usage guide Direct reporting for typical speech 225	
7.22	Usage guide Indirect reporting and paraphrasing 225	
7.23	Usage guide Noun clauses and lexical grammar 226	
7.24	Usage guide Noun clauses and relative clauses 226	
7.25	Usage guide Using noun clauses to make your writing more precise . .226	
7.26	Problems with noun clauses and reporting 227	

Chapter 7 — Noun clauses and reporting

7.1 Noun clauses in context

Noun clauses begin with *that* or a *wh* word (*whether, what, how,* etc.). These clauses function like nouns, usually as subjects or after verbs. Some noun clauses with *that* follow a noun or an adjective (see 7.8), completing its meaning. (These are sometimes called complements.)

KEY
Ch. 6 = Chapter 6
Ex. 23 = Exercise 23
5.2 = Chapter 5, section 2
2.14.3 = Chapter 2, section 14, subsection 3
(a) = an example

HIGH PRIORITY

■ **Exercise 1** Based on what you already know about noun clauses, can you identify noun clauses in the passage below? (If you prefer, read 7.2 and 7.3 first.) The first two noun clauses are already underlined.

> When you buy something, you want to know exactly <u>what you're getting</u>, and you probably assume <u>that the seller will provide information</u>. The truth is that sellers don't always operate that way. In this regard, the term *caveat emptor* applies. *Caveat emptor* is a Latin phrase translated as "Let the buyer beware." It expresses the idea that buyers are responsible for determining whether they are getting a fair deal. There is of course an implied guarantee that the product is what the seller claims it to be, but *caveat emptor* suggests that buyers must be aware that they take on some risk with any purchase.

7.2 What are noun clauses?

A noun clause is a clause that functions as a noun, usually as a subject or an object. Some noun clauses begin with *that*, but we often omit *that* (a). Other noun clauses begin with a *wh* word or phrase (b, c). The *wh* word *whether* can sometimes be replaced by *if* (c). We use noun clauses to describe ideas, thoughts, feelings, and speech (7.9). Some uses of noun clauses can be described as **reporting** (7.9-7.14).

a. *Do you think **(that) most people are honest**?*	We often omit *that*, especially after common verbs like *think* and *know* (see 7.17, "When to include *that*").
b. *Before buying a used car, you should find out **how many owners it has had**.*	Notice the word word order: *it has*, not *has it*. (See 7.4.)
c. *It's important to ask **whether the car has every been in an accident**. You want to know **if it has been damaged**.*	*Whether* and *if* are often but not always interchangeable. (See 7.4.) Don't use them together (*whether if*).

7.3 Noun clauses with *that* or no marker

We can use *that* clauses as subjects (a), as delayed subjects after empty *it* (b), after BE (c), and as appositives (d). We use them as **complements** after many verbs (e), certain nouns (f), and certain adjectives (g).

a. Everyone expected the Jets to win. **That they won by only two points** was a surprise.	See 7.5
b. It was a surprise **that they won by only two points**.	
c. The surprise of the tournament was **that the Jets won by only two points**.	See 7.6
d. The big news of the week, **that the Jets won by only two points**, surprised everyone.	See 8.15
e. Do you believe **that it is always wrong to lie**? Most people find **that "white lies" are sometimes necessary**.	See 7.7
f. The idea **that marriage should be based on love** is rather new.	See 7.8.1
g. I wasn't aware **that there was an entry fee**. I'm afraid that **I don't have any money**.	See 7.8.2

Noun clauses may have clauses inside them, including structures before the subject of the noun clause (h). Sometimes elements inside a noun clause are set off by commas or other punctuation (j).

h. Most people know **that when they buy a car they are taking a risk**.	*That* is separated from the subject of the clause by an adverbial clause (Ch. 9).
i. I know **that what I did was wrong**.	The subject of the *that* clause is another noun clause, introduced by a *wh* word.
j. They say **that**, in politics, **anything can happen**.	The noun clause is interrupted by a phrase.

We do not use a *that* clause (with or without *that*) after a preposition (k-n). At the beginning of a sentence, we do not use a *that* clause with no *that* (o).

    k. WRONG: *I don't agree with people keep monkeys as pets.* ⟶ *I don't think people should keep ... / I don't agree with (people) keeping ...*

    l. WRONG: *Instead of you stay at a hotel, why don't you stay with us?* ⟶ *Instead of staying ...*

    m. WRONG: *They always complain about they have too much to do.* ⟶ *complain that they have / complain about having*

    n. WRONG: *I'm worried about my paper is too short.* ⟶ *I am worried that my paper is too short.*

    o. WRONG: *People go hungry is a shame.* ⟶ *That people go hungry is a shame. / It's a shame that people go hungry.*

Chapter 7 — Noun clauses and reporting

7.4 Noun clauses beginning with *wh* words

I don't know why I'm so hungry.

7.4.1 Embedded questions Some noun clauses begin with *wh* words, like questions. They are sometimes called embedded questions. They often follow verbs like *ask, find out, know,* and *wonder*. They can also follow BE (e). Unlike questions, they do not have auxiliary + subject word order (see 2.11), and they do not require the auxiliary DO. When a *wh* word introduces a noun clause, we do not use *that*.

a. *I wonder **what my family is doing now**.*	what ~~is my family~~ doing
b. *They always ask **when we can come again**.*	when ~~can we~~ come
c. *We found out **where they keep the money**.*	where ~~do~~ they keep
d. *I don't know **why I'm so hungry**.*	~~that why, why that~~
e. *I want to talk to you. That's **why I'm here**.*	

7.4.2 Whether and if We use *whether* to introduce an embedded question that is similar to a yes/no question (f). We often use *if* instead of *whether*, especially in conversation after the verbs *see, know,* and *find out*. We can include *or not* after *whether* or at the end (g). (See 10.10 for the use of *whether* in conditionals). We use *whether* but not usually *if* when the clause is at the beginning of a sentence (h), after a preposition (i), or after a form of BE (j).

f. *I want to know **whether/if they take credit cards**.* (Compare: *Do they take credit cards?*)
g. *I asked **whether or not** the tip was included. I asked **whether** the tip was included **or not**.*
h. *They say coffee is bad for you. **Whether (if) it's true** I don't know.*
i. *Can you get a student discount? It depends on **whether (if) you have your ID**.*
j. *One question related to capital punishment is **whether (if) it really deters crime**.*

7.4.3 Punctuation The punctuation depends on the whole sentence, not the *wh* clause. See also 7.9.

k. *I want to know **who is in charge**.*	The **sentence** is a statement, so we use a period.
l. *Do you know **who is in charge**?*	The **sentence** is a question, so we use a question mark.

7.4.4 Noun clauses that are like relative clauses Some noun clauses with *wh* words are similar to relative clause constructions (Ch. 8).

m. *I found **what I was looking for**.*	I found the thing(s) that I was looking for. (8.5, 8.19)
n. *This is **where we keep our supplies**.*	This is the place where we keep them. (8.7)

7.4.5 Grammatical roles of *wh* clauses We can use *wh* clauses as we use nouns, including after prepositions (o). We can use them after *the issue of, the problem of,* and *the question of* (p).

o. *Economists spend a lot of time thinking **about what motivates people**. They are interested **in why people make certain decisions instead of others**.*
p. *We still have to discuss **the issue of how we should spend our refund**.*

Do you know what to do?

7.4.6 Wh words + infinitives A *wh* clause that includes *should* can often be paraphrased by a phrase with an infinitive (*ask **what to do**, remember **how to log in***). (See also 6.17). These phrases generally include the idea of *should* or *can*.

Sentences with *wh* clauses	Paraphrases with infinitive phrases
o. *Do you know what you should do if you encounter a bear?*	p. *Do you know what to do if you encounter a bear?*
r. *The problem of how we can dispose of toxic waste has not been solved.*	s. *The problem of how to dispose of toxic waste has not been solved.*

7.4.7 Verbs that often introduce *wh* clauses Verbs that are often followed by a *wh* clause are listed below. After some, a pronoun appears, representing an indirect object, usually optional. Parentheses around a word mean that it is optional.

Verbs followed by a *wh* clause – in typical phrases		
ask (them) who he is	**guess** what will happen	**remember** when you arrived
don't **care** what I do	**imagine** how much fun it will be	**remind** me what day it is
decide what you want	**indicate** whether you need help	**say** what he wanted
determine how old it is	**judge** how long it will take	**see** what works best
discover who it was	doesn't **know** how it started	**show** (us) where it is
discuss what happened	**measure** how much we learn	**tell** (them) who you are
figure out how it works	**predict** how it will end	**understand** why you're angry
find out how much it costs	don't **realize** how hard it is	**wonder** what the problem is
forget where you parked		

■ **Exercise 2** Find two *that* clauses after verbs, three clauses beginning with *wh* words, one *that* clause after BE, two *that* clauses after nouns, and one *that* clause after an adjective. (*When you buy something* is an adverbial clause; see Ch. 9.)

When you buy something, you want to know exactly what you're getting, and you probably assume that the seller will provide information. The truth is that sellers don't always operate that way. *Caveat emptor* is a Latin phrase translated as "Let the buyer beware." It expresses the idea that buyers are responsible for determining whether they are getting a fair deal. There is of course an implied guarantee that the product is what the seller claims it to be, but *caveat emptor* suggests that buyers must be aware that they take on some risk with any purchase.

Chapter 7 — Noun clauses and reporting

■ **Exercise 3** Choose the correct forms.

1. Stonehenge is an ancient monument in England. Historians believe __ was built more than 4,000 years ago.
   (a) that Stonehenge it   (b) that it   (c) Stonehenge that   (d) that

2. They know __ built in six stages.
   (a) it was   (b) it that   (c) it   (d) that it

3. They don't know __ built it.
   (a) who was   (b) that who   (c) how   (d) who

4. __ the Jets won by only two points.
   (a) Was a surprise that   (b) It was a surprise that
   (c) That was a surprise   (d) A surprise that

5. That the Jets won by only two points __ a big surprise.
   (a) it was   (b) that was   (c) was   (d) that it was

6. The big surprise of the week __ won by only two points.
   (a) the Jets   (b) that the Jets   (c) it was that the Jets   (d) was that the Jets

7. Do you believe __ always wrong to tell a lie?
   (a) it is   (b) that is   (c) is that   (d) is it

8. The idea that marriage should be based on love __ new.
   (a) it's rather   (b) rather   (c) is rather   (d) that is rather

9. I wasn't aware __ there was a fee.
   (a) of   (b) that   (c) about   (d) is that

10. I know __ I did was wrong.
    (a) that what   (b) what that   (c) it that   (d) that

11. They say ___, in politics, anything is possible.
    (a) so   (b) it   (c) what   (d) that

12. Instead of __ at a hotel, why don't you stay with us?
    (a) you stay   (b) that you stay   (c) staying   (d) to stay

■ **Exercise 4** Combine the sentences, following the example.

> *How did the game end? I wonder.* ⟶ *I wonder how the game ended.*

1. What is my family doing now? I wonder.
2. When can they come again? He always asks.
3. Where do they keep the money? We need to find out.
4. Why am I hungry? I don't know.
5. Do they take credit cards? I have to ask.
6. Is the tip included? I'll ask.
7. Who is in charge? I want to know.
8. What does e.g. mean? Do you know?
9. What is a sonnet? Do you know?
10. What does ASAP mean? Can you tell me?
11. What does PDQ mean? Do you have any idea?
12. When can we take a break? I wonder.

■ **Exercise 5** Choose one item from each column to produce a sentence with a noun clause.

Example: I found what I was looking for.

	√ I found	where	she had a headache.
1	She said	when	√ I was looking for.
2	We learned	√ what	they were coming.
3	This closet is	that	paragraphs are structured.
4	They didn't tell us	how	we keep our supplies.

5	I wonder	what time	his car was.
6	He forgot	how long	we had a lot to do.
7	We all knew	where	the storm will last.
8	She doesn't know	that	her appointment is

■ **Exercise 6** Use the words to complete the sentence. **Omit one word.** There may be more than one way.

1. People often ... from / ask / they / where / international students / to / are
2. Historians don't ... temple / Stonehenge / know / a / was / whether / if
3. I don't ... that / eligible voters / understand / some / why / don't vote
4. I don't care. You can ... to / want / do / do / you / that / what

■ **Exercise 7** Add a form of DO where it is needed. Some of the blanks should remain empty.

When you're chatting online with a stranger, how __ you decide how much to tell the person about yourself? If they want to know how old are you, __ you answer honestly? If they ask how much money __ you make, __ you tell a white lie? How __ you answer personal questions depends on how much __ you trust the stranger you are chatting with. One strategy some people use is to respond to a question with a question: *Why __ you want to know?* If the other person can't give you a good answer, maybe it's good idea to say good-bye.

7.5 Noun clauses as subjects and delayed subjects

It's clear that you're well-qualified.

We can use a *that* clause as a subject to express a fact (*you are well qualified*) and comment on it (*it's clear*). More commonly, we use empty *it* at the beginning and place the *that* clause at the end as a delayed subject. (See also 7.19, 7.20, and Ch. 6.7.)

a. ***That you are well-qualified** is clear. It is clear **that you are well-qualified**.*

Below, empty *it* expressions often used with *that* clauses appear in groups with related meanings.

*It's **clear / true / obvious** that we need a new manager.*
*It's **certain / (un)likely / (im)possible / doubtful** that things will change.*
*It was **lucky / fortunate / a good thing** that we had some food.*
*It is **interesting / amazing / surprising** that business is so good.*
*It's **unfortunate / too bad / a pity / a shame** that no one helped you.*
*It **turned out / happened** that only one person applied for the job.*
*It **doesn't matter / makes no difference** that you have no experience.*

- Some expressions with empty *it* (*It is essential*) are used with a subjunctive verb in the *that* clause (7.7.3).
- With *turn out* and *happen*, we do not use a *that* clause as a subject at the beginning of the sentence.

We often use a *wh* clause as a subject or a delayed subject after expressions such as *It doesn't matter, It makes no difference, It's not clear, It is unknown,* and *It remains to be seen*.

b. ***What you do** makes no difference. It makes no difference **what you do**.*
c. ***Whether it works** remains to be seen. It remains to be seen **whether it works**.*

The reason is that...

7.6 That clauses after BE

We can use a noun such as *problem, reason, result, truth, idea* or *point* as a subject followed by BE and a *that* clause. There is no comma after the subject. It is a mistake to omit BE and *that* (e).

a. *I like having guests.* **The problem is that** *sometimes they don't know when to leave.*
b. **The reason** *for the detour* **was that** *the bridge was closed.*
c. **One result** *of improved healthcare* **is that** *infant mortality has decreased.*
d. *He says he's in the film business, but* **the truth is that** *he just blogs about movies.*
e. WRONG: *Another result of improved health care, people are living longer.* → *Another result...* **is that** *people are....*

■ **Exercise 8** **One or two** of the underlined parts are wrong. The others have no mistakes. Find and fix the mistake(s).

When you order a sandwich made with square slices of bread, it's always cut diagonally, from corner to corner. It makes no <u>difference what</u> kind of sandwich it is; it's always cut the same. One reason they cut sandwiches this way <u>is that it's</u> the easiest way to make the two parts equal in size. A more important <u>reason it</u> maximizes the view of <u>what's inside</u>. It's <u>obvious that</u> restaurant owners have <u>figured out what</u> makes a sandwich look appetizing.

■ **Exercise 9** Put the words in the right order to make a sentence. Add empty *it*, a BE verb if it is needed, and *that*.

Example: It's raining really hard. *a good thing / an umbrella / brought / I* → It's a good thing that I brought an umbrella.

1 Children are natural language learners. *languages / than adults / obvious / they / more easily / learn*
2 You can always learn new things. *are / old / doesn't / you / how / matter*
3 Some birds migrate hundreds of miles. *can fly / amazing / without / so far / they / losing their way*
4 Libraries are a great free resource. *more people / them / use / don't / a shame*
5 Anyone can read books in the library. *have a card / you / no difference / or not / whether / makes*

■ **Exercise 10** Paraphrase your answers from exercise 9 with the noun clause at the beginning.

■ **Exercise 11** Fill the blanks using the words that are provided: one, two or three words.

is (x4)   *it*   *that* (x3)   *they* (x2)

Community colleges, where students earn two-year degrees, have grown dramatically in recent years. One of the main reasons __ generally cost less than four-year colleges. Not only is tuition lower, but because there are so many community colleges, __ likely __ a student can choose one near home, which may save the cost of living in a dorm. One disadvantage of community colleges __ don't usually offer financial aid, but even without financial aid, most students find them cheaper than four-year schools. Another advantage of community colleges __ flexible scheduling, which makes them attractive to working adults, who can study in the evening and on weekends.

Chapter 7

■ Exercise 12 Choose the correct forms.

1. After their first American tour ___ that the Beatles were going to be hugely popular in the U.S.
   (a) it was clear   (b) was clear   (c) it was clearly that   (d) was clearly

2. You can't see the doctor today. ___ how long you wait. She's not in.
   (a) It's no difference   (b) It makes no difference
   (c) There's no difference   (d) It's no different

3. I'd like to get the student discount. ___ I don't have my ID?
   (a) Is it matter that   (b) Does it matter that   (c) Is a matter that   (d) Does that matter if

4. One difficulty with English spelling ___ have so many exceptions.
   (a) the rules   (b) is the rules   (c) because the rules   (d) is that the rules

5. One consequence of increased employment opportunities for women ___ fewer talented women choose to go into teaching.
   (a) it is that   (b) it is   (c) is that   (d) that is

Did you know that tigers are almost extinct?

7.7 *That* clauses after verbs

We use *that* clauses after many verbs, especially verbs of thinking and communication. With most of these verbs we do not include an indirect object (7.1). With some, an indirect object is optional (7.2a) and with some it is required (7.2b). The verb *wish* has unique patterns (7.7.4).

7.7.1 Verb + *that* clause: know that it works
These verbs mostly describe thinking events.

They **argue** that the law is unfair.	When did you **learn** that you had been hired?
From my name people **assume** that I'm French.	They **maintain** that no laws were broken.
I **believe** that most people are honest.	This **means** that I can retire next year.
We **conclude**d that no one was at fault.	No one **notice**d that she had left.
We **decide**d that it was too expensive.	We **observe**d that the weather was changing.
They **discover**ed that a child was missing.	We **pretend**ed that we were Canadian.
I **doubt** that anyone will object.	I've **read** that Bali is a beautiful place.
Do you **expect** that there will be trouble?	Do you **realize** that we're almost finished?
Do you **feel** that things are getting getter?	She regrets that she can't join us.
I **find** that I need more sleep these days.	I didn't **remember** that it was Sunday.
Don't **forget** that we have a test.	We **speculate**d that the fire began in the kitchen.
I **guess** that I should have looked at a map.	I **see** that you got a haircut.
Did you **hear** that class is canceled?	**Suppose** that someone asked you for money.
I **hope** that your test goes well.	Do you **think** that there is life after death?
Imagine for a moment that it is 1492.	I **understand** that you're looking for work.
Did you **know** that tigers are almost extinct?	

7.7.2 Verb + indirect object + *that* clause
These verbs mostly describe talking events, with a listener.

Don't say it's too late.

7.7.2a Verbs with an optional indirect object after *to* (except for *agree with*)	
He **admit**ted (to us) that he had failed.	They **indicate**d (to us) that the road was clear.
I **agree** (with you) that this is a great city.	He **insist**ed (to me) that he would pay next time.
He **claim**ed (to them) that he had a license.	They didn't **mention** (to us) that he had left.
I **concede**d (to them) that I'd made mistakes.	He **prove**d (to them) that he was innocent.
He **complain**ed (to us) that it was too noisy.	We **report**ed (to the media) that we had won.
I **emphasize**d (to him) that no one was hurt.	They **say** (to everyone) that they never make exceptions.
She **explain**ed (to me) that she needed time.	
She **implie**d (to us) that wasn't comfortable.	The findings **suggest** (to us) that exercise helps.

Don't tell me it's too late.

7.7.2b Verbs with an optional or required indirect object – without *to*	
He **advise**d (me) that the property was unsafe.	**Promise** (me) that you won't tell anyone.
He **convince**d us that we were mistaken.	They **remind**ed me that it was Sunday.
They **inform**ed us that there would be a delay.	Parents **teach** (us) that we should be honest.
When did they **notify** you that we had won?	Research **show**s (us) that sleep helps memory.
I **persuade**d him that it would be OK.	Please don't **tell** me that it's too late.
I **pointed out** (to him) that his shoe was untied.	The guard **warn**ed (us) that it was dangerous.

The verbs in 7.7.2b can be passive (Ch. 5). The *that* clause then directly follows the verb.

We were **warned** that it was dangerous. I was **reminded** that it was Sunday.

Chapter 7 Noun clauses and reporting

■ **Exercise 13** Using a dictionary, choose the verb that matches the underlined verb most closely.

1. Diane Ravitch <u>argues</u> that schools have overemphasized testing in recent years.
   (a) proves   (b) claims   (c) concedes   (d) implies

2. Ravitch <u>concedes</u> that testing is necessary but argues that it can be overdone.
   (a) explains   (b) says   (c) admits   (d) implies

3. If we're going to eat out on New Year's eve, I <u>imagine</u> we'll need reservations.
   (a) determine   (b) realize   (c) suppose   (d) notice

4. We <u>learned</u> that our building was going to be remodeled.
   (a) decided   (b) regretted   (c) discovered   (d) guessed

5. I <u>doubt</u> that anyone will care if we park here.
   (a) don't say   (b) don't agree   (c) don't pretend   (d) don't think

6. The police <u>concluded</u> that there was no reason to arrest anyone.
   (a) argued   (b) determined   (c) explained   (d) hoped

7. At the annual meeting, the treasurer <u>reported</u> that earnings had declined.
   (a) emphasized   (b) found   (c) complained   (d) said

8. How did Calvin <u>persuade</u> his boss that he deserved a second chance?
   (a) convince   (b) advise   (c) notify   (d) show

■ **Exercise 14** Fill the blanks using the words that are provided: one or two words. All but one of the verbs should be in past tense. There is more than one correct way.

admit	agree	complain	promise	warn
to	with	him	that (x2 or 3)	

One weekend, Brad had a very loud party. His downstairs neighbors __ the landlord __ his party had kept them awake all night. They said it sounded like a riot. Brad __ the party had been loud, but he didn't __ them __ it sounded like a riot. Still, he __ the next party would be quieter. They __ they'd call the police next time if it wasn't.

Fill the blanks with one, two, or three words. Four of the forms should be in past tense. There is more than one correct way. Some words may be used more than once.

explain	insist	persuade	prove	remember
tell	to	me	them	that

When I was seven, I __ my parents that I wanted a dog. They __ me that dogs require a lot of care, but __ I would do everything. I even got a book on dog care from the library to show __ I was serious. I finally __ that I deserved a chance to __ I meant what I said. We got a dog. I __ that I fed and walked the dog faithfully every day, for about a week.

insist that he leave

7.7.3 Verbs and other expressions followed by a subjunctive *that* clause

- After verbs like *demand* and *recommend* and expressions like *It's important*, we can use a *that* clause with a subjunctive verb: a base form verb, with no *–s* or other marker (a).
- The negative subjunctive is *not* and a base form (b). The base form is used even for a past situation (c).
- Instead of the subjunctive, we sometimes use *should* (d).
- A subjunctive *that* clause describes an event or situation that is required or preferred, not a fact.
- With *insist*, *suggest*, and a few other expressions, we can use both subjunctive and non-subjunctive verbs depending on the meaning (e, f).
- Most expressions that allow subjunctive clauses also allow other patterns.

a. *It's important **that she participate**.*
b. *My teacher prefers that we **not use** / **don't use** dictionaries during tests.*
c. *We asked **that our money be** refunded.* (is/was refunded)
d. *They suggested **that the price (should) be raised**.*
e. *They insist that this drug **is** safe.* (They say firmly that it is safe.)
f. *They insist that all drugs **be** properly labeled.* (They say they must be labeled.)

The box includes verbs and other expressions that may be used with the subjunctive. The verbs usually do not have an indirect object (*demand him, recommend us, suggest them*).

*They always **ask** that people park in the back.*	*They **require** that students live on campus.*
*The protesters **demanded** that the president resign.*	*It's **crucial** that doors be kept locked.*
*You should **insist** that she apologize.*	*It's **essential** that his wishes be respected.*
*I **prefer** that you go outside to smoke.*	*It's **important** that everyone cooperate.*
*We **recommend** that you not travel alone.*	*It **isn't necessary** that everyone attend.*
*We **request** that you not call after 10 p.m.*	*It's **urgent** that he contact us at once.*
*They **suggest**ed (to us) that she be vaccinated.*	*It's **vital** that we keep in touch.*

- Avoid these common mistakes:

g.	WRONG: *We recommend you to make a reservation.* →	*We recommend (that) you make a reservation.* *We recommend making a reservation.* (6.6)
h.	WRONG: *They suggested me to come back later.* →	*They suggested (that) I come back later.* *They suggested coming back later.* (6.6)
i.	WRONG: *I prefer that I go to bed early.* →	*I prefer to go to bed early.* (6.10)

7.7.4 Noun clauses after *wish* and *hope*   *I wish I were*

- In a *that* clause after *wish*, we use verbs in the past tense for **unreal** (imaginary) present or future events (a). We often omit *that*.
- If the verb is BE, we use *were* for all subjects (b).
- For unreal **past** events, we use past perfect (c).
- We can use *could* in a clause after *wish* to express an unreal present or future situation (d).
- We sometimes use *wish* followed by an object and a noun like *luck* or *success* (e).
- We do not use *wish* to express a hope. Instead we use *hope*. After *hope*, we can use present or future for a future event (f, g).
- The grammar of *wish* clauses is similar to the grammar of conditional sentences (Ch. 10). (The term *subjunctive* is sometimes used for verbs after *wish* as well as for the structure described in 7.7.3.)

Wish for unreal events	
a. **I wish I lived** in New York, but here I am in St. Paul. **I wish I could move.**	In fact, **I don't live** in New York. **I can't move.** Compare: **If I lived** in New York, my life would be more exciting. **If I could move** there, I would. See 10.6
b. I wish **I were** stronger. **I wish he were** ... **I wish she were** ... **I wish it were** ...	Use *wish (someone)* **were** in academic writing. Informally, we sometimes use *was*.
c. I did not speak to my advisor. I **wish I had spoken** to her.	Compare: *If I* **had spoken** to her, I would have known what to do. (See 10.4.)
d. I have a test tomorrow. **I wish I could** get a perfect score, but that would be a miracle.	The sentence shows that you don't think a perfect score is possible. Don't say *I wish I could* if you **hope** that you **will**.
e. Wish me luck! I wish you happiness and health in the coming year.	
Hope for possible events	
f. **I hope** the test **is / will be** easy. (I ~~wish the test is~~ / ~~will be~~ ...)	
g. **I hope** you **have** a good summer! (I ~~wish~~ you have ...)	

■ **Exercise 15** Choose the correct forms.

1. It was rude of Kyle to speak to you that way. You should __ that he apologize.
   (a) tell him   (b) wish   (c) hope   (d) insist

2. We need to be cautious. It's essential that we __ anything we will later regret.
   (a) not do   (b) didn't do   (c) not to do   (d) not doing

3. Don't let the room get too hot. It's __ that it stay cool.
   (a) fortunate   (b) usual   (c) important   (d) comfortable

4. The robber demanded that the money __ put into a paper bag, but they didn't have one.
   (a) is   (b) be   (c) will be   (d) to be

5. Sometimes I miss my family and wish I __ home again.
   (a) am   (b) will be   (c) go   (d) were

6. I start my new job next week. I __ that I can do well enough to earn a promotion soon.
   (a) want   (b) hope   (c) wish   (d) would like

7. I'm not really ready to start working. I __ that I could afford to wait a while.
   (a) would like   (b) hope   (c) wish   (d) prefer

8. Looking back on their busy lives, people often say they wish they __ more time with family.
   (a) had spent   (b) have spent   (c) spent   (d) would spend

■ **Exercise 16** Advice columns like "Dear Abby" and "Ask Amy" give readers advice on problems that they describe in letters to the columnist. Using the words provided, complete the two letters and responses below. Most of the verbs (not all) should be in the subjunctive form (7.7.3). There is more than one way.

be   follow   forget   important   prefer   put   require   respect   not share   suggest

Dear Gaby: My son and his girlfriend Angelina are planning to spend a weekend with us this summer. He has asked that we __ them in his old bedroom, like a married couple, instead of putting her in the guest room. I'm not comfortable with that. I don't __ that he __ my rules in his own home, but this is my home. My husband insists that I __ old-fashioned and __ that I just __ about it. Should I listen to him? I usually don't.
— Old-fashioned Mom in Missouri

Dear OFM: Tell your son you __ that he and Angelina __ a room when they are your guests. There's no need to apologize. It's __ that he __ your wishes in your house.

be (x2)   demand (x2)   insist   leave (x2)   love   not make   prefer   stay

Dear Gaby: My mother's 14-year-old dog, Max, is not welcome in my home. He jumps on the furniture and smells bad. Still, she __ that he __ included whenever we get together, as if he were a member of the family. I've always suspected that she __ Max more than me. Can I __ that she __ him at home when she visits? – Maxed out

Dear Maxed: Be careful. It's crucial that you __ this a big issue. __ that she __ the dog at home is going too far. Tell Mom you __ that Max __ outside. If she __ that he __ allowed inside, hold your nose and welcome him. He'll be gone in a few years and you'll probably miss him.

7.8 *The fact that* and other nouns and adjectives followed by *that* clauses

> **The discovery that rats carry disease led to improvements in public health.**

- We can use *that* clause complements after certain nouns. The most common expression is *the fact that*.
- The nouns in these constructions are usually unmodified, singular, and definite (preceded by *the*).
- Among those that are often indefinite (without *the* but with *a/an* if the noun is countable) are *chance, evidence, feeling, indication, possibility,* and *sign*.
- We never use *which* instead of *that* in these constructions.

   I had **a/the feeling that** I was being watched. **The fact that** I was alone made me nervous.

The nouns that appear together in 7.8.1 have related meanings. Check a dictionary to learn how they differ.

We can use *that* clause complements after some adjectives. The adjectives that appear together in 7.8.2 have related meanings. Check a dictionary to learn how they differ.

7.8.1 Nouns that can be followed by a *that* clause – in typical phrases

> the **fact / discovery / finding / knowledge** that rats carry disease
> the **news / report / observation** that businesses are doing better
> the **idea / thought / notion** that pets are like family members
> the **assumption / belief / view** that everyone should learn to read
> the **feeling / impression / perception / sense** that we have met before
> the **hope** that we will succeed, the **fear** that we will fail
> the **chance / possibility / likelihood** that you will live to be 100
> the **claim / hypothesis / conclusion / suggestion** that smokers have low self-esteem
> no **evidence / indication / sign** that anything was wrong
> your **demand / proposal / request / suggestion** that the rules be changed
> **There's no doubt** that people can be healthy without eating meat.

- After *demand* and *request*, we use a *that* clause with a subjunctive verb (7.7.3). After *suggest*, the noun clause may or may not have a subjunctive verb, depending on the meaning that *suggest* expresses (7.7.3).
- *Doubt* is most often used in the expression *There is no doubt that...*

7.8.2 Adjectives that can be followed by a that clause – in typical sentences

> **I'm sure that we will win.**

> I'm **sure / confident / certain / positive** that we will win.
> We were **amazed / surprised / shocked** that the price was so high.
> I was **angry / annoyed / irritated / upset** that they were so rude.
> We were **sad / sorry / disappointed** that we had to leave our old home.
> Are you **afraid / concerned / worried** that you might get sick?
> You should be **happy / glad / pleased / relieved** that you don't have to pay more.
> We are **grateful / thankful** that we live in a peaceful place.
> I wasn't **aware** that you grew up in Spain./ I was **unaware** that you grew up in Spain.
> They are **proud** that their daughter is so strong.

We can use prepositional phrases after some of these nouns and adjectives, but we do not use a *that* clause, with or without *that*, after a preposition.

   a. WRONG: She talked about her fear of she will lose her job. ⟶ her fear of losing, her fear that she will lose…
   b. WRONG: I'm thankful for you helped me. ⟶ thankful for your help, thankful that you helped me

■ **Exercise 17** Rewrite the second sentence using the information from the first sentence in a noun complement (beginning with *that*) inside it.

Rats carry disease. This discovery led to improvements in public health. ➡ ***The discovery that rats carry disease*** *led to improvements in public health.* Note that *this discovery* becomes *the discovery.*

1. Consumer confidence is on the rise. Business leaders are encouraged by this news.
2. Pets are treated like family members. International visitors are sometimes struck by this fact.
3. We assume that everyone should learn to read. This assumption was not universal 100 years ago. (Don't include *We assume.*)
4. I felt as if we had met before. I couldn't get over the feeling. (Don't include *I felt as if.*)
5. The parents hoped that their daughter would graduate from college. This hope motivated them to work hard.
6. We feared that someone might be hurt. This fear made us nervous.
7. It's possible that you will live to be 100. Do you ever think about the possibility?
8. Some people claim that girls can't learn math. This claim is offensive to many people.
9. It was found that smoking is unhealthy. This evidence led to health warnings on cigarette packages.
10. The shareholders demanded that the CEO resign. Discussion at the meeting was dominated by this demand.

■ **Exercise 18** Write a paraphrase of the sentence using **one** of the four words. Do not use the underlined words.

1. I <u>know for sure</u> that I locked the door. *doubtful / positive / upset / glad*
2. We were <u>happy</u> that the problem was solved. *upset / aware / relieved / surprised*
3. The coach was <u>annoyed</u> that we ignored his advice. *angry / disappointed / afraid / aware*
4. I <u>knew</u> that not everyone agreed with me. *proud / pleased / aware / grateful*
5. I'm <u>amazed</u> that such a famous film is so boring. *grateful / sad / surprised / doubtful*

■ **Exercise 19** Choose the correct forms.

1. Though experts argue about the details, __ doubt that the world is becoming warmer.
   (a) there is not   (b) there is no   (c) it is not   (d) it is no

2. We never considered the possibility __ our flight would be canceled.
   (a) of   (b) for   (c) that   (d) if

3. I'm grateful __ I live in a city where the arts are taken seriously.
   (a) that   (b) for   (c) about   (d) as

4. We were thankful __ their help when we were stuck with no place to stay.
   (a) of   (b) that   (d) to   (d) for

5. Growing up, Tyler's character was shaped by __ that there were no other kids around.
   (a) a fact   (b) the fact   (b) that fact   (c) the fact was

7.9 Reporting with noun clauses and other structures

We can report what people say **directly**, using the original words (*He said, "I'm ready"*) or **indirectly** (*He said he was ready*). The box shows the basics of reporting complete sentences. Details are in later sections. In general, when we speak of the grammar of reporting, the rules apply not only to speaking but to written communication and thoughts.

In both direct and indirect reporting, we use an **attribution phrase** (*They say, She asked*) referring to the source of the words. In the box, the reporting verbs are present tense. Past reporting verbs often affect tenses in the following clause (7.10).

Reporting complete sentences directly and indirectly: common patterns

Direct reporting	Indirect reporting
After the attribution phrase, use a comma. Put quotation marks around the reported words. Put the end punctuation (. ? !) inside the quotation marks.	Do not use quotation marks. Do not put a comma before the reported words. Use end punctuation (. ? !) that fits the whole sentence, not the reported part
1. *She asks, "What is wrong?"*	2. *She asks what is wrong. (?)*
Do not use *that* in direct reporting of a complete sentence.	Use *that* (optionally) for an indirectly reported statement.
3. *She says ~~that~~, "I want to know."*	4. *She says (that) she wants to know.*
Report the exact words. (For exceptions, see a composition textbook. Look up *brackets* in the index.)	Use pronouns that reflect your own perspective (as the person reporting), not the perspective of the person whose words you are reporting.
5. *She says, **"My phone isn't working."***	6. *She says **her phone isn't working.***
To report a question, use *ask* or *say*.	To report a question indirectly, use *ask*.
7. *She **asks / says**, "What's wrong with it?"*	8. *She **asks** what is wrong with it.*
To report a command (an imperative) directly, use *say*.	To report a command indirectly, use an infinitive after *tell* or *ask* + an indirect object (less commonly *say*, with no indirect object).
9. *She says, "Call me."*	10. *She **tells me / asks me / says to** call her.* (~~told to~~, said ~~me~~, said ~~to me~~)

The attribution phrase in direct reporting may be between parts of a sentence (11) or at the end (12), and an attribution phrase may go with more than one sentence (11). Notice the punctuation.

11 *"Unfortunately," he said, "my flight was canceled. I'll have to take the next one."*
12 *"You can trust me," he said. "How can I be sure?" she asked.*

Exercise 20 Punctuate the sentences. Add periods, commas, question marks, and quotation marks where they are needed. Indicate which letters should be capitalized. Fill the blanks with appropriate forms. When a verb is required, use present tense. The sentences are from 7.9. To check your answers, look at the same-numbered sentences in 7.9.

Direct reporting	Indirect reporting
1. She asks what is wrong	2. She asks what is wrong
3. She says I want to know	4. She says that she wants to know
5. She says my phone isn't working right	6. She says ___ phone isn't working right
7. She ___ / ___ what's wrong with it	8. She ___ what is wrong with it
9. She says call me	10. She ___ ___ / ___ ___ / ___ ___ call her
11. Unfortunately he said my flight was canceled I'll have to take the next one (direct)	
12. You can trust me he said how can I be sure she asked (direct)	

Exercise 21 Write an indirect report for each directly reported sentence and vice versa.

1. He always asks, "What's on TV?"
2. She says that TV is boring.
3. He says, "I like it."
4. She says that she prefers to read.

Exercise 22 Choose the right forms. More than one answer may be correct.

1. The researchers say ___ need more money.
   (a) that   (b) they   (c) to   (d) that they

2. We ___ our good luck would continue.
   (a) wondered   (b) wondered whether   (c) wondered if   (d) wondered that

3. When they ___ I put up with so much inconvenience, I couldn't answer.
   (a) said why do   (b) asked why do   (c) said why   (d) asked why

4. My parents always told me ___ friends.
   (a) I should be kind to my   (b) that should be kind to my
   (c) you should be kind to your   (d) that I should be kind to my

5. At the lab, the employee at the desk always asks ___ sign in.
   (a) to you   (b) you to   (c) to   (d) you

6. The little boy ___ , "Is this bike yours?"
   (a) asked to me   (b) asked me   (c) asked   (d) said

7. The sign on the door ___ , "Back in ten minutes."
   (a) said that   (b) told that   (c) said   (d) told

7.10 Tenses, modals, and adverbials in reporting

In an indirect report with a past tense verb (*said, asked*), we usually **backshift** verbs in the following clause. For example, *He said, "I am ready"* becomes *He said he **was** ready.*

Direct reporting	Indirect reporting	
a. I said, "I **work** hard."	I said I **worked** hard.	Present (progressive) → past (progressive)
b. I said, "I **am working** hard."	I said I **was working** hard.	
c. I said, "I **have worked** hard."	I said I **had worked** hard.	Present perfect, past, or past perfect → past perfect
d. I said, "I **worked** hard."		
e. I said, "I **had worked** hard."		
f. I said, "I **have been working** hard."	I said I **had been working** hard.	Present perfect progressive, past progressive, past perfect progressive → past perfect progressive
g. I said, "I **was working** hard."		
h. I said, "I **had been working** hard."		
i. I said, "I **will** work hard."	I said I **would** work hard.	will → would
j. I said, "I **can** work hard."	I said I **could** work hard.	can → could
k. I said, "I **may** work late."	I said I **might** work late.	may → might
l. I said, "**Shall** I work late?"	I asked if I **should** work late.	shall → should
m. I said, "I **should** work harder."	I said I **should** work harder.	*Should, could, would, must,* and *ought*: no change.
n. I said, "This is a difficult issue."	I said it was a difficult issue.	Pronouns and adverbials reflect the time and place of the reporting.
o. I said, "We need help now."	I said we needed help right away.	

We often do not backshift when the words we are reporting are still true (2). We almost always backshift after *thought, realized,* and *knew* (4).

Direct reporting	Indirect reporting	
1. He said, "I have a job."	2a. He said he **has** a job. OR	He still has a job.
	2b. He said he **had** a job.	The sentence does not indicate whether he still has a job or not.
3. I thought, "Something wrong."	4. I thought something was wrong.	Back-shifting is required. - ~~I thought something is wrong~~.

He asked who they were.

7.11 Reporting questions

When we report a question indirectly, we usually use *ask* and a noun clause beginning with a *wh* word. To report a *yes/no* question, we use *whether* or *if* (2). We do not use question word order (2.14); the subject precedes the verb (4). We do not use auxiliary DO. (See also 7.4.)

Direct reporting	Indirect reporting
1. *I said, "Will it hurt?"*	2. *I asked **whether** / **if** it would hurt.*
3. *He said, "Who **are** they?"*	4. *He asked who **they were**. (were they)*
5. *She always asks me, "Why do you work so hard?"*	6. *She always asks me why (do) I work so hard.*

■ **Exercise 23** Write an indirect report for each directly reported sentence and vice versa. Follow the rules for tense backshifting (7.10).

1. He said, "I have an extra ticket for Friday."
2. She said she was working Friday.
3. He said, "I forgot."
4. She asked if he knew what else he had forgotten.
5. He said, "Is it your birthday today?"
6. She said it was his.

7. He said, "I can't find my watch."
8. She asked if it was by the bed.
9. He said, "I looked there."
10. She asked where he had last seen it.
11. He said, "I don't know."
12. She said he should look on his wrist.

13. She said, "You look tired."
14. He said he had been working too hard.
15. She asked, "What are you working on?"
16. He said he was writing a novel.
17. She said, "How many pages have you written?"
18. He said he hadn't started yet.

■ **Exercise 24** **One** of the underlined parts in each item is a mistake. Find it and correct it.

1. A first-grade teacher <u>asked the children</u> in her class what they <u>wanted</u> to be when they <u>grow up</u>. Everyone answered and then one boy <u>asked the teacher</u> what she wanted to be when she grew up.

2. In a lesson about dinosaurs, a teacher asked her students <u>whether</u> anyone knew why there <u>are</u> no dinosaurs today. One child said people <u>catch</u> them and <u>put</u> them all in museums.

3. When I was about five, my sister explained <u>to me</u> that most doctors and lawyers <u>were</u> rich. She said that people with other jobs <u>didn't</u> have so much money. After learning that, I thought people <u>buy</u> their jobs and only rich doctors and lawyers <u>had</u> the money to buy good ones.

4. A kindergarten teacher asked her pupils why it <u>was</u> important not to drink from another person's glass. Cassie said that you <u>could</u> get germs that way. Mario said it <u>was</u> impolite. Sam said, "At my house, most of the glasses <u>had</u> beer in them!"

5. A four-year-old <u>asked her daddy</u> where babies <u>come</u> from, and he <u>said</u>, "From the hospital." Later she had to go to the hospital for minor surgery. Before they went, she asked her daddy if <u>she's</u> going to get a baby at the hospital too.

Chapter 7   Noun clauses and reporting   Grammar Advantage **217**

■ **Exercise 25** Below are some questions often asked in job interviews. Report each question directly and indirectly. (Hints for changes in the indirect report are in parentheses.) *Use They ask* or *They may ask*. (*They* may represent a group or, informally, an individual.)

1. Why do you want this job? (Indirect: *this* → *the*.)
2. How did you find out about the job?
3. How has your education prepared you to work here? (Indirect: *here* → *there*.)
4. What are your strengths?
5. What are your weaknesses?
6. Are you willing to relocate?
7. What do you know about our company? (Indirect: change *our*.)
8. Why did you decide to leave your current job?
9. Where would you like to be in your career five years from now? (Indirect: *in five years*)
10. How do you cope with stress on the job?
11. How do you want to improve yourself in the next year?
12. How would you describe your working style?
13. Who has influenced you most?
14. Who are your heroes?
15. What salary are you seeking?
16. Are you able to start work tomorrow? (Indirect: *the next day*.)
17. Do you have any questions for us? (Indirect: Change *us*.)

■ **Exercise 26** Imagine you have met someone at a friend's party. To make small talk, which questions below might you ask and which would you not ask? Create sentences beginning with *I might/would ask* OR *I would not ask*… (Use *him, her* or *them*.)

Examples:

Are you having a good time? → I would not ask whether he (she) is having a good time.
What kind of music do you like? → I might ask what kind of music he (she) likes.

1. Are you employed?
2. Do you like to travel?
3. How long have you lived in this city?
4. Where do you live?
5. Have you seen any good movies lately?
6. Do you have any plans for the weekend?
7. What sign of the zodiac were you born under?
8. What TV shows do you like?
9. How did you meet our host?
10. How much money do you make?
11. Are you religious?
12. Are you interested in politics?
13. Who do you live with?
14. Do you have a family?
15. Where did you grow up?
16. When is your birthday?
17. Are you married?
18. Are you a morning person?

■ **Exercise 27** Gertrude Stein was a 20th-century writer. She was famous for being described (especially by herself) as a genius, for expecting others (especially Miss Toklas, her lifelong companion) to do everything for her, and for writing books that no one understood. She did not like to use conventional punctuation. The passage below, from one of her books, uses a lot of directly reported speech, but it is not punctuated in the usual way. As a result, it may be hard to read. Rewrite it using conventional punctuation. The first line, indirectly reported, needs no change. Start with the second line.

There was [a photographer] who came in and said he was sent to do a layout of me. A layout, I said yes he said what is that I said oh he said it is four or five pictures of you doing anything. All right I said what do you want me to do. Well he said there is your airplane bag suppose you unpack it oh I said Miss Toklas always does that oh no I could not do that, well he said there is the telephone suppose you make a phone call well I said yes but I never do Miss Toklas always does that, well he said what can you do, well I said I can put my hat on and take my hat off and I can put my coat on and I can take it off and I like water I can drink a glass of water all right he said do that so I did that and he photographed while I did that.

*Gertrude Stein, *Everybody's Autobiography* (slightly adapted)

He told us to stop.

7.12 Reporting commands and requests

- We use infinitives to report commands (2.15.2) indirectly, usually with *tell* as the reporting verb (2a). We sometimes use *say* (2b).
- *Tell* requires an indirect object (*tell **someone** to*). *Say* does not usually allow an indirect object (*say someone to*).
- To report a request in the form of an imperative, we use *ask* and an infinitive, usually with an indirect object (4).
- To indirectly report a request in the form of a question (6), we follow the rules for reporting questions (6a; see 7.10) or use an infinitive (6b).

Direct reporting	Indirect reporting
1. *He said, "Stop." He said, "Don't Move."*	2a. *He told us to stop. He told us not to move.* (He told to)
	2b. *He said to stop. He said not to move.* (said me, said to me)
3. *She said, "Please call me Ann." She said, "Please don't interrupt."*	4. *She asked us to call her Ann. She asked us not to interrupt.* (The indirect object *us* is required because it provides the implied subject of *call*: **We** will call her Ann.)
5. *She said, "Can I join you?"*	6a. *She asked (me) whether/if she could join us.* (could she)
	6b. *She asked to join us.* There is no indirect object (asked me).

7.13 Verbs that are not followed by a *that* clause

Most verbs (*criticize, discuss, talk, want*) are not followed by a *that* clause or direct reporting even if they seem similar to the verbs in 7.7.

WRONG	REVISED
1 *They criticized that he was rude.* →	*They criticized him for being rude.*
2 *He talked that things had changed.* → / *about the fact that things had changed.*	*He talked about how things had changed* / *He said that things had changed.*
3. *She talked, "It doesn't matter."* →	*She said (that) it didn't matter.*
4. *They want that we remain here.* →	*They want us to remain here / prefer that we remain here.*
5. *He described that everything looked new.* →	*He said that everything looked new.*

■ **Exercise 28** Choose the best answer. More than one may be correct.

1. When the sales clerk started demonstrating a more expensive product, I __ make it short.
   (a) said to   (b) told him to   (c) said that   (d) told him that

2. College teachers often __ call them by their first names.
   (a) ask students to   (b) ask students   (c) tell students to   (d) tell students

3. Did the teachers at your university tell you __ cite Wikipedia as a source?
   (a) not   (b) don't   (c) not to   (d) that not

4. They __ that the concert was sold out.
   (a) told   (b) said   (c) asked   (d) talked

5. The clerk __ that we should buy the service agreement.
   (a) wanted   (b) told   (c) asked us   (d) said

6. Have you ever asked __ record a lecture so you can listen to it later?
   (a) for   (b) if you could   (c) that you   (d) to

Chapter 7

■ **Exercise 29** Fill the blanks using appropriate forms of the words. Use one or two words in a blank.

| ask | be | I | have (x2) | me (x3) | to (x2) | should |
| sound | take (x2) | talk | that | would | | |

When I was about to leave for the U.S., I asked my grandmother for advice. She told __ work hard and go to bed at a reasonable hour. She reminded __ I __ promised to call or write at least once a week. When I __ my favorite teacher, she said I __ a wide variety of courses and follow a strict study schedule. I began to think, "This __ like a lot of work!" Then I __ to my father. He told __ fun courses as well as difficult ones. He said that I __ be young only once and that universities __ great places to try new things. He said that he __ enjoyed his college days and recommended __ do the same.

I insisted on paying.

USAGE GUIDE

7.14 Reporting special types of speech indirectly

- Reporting suggestions, demands, accusations, and other specific types of speech indirectly involves a variety of verbs and patterns, mostly related to infinitives and gerunds. Some of these are shown below.
- The indirect reports do not correspond to particular direct reports; the direct reports in parentheses are just examples.
- We do not usually use these verbs in direct reporting. For direct reporting of any speech, we can use *say*.

a. He **accused me of copying**. ("You copied this paper." "This paper is copied.")
b. She **advised us to keep quiet**. ("You should keep quiet." "If I were you, I'd keep quiet.")
c. He **criticized me for laughing**. ("It was rude to laugh." "You shouldn't have laughed.")
d. He **demanded to talk to the chef**. ("I demand to talk to the chef!" "Let me talk to the chef!")
e. I **insisted on paying**. ("I insist on paying." "I'm paying. Don't argue with me.")
f. She **invited us to sit down**. ("Please sit down." "Would you like to sit down?")
g. I **offered to carry her bag**. ("Can I carry your bag for you?" "Let me carry your bag.")
h. I **suggested going to dinner**. ("Let's go to dinner." "Why don't we go to dinner?")

All of these verbs occur in other patterns (*suggested that we go, advised keeping*), but all of them also are not allowed in certain patterns (*suggested me to, criticized that I*).

■ **Exercise 30** Paraphrase the direct report indirectly, using the suggested verb.

1. He said (to me), "You copied my paper!" *accuse*
2. She said (to us), "You should keep quiet." *advise*
3. He said (to me), "You shouldn't have laughed." *criticize*
4. He said, "Let me talk to the chef!" *demand*
5. I said, "I'm paying!" *insist*
6. She said (to us), "Please sit down." *invite*
7. He said, "Can I pay?" *offer*
8. I said, "Let's go to dinner." *suggest*

■ **Exercise 31** Paraphrase each report indirectly, using one of the suggested verbs. For most some of them, there is more than one possibility. If pronouns are required, use *him* and *his*.

    accuse   advise   criticize   demand   insist   invite   offer   suggest

1. She said, "Let's order a pizza."
2. She said, "You should quit smoking."
3. She said, "Please join me."
4. She said, "You never pay attention."
5. She said, "You stole my fork!"
6. She said, "Leave me alone!"
7. She said, "May I pay for your ticket?"
8. She said, "I'm paying for your ticket!"

Usage Guide

■ **Exercise 32** Using a dictionary, fill the blank with the word that fits best in terms of grammar and meaning. Relevant sections are given in parentheses. A few of the words have not been introduced; they are in italics. You may want to add them in a marginal note to the appropriate section. In some cases, more than one of the words is correct, with a difference in meaning.

claim (7.7.2a)   judge (7.4)   question (7.4)   suggest (7.7.2a)

1. The authors ___ that their findings might be related to age.
2. The authors ___ the assumption that more exercise is always a good thing.
3. One job of a teacher is to ___ whether students are prepared to go to the next level.
4. Most scholars dismiss the ___ that Shakespeare did not write the works generally attributed to him.

imply (7.7.2a)   *measured* (7.4)   observe (7.7.1)   *speculated* (7.7.1)

5. The lecturer said nothing directly about standardized tests, but in his conclusion he ___ that he is critical of them.
6. "Are these two conditions linked? Quite possibly!" the lecturer said. In other words, the lecturer ___ that the two conditions are linked.
7. The project began when the author ___ that he always performed better on tests after eating chocolate.
8. We ___ how much the participants remembered by giving them a test.

advise (7.7.2b)   *determine* (7.7.1)   explain (7.7.2b)   *predict* (7.7.1a)

9. How can you ___ to your parents that you need money again?
10. Experts ___ that the world's population will double in the next 100 years.
11. The committee is expected to ___ that services be reduced.
12. We need to ___ whether more funds are needed.

finding (7.8.1)   issue (7.4.5)   perception (7.8.1)   proposal (7.8.1)

13. The researchers were surprised by the ___ that 73% of the participants preferred product B.
14. You're ignoring the ___ of how much we should emphasize competition.
15. No one supported Ryan's ___ that we adjourn.
16. There is a widespread ___ that the candidate is less trustworthy than her rivals.

positive (7.8.2)   possible (7.5)   surprised (7.8.2)   unaware (7.8.2)

17. I was ___ that I didn't sleep well after such a hard day.
18. I read the paper carefully, but it's ___ that I misunderstood a few things.
19. Are you ___ that you didn't make any mistakes?
20. Pay attention to your work. You seem ___ that you're making lots of errors.

USAGE GUIDE

According to the author...

7.15 *According to* and other phrases for attribution or commenting

We can indicate the source of information in direct and indirect reports with the phrase *according to* at the beginning of a sentence (a), between parts (b), or at the end (c). We do not use *according to ~~me~~*.

  a. *According to Nicholas Kristof, gender inequality is the greatest moral challenge of the 21st century.*
  b. *The international community has not fulfilled its commitments to women's equality, according to a United Nations report.*
  c. *The education of girls, according to UNICEF, is one of the keys to women's empowerment.*

In the same way that we use phrases such as *they say, we agreed*, and *it is true* before noun clauses, we can use these phrases between parts of a sentence (d) or at the end (e) to indicate the source of the information (d, e) or comment on it (f). *That* is not included.

  d. *Success, my father always said, comes from a combination of effort and opportunity.*
  e. *Fresh vegetables may have fewer nutrients than frozen ones, research has shown.*
  f. *Individualism, it can be argued, is the core American value.*

We can introduce an attribution phrase with *as* (*as the author says, as Jones argues*). Using *as* indicates our agreement with the reported information.

g. *True learning, as Harris says, requires engagement.*	The writer of the sentence agrees with Harris.
h. *Sports, Harris says, are a waste of time.*	The writer may or may not agree.

7.16 Directly reporting parts of sentences

We often quote sentence parts — clauses, phrases, and individual words — rather than reporting a whole sentence directly. We do this often in combination with paraphrasing from an article or book. The example below illustrates the use of quoted sentence parts in combination with paraphrasing. As in the example, we often use quotation marks around a title as well.

In "The Yin and Yang of American Culture," Eun Kim criticizes American society for being "**preoccupied with choices.**" For example, she points to "**soda, ice cream, chips, and juice in seemingly endless flavors**" in stores. According to Kim, Americans should "**relinquish their preoccupation with choices**." Doing so, she suggests, could be "**a liberating experience.**"	← a title ← An adjective phrase ← A noun phrase ← A predicate (2.2.4) ← A noun phrase

When you quote, it's important to make sure that you are either quoting a complete sentence (a) or quoting a sentence part <u>and</u> fitting it correctly into your own sentence (b).

  a. According to Kim, "Having no choice can be a blessing at times." This is correct if Kim uses these exact words. After *According to X*, we expect a complete sentence.
  b. Kim describes the lack of choice as "a blessing at times." After *describe X as*, we expect a phrase, not a complete sentence. WRONG: Kim describes the lack of choice as "Having no choice can be a blessing at times."

Usage Guide

7.17 When to include *that*

When should you avoid omitting *that*?

If you always include *that* – even when it could be omitted – you are less likely to make mistakes. Under certain conditions, we tend to avoid omitting *that*:

- When we have *that* clauses joined by *and* (a)
- When the *that* clause follows a noun (b)
- When there is a word (like an adverb) between the verb and the *that* clause (c)
- When the *that* clause begins with something (like an adverb) other than the subject (d)
- When the *that* clause follows a form of BE (e).

　a. She says **that** she loves movies **and that** Ang Lee is her favorite director.
　b. The idea **that** form follows function was popularized by the architect Louis Sullivan.
　c. You need to explain clearly **that** these ideas are from a source.
　d. He told me **that** last week he had to go to the hospital.
　e. One problem with rental bikes is **that** they usually don't include a helmet.

7.18 *Feel like, look like, sound like, seem like*

After *feel, look, sound,* and *seem,* we can use *like* before a noun clause (a). We don't include *that*. We can also use empty *it*, with the noun clause as a delayed subject (b) (7.5, 2.9).

　a. The dog looks like he wants to go out again. I feel like I'm his servant.
　b. ~ It seems like he's in charge. ~ It sounds like you and the dog need to have a talk.

7.19 *Like it that..., make it clear that...* etc.

We can use empty *it* and a *that* clause after verbs of liking and disliking (a). This usage is somewhat informal. We can use empty *it* optionally in the expression *make it clear*, followed by a *that* clause or a *wh* clause (b). Less commonly, we use other adjectives after *make it*, including *(un)likely, inevitable, possible. It* is required. We use infinitives in similar constructions (6.8).

　a. Her brothers **hate it / don't like it that** she gets good grades without trying.
　b. You need to **make (it) clear that** this is your own idea / how your idea is different from his.
　c. Deforestation **makes it likely that** many species will soon become extinct.

7.20 *Consider, find, regard,* and *see*

How to avoid overusing "I think"

The examples show how we can use constructions with *consider, find, regard,* and *see* with noun clauses and other constructions to avoid overusing *think*.

a. We **consider it likely that** rural areas will continue to lose population. We **consider it unfortunate that** this problem has received so little attention.	After *consider it* we use adjectives that express likelihood or an evaluation. The *it* is empty *it* (7.5). We do not usually include *is* (*consider it is unlikely*).
b. I **found it interesting that** only two people applied for the job.	After *find it* we use adjectives that express an evaluation.
c. I **regard it / see it as essential that** we not let this opportunity pass.	After *regard it* and *see it* we use *as* before the adjective. If the adjective expresses urgency, the verb may be subjunctive (7.7.3).
d. I **consider/find** quiz shows boring. I **see** them as/**regard** them as a waste of time.	*Consider/find* + object + description *Regard/see* + object + *as* + description

Usage Guide

■ **Exercise 33** Put the words in the right order to create a sentence. Add empty *it*, a BE verb if it is needed, and *that*.

1. We weren't worried about the storm. *wouldn't / looked / last long / it* (x 2) / *like*

2. Jacob didn't feel welcome. *was / like / intruding / felt / he* (x 2)

3. I guess the party was a success. *everyone / a good time / like / sounds / had / it*

4. People are so busy! *seems / they / like / no time / have / to relax / it*

5. The kids were not happy. *had to stay / that / didn't / it / they* (x 2) / *indoors / like*

6. Two of my co-workers have quit. *likely / makes / that / be promoted / it / that / I'll*

■ **Exercise 34** Match words from each column to create a sentence. Add *it, as*, and *that* when you need them. There is more than one correct way.

Example: *I found it funny that all of us showed up wearing the same colors.*

0. √ I found	essential	no one qualified for financial aid.
1. The girls regard	unfortunate	every student participate.
2. We found	unfair	He will get a pay raise within a year.
3. The teachers see	likely	√ all of us showed up wearing the same colors.
4. Adam considers	√ funny	only boys are allowed to play football.

5. Sarah found	beneficial	all my classes were scheduled on just two days.
6. We considered	convenient	his children grew up in a bilingual neighborhood.
7. He saw	annoying	our son develop good table manners.
8. I found	important	she had to wait so long.

■ **Exercise 35** Choose the right forms.

1. The waiter said that the fish was fresh and ___ one of their most popular dishes.
   (a) seemed as   (b) considered that   (c) regarded that   (d) that it was

2. Just when ___ we were going to be able to enjoy a quiet evening, the phone rang.
   (a) it seemed as   (b) it seemed like   (c) seemed as   (d) seemed like

3. Negative attitudes on both sides made ___ a compromise could be reached.
   (a) it unlikely that   (b) unlikely that   (c) to be unlikely   (d) it was unlikely

4. Do you ___ it as important that husbands and wives share housework equally?
   (a) consider   (b) think   (c) see   (d) feel like

5. We consider ___ important that meetings start on time.
   (a) it's   (b) it   (c) that   (d) as

Usage Guide

7.21 Recreated or typical speech in academic writing

Two ideas for using reporting in academic writing

We use directly reported speech not only when we quote an individual's words but when we recreate speech from memory or imagine typical speech. These examples show how.

7.21.1 Direct reporting for recreated speech Julia Tabbut tells a story that could be used in a paper about cross-cultural learning. She recreates the speech that she recalls. She also includes indirect reporting (of a thought): *Then I realized that all along they...*

A few years ago I spent six months living in Sri Lanka. When my British friends and I were walking in the village (never in cities or towns), Sri Lankans would often stop us and ask, "Where are you going?" We never wanted to answer. "They think they need to know everything we're doing," complained my friends. "How rude!" But I like to think the best of people, so I thought, "Well, maybe they just want to practice their English, and that's the only phrase they know." Then I made friends with more Sri Lankan people, and I learned more of the language, and when I walked through villages with my Sri Lankan friends, I was really surprised. "Koheda yanne?" people always asked us. That, of course, means "Where are you going?" And my Sri Lankan friends always answered! Then I realized that all along they were just being friendly, and also being kind enough to translate for us. We had been rude to not answer them!
  - Julia Tabbut

7.21.2 Direct reporting for typical speech In this excerpt from a book on American culture, Gary Althen uses direct reporting to support the main point of a paragraph. He reports not what an individual said but what people typically say. Althen also includes indirect reporting (of a thought): *The have the idea that what happens...*

Americans are generally less concerned about history and traditions than are people from older societies. "History doesn't matter," many of them will say. "It's the future that counts." They look ahead. They have the idea that what happens in the future is within their control, or at least subject to their influence...   - Gary Althen, *American Ways*, 3rd ed., p. 15

7.22 Indirect reporting and paraphrasing

Paraphrasing, an important skill in academic writing, involves more than the minimal changes that we make in indirect reporting. Compare the indirect report below with the paraphrase. Proper paraphrasing in academic writing involves significant changes.

Direct reporting (quoting)	Indirect reporting (not a true paraphrase)	An acceptable paraphrase
He said, "With old friends and former foes, we'll work tirelessly to lessen the nuclear threat and roll back the specter of a warming planet."	Not acceptable: *He said that with old friends and former foes, he would work tirelessly to lessen the nuclear threat and roll back the specter of a warming planet.*	*In his inaugural address, the president promised to work with allies and former enemies to combat nuclear proliferation and global warming.*

— President Barack Obama's first inaugural address

Usage Guide

Lexical grammar: the grammar of individual words

7.23 Noun clauses and lexical grammar

Noun clauses, like gerunds and infinitives, involve not only general grammar rules but facts about particular verbs and groups of verbs — that is, lexical grammar. First, many verbs, nouns, and adjectives may be followed by more than one type of complement. Sometimes the same verb has different patterns depending on the meaning. When you learn a verb, you also have to learn what types of complement it takes, if any. Examples in a dictionary or online may help. Second, verbs with similar meanings may have different patterns. The choice may seem arbitrary. Third, the grammar of noun clauses, like the grammar of gerunds and infinitives, also involves noun and pronoun objects. Again, which verbs allow which patterns may seem arbitrary.

Noun clause or relative clause?

7.24 Comparing noun clauses with relative clauses

Noun clauses	Relative clauses

That introduces the clause, but it is not a subject or an object (a).
 	
a. *Who introduced the idea that <u>form follows function</u>?*
    SUBJECT VERB OBJECT
	That is either a subject (b) or an object (c) in the relative clause.
	
	b. *We need an idea <u>that</u> will impress people.*
	    SUBJECT VERB OBJECT
	c. *They liked the idea <u>that</u> we suggested.*
	    OBJECT VERB
	    SUBJECT

Which cannot introduce a noun clause. WRONG: *the idea ~~which~~ form follows function*	Also correct: *the/an idea which ....*
Only **certain nouns** (7.8.1) can be followed by a noun clause.	**Any noun** can be followed by a relative clause.

Precise writing with noun clauses

7.25 Using noun clauses to make your writing more precise

Noun clauses can help you make your writing more precise. For example, if you wish to summarize and comment on something you have read, you can say more than "I agree with the author" or "I agree with the article."

Less precise:	More precise, with noun clauses:
I agree with the article.	*I agree **that the use of laptops during lectures can be a distraction**, but I question **whether banning them is the best response**.* (See 7.3 and 7.4.)
We need to think about the future.	*We need to think about **how technology is likely to evolve in the next decade**.* (7.4)
The author's suggestion surprised me.	*The author's suggestion **that students should be prohibited from using laptops in class** surprised me.* (7.8.1)

Chapter 7 — Noun clauses and reporting

7.26 Problems with noun clauses and reporting

Problems	Revisions	Comments
1. They told me that how I could save money. They told me how that I could save money.	They told me that I could save money. OR They told me how I could save money.	Use a *that* clause or a *wh* clause. Don't mix the two. (7.2, 7.4)
2. Do you agree with marijuana should be legal?	Do you agree that marijuana should be legal? OR Do you agree with the author that…	Don't use a *that* clause after a preposition. (7.2, 7.8)
3. I asked what did it mean? I don't know how will it end.	I asked what it meant. I don't know how it will end.	Don't use question grammar (DO, auxiliary + subject order) in noun clauses. (7.4)
4. Tell me what happened?	Tell me what happened.	The whole sentence, not the noun clause, determines the punctuation. (7.4)
5. She didn't know the job was taken or not.	She didn't know whether the job was taken (or not).	Use *whether* for an embedded yes/no question. (7.4)
6. I wonder whether if they know.	I wonder whether they know. OR I wonder if they know.	Use *whether* or *if*, not both. (7.4)
7. Why is important that we wait?	Why is it important that we wait?	Don't omit empty *it*. (7.5)
8. I need to revise my paper. The main reason, it's too long.	The main reason is that it's too long.	Remember the BE verb and *that*. (7.6)
9. He said me that it was free. He told that it was free. He explained me that it…	He said that OR told me that it was free. OR I was told that it was free. He explained (to me) that it was…	Use an indirect object after *tell* but not *say* or *explain*. For other verbs and patterns, see 7.7.
10. I wish I can help you. I hope I could help you.	I wish I could help you. I hope I can help you.	See 7.7.4 for patterns with *wish* and *hope*.
11. What do you think of the idea which boys and girls should be educated separately?	What do you think of the idea that boys and girls should be educated separately?	Use *that*, not *which*, to introduce a noun complement. (7.8) (*Which* may be used in a relative clause. See Ch. 8.)
12. She said enjoy yourselves.	She said, "Enjoy yourselves." OR She told us to enjoy ourselves.	Don't mix direct and indirect reporting. (7.9)
13. He said that "I don't care."	He said, "I don't care." He said that he didn't care.	Don't use *that* with direct reporting. (7.9)
14. They said if they could help.	They asked if they could help.	Report a question with *ask*. (7.9, 7.11)
15. I didn't realize I am late. I thought I am on time.	I didn't realize I was late. I thought I was on time.	Follow rules for backshifting when required. (7.10)
16. He told me that don't worry.	He told me not to worry. He told me, "Don't worry."	Rules for reporting commands: 7.12.
17. They talked that the weather was great.	They said that everything was fine. They talked about the great weather.	Use noun clauses only after verbs that allow it. (7.12)

Chapter 8

Relative clauses

IN THIS CHAPTER

Adding complex information to nouns

using grammar for tight writing

adding detail and color to your writing

Chapter 8
Relative clauses

Chapter 8: Relative clauses 231

8.1	Relative clauses in context	233
8.2	What are relative clauses?	233
8.3	Subjects: *a woman who was lost*	234
8.4	Objects: *the woman (whom) we helped*	234
8.5	Objects of a preposition: *the friends we stayed with*	235
8.6	Whose: *a woman whose name I've forgotten*	238
8.7	*Where, when, why* and *the way*	239
8.8	Restrictive and nonrestrictive clauses	242
8.9	Relative clauses that modify a sentence	244
8.10	Clauses with *of whom* or *of which*	244
8.11	Relative clauses like (*the candidate*) *they say will win*	244
8.12	Reduced relative clauses	245
8.13	Phrases like *a book belonging to the library*	247
8.14	Past participle or *–ing* form?	248
8.15	Appositives	249
8.16	Adjectives and prepositional phrases after nouns	250
8.17	Nonrestrictive reduced clauses	250
8.18	Relative clauses that modify pronouns	251
8.19	Headless relative clauses	252
8.20	Infinitive relatives	252
8.21	Relative clauses and sentence structure	255
8.22	Relative clauses compared to other structures that modify nouns	256
8.23	Usage guide Grammar checkers' advice on *that* and *which*	257
8.24	Usage guide Using relative clauses to express details	257
8.25	Usage guide Avoiding wordy relative clauses	257
8.26	Usage guide Relative clauses in definitions	258
8.27	Usage guide Using relative clauses for a tight writing style	259
8.28	Problems with relative clauses	264

Chapter 8 — Relative clauses

8.1 Relative clauses in context

People who live in glass houses shouldn't throw stones. The underlined words are a relative clause. A relative clause can follow a noun in any part of a sentence. It often begins with *who* or *that* or *which*.

KEY
Ch. 6 = Chapter 6
Ex. 23 = Exercise 23
5.2 = Chapter 5, section 2
2.14.3 = Chapter 2, section 14, subsection 3
(a) = an example

■ **Exercise 1** Based on what you already know, identify relative clauses in the passage. (If you prefer, first read 8.2.) The first two relative clauses are already underlined.

How do you find a major <u>that matches well with the things you enjoy doing</u> (your interests), the things <u>that you're good at</u> (your skills), and the things that you believe in (your values)? One tool that many college counselors recommend is based on occupational themes. The psychologist John Holland created this scheme on the basis of two observations: People tend to seek out careers that fit their personalities, and careers can be classified according to the type of personalities that flourish in them.

In using this method, counselors ask students to answer a series of questions about their preferences. Their answers reveal how well their personalities match six themes, which are identified by the letters RIASEC. These letters stand for six personal attributes: *realistic, investigative, artistic, social, enterprising,* and *conventional*. Students who score high on the attribute *realistic*, for example, are likely to do well in fields like engineering, which requires solving concrete problems in an organized and structured way. Students who score high on the attribute *enterprising* are likely to thrive in business, which requires competition and persuasion.

8.2 What are relative clauses?

- Relative clauses give information about people, things, and places. They are subordinate clauses connected to a noun or noun phrase in another clause (a).
- A relative clause immediately follows the noun it modifies (b).
- Relative clauses are usually introduced by a relativizer (a relative pronoun): *that, which, who, whom,* or *whose* (c-f).
- We normally use *who/whom* for people and *which* or *that* for things.
- We can sometimes omit the relativizer (g); see 8.4.
- Some relative clauses can be reduced (h); see 8.12.

a.	We helped a woman **who was lost**.	The relative clause modifies a *woman*.
b.	The map **that she was using** looked old. (The map looked ~~old that she~~....)	
c.	People **who** live in glass houses shouldn't throw stones. (~~which~~)	
d.	A clause is a structure **that / which** includes a subject and a verb. (~~who~~)	
e.	They help children **whose** parents can't support them. (children ~~who their~~) (8.6)	
f.	The town **where** I grew up had no high school. (~~that~~) (8.7)	
g.	The map **she was using** looked old (8.4).	
h.	We ate clams (that were) cooked over an open fire and chatted with people (who were) passing by (8.12).	

a woman
who was lost

8.3 Clauses with relativizers that function as subjects

- We use the relativizer *who*, *that*, or *which* as the subject in a relative clause (a-c).
- We use a plural verb if the noun in the main clause is plural (b).
- We don't omit a subject relativizer (e, f, g).
- The clause normally comes right after the noun it modifies (h). This is true for all types of relative clauses.

a. *We helped a woman **who / that was lost**.*	**She** was lost.
b. *Other people **who / that were (was) passing by** didn't notice her.*	**They** were passing by. *People* is plural, so *were* is used in the relative clause.
c. *She had a map **which / that looked really old**.*	**It** looked old.
d. *The map **which / that caused the problem** looked really old.*	**It** caused the problem.
e. *I have a map **that** shows all the tourist attractions.*	*I have a map shows* … *That* is needed as the subject of the clause.
f. *There's a doorman **who** can give us directions.*	*There's a doorman can* … *Who* is needed as the subject of the clause.
g. *There are some people **who** live their whole lives without leaving their hometown.*	*There are some people live* … *Who* is needed as the subject of the clause.
h. *The map that caused the problem looked old.*	*The map looked old that* …

the woman
(whom) we helped

8.4 Clauses with relativizers that function as objects:

- We use the relativizer *whom*, *who*, *which*, *that*, or Ø as the object in a relative clause (a–c). *Whom* is formal.
- The relative clause usually immediately follows the noun it modifies (d, e).
- We do not include an object pronoun in the relative clause (f).

a. *We didn't know the woman **whom / who / that / Ø** we helped.*	We helped **her**.
b. *The woman **whom / who / that / Ø** we helped was a stranger.*	
c. *Where did she get the map **which / that / Ø** she was using?*	She was using **it**.
d. *The map **which / that / Ø** she was using looked really old.*	
e. *The map looked really old that she was using.*	Use the word order in d.
f. … *the woman whom / that / Ø we helped her. The map that / which / that / Ø she was using it* …	

8.5 Clauses with relativizers that are objects of a preposition

- We use *whom, which, who, that* or *Ø* as the object of a preposition in a relative clause.
- We sometimes begin the clause with the preposition, followed by *which* or *whom*, in formal style.
- We do not include the object pronoun in the relative clause (e).

a.	Here's a photo of the friends **with whom** we stayed. *whom / who / that / Ø* we stayed **with**.	We stayed **with them**.
b.	This is the house **in which** I grew up. *which / that / Ø* I grew up **in**.	I grew up **in it**.
c.	The man **for whom** the town was named lived here. *whom / who / that / Ø* the town was named **for** lived here.	The town was named **for him**.
d.	*The friends* **to whom** I am closest live on a farm. *whom / who / that / Ø* I am closest **to** live on a farm.	I am closest **to them**.
e.	... the friends *whom / who / that / Ø* we stayed with ~~them~~. ... the house that I grew up in ~~it~~.	

the friends **we stayed with**

the friends **with whom we stayed**

■ **Exercise 2** Read the passage and identify:

- five relative clauses in which the relativizer functions as a subject (there are 12; 8.3)
- two relative clauses in which the relativizer functions as an object (there are five; 8.4)
- three in which the relative clause functions as the object of a preposition (there are six; 8.5)
- two that do not include a relativizer (there are six; 8.4 and 8.5).

How do you find a major that matches well with the things you enjoy doing (your interests), the things you're good at (your skills), and the things you believe in (your values)? One tool that many college counselors recommend is based occupational themes. The psychologist John Holland created this scheme on the basis of two observations: People tend to seek out careers that fit their personalities, and careers can be classified according to the type of personalities that flourish in them.

In using this method, counselors ask students to answer a series of questions about their preferences. Their answers reveal how well their personalities match six themes, which are identified by the letters RIASEC. These letters stand for six personal attributes: *realistic, investigative, artistic, social, enterprising*, and *conventional*. Students who score high on the attribute *realistic*, for example, are likely to do well in fields like engineering, which requires solving concrete problems in an organized and structured way. Students who score high on the attribute *enterprising* are likely to thrive in business, which requires competition and persuasion.

At the same time, counselors often point out that the major you choose will not necessarily determine the career you end up in. Some studies indicate that most people work in careers that aren't directly related to their undergraduate majors. Even if the job you get is related to your major, we live today in a world in which many people change careers several times. There are doctors who decide to become lawyers, and computer programmers who go into teaching. Moreover, some jobs that exist today will be obsolete in a few years, and careers that we haven't yet dreamed of will be available. As one counseling service put it, "The connection between the major that you choose now and the career that you'll find yourself in ten years from now is likely to be very small."

■ **Exercise 3** In the passage above, identify three relativizers that could be omitted (there are four).

HIGH PRIORITY

■ **Exercise 4** **Two or three** of the items below include mistakes. Find and fix them. Don't change anything in the other items.

1. People who don't read have no advantage over people who can't read.
2. Have you heard about the store in New York sells new husbands?
3. Do you still keep in touch with the friends you made in high school?
4. It's hard to write about a topic that you don't know very much about it.
5. A year in which the month of February has 29 days is called a leap year.
6. A paradox is a statement which seems to contradict itself, like "Less is more."
7. I'm always spending money I don't have on things I don't need.
8. Too many drivers these days are busy doing things that shouldn't be doing, like texting.

■ **Exercise 5** In the sentences below (based on Ex. 2), fill each blank with one or two words or Ø. To make the right choices, you need to think about the overall sentence structure, not just the structure of relative clauses. If you wish, review Ex. 2 first (for the content).

who   which   that   it   you   they   Ø

1. How do you find a major _____ matches well with the things you enjoy doing, the things you're good at, and the things _____ you believe in? One tool _____ many college counselors recommend _____ is based occupational themes.

2. People tend to seek out careers _____ fit their personalities, and careers _____ can be classified according to the type of personalities _____ flourish in them.

3. Students _____ score high on the attribute *realistic*, for example, are likely to do well in fields like engineering, which requires solving concrete problems in an organized and structured way. Students who score high on the attribute *enterprising* _____ are likely to thrive in business, which _____ requires competition and persuasion.

4. Most people _____ work in careers _____ aren't directly related to their undergraduate majors. Even if the job you get _____ is related to your major, we live today in a world in _____ many people change careers several times.

5. There are doctors _____ decide to become lawyers, and computer programmers _____ go into to teaching. Moreover, some jobs _____ exist today _____ will be obsolete in a few years, and careers that we haven't yet dreamed of _____ will be available.

6. As one counseling service put it, "The connection between the major that you choose _____ now and the career that _____ will find yourself in ten years from now _____ is likely to be very small."

Chapter 8 — Relative clauses — Grammar Advantage 237

■ **Exercise 6** Use the information from the second sentence to create a relative clause in the first one. Example: *I went to a wedding. I'll never forget it.* → *I went to a wedding (that) I'll never forget.*

1. At my sister's wedding, there was a soloist. She sang *"What's love got to do with it?"*
2. A band played at the party afterward. They performed hits from the nineties.
3. They played an old song. It always makes me cry.
4. Some of the songs made people get up and dance. My sister requested the songs.
5. Last year I went to a wedding. It lasted two hours.
6. A guest fell asleep. He was sitting right in front.
7. The priest talked really slowly. He performed the ceremony.
8. He told a long story. I didn't understand it very well.
9. I sat next to some people. I didn't really like them.
10. Do you remember the old man? We met him after the ceremony.
11. The man had a beard. I'm talking about him.
12. He told us about a group of musicians. He used to play with them.
13. If I get married, I want a simple ceremony. It won't last very long.
14. A short ceremony is best. People will remember it.
15. There might be songs. Everyone can sing along with them.
16. I won't invite any boring people. They don't know how to have fun.

■ **Exercise 7** Read the sentence on the right, followed by the question. Then expand the question, using a relative clause based on the first sentence. In the relative clause, use *you* and the pattern with the preposition at the end, as in the example.

0. You went to a movie.   How was it?   *How was the movie you went to?*
                                                    [Note: **the** movie]
1. You were looking at a magazine.   Where is it?
2. You live in a dormitory.   What's the name of it?
3. You were working on a project.   Did you finish it?
4. You were studying for a test.   Did you pass it?
5. You stayed at a hotel.   How was it?
6. You were looking for a book.   Did you find it?
7. You were listening to a podcast. Was it interesting?
8. You work at a lab.   Where is it?
9. You were studying with friends.   Who were they?
10. You were talking to a woman.   Who was she?

■ **Exercise 8** Expand each sentence with a relative clause based on the sentence in Ex. 7 with the same number. In the relative clause, use *I*. For example:

HIGH PRIORITY

0. The movie was great.   *The movie (that) I went to was great.*
1. The magazine is on the table.
2. The name of the dormitory is Sanford.
3. I finished the project.
4. I passed the test.
5. The hotel was a dump.
6. I found the document.
7. The podcast was interesting.
8. The lab is downtown.
9. The friends were my housemates.
10. The woman is a neighbor.

■ **Exercise 9** Relative clauses beginning with phrases like *in which* and *through which* (8.5) are common after certain nouns, especially in academic writing. The box below includes typical phases.

a case / context / situation / system **in which**	*the point / rate* **at which**
the circumstances **in / under which**	*the process* **by / through which**
the degree / extent **to which**	*the manner / way* **in which**

Complete each sentence with a preposition + *which*. Look up words you are not familiar with.

0. Can you imagine a situation … you would steal something? *Can you imagine a situation* **in which** *you would steal something?*
1. *Effect* is usually a noun, but there are some contexts … it is used as a verb.
2. An autocracy is a system … one person has unlimited power.
3. There are situations … telling a lie is the right thing to do.
4. Are there circumstances … the military should take over the government?
5. People usually don't realize the extent … emotions influence their decisions.
6. In science classes, power is sometimes defined as the rate … work is done.
7. In the Fahrenheit scale, what is the point … water boils?
8. Compromise is the process … opposing sides come to an agreement, with each giving something up.
9. In arguing against capital punishment, people sometimes point to cases … innocent people have been sentenced to death.
10. It's important for parents to be aware of the degree … a child may be influenced by her parents' bad habits.

a woman
whose name
I've forgotten

8.6 Relative clauses with *whose*

We use *whose* plus a noun to show possession. The noun after *whose* can be a subject (a) or an object (b) in the relative clause.

a. *I met a man* **whose ancestors immigrated from Poland**.	**His** ancestors immigrated.
b. *I bought my bike from a woman* **whose name I've forgotten**.	I've forgotten **her** name.

We can use *whose* with a place (c), an organization (d), or a thing (e) as well as a person.

c. *My ancestors came from a village* **whose name** *I can't pronounce.*
d. *I want to work for a company* **whose management shares my values**.
e. *This is an idea* **whose time has come**.

Chapter 8 — Relative clauses

8.7 Clauses with *where*, *when*, *why* and *the way*

We can use the relativizer *where* in a clause after a noun referring to a place, such as *area*, *city*, *house*, or *town* (a) as an alternative to a relative clause with a preposition plus *which*, *that*, or Ø (b). We often omit the relativizer *where* after the noun *place*, but not usually after other nouns (d).

a. *That's the town*	*where we stayed.*		We stayed **there**.
b. *That's the town*	*that / which / Ø* *in which*	*we stayed **in**.* *we stayed.*	We stayed **in that town**.
c. *We've come to a point*	*where* *at which*	*we need outside help.*	We need outside **help at this point**.
d. *Do you remember **the place we ate** / the restaurant **where** we ate?* (~~the restaurant we ate~~)			

Relative clauses after such nouns may instead require relativizers that are subjects (e) or objects (f). The choice of relativizer depends on the role of the relativizer **inside** the relative clause.

e. *That's the town **that / which** won an award.* (~~where~~)	**It** won an award. *That/which* is a subject (8.3).
f. *That's the town **that / which / Ø** I prefer.* (~~where~~)	I prefer **it**. *That/which* is an object (8.4).
g. *That's the town **where** I got my first job.* (~~that~~, ~~which~~)	I got my first job **there**.

We can use *when* as a relativizer after nouns referring to a period of time, such as *age*, *century*, *era*, and *season* (h). After common nouns referring to time, such as *moment*, *month*, *time*, and *week*, we can use *when*, *that*, or Ø, but not *which* (i).

h. *I grew up in an era **when** food was scarce. Winter is the season **when** nothing grows.*
i. *Is June a month **when / that / Ø** you're free? That was the week **when / that / Ø** I was sick.* ~~which~~

We use *why*, *that*, or Ø after the noun *reason*. After *the way*, we use *that* or Ø or *in which* (not *how*).

k. *There are many reasons **why / that / Ø** people decide to emigrate.*
l. *Can you describe the way*   *that / Ø*   *you prepare for tests?* (the way ~~how~~)
                        in which

■ **Exercise 10** Create sentences by choosing one part from each column, transforming the sentences in the last box into relative clauses with *whose*. Use each part once.

Example: *This is an idea **whose time has come**.*

√ This is an idea	children	Her life changes when she wins the lottery.
1. You should never marry	√ time	They did not release their names.
2. Barack Obama was	a man	√ It has come.
3. Do you feel sorry for	a 20th Century artist	His first wife calls him every day.
4. Andy Warhol was	two suspects	Their parents don't know how to say "No."
5. We saw a movie about	the first modern president	His work is full of pop culture references.
6. The police questioned	a waitress	His father was born in another country.

■ **Exercise 11** Create sentences by matching the parts, transforming the sentences in the second box into relative clauses with *where, when, why,* or *Ø*. Use each part once.

Example: *Near the end of the game, there was a moment **when I thought we were going to win**.*

√ Near the end of the game there was a moment …   You felt proud.
1. They want to live in a neighborhood …   I can park for free.
2. Can you remember a time …   People know their neighbors.
3. In France, August is the month …   √ I thought we were going to win.
4. I never stay in a hotel room …   Smoking is allowed.
5. In our family, there are lots of reasons …   Most people take a vacation.
6. Can you direct me to a place …   We don't spend holidays together.

■ **Exercise 12** Choose the best answer.

1. The Red Cross helps people __ have been disrupted by natural disasters.
   a. that their lives   b. whose lives   c. lives which   d. who their lives

2. Why do Sara's parents always complain about the way __ she dresses?
   a. how   b. when   c. that   d. which

3. We're going to visit a village where __ an earthquake a few years ago.
   a. there was   b. it had   c. had   d. was

4. We live in an era __ people are more cynical.
   a. where   b. that   c. which   d. when

5. Driving a car is expensive in countries __ have to import all their oil.
   a. where   b. they   c. who   d. that

6. In all your travels, what is the country __ you remember best?
   a. in which   b. whom   c. Ø   d. where

7. In countries __ there is plenty of oil, there is less incentive to develop alternative energies.
   a. which   b. where   c. that   d. who

Chapter 8

Exercise 13 Each numbered item is followed by some sentences. For each sentence, decide whether it can be transformed into a relative clause and added to the numbered sentence. In order to become a relative clause, the sentence mus include a pronoun that refers to a noun in the first sentence. For each set, more than one relative clause can be created. The sentences you create for each numbered item will all begin the same.

Example: The company purchased a building.
    I work for it. → The company **that I work for** purchased a new building.
    It rises 40 stories. → The company purchased a building **that rises 40 stories**.
    I was surprised. *No relative clause is possible, because there is no pronoun in the sentence that refers to the company or the building.*

1. This is the software.
   a. It caused all our problems.
   b. We read about it.
   c. The old software was better.
   d. Everyone hated it.
   e. Software design is difficult.

2. The official no longer works here.
   a. You spoke with her.
   b. She used to be at this desk.
   c. You need her signature.
   d. There are no other officials on duty.
   e. I'm very disappointed.

3. The train almost hit a man.
   a. He had fallen asleep on the tracks.
   b. It passes through my neighborhood.
   c. You need to be careful where you fall asleep.
   d. We hear it every night.

4. The flight was canceled because of a storm.
   a. The whole airport was shut down.
   b. It shut down the whole airport.
   c. We were hoping to take it.
   d. The pilots got a day off.
   e. We had tickets for it.

Exercise 14 The statements below are things people might say about restaurants they like. Use each one to complete the sentence *We like restaurants ...* as in the example. Remember to omit *they*, *them*, or *there* in the relative clause (*restaurants that ~~they~~ are frequented by celebrities*, *restaurants where you can see interesting people ~~there~~*, *restaurants our friends recommend ~~them~~*).

They attract celebrities. → *We like restaurants* **that attract celebrities.**

1. They have specials all the time. → *We like restaurants ...*
2. Our friends like them. → *We like restaurants ...*
3. Not everyone knows about them.
4. We can relax there.
5. The waiters there don't chat too much.
6. They're not full of people talking on cell phones.
7. Their names are easy to pronounce.
8. You can see interesting people there.
9. The waiters there remember us.
10. They change their menu from time to time.
11. Children are welcome there.
12. Guide books recommend them.
13. We can go to them again and again without getting bored.
14. The lighting is romantic.

Commas or no commas? Which or that?

8.8 Restrictive and nonrestrictive clauses

- **Restrictive** relative clauses **identify what kind of** person or thing we are talking about.
- They restrict or **limit the reference** of the noun to which they are attached.

a. *Do you remember the author **we met**?*	Which author? <u>This one.</u>
b. *I like movies **that make me think**.*	What kind of movies? <u>This kind.</u>

- **Nonrestrictive** relative clauses **add extra information** about a person or thing.
- We put one comma before the clause and one after it, if the sentence continues (c).
- We often use nonrestrictive relative clauses after nouns for whole groups (d) and proper nouns (e).
- A relative clause after a proper noun (with a capital letter) is always nonrestrictive. We use commas, and we don't use *that* (f). This is also true for clauses beginning with *where* and other relativizers (8.7).
- Restrictive relative clauses do not require commas (g).

c. *This is a good book. The author, **who also writes for TV**, knows how to create suspense.*	The relative clause does not limit the reference. It just adds extra information.
d. *Bald eagles, **which almost became extinct in the 20th century**, have recently come back.*	*Bald eagles* refers to the whole species. The relative clause just adds information.
e. *They live in Hawaii, **which has perfect weather all year**. (~~that~~)*	After *Hawaii*, a proper noun, commas are required. The clause just adds information. For the use of *where*, see 8.7.
f. *They live in Hawaii, **where the weather is perfect all year**.*	
g. *The class **that I like best** is not the easiest one.* (There are no commas.)	Commas would be a mistake because the clause is restrictive. It tells which class.

We can decide to make a clause restrictive or nonrestrictive depending on our beliefs.

h. *Nurses, who work as hard as doctors, should be paid as well.*	All nurses work as hard as doctors and should be paid as well.
i. *Nurses who work as hard as doctors should be paid as well.*	Some nurses work as hard as doctors and should be paid as well.

Restrictive relative are sometimes called *defining* or *essential* relative clauses, because the information they provide is necessary for the meaning and cannot be removed. A nonrestrictive relative clause (non-defining, non-essential) can be removed. Removing a nonrestrictive clause does not change the idea of the main clause.

A nonrestrictive relative clause is a kind of interruption of the sentence. Like other interruptions, it can sometimes be marked by long dashes or parentheses (instead of commas).

i. *The author of this book (who also writes for TV) knows how to create suspense.*
j. *The author of this book — who also writes for TV — knows how to create suspense.*

Sometimes, especially after an indefinite noun phrase, we can use a restrictive or nonrestrictive relative clause with little or no difference in meaning.

k. *The city has a tourist office that / which provides free maps.*	The sentences are interchangeable.
l. *The city has a tourist office, which provides free maps.*	

■ **Exercise 15** Here is a list of characteristics from 8.8, in note form and in random order. Copy the right ones under each heading. List five points under each one.

Don't use *that*
No commas
Often follow proper nouns
Not necessary
Don't omit the clause

Often use *that*
Commas
Don't follow proper nouns
Necessary
The clause can be omitted

Restrictive relative clauses	Nonrestrictive relative clauses

■ **Exercise 16** Complete the sentences below — about a famous political family — by adding words (or Ø) from the group listed below and commas where they are needed. The short blanks are for commas — if they are needed. (Eleven commas are needed.)

who   which   where   that   Ø

Example: Joseph P. Kennedy III, **who** was elected to Congress in 2012, was born in 1980.

1. *Kennedy* is the most famous of all the names __ people associate with American politics.

2. Joseph P. Kennedy __ ____ served as ambassador to Britain in the 1930s __ had nine children.

3. In Boston __ ____ the Kennedy children grew up __ they were known for their competitiveness.

4. John Kennedy __ ____ became president in 1960 __ was assassinated after only three years in office. His death __ ____ shocked the nation __ is remembered by every American __ ____ was alive at the time.

5. John was the only Kennedy son __ ____ was ever elected president.

6. Robert Kennedy __ ____ who served as John Kennedy's attorney general __ might have been elected president in 1968 if he too had not been assassinated.

7. The Kennedy brother __ ____ had the longest career __ was Edward __ ____ served in the U.S. Senate from 1962 until his death in 2009.

8. The Kennedy family members __ ____ did not go into politics __ had distinguished careers in other fields.

We won, which put us in first place.

8.9 Relative clauses that modify a sentence

We often use *It*, *This* or *That* as the subject of a sentence to comment on the preceding sentence. As an alternative, we can use a nonrestrictive relative clause introduced by *which* (not *that*). Similarly, we can use the phrases *in which case* and *at which point*.

a.	*We won.* **It put** *us in first place.*	b.	*We won,* **which** *put us in first place.*
c.	*The company is doing well now.* **This means** *they can invest in new equipment.*	d.	*The company is doing well now,* **which means** *they can invest in new equipment.*
e.	*Maria and Peter finally got married.* **That made** *their parents very happy.*	f.	*Maria and Peter finally got married,* **which made** *their parents very happy.*
g.	*There may be a flood.* **In that case** *people will be evacuated.*	h.	*There may be a flood,* **in which case** *people will be evacuated.*
i.	*Prices fell.* **At that point** *the CEO quit.*	j.	*Prices fell,* **at which point** *the CEO quit.*

some of whom

all of which

the best of which

8.10 Clauses with *of whom* or *of which*

We can use a quantifier (or a noun such as *part*) plus *of whom* or *of which* in relative clauses. These clauses are usually nonrestrictive, so we use commas. Quantifiers include numbers (*two, a hundred*), *none, some, half, most, all,* and *both*. We can also use superlative phrases (*the best, the longest, the most difficult*) and ordinal numbers (*the first, the second*).

a. *My great grandparents had nine children,* **two of whom** *became doctors.*
b. *In the northern region,* **most of which** *is mountainous, farming is difficult.*
c. *They have a lot of land,* **part of which** *they rent to a neighboring farmer.*
d. *Japan has four main islands,* **the largest of which** *is Honshu.*

8.11 Relative clauses like *(the candidate) they say will win*

We can use a noun clause after words like *they say* and *I think* inside a relative clause. The relativizer can function as a subject (a) or an object (b) within the relative clause. A noun clause inside such a relative clause does not usually include *that* (*they said* ~~that~~, *I think* ~~that~~). Though we do not normally omit a relativizer that functions as a subject (8.3), in these clauses we can.

a.	*I support the candidate* **that / who / Ø** *they say will win.*	*They say that* **she/he will win**.
b.	*That's the course* **that / which / Ø** *I think I'll take.*	*I think that I'll take* **it**.

■ **Exercise 17** Combine the sentences, transforming the second one into a relative clause.

1. At my company, we have all our meetings standing up. It saves a lot of time.
2. Maria and Peter got divorced. It made their parents very unhappy.
3. Maria started looking for a new husband. That surprised everyone.
4. Peter became a priest. That means he can never marry.
5. The patient takes vitamin supplements. She thinks they will prevent cancer.
6. Her doctor prescribed some pills. She says they are making her sick.
7. I chose a password. I thought I would never forget it.
8. I forgot my password. It made it impossible for me to access my account.
9. We interviewed 10 applicants. All of them were well-qualified.
10. The U.S. consists of 50 states. The largest is Alaska.
11. Land in the West is not well-suited to many types of agriculture. Most of it is quite arid.
12. We develop our eating habits early in life. This makes them difficult to change.

8.12 Reduced relative clauses

a house **built in 1920**

a person **running for office**

We can shorten a relative clause with *who, that,* or *which* + a form of BE by omitting the relativizer and BE verb, leaving only a past participle for a passive verb (a) or an *–ing* form for a continuous verb (b). Only clauses with *who, that,* or *which* + BE can be reduced this way.

   a. *They bought a house* that /which was *built in 1920.* → *They bought* **a house built** *in 1920.*
   b. *A person* who is *running for office needs funds.* → *A* **person running** *for office needs funds.*

You have to omit **both** the relativizer and the BE verb (a, b). It is a mistake to omit just one.

   c. *They bought a house* ~~that/which built~~ *in 1920. They bought a house* ~~was built~~…
   d. *A person* ~~who running~~ *for office needs funds. A person* ~~is running~~ *for office needs…*

Reduced relative clauses do not have any tense. We interpret the tense from the context, using information from the main verb and our understanding of the situation.

e. *The money* **goes** *to researchers* **working** *on AIDS.*	They **are** working…
f. *Some men* **working** *on a water pipe* **caused** *an outage.*	They **were** working…
g. *I* **want** *to find more articles* **related** *to my topic.*	They **are** related…
h. **Jesus spoke** *a language* **related** *to Arabic and Hebrew.*	It **was** related….

Past participles in reduced relative clauses often represent stative passives (Ch. 5) as in *who are accustomed* or *which is associated.* Some of these, in typical phrases, appear below.

men **accustomed to** *giving orders*	*the steps* **outlined in** *the manual*
areas of the brain **associated with** *pleasure*	*objects* **made of** *ivory*
discrimination **based on** *gender*	*smokers* **married to** *non-smokers*
a committee **composed of** *students*	*elements* **named after** *people*
citizens **concerned about** *crime*	*people* **opposed to** *capital punishment*
habits **linked to** *longevity*	*problems* **related to** *aging*
cities **located on** *fault lines*	*a building* **scheduled for** *demolition*

We sometimes reduce a relative clause with a passive **continuous** verb (4.7):

   i. *The city council is trying to come up with a name for a new park. Some of the names being considered are controversial.*

■ **Exercise 18** Reduce the relative clauses that can be reduced. Don't change the others.

HIGH PRIORITY

1. Cars that are powered by electricity require frequent recharging.
2. They talked to a man who was known as Big Al about a car that he wanted to sell.
3. A person who is walking can sometimes get around faster than a person who is driving.
4. Commuters who are riding bikes are a common sight in cities where the weather is mild.
5. People who eat meat sometimes don't understand the motivations of vegetarians.
6. We ate clams that were baked over a fire and chatted with people who were passing by.
7. Smokers who are married to non-smokers have a strong incentive to quit.
8. The vice-president can become president according to procedures that are outlined in the constitution.

HIGH PRIORITY

■ **Exercise 19** Choose the correct answers. For most of the items, more than one is correct.

1. We went to a historic re-enactment in a town __ after a Civil War hero.
   a. that was named   b. that named   c. was named   d. named

2. This office gets a lot of calls from people __ for work.
   a. who looking   b. looking   c. are looking   d. who are looking

3. There was a concert of Renaissance music __ on ancient instruments.
   a. played   b. was played   c. which played   d. which was played

4. Music __ on ancient instruments sounds different.
   a. plays   b. playing   c. play   d. played

5. I gave a few coins to a guitarist __ by the subway entrance.
   a. played   b. was playing   c. playing   d. who was playing

6. The biologist started a research project __ wolves and deer on Isle Royale.
   a. that involved   b. involving   c. involved   d. involve

7. Smokers __ to nonsmokers have a high incentive to quit.
   a. who married   b. married   c. marrying   d. who are married

8. Is it hard for you to read comments __ by hand?
   a. writing   b. written   c. that write   d. wrote

HIGH PRIORITY

■ **Exercise 20** Combine the sentences, based on summaries of movies, to create one sentence. Use relative clauses and reduced relative clauses. Example: *A soldier falls in love with a young woman. He is trapped behind enemy lines. Her husband has recently died.* ➙ *A soldier trapped behind enemy lines falls in love with a young woman whose husband has recently died.*

1. A rich young woman is helped by a man. She is running away from her family. He turns out to be a reporter looking for a story.

2. A young math genius meets a psychologist. The young genius is working as a janitor. The psychologist helps him find direction in his life.

3. A private detective accidentally discovers a murder scheme. He is investigating a case in Los Angeles. The murder scheme is related to water rights.

4. A man invites his wife's lover to meet him. The man loves games and theater. This leads to a dangerous battle of wits.

5. An alien infant grows up with superhuman abilities. He is raised on earth. They can help him save the world.

6. A paleontologist is pursued by a rich young woman. He is trying to get a million-dollar donation for his museum. She has a leopard. It is named Baby.

7. Thor battles a race of Dark Elves. They are led by Malekeith. He threatens to plunge the world into darkness.

8.13 Reduced relative clauses with stative verbs

We do not normally use verbs like *belong* (stative verbs) in the continuous aspect (*is belonging*). However, we use many stative verbs in the *-ing* form in reduced relative clauses.

| a. *Do you know a word **meaning** "very big"?* | = *a word that means* |
| b. *The U.S. bought some land **belonging** to France.* | = *land that belonged* |

With verbs that express communication, such as *show*, we use phrases like *a chart showing income growth* (= *a chart that shows/showed income growth*). Some of these verbs and some stative verbs, in typical phrases, appear below.

*a book **belonging to** the library*	*an accident **involving** four cars*
*foods **containing** additives*	*a name **meaning** "hope"*
*a team **consisting of** girls and boys*	*people **needing** assistance*
*matters **concerning** students*	*symbols **representing** sounds*
*numbers **corresponding to** names*	*a message **saying** hello*
*a report **describing** recent events*	*a chart **showing** income growth*
*a paragraph **explaining** your results*	*data **suggesting** other conclusions*
*papers **including** references*	*students **wishing** to enroll*

The verbs in such phrases are interpreted as simple tenses, not continuous (*a name that means "hope,"* not *that is meaning*). With a verb that expresses an action, we usually interpret the *-ing* form in a reduced relative clause as continuous (8.12):

c. *I took a picture of **a woman smoking** a cigar.* (She was smoking at the moment.)
d. *I once met a woman **who smoked** cigars* (*a woman smoking* cigars). (It was her habit.)

When in doubt, it is best to use a full relative clause rather than a reduced clause.

a book **belonging to the library**

a chart **showing income**

-ed or -ing?

8.14 Past participle or –ing form?

Transitive verbs (2.4.1) can be active or passive (Ch. 5), so they can appear in reduced relative clauses as –*ing* forms (a) or past participles (b). Intransitive verbs cannot be passive, so they appear in reduced relative clauses only as –*ing* forms (c). Remember: *a team **that consisted** of girls and boys* = *a team **consisting** ...*, not ~~*a team consisted*~~.

a. *I saw an accident **involving** four cars.*	The accident **involved** four cars. (active)
b. *The cars **involved** in the accident were towed.*	The cars **were involved**. (passive)
c. *She coached a team **consisting** of girls and boys.*	= a team **that consisted** of… (active)

■ **Exercise 21** Find and fix **one or two** mistakes in this passage from a course syllabus. Focus on the underlined words.

Students <u>taking</u> this class for graduate credit are <u>required</u> to write a ten-page paper <u>showing</u> how Knapp and Vangelisti's model of relationships <u>applies</u> to a relationship they have <u>experienced</u>. Include a section <u>explaining</u> the model. Use only the sources <u>suggest</u> on the assignment sheet <u>attached</u> to the syllabus. Follow the format guidelines <u>described</u> on page 12 of your text.

■ **Exercise 22** Identify the relative clauses and reduced relative clauses, and fix **one** mistake in each item. Focus on the underlined words.

1. Memorial Day, <u>celebrated</u> in the US on the last Monday in May, <u>is</u> a national holiday <u>honors</u> members of the military and citizens who have <u>died</u> in wars. On Memorial Day some people <u>visit</u> cemeteries, but more people <u>go</u> to malls, where stores <u>offer</u> Memorial Day sales.

2. Memorabilia are objects <u>valued</u> by collectors because they are <u>connected</u> with people or things <u>considered</u> important. For example, people may <u>collect</u> old movie posters, early signs and artifacts <u>advertising</u> Coca-cola, or objects <u>associate</u> with the Beatles. Collectors will <u>pay</u> thousands of dollars for a baseball <u>signed</u> by a famous player or a drawing that John Lennon <u>made</u> on a napkin.

3. A memorial is something that <u>reminds</u> people of a famous event or a person who has <u>died</u>. One example is the Washington Monument, which <u>honoring</u> the first president. At the scene of a fatal bicycle accident, people who <u>remember</u> the victim sometimes <u>set</u> up an informal memorial <u>consisting</u> of an old bicycle <u>painted</u> white, along with flowers and messages.

4. Shangri-La is an imaginary place <u>describe</u> in the novel *Lost Horizon*. It is a land in which people <u>seem</u> to stay young forever, an eternally happy land <u>isolated</u> from the violence of the world. In 2001, a county in China, <u>hoping</u> to attract tourists, <u>changed</u> its name to Shangri-la

5. In 1516, Thomas More <u>published</u> a book <u>called</u> *Utopia,* <u>described</u> a place where everything is perfect and people live in harmony. The word *utopia* has come to be used for any ideal society that is free of the political and social troubles that people <u>experience</u> in the real world.

6. In the U.S. in the early part of the 19th century, people <u>established</u> utopian communities <u>founded</u> on religious or ethical principles. A community <u>calling</u> New Harmony, <u>established</u> in Indiana in 1925, was <u>based</u> on principles of economic and political equality.

Chapter 8 — Relative clauses — Grammar Advantage 249

■ **Exercise 23** Choose the correct forms.

1. An extinct species is one __ no longer exists.
   (a) that it   (b) it   (c) Ø   (d) which

2. Insulation is material that heat or cold can't easily pass __.
   (a) through   (b) through it   (c) through that   (d) it through

3. A hook is a curved piece of metal or other material __ you can hang things on.
   (a) on which   (b) on that   (c) which   (d) where

4. Fossils are the remains of animals and plants __ become as solid as rock over a long period.
   (a) whose   (b) that   (c) Ø   (d) they

5. Until recently, no examples of well-preserved feathers had been found in fossils from the cretaceous period, __ ended in mass extinctions about 65 million years ago.
   (a) that   (b) it   (c) that it   (d) which

6. Modern feathers consist of thousands of fibers __ together by tiny hooks.
   (a) that held   (b) held   (c) are held   (d) they are held

7. Small differences in that basic design have resulted in feathers that create a waterproof coat and others that __ insulation from extreme cold.
   (a) provide   (b) providing   (c) they provide   (d) provided

8.15 Appositives

*Washington, **the first president**, was quite tall.*

We can add information about a noun by adding another noun or noun phrase after it, separated by commas. This is called an appositive. It is another type of reduced relative clause (8.12).

| a. George Washington, **the first president**, was quite tall = Washington, **who was** the … |
| b. Their houses are made of adobe, **a kind of brick**. = … adobe, **which is** a kind |

An appositive can help you write more concisely, avoiding unnecessary words.

| c. They practice kendo, ~~which is~~ a traditional Japanese sport. | *Which is* is not wrong, but the sentence is more concise without it. |

We sometimes add a relative clause after the noun inside the appositive (d, e, f). Then the final comma usually goes at the end of the relative clause, not after the noun (d). We sometimes place an appositive or a reduced relative clause **initially** in the sentence, separated by a comma (g).

  d. Steve Jobs, the technology innovator **who co-founded Apple**, died in 2011.
  e. Their houses are made of adobe, a kind of brick **(that is) made from earth**.
  f. Garrison Keillor wrote stories about Lake Wobegon, a town *"where all the women are strong, all the men are good-looking, and all the children are above average."*
  g. **A Minnesotan native, / Born in Minnesota**, Keillor was a keen observer of local culture.

Avoid this comma mistake with an appostive:

  h. WRONG: *My country Norway has a long history of shipbuilding.* → *My country, Norway, has…*

8.16 Adjectives and prepositional phrases after nouns

We sometimes add information after a noun by adding an adjective phrase (a) or a prepositional phrase (b). These adjective phrases and some prepositional phrases can be paraphrased with relative clauses.

a. *Children **younger than 12** eat free.*	= *Children who are younger ....*
b. *I need to talk to the person **in charge of admissions**.*	= *... the person who is in charge ...*

8.17 Nonrestrictive reduced clauses

Reduced relative clauses, including adjective phrases and prepositional phrases (8.16), may be non-restrictive (8.8), with commas.

a. *We visited Bizen, known for its beautiful pottery.*	= *... Bizen, which is known for ...*
b. *My uncle, wearing a woman's hat, looked very funny.*	= *My uncle, who was wearing ...*
c. *Josh, too young to understand the joke, didn't laugh.*	= *Josh, who was too young ...*
d. *Dr. Wu, in charge of admissions, made the decision.*	= *Dr. Wu, who is in charge ...*

■ **Exercise 24**   Combine the two sentences by transforming the second one into an appositive. If there is a third sentence, transform it into a relative clause inside the appositive.

1. The U.S. army once used a secret code based on Navajo. It is an American Indian language.
2. Linguistics has applications in almost every facet of life that involves communication. It is the study of human language.
3. Parts of the Atacama Desert get an average of one millimeter of rain a year. It is the world's driest place.
4. Tabbouleh is made with bulgur, tomatoes, and parsley. It's a popular dish in many countries.
5. Grandma Moses died at 101. She was an artist. She began painting in her seventies.
6. Oscar Niemeyer died at 104. He was an architect. He designed many buildings in Brazil.

■ **Exercise 25**   **Two or three** of the items below include mistakes. Find and fix them. Don't change anything in the other items.

1. The ancient Greeks invented an engine powered by steam.
2. Downtown, a person walking can sometimes get somewhere faster than a person driving.
3. The award went to a research team that working on AIDS.
4. There was a short power outage caused by workers digging up the street.
5. Today there's a lot of work being done on artificial intelligence.
6. The competition was won by a group consist of students representing five universities.
7. Aramaic, the language spoken by Jesus, was related to Hebrew and Arabic.
8. Bizen, a town known for pottery and swords, is in Hokkaido, Japan's northern island.

Chapter 8

■ **Exercise 26** Fill each blank with a form of the verb that is provided after the first sentence. You will need some past participles and some *-ing* forms.

1. There was an accident … three cars.   *involve*
2. The cars … in the accident were blocking the highway.
3. An accident at the same intersection last week … four cars.
4. I once saw an accident … five cars.

5. We have to write a paper … a literature review.   *include*
6. The ideas … in this paper come from many sources.
7. Paragraphs that … quotations require in-text references.
8. This paper … ideas from many sources.

9. Last week's news was dominated by a flood … half the city.   *affect*
10. A flood that … half the city dominated the news.
11. The areas … by the flood were without power.
12. The flood … thousands of people.

13. A report that … company secrets is worth a lot to rival companies.   *contain*
14. Someone at our company leaked a report … company secrets.
15. The secrets … in the report are related to finances.
16. The report … valuable secrets.

17. Some chapters in this text … lots of topics.   *cover*
18. We have to read a chapter … several topics.
19. The topics … in Chapter 2 are very important.
20. The professor always … important topics in the lectures.

21. This paper … several famous battles.   *describe*
22. It includes a section … the Punic Wars.
23. Most of the battles … in the paper took place centuries ago.
24. The parts that … 20th century battles are based on firsthand accounts.

25. Cigarette labels include a warning … by law.   *require*
26. The law … health warnings has been in effect for many years.
27. Some people think laws that … health warnings should be on sugary soft drinks as well.
28. Currently there are no laws … health warnings on junk food.

8.18 Relative clauses that modify pronouns

*one **that will fit me***

Restrictive relative clauses (including reduced clauses) can modify pronouns and quantifiers like *one, the one(s), anyone, someone, everyone, no one, anything, something, everything, all,* and *nothing*. We do not usually use relative clauses after personal pronouns (*I, she, it,* etc.).

a. **Anyone (who is) looking for a job** in a recession knows how depressing it can be.
b. I need to borrow a sweater or a jacket. Do you have **one/anything that will fit me**?

We sometimes use *those who* or *those which/that* instead of *people who* or *the ones that*.

c. Anyone can apply for this scholarship, but only **those who** really need it will be considered.
d. I didn't understand any of the answers, so I just picked **those that** seemed more reasonable.

What matters is...

8.19 Headless relative clauses

As an alternative to *the thing(s) that/which ...* we can use a clause beginning with *what*, sometimes called a headless relative clause. For the idea of "anything that" or "anyone who," we can use clauses with *whatever* and *whoever*. We don't use just *who*. (See also Chapter 7.)

a.	*I took only **what I could carry**.*	I took only the things that I could carry.
b.	*Waiter, this isn't **what I ordered**.*	This isn't the food that I ordered.
c.	***What matters most** is content.*	The thing that matters most is content.
d.	*Take **whatever you want**.*	Take anything that you want.
e.	***Whoever said that** is a liar. (Who said that is ...)*	No matter who said that, he or she is ...

These clauses can be adverbial (in addition to functioning as subjects or objects). They are similar to adverbial clauses with *wherever, whenever,* and *however*. See Chapter 9.

f.	***Whatever happens**, we'll stay together.*	No matter what happens ... (10.15)
g.	***Whoever wins**, I'm going to be disappointed.*	No matter who wins ... (10.15)
h.	***Wherever I go**, I run into someone I know..*	No matter where I go ... (9.12)
i.	*Use my bike **whenever you want to**.*	... any time you want to. (9.7)
j.	*I'll stay till the end, **however long it takes**.*	... no matter how long it takes. (10.15)
	This use of *however* is not related to the **transition expression** *however* (3.10).	

a book for you to read

the first man to walk on the moon

8.20 Infinitive relatives

An infinitive relative consists of an infinitive, sometimes preceded by a phrase with *for*, in a structure that is similar to a relative clause. *Can, should, must, have to,* or *want to* is implied. After superlative expressions or phrases with an ordinal number, we can use an infinitive phrase instead of a relative clause. We sometimes use *in which* or *with which* and an infinitive (f) (6.18).

a.	*This is my list of places **to visit** (them) **before I die**.*	= places **that I want to** visit
b.	*They're looking for someone **to keep the books**.*	= someone **who can** keep
c.	*The paper **for you to sign** (it) is on the table.*	= the paper **that you have to** sign
d.	*Neil Armstrong was the **first man to walk on the moon**.*	= the first man **who walked**
e.	*Who is the **oldest** athlete **to compete in the Olympics**?*	= athlete **who has ever competed**
f.	*You have an hour **in which to revise** your work.*	You must/can revise it in an hour.

Exercise 27 Answer each question with a sentence or phrase that includes a relative clause.
Example: *One donut fell into the dishwater. One donut fell into the kitty litter. Which donut would you rather have?* ➔ *I would rather have the one / the donut that fell into the dishwater.*

1. Two people were interviewed for a job. One asked a lot of questions in the interview. One didn't ask any questions. Which one made a more favorable impression?

2. Two beds are for sale. Princess Diana once slept in one of them. George Washington once slept in the other one. Which bed would you buy?

3. There are two apartment buildings. A famous politician lives in one apartment building. A famous movie star lives in the other. Which building would you rather live in?

4. There are two boys. They both have a problem. One boy's mother hates him. One boy's sister hates him. Which boy will have a happier life?

5. There are two doctors. One doctor charges too much. One doctor got bad grades in medical school. Which doctor would you go to?

6. There are two rooms. In one room, a murder was committed. In one room, there's a strong smell of rotten eggs. Which room would you rather spend the night in?

7. There are two women; each has a husband. One woman's husband is a pilot. One woman's husband is a fire fighter. Which woman has more to worry about?

8. I studied two subjects. I studied one subject by myself at home. I studied one subject in class. Which subject do you think I prefer?

9. You have two drawings. You paid $100 for one of them. Your best friend drew the other one. Which drawing is worth more to you?

10. There are two people. They both love to cook. One person cooks French food. One person cooks Chinese food. Which person would you rather visit?

11. There are two countries. In one, a group of generals has most of the power. In one, a group of businessmen has most of the power. Which country would you rather live in?

12. There are two people. Both of them plan to have children. One person wants to have ten children. One person wants to have two children. Which person will have a happier life?

13. There are two women. One woman has lived in a convent all her life. One woman has been in the army all her life. Which woman would you rather have lunch with?

14. There are two children. I took one child to an art museum. I took one child to the zoo. Which child had a better time?

15. I have two drawings by the famous artist Picasso. The artist signed one of them. He forgot to sign the other. Which drawing is worth more?

16. You have two friends. One friend's wife died. One friend's mother died. Which friend would you visit first?

17. I waved at one professor. I winked at one professor. Which professor was more surprised?

■ **Exercise 28** Imagine that you are looking for someone to share your life. Transform each statement into a relative clause to complete the sentence *I'm looking for someone ...* as in the example.

This person has a career. ⟶ *I'm looking for someone **who has a career**.*

1. I can trust this person. ⟶ *I'm looking for someone ...*
2. I can depend on this person.
3. This person doesn't interrupt me.
4. This person likes animals.
5. This person's family lives far away.
6. My dog likes this person.
7. This person's parents have a good marriage.
8. My parents like this person.
9. I can talk to this person about anything.
10. This person understands me.

■ **Exercise 29** Complete each sentence with a headless relative clause beginning with *what* (8.19) using the words below.

I (x4)   she   we   they   ate   expected   learned   meant   ordered   said   wanted

1. This gift is perfect. It's exactly ...
2. We had nothing but bread and cheese, so that's ...
3. The waiter made a mistake. This isn't ...
4. They were surprised by the result. It wasn't ...
5. The reporter misquoted me. That's not ...
6. I always talk to my daughter after school. We talk about ...
7. You misinterpreted me. That's not ...

■ **Exercise 30** Paraphrase the clause in italics, using a headless relative clause. This type of sentence, sometimes called a *wh* cleft, allows us to move a noun phrase to the end of the sentence, for greater emphasis. Example: They're very traditional. *Family comes first.* ⟶ *What comes first is family.*

1. My composition teacher says that *content matters most*.
2. If a person wants to lose weight, *a combination of dieting and exercise works best*.
3. The instructions were not at all clear. *Total confusion followed*.
4. Some us did well and some didn't. *Motivation made the difference*.
5. When I feel under pressure, *meditation helps me most*.
6. I don't like my job. *The lack of variety bothers me more than anything*.
7. This company cares about only one thing. *Profit comes first*.
8. We won the game. *A foul by the other team saved us*.

■ **Exercise 31** Identify the infinitive phrases that are used like relative clauses in the sentences below. Find and fix **two or three** mistakes. Most of the sentences have no mistake.

1. In 1869, Wyoming became the first state to give women the right to vote.
2. The oldest athlete ever to compete in the Olympics was Oscar Swahn, a 72-year-old shooter.
3. Coffee shops nowadays have become places for people to do business.
4. When no one is in charge, there is no one can be held accountable.
5. Taxpayers deserve a clean environment in which to live and work and play.
6. A "bucket list" is a list of things to do them before you die.
7. The waiting room has toys for kids to play with while their parents are seeing the doctor.
8. There are lots of resources for students to take advantage of when they need academic help.

Chapter 8

8.21 Relative clauses and sentence structure

Using relative clauses and related structures well requires attention to the overall structure of sentences. Avoid fragments (a). Don't use extra subjects (b). Don't use relativizers when you need other ways of connecting, like *so* and *and* (b, c).

Problem sentences:	Revisions:
a. When a person dies, his or her property goes to relatives. For this action we use the verb *inherit*. ~~Which is related to the word *heir*, meaning *a person who inherits something*~~.	For this action we use the *verb inherit*, which is related to the word ... / ... we use the verb *inherit*. This verb is related to the word ...
b. Sometimes a person who dies he has no family nearby, ~~which city officials have to try to find family elsewhere~~.	Sometimes a person who **dies has** no family nearby, so city officials have to ... / ... **which means that** city officials have to ...
c. In 2012, in Carson City, Nevada, city officials who were looking for a deceased man's heirs ~~and~~ finally found a cousin in California.	... city officials who were looking for a deceased man's **heirs finally found** a cousin in California. / city officials were looking for a deceased man's heirs and ...

■ **Exercise 32** Fill the blanks that need filling. Most of the blanks should remain blank (Ø). Some require a word from the set provided. Keep in mind the overall structure of the sentence.

1. A California teacher inherited a fortune in gold coins __ discovered by workers __ cleaning the home of her cousin, __ had quietly saved a treasure __ worth more than $7 million before he died in 2012.

    Ø were that and Ø who they were
    Ø who he that
    Ø were that and

2. A judge __ certified that Arlene Magdanz __ was the only heir to the treasure, __ valued at $7.4 million, __ found in the modest home of Walter Samaszko.

    Ø who he that was, Ø she who and
    Ø were that and
    Ø were that and

3. Samaszko __ lived quietly in Carson City, Nevada, for more than 40 years, __ no one knew of his wealth. Records __ showed that he lived on just $500 a month from his stock accounts, according to Alan Glover, a city official.

    Ø she who was
    Ø and who which
    Ø they that which

4. Samaszko apparently __ had no living family in Carson City, so genealogical researchers __ looked for relatives elsewhere __ eventually found Magdanz.

    Ø he who that
    Ø who were they
    Ø they were and

5. A crew __ hired by Glover to clean up the man's house __ discovered boxes of gold coins in the garage. Later more boxes __ were found, __ Glover said the coins, __ wrapped in foil, __ were enough to fill two wheelbarrows.

    Ø were that who
    Ø were they who
    Ø that they which Ø which and
    Ø which they were Ø and they that

6. In addition to the gold, Samazko __ had money, stock, and bank accounts __ totaling $165,570, a 1968 Ford Mustang, __ appraised at about $17,000, and $5,330 in other property in the home.

    Ø who he that
    Ø were that they
    Ø was that and

8.22 Relative clauses compared to other structures that modify nouns

Relative clauses are similar to other structures that follow nouns, but they differ in important ways. See also 7.24.

Relative clauses:		
... the idea **that changed my mind** ...	The underlined parts are not complete by themselves. They could not be sentences. You can make them into sentences by "borrowing" the noun they modify: **The idea** changed your mind. They suggested **the idea**. They talked about **the idea**.	Any noun can be followed by a relative clause: - the book / incident / event that changed your mind ... - the movie / class / solution that they suggested ... - the topic / actor / trips that they talked about
... the idea **that / Ø they suggested** ...		
... the idea **that / Ø they talked about** ...		
Nouns with *that* clause complements (not relative clauses):		
... the idea **that <u>music helps learning</u>** ...	The underlined part could be a sentence by itself. *That* introduces the clause but has no grammatical role in it. *Which* cannot be used.	Only certain nouns can be followed by a noun clause complement: *claim, idea, fact, news, possibility, evidence*, etc. (See 7.8.1)
Nouns with infinitive complements:		
... my effort **to improve** ... the ability **to write poetry**	Only certain nouns can be followed by infinitive complements: *failure, plan, tendency*, etc. (See 6.23)	
Nouns complements with *of* and a gerund		
... the process of **learning English** ... his habit of **interrupting people**	Only certain nouns can be followed by this type of complement. (See 6.22)	

Understanding complements of nouns can help you avoid errors with relative clauses:

a. The idea ~~which~~ the earth was round was proven by Magellan's voyage. → that
b. She has the ability ~~that she can~~ sleep through anything. → to
c. I'm annoyed by their habit ~~that they play~~ loud music late at night. → of playing

■ **Exercise 33** Two or three of the underlined parts have mistakes. Fix them.
1. We were encouraged by the <u>news that unemployment was declining.</u>
2. The reporter was criticized for including opinions in the <u>news that he reported</u>.
3. The company had to abandon its <u>plan to expand to overseas markets</u>.
4. The nation was overjoyed by the<u> news which the queen had given birth to a son</u>.
5. The <u>plan that we finally adopted</u> was similar to the one we started with.
6. We learned a lot from the <u>process of trying to write our ideas as concisely as possible</u>.
7. I was annoyed by my sister's <u>habit that she interrupted people all the time</u>.
8. There was controversy about the <u>process which they used</u> for deciding how to cut costs.

Usage Guide

8.23 Grammar checkers' advice on *that* and *which*

What do grammar checkers say about *that* and *which*?

Grammar checkers in word-processing programs sometimes give advice related to *that* and *which*. They may suggest using *which* instead of *that* after a comma:

a. In 1919, Congress passed the 20th **amendment, that** gave women the right to vote.
    → **amendment, which**

In the sentence above, this is good advice. The relative clause is nonrestrictive, so *which* is right (8.8). When there is no comma, grammar checkers may suggest using *that* instead of *which*:

b. A paradox is a **statement which** seems to contradict itself, like "Less is more."
    → **statement that**

In this case, with a restrictive relative clause, *which* is not a mistake, but many writers prefer *that*. If you follow the advice in cases like these, you will usually not make a mistake. The advice of grammar checkers can be useful, if you judge it carefully.

8.24 Using relative clauses to express details

Avoiding overused words like *good*

If you tend to write phrases with overused adjectives — *a good person, a bad leader, an interesting book* — relative clauses can help you add detail and color to your writing. They allow you to describe people and things in terms of actions. *Good people* might be good in different ways. Writers sometimes prefer to specify one way. They select one detail (or more) to represent a quality and express it in a relative clause.

a good boss	a boss who knows how to bring out the best in employees
a good friend	a friend you can depend on
a good teacher	a teacher who knows her subject and can make it come alive
a bad decision	a decision I will regret for the rest of my life
a bad day	a day when nothing goes right
interesting movies	movies that make you think
interesting places	places that you could visit again and again without getting bored
a rich person	a person who drives a Ferrari and wears a Rolex
a poor person	a person who doesn't know where her next meal is coming from

8.25 Avoiding wordy relative clauses

Sometimes a relative clause with the verb BE or HAVE is wordy and can be replaced by a more concise structure.

a. Avoid wordy relative clauses:	Use more concise structures:
b. Children who are healthy learn better. →	Healthy children learn better.
c. We read books which were written by women. →	We read books by women.
d. I want an apartment which has parking. →	I want an apartment with parking.

Sometimes a wordy relative clause with *which is* can be revised as (d). Notice the colon (:).

| d. Many industrialized countries have a demographic problem, which is that the population is aging fast and not replacing itself. → | Many industrialized countries have a demographic problem: the population is aging fast and not replacing itself. |

Avoiding "which is"

A reflex is an action you perform unconsciously.

USAGE GUIDE

8.26 Relative clauses in definitions

We often use relative clauses and reduced relative clauses we when define or explain a term, using the pattern below. We cannot omit the noun before *that* or *who(m) / whose* (g).

Term		Category	Differentiating information
a. *A prodigy*	*is*	*a person*	*who shows exceptional talent as a child.* (8.3)
b. *A reflex*	*is*	*an action*	*you perform unconsciously.* (8.4)
c. *A key pal*	*is*	*someone*	*you correspond with through email.* (8.5)
d. *A widow*	*is*	*a woman*	*whose husband has died.* (8.6)
e. *A chat room*	*is*	*a virtual space*	*where strangers can interact online.* (8.7)
f. *Chili*	*is*	*a stew*	*made with meat, tomatoes, and peppers.* (8.2)
g. *A prodigy is* ~~*who shows*~~ ... *Your daily routine is* ~~*that you do*~~ ...(*everything that you do ...*)			

■ **Exercise 34** In the questions below, identify the relative clauses. Then choose a term from the list at the end to answer each question. The terms are typical terms used at American universities.

1. What do you call a document that describes the content and expectations of a course?
2. What do you call a test you take after missing a test in class?
3. What do you call a graduate student who helps a professor with teaching duties?
4. What do you call a course you have to take before you register for another course?
5. What do you call an temporary job that gives a student work experience (for example, in a company)?
6. What do you call a place where students can go for help with academic papers?
7. What do you call a room where students can go to study between classes?
8. What do you call an essay in which you share an insight gained from your experience?
9. What do you call the subject area in which you concentrate your studies?
10. What do you call a building where students live on campus?
11. What do you call a test that covers all the material from a course up to the time of the test?
12. What do you call the part of an article in which the author reviews previous research?

___ an internship   ___ a cumulative exam   ___ a study lounge
___ a literature review   ___ a prerequisite   ___ a syllabus
___ a major / your major   ___ a personal experience essay ___ a teaching assistant
___ a make-up test   ___ a residence hall / a dormitory ___ a writing center

■ **Exercise 35** Without looking at the questions in exercise 34, write definitions for the terms above. Then compare your definitions with those in the questions.

■ **Exercise 36** Write definitions of words below that you know, using relative clauses or reduced relative clauses (8.12). If you use a dictionary, don't copy the definition. Learn it and then write it as you remember it.

an adverb	a conformist	a garage	an orchard	a theater
an atheist	a couch potato	a hypochondriac	a panhandler	a vegan
a bucket list	a fair weather friend	a lounge	a pet	a werewolf
a casino	a flea market	a mentor	a polyglot	a widower
a commuter	a friend	an optimist	a studio	a witness

Usage Guide

8.27 Using relative clauses for a *tight* writing style

Tight writing can improve your style.

- Writing can be described as **loose** or **tight**.
- Loose writing has short, simple sentences, each with a small amount of information.
- Tight writing has longer, more complex sentences, each with more information.
- In academic work, tight writing is preferred and often makes use of relative clauses.
- Look at the two different versions of the same information in the table below.
- Notice how the relative clauses in Passage B are used to make a tighter connection between the two pieces of information.

Passage A: Loose writing	Passage B: Tight writing
In 1902, six men in northern Minnesota started a company. It eventually became 3M.	*In 1902, six men in northern Minnesota started a company that eventually became 3M.*
Later the company moved from northern Minnesota to the St. Paul area. It still has its headquarters there.	*Later the company moved from northern Minnesota to the St. Paul area, where it still has its headquarters.*
3M employs many researchers. They improve existing products and develop new ones.	*3M employs many researchers who improve existing products and develop new ones.*
In 1974, one of their researchers developed an adhesive. (His name was Spencer Silver.) It seemed too weak to be useful but it later became the basis of post-it notes. Post-it notes are also known as "sticky notes." They are one of 3M's best-known products.	*In 1974, one of their researchers, Spencer Silver, developed an adhesive which seemed too weak to be useful but which later became the basis of post-it notes (sometimes called "sticky notes"), one of 3M's best-known products.*

■ **Exercise 37** Study the differences between the two passages above. How many sentences appear in the loose version? How many in the tight version? Identify the relative clauses, one appositive, and one reduced relative clause in the tightly written version.

■ **Exercise 38** Writing tightly requires careful attention to overall sentence structure. Considering overall sentence structure, complete the passage without looking above. **Five or six** blanks should be left blank (Ø). Others require one of the words provided. There may be more than on way.

   Ø   and   he   it   that   who   where

In 1902, six men in northern Minnesota __ started a company __ eventually became 3M. Later the company __ moved from northern Minnesota to the St. Paul area, __ __ still has its headquarters. 3M employs many researchers __ improve existing products __ develop new ones. In 1974, one of their researchers, __ Spencer Silver, __ developed an adhesive __ seemed too weak to be useful but __ later became the basis of post-it notes (__ also sometimes called "sticky notes"), __ one of 3M's best-known products.

■ **Exercise 39** Cover the words in the "Passage B" box above. Reconstruct it by looking only at the left box, combining sentences using relative clauses, two appositives, and one reduced relative clause.

Usage Guide

■ **Exercise 40** The sentences below, based on Shakespeare's *Romeo and Juliet*, include several relative clauses and related structures (in a tight writing style – 8.26). Identify the relative clauses, reduced relative clauses (8.12), and appositives (8.15). In parentheses after each item is a suggestion of what you should be able to find and which part of the chapter to consult if you have difficulty. Note: In summarizing the events in a story or drama, we typically use present tenses.

1. The story takes place in Verona, an Italian city-state dominated by a few rich and powerful families. In addition to the young lovers, the characters include Mercutio and Tybalt, both of whom are killed early in the story. Friar Lawrence, a priest, plays an important role in the plot. (Look for an appositive with a reduced relative clause [8.13 d], a relative clause with a quantifier [8.10], an another appositive [8.15].)

2. Romeo and Juliet, teenagers whose families are enemies, meet at a party given by Juliet's family, the Capulets. (Look for two appositives, one of which includes a relative clause [8.15].)

3. After the party, Romeo secretly hides in the Capulets' garden, where he sees Juliet at her window and delivers a famous speech about how beautiful she is. When he hears her speak his name he calls out to her, and they declare their love for each other. (Look for a relative clause [8.7].)

4. Romeo goes to see Friar Lawrence, who agrees to perform a secret marriage which he thinks might end the bad feelings between the two families. (Look for two relative clauses [8.3, 8.11].)

5. In the streets of Verona, Romeo becomes involved in a fight with a group of Capulet men. Tybalt, Juliet's cousin, kills Romeo's friend Mercutio, and Romeo kills Tybalt. As punishment, Romeo is exiled from Verona. His mother, Lady Montague, dies of grief. (Look for two appositives [8.15].)

6. Juliet's parents, unaware that their daughter is secretly married, arrange for her to be married within three days to another man. She seeks the advice of Friar Lawrence, who gives her a potion he says will make her fall into a deep sleep that resembles death. (Look for a reduced relative clause beginning with an adjective [8.16] and three relative clauses [8.3, 8.11].)

7. The potion works. The Capulets, sure that she is dead, put Juliet to rest in the family tomb. According to Friar Lawrence's plan, Romeo will visit the tomb after she wakes up and secretly take her away. (Look for a reduced relative clause beginning with an adjective [8.16].)

8. Friar Lawrence writes Romeo a message in which he explains the plan. Romeo never receives the message. He only hears that Juliet is dead. (Look for a relative clause [8.5].)

9. Romeo rushes to Juliet's tomb, where he swallows a bottle of poison he has purchased from an apothecary. When Juliet wakes up, she sees he is dead, which drives her to kill herself with his dagger. The Montagues and the Capulets, saddened by the deaths, agree to live peacefully. (Look for three relative clauses [8.7, 8.4, 8.9] and a reduced relative clause [8.12].)

Usage Guide

■ **Exercise 41** Using relative clauses and related structures, revise the sentences using a tighter writing style (8.26). For conciseness, use an appositive instead of a relative clause when you can (8.15). For example: *Juliet's parents want her to marry Paris. He is a young man. She does not love him.* ⟶ *Juliet's parents want her to marry Paris, ~~who is~~ a young man she does not love.*

1. The story takes place in Verona. Verona is an Italian city-state. It is dominated by a few rich and powerful families.

2. In addition to the young lovers, the characters include Mercutio and Tybalt. Both of them are killed early in the play.

3. Friar Lawrence is a priest. He plays an important role in the plot. (*There are two ways.*)

4. Romeo and Juliet meet at a party. It is given by Juliet's family. They are teenagers. Their families are enemies. Juliet's family is the Capulets.

5. After the party, Romeo secretly hides in the Capulet's garden, There he sees Juliet at her window and delivers a famous speech about how beautiful she is.

6. Romeo goes to see Friar Lawrence. Friar Lawrence agrees to perform a secret marriage. He thinks this marriage might end the bad feelings between the two families.

7. Tybalt (he is Juliet's cousin) kills Romeo's friend Mercutio, and Romeo kills Tybalt. As punishment, Romeo is exiled from Verona. His mother dies of grief. She is Lady Montague.

8. Juliet's parents arrange for her to be married within three days to another man. They are unaware that their daughter is secretly married.

9. She seeks the advice of Friar Lawrence. He gives her a potion. He says it will make her fall into a deep sleep. This sleep will resemble death.

10. The Capulets put Juliet to rest in the family tomb. They are sure she is dead.

11. Friar Lawrence writes Romeo a message. In it he explains the plan.

12. Romeo rushes to Juliet's tomb. There he swallows a bottle of poison. He has purchased it from an apothecary.

13. When Juliet wakes up, she sees that he is dead. This drives her to kill herself with his dagger.

14. The Montagues and the Capulets agree to live peacefully. They are saddened by the deaths.

■ **Exercise 42** Make notes on the story of Romeo and Juliet, writing down names and main events in note form. Then, using your notes, reconstruct the story in your own words, using relative clauses and related structures appropriately. As we usually do in writing about the events of a drama, use mainly present tenses.

Test yourself

■ **Exercise 43** Choose the correct forms. **One, two, or three** answers may be correct.

1. Did you read about the passengers __ were stuck on a plane for five hours?
   (a) they   (b) who   (c) Ø   (d) which

2. Adam spent a lot at the bookstore. Some of the books __ were really expensive.
   (a) he bought   (b) that bought   (c) that he bought them   (d) he bought which

3. They showed us some pictures of the area they __
   (a) lived   (b) lived in   (c) lived in it   (d) lived in which

4. The evidence __ was found at last in a storeroom at the national museum.
   (a) that scholars had been searching for it   (b) that scholars had been searching
   (c) for which scholars had been searching   (d) that scholars had been searching for

5. This book is for students __ first language isn't English.
   (a) who   (b) whose   (c) which   (d) that

6. They lived in a small town in southern Germany
   (a) the name I can't remember it   (b) that I can't remember the name
   (c) whose name I can't remember   (d) that I can't remember its name

7. I remember one small village in France __ we lived for a month.
   (a) that   (b) when   (c) which   (d) where

8. Can you remember a time __ you felt proud?
   (a) when   (b) that   (c) Ø   (d) which

9. There are good reasons __ some people choose not to have children.
   (a) why   (b) which   (c) for   (d) Ø

10. The Roman Empire __ stretched from the British Isles to Egypt.
    (a) , which lasted for hundred of years,   (b) , that lasted for hundreds of years,
    (c) which lasted for hundreds of years   (d) that lasted hundreds of years

11. I always read my papers aloud, __ helps me catch mistakes.
    (a) it   (b) which   (c) that it   (d) that

12. J.S. Bach had 20 children, only __ survived into adulthood.
    (a) ten   (b) ten of them   (c) ten of which   (d) ten of whom

13. We had to draw a diagram, part of __ consisted of a triangle inside a circle.
    (a) it   (b) that   (c) which   (d) whose

14. She takes vitamin supplements __ will prevent cancer.
    (a) that she says   (b) that she says they   (c) which she says that   (d) which she says

15. Microbiology is the study of tiny organisms __ microbes.
    (a) calling   (b) called   (c) that are called   (d) that called

Chapter 8

USAGE GUIDE

16. People ___ for work know how frustrating it can be.
    (a) are looking   (b) who are looking   (c) that they are looking   (d) looking

17. One of the men working in the building ___ helped me find the right office.
    (a) Ø   (b) he   (c) who   (d) which

18. In my presentation, I handed out a chart ___ my results.
    (a) summarizing   (b) summarized   (c) that summarized   (d) which summarized

19. The ideas ___ in this chart are important.
    (a) summarizing   (b) summarized   (c) that are summarized   (d) are summarized

20. Bizen is in Hokkaido ___ .
    (a) Japan's northern island
    (b) Japan's northern island
    (c) which is Japan's northern island
    (d) is Japan's northern island

21. Tourists to Hokkaido should be sure to visit Bizen, ___ for pottery and swords.
    (a) which famous   (b) that is famous   (c) famous   (d) which is famous

22. We visited Bizen, ___ known for pottery and swords.
    (a) a town   (b) which   (c) Ø   (d) which is a town

23. During the hike, you'll have to carry ___ you need in your backpacks.
    (a) what   (b) everything   (c) that   (d) all that

24. There is an organization that gives food to ___ needs it.
    (a) who   (b) whoever   (c) anyone who   (d) anyone

25. Josh ___ didn't laugh.
    (a) too young to understand the joke
    (b) too young to understand the joke,
    (c) was too young to understand the joke
    (d) was too young to understand the joke,

26. They have interpreters on staff to help ___ don't speak English.
    (a) those who   (b) people   (c) who   (d) people who

27. In this clinic we have toys for children ___ with while their parents talk to the doctor.
    (a) who play   (b) that play   (c) to play   (d) playing

28. Neil Armstrong was the first man ___ on the moon.
    (a) walked   (b) to walk   (c) who walked   (d) to walking

29. Leonardo da Vinci is best known for his paintings, one of which, the Mona Lisa, ___ probably the most famous painting in the world.
    (a) is   (b) and   (c) that is   (d) Ø

30. There is an increasing concern over the fate of young men who are pressured to become gang members ___ beaten or even killed if they refuse.
    (a) Ø   (b) are   (c) and   (d) who

8.28 Problems with relative clause

	Problems	Revisions	Comments
1.	The book was about zombies that I read.	The book that I read was about zombies.	Put the relative clause right after the noun it modifies. (8.2)

- Exception: Sometimes another modifier — usually a reduced relative clause (8.12) or a prepositional phrase — comes first: *I met a student **from China** who plays ping-pong.*

	Problems	Revisions	Comments
2.	I have a friend needs a job. I have a friend who/that	I have a friend who needs a job.	Don't omit a subject relative pronoun. (8.3)
3.	I have a friend that he needs a job.		Don't use an extra pronoun (or noun). (8.3, 8.4, 8.5)
4.	Is this the book (that) you were looking for it?	Is this the book (that) you were looking for?	
5.	The music they listen is called cumbia.	The music they listen to (to which they listen) is called cumbia.	Don't omit a necessary preposition. (8.5)
6.	I met a girl that her mother is in the army.	I met a girl whose mother is in the army.	Use *whose* for a possessive relative clause. (8.6)
7.	Do you know of a coffee shop that we can meet?	Do you know of a coffee shop where we can meet? (that we can meet at)	Use *where* (8.7) or *that* + a preposition (8.5) appropriately.
8.	I need to find a coffee shop where has WiFi.	I need to find a coffee shop that has WiFi.	Don't use *where* (8.7) when you need a relativizer that is a subject or object. (8.4)
9.	The shops where I prefer are all near the campus.	The shops that I prefer are all near the campus.	
10.	Germany, that has no oil resources, is a leader in solar energy.	Germany, which has no oil resources, is a leader in solar energy.	With a nonrestrictive relative clause, use commas and don't use *that*. (8.8)
11.	Germany which has no oil…		
12.	A pediatrician is a doctor, who treats children.	A pediatrician is a doctor who treats children.	With a restrictive relative clause, don't use commas. (8.8)
13.	A person who running for office needs funds.	A person running for office needs funds.	When you reduce a relative clause, don't keep the relative pronoun. (8.12)
14.	They bought a house that built in 1920.	They bought a house built in 1920.	

Problems	Revisions	Comments
15. I included a table summarized my results.	I included a table summarizing (that summarized) my results.	Use an *-ing* word in a reduced relative clause for active voice. (8.12, 8.13, 8.14)
16. The results summarizing in the table are significant.	The results summarized (that are summarized) in the table are significant.	Use a past participle in a reduced relative clause for passive voice. (8.12, 8.14)
17. This is everything what I need.	This is everything that I need. This is what I need.	Don't use *what* except in a headless relative. (8.18, 8.19)
18. There is a free bus, it is very convenient.	There is a free bus, which is very convenient.	A relative clause can sometimes help you fix a comma splice. (2.19 and Appendix B)
19. There were three buses, two of them were full.	There were three buses, two of which were full.	
20. There are many students live alone.	There are many students who live alone (many students living alone). More concise: Many students live alone.	After *There is/are* and a noun, don't use a finite verb. Use a relative clause or reduced relative clause or don't use *There is/are*.
21. In the 1960s, Congress passed an important law. The Voting Rights Act, which made discriminatory voting practices illegal.	In the 1960s, Congress passed an important law, the Voting Rights Act, which made discriminatory voting practices illegal. In the 1960s, Congress passed an important law. The Voting Rights Act made discriminatory voting practices illegal.	Check your overall sentence structure to avoid fragments and other sentence structure problems. (8.21)

Chapter 9

Adverbial clauses

IN THIS CHAPTER
Adding information about time, reason, result, contrast, and manner

expressing the same meaning in different ways

stylistic variety

Chapter 9
Adverbial clauses

Chapter 9: Adverbial clauses 269

9.1	Adverbial clauses in context	271
9.2	Meanings that adverbial clauses express	271
9.3	How do you introduce an adverbial clause?	272
9.4	Conjunctions or prepositions?	272
9.5	Connecting an adverbial clause and a main clause	273
9.6	Avoiding fragments with adverbial clauses	273
9.7	Time clauses	277
	9.7.1 *When, whenever, while, as*	277
	9.7.2 *After, as soon as, before, by the time, since, until*	277
	9.7.3 Reduced adverbial clauses like *after finishing*	278
	9.7.4 Time clauses about the future: *When I will*	278
	9.7.5 Usage guide *When* or *while* or *as*?	279
	9.7.6 Usage guide *Before* and *until*	279
	9.7.7 Usage guide *By the time* and *before*	279
	9.7.8 Usage guide *Two years after* and similar expressions	279
	9.7.9 Usage guide *Since before* and *until after*	280
	9.7.10 Usage guide *Once* and *now that* for stylistic variety	280
9.8	Reason, result and purpose	283
9.9	Reason clauses and phrases	283
	9.9.1 Reason clauses	283
	9.9.2 Reason phrases with prepositions	283
9.10	Result clauses with *so* and *so that*	284
9.11	Result clauses with separate parts	284
9.12	Purpose clauses and phrases: *to, in order to, so (that), so as to*	285
9.13	*For* and *to* in descriptions of the purpose of an object or action	286
9.14	Usage guide *So little* and *so few...that* before a result clause	286
9.15	Usage guide *Such a disaster* and similar expressions	286
9.16	Usage guide Lexical grammar: *Thank you for not smoking*	287
9.17	Usage guide Using subordination to write more tightly: *so/such*	288
9.18	Usage guide Purpose infinitives in front position	288
9.19	Contrast and concession clauses	291
	9.19.1 Contrast Clauses	291
	9.19.2 Concession clauses: *although, though, even though, even if*	291
9.20	Manner clauses: *as, just as, as if, as though, like*	292
9.21	Place clauses: *where, wherever, everywhere*	292
9.22	Usage guide Four ways of expressing contrast	293
9.23	Usage guide Lexical grammar: *look like / as if / as though*	293
9.24	Usage guide Reduced clauses of contrast, manner, and place	294
9.25	Problems with adverbial clauses and related structures	298

Chapter 9 — Adverbial clauses — Grammar Advantage **271**

9.1 Adverbial clauses in context

Adverbial clauses are subordinate clauses that give information such as time and reason. They answer questions like *When, Why, How,* and *Under what conditions?*

KEY
Ch. 6 = Chapter 6
Ex. 23 = Exercise 23
5.2 = Chapter 5, section 2
2.14.3 = Chapter 2, section 14, subsection 3
(a) = an example

■ **Exercise 1** Based on what you already know about adverbial clauses, underline the adverbial clauses in the following text. The first adverbial clause, expressing a condition, is underlined. Find adverbial clauses that express *time, reason, manner, purpose, contrast,* and *place*. Look at 9.2 first if you wish.

<u>If you are a typical student</u>, maybe this sounds like you. When you study, you always have your phone at hand. You keep it handy because you don't want to miss anything. You act as if studying does not require uninterrupted attention.

In fact, it might be better to turn your phone off so that you can avoid interruptions. Most of us like to think we are good at multi-tasking, but when we divide our attention among tasks, the quality of our work generally goes down. Though we may think we can pay attention to many things at once, interruptions make us less efficient.

Of course no one wants to miss out on anything. But while it's unfortunate to miss out on updates from friends, it may be even worse to miss the chance to do well on an important task.

So think about it. It's great to have your phone with you wherever you go, but sometimes you ought to turn it off.

9.2 Meanings that adverbial clauses express

Condition	a. *If you are a typical student*, maybe this sounds like you.
Time	b. *When you study*, you always have your phone at hand.
Reason (cause)	c. You keep it handy *because you don't want to miss anything*.
Manner	d. You act *as if studying does not require uninterrupted attention.*
Purpose or result	e. Shouldn't you turn your phone off *so that you can avoid interruptions?*
Concession	f. *Though we may think we can pay attention to many things at once*, interruptions make us less efficient.
Contrast	g. *While it's unfortunate to miss out on updates from friends*, it might be even worse to miss your chance to pass an exam or write a good paper.
Place	h. You can take your phone *wherever you go*, but sometimes you have to turn it off.

- Punctuation note: We usually use a comma after an adverbial clause at the beginning of the sentence. There is usually no comma if the adverbial clause is at the end.

9.3 How do you introduce an adverbial clause?

- An adverbial clause begins with a subordinating conjunction that connects the clause to the rest of the sentence.
- We use only one subordinating conjunction to introduce an adverbial clause (*after when you finish ..., because that I was late ...*).
- Some conjunctions are used for more than one meaning. For example, *while* can express both time and contrast. These conjunctions appear in boldface below.

Time (9.7)	*after, as, as soon as, before, by the time,* **now that**, *once,* **since**, *until, when, whenever,* **while**
Reason (9.9)	*because, as, since,* **now that**
Result (9.10, 9.11)	*so, so that, so ... that, such ... that*
Purpose (9.12)	*to, in order to, so as to,* * **so (that)**, *in order that, (in order) for*
Contrast (9.19.1)	**while**, *whereas*
Concession (9.19.2)	*although, though, even though*
Manner (9.20)	**as**, *just as, as if, as though, like*
Place (9.21)	*where, wherever, everywhere*
Condition (Ch. 10)	*if, unless, since, as long as, whether or not, no matter...*
* In the purpose group, *to, in order to,* and *so as to* introduce phrases, not clauses.	

9.4 Conjunctions or prepositions?

After, before, since, and *until* are both conjunctions (*after we ate*) and prepositions (*after lunch*). *Although, because, unless,* and *while* can be difficult because the corresponding prepositions have different forms.

a. **Although we had delays**, we weren't too late. ≈ **Despite delays**, we weren't too late.
b. **Because it costs so much**, we don't fly first-class. ≈ **Because of** the cost, we...
c. **While you're talking on the phone**, do you gesture? ≈ **During** a phone conversation, do...

Conjunction + clause		Preposition + noun phrase
after they left	≈	after their departure
before class begins	≈	before class
since they arrived	≈	since their arrival
until the assignment is due	≈	until the due date
although it was raining	≈	**despite / in spite of** the rain
because it is unhealthy	≈	**because of / due to** the health risks
while we were on vacation	≈	**during** our vacation
unless I get a scholarship	≈	**without** a scholarship

9.5 Connecting an adverbial clause and a main clause

After an adverbial clause, we don't introduce the main clause with a conjunction.

a. ***Although*** *this cheese smells bad, it tastes good.* (~~but~~ *it tastes good*)

Also correct: This cheese smells bad, but it tastes good.

b. ***Because*** *children are natural language learners, they don't have to study.* (~~so~~ *they don't...*)

Also correct: Children are natural language learners, so they don't have to study.

Although it rained, we played outside.

It rained, but we played outside.

9.6 Avoiding fragments with adverbial clauses

When an adverbial clause is used without a main clause, it is a fragment. We use fragments in conversation, but we avoid them in writing. See also 2.19.

Avoiding fragments

Correctly punctuated sentences	Incorrect punctuation (with fragments)
a. *Basketball is popular because you don't need much equipment and you don't need a lot of space.*	WRONG: *Basketball is popular. Because you don't need much equipment and you don't need a lot of space.*
b. *Some parents still believe the theory that vaccines cause autism even though there is no evidence to support it.*	WRONG: *Some parents still believe the theory that vaccines cause autism. Even though there is no evidence to support it.*
c. *When the telephone was invented in the late 19th Century, it was expected to be used primarily by businesses, not for everyday communication among ordinary people.*	WRONG: *When the telephone was invented in the late 19th Century. It was expected to be used primarily by businesses, not for everyday communication among ordinary people.*

■ **Exercise 2** The passage below includes six adverbial clauses. The first, a conditional clause, is identified. Identify the other five: clauses of concession, manner, purpose, reason, and time.

HIGH PRIORITY

> Most American parents send their children to public schools. But <u>if they are not satisfied with the school system</u>, some parents look for alternatives. Though some parents choose a private school, others decide to educate their children at home. This is called home schooling, and it is a growing movement in the U.S. Most home-schooling parents choose this option because they object to ideas or teaching methods in the public schools At home, they can teach their children as they believe they should be taught. When parents make this choice, they need to investigate the legal implications so that they don't violate compulsory education laws.

■ **Exercise 3** Rewrite the two sentences as one sentence, using the subordinating conjunction to create an adverbial clause. Sometimes the adverbial clause will be the first part and sometimes it will be the second part.

1 You learn a new word. You should learn how to use it. *when*

2 Experts say you should eat something. You finish lifting weights. *as soon as*

3 My friend from Morocco uses an English name. It's hard for Americans to pronounce her real name. *because*

4 Always proofread your writing. You can catch at least a few mistakes. *so that*

5 There are exceptions. Most people are friendly. *although*

6 You travel. You can find friendly people. *wherever*

7 The weather is good. The crops will grow. *if*

■ **Exercise 4** Focusing on the underlined parts, find and correct **two or three** problems. There is more than one way.

Because people want to avoid making others uncomfortable, they often use alternative words or phrases, such as *passed away* instead of *died*. These expressions are called euphemisms. Although many euphemisms are used simply to avoid discomfort, but some are used intentionally to disguise unpleasant news. For example, when civilians die in military strikes, the euphemism *collateral damage* may be used. When military personnel are killed by their own side, the cause of death is described as *friendly fire*. Because the words *kill* and *death* are missing from both expressions, so we tend not to think about the awfulness of the events.

In a similar way, the verb *euthanize* is used to describe the killing of a wild animal that is active in a place where humans don't want it – even though *euthanize* traditionally refers to ending someone's life in order to save him or her from further suffering. A bear that is "euthanized" dies not because it is suffering but because it makes people nervous.

■ **Exercise 5** Choose the correct forms. More than one form may be correct.

1. They weren't very successful because ___ .
   (a) they didn't work hard   (b) not enough preparation
   (c) no one cooperated   (d) a shortage of money and time

2. The proposal failed because of ___ .
   (a) no one liked it   (b) too complex
   (c) a lack of interest   (d) problems with funding

3. Be sure to check the prerequisites ___ try to register.
   (a) before that you   (b) before   (c) before you   (d) before to

4. ___ the short growing season, Iowa is an important agricultural state.
   (a) Although   (b) Despite   (c) In spite of   (d) Though

5. ___ earth's orbit is elliptical, so the speed of the earth varies.
   (a) The   (b) Because   (c) Because of   (d) Because of the

6. The dorms are cleaned ___ the students are away for the summer.
   (a) during   (b) when that   (c) while   (d) despite

7. No one has felt safe since ___
   (a) when the war began   (b) the beginning of the war
   (c) the war began   (d) that the war began

Chapter 9

Exercise 6 Complete the text with these conjunctions and prepositions.

because   because of   despite   during   unless   until   while

_____ her age, my friend Samantha still plays tennis. It's hard to believe she's 67 _____ she plays like a 20-year-old. She often asks me to take photos of her _____ she's training or playing. _____ her retirement, she plans to put them in a scrapbook. _____ her love of the game, she doesn't plan to retire _____ she's 100. _____ she breaks a leg, I think she'll do it.

Exercise 7 Write a sentence that is similar in meaning, using the conjunction or preposition that is supplied. If the sentence requires a clause, remember to include a subject and verb.

1. We didn't want to interrupt them during their negotiations. *while*
2. Some people enjoy living in the North despite the harsh winters. *even though*
3. Mr. MacDonald has gone on two world cruises since his retirement. *since*
4. They say they won't go without us. *unless*
5. Unemployment remains high because the economy is slow. *because of*

Exercise 8 Choose between the alternatives or choose *both correct*.

1. A whiplash is an injury to the neck caused when the head moves forward and then back suddenly [during / while / *both correct*] a car crash or other similar accident.
2. A will is an official document that states what a person wants to happen to their property and their money after [they die / their death / *both correct*].
3. A zip file is a computer file that has been reduced in size so that [to use less space / it uses less space / *both correct*].
4. A prenuptial agreement is an agreement by a couple before [they get married / their marriage / *both correct*] about how their property will be divided up if they get divorced.
5. They won't let you get on a plane these days [unless / without / *both correct*] a valid ID.

■ **Exercise 9** Add punctuation. If you punctuate correctly, each item has two or three sentences. Be careful to avoid fragments (9.6).

1. Parents choose to homeschool their children
   because they object to the public school curriculum
   or simply because they believe they can do a better job of teaching their own child
   since homeschooling parents tend to be well-educated and highly motivated
   they sometimes really can do a good job

2. Homeschooling regulations vary from state to state
   Missouri, for example, has only minimal requirements
   while New York requires state tests and curriculum approval

3. Homeschooling isolates students from their peers
   because parents understand that this can inhibit the learning of social skills
   they often join associations
   so that they can contact other homeschoolers and cooperate on group activities

4. Some schools allow homeschoolers to participate in public school clubs and teams
   when schools offer this opportunity
   they can often receive additional funding to cover the costs

5. Do homeschooled children learn as much as their peers in public school
   In order to support their belief that homeschooling is a reasonable alternative
   homeschooling advocates have argued on the basis of research that it is effective
   however, the research has been criticized
   because there are many factors besides schooling that contribute to a child's success
   and it's misleading to compare a select group, homeschoolers, with all public school students

9.7 Time clauses

| after | as soon as | by the time | once (9.7.10) | until | whenever |
| as | before | now that (9.7.10) | since | when | while |

9.7.1 When, whenever, while, and as

a.	**When** they are born, babies can't tell the difference between similar colors.	When = at that point.
b.	I always took the bus **when** I was a student.	When = during that period.
c.	He will call when he **arrives / has arrived**. (*when he will arrive*, *when he arrived*)	In time clauses referring to future actions or events, we usually use present tenses, not will.
d.	We used to live just outside Chicago. **Whenever** we went into the city, we took the train.	When = every time, any time
e.	Surgery sometimes involves stopping the heart while the patient is kept alive by a machine. (*when*)	We often use *while* or *as* when we describe two activities that continue during the same period.
f.	Why do they always call **while** we're having dinner? (*while we have*)	We often use *while* for an event that is interrupted by another. The while clause usually has a continuous verb.
g.	**As** the Arctic ice melts, sea levels have been rising.	We often use *as* to describe changes that take place together.

- *While* and *when* are often interchangeable if the time clause has a continuous tense.

9.7.2 After, as soon as, before, by the time, since, and until

h.	Prosperity returned **after** the war ended.	= at a later time
i.	Do you fall asleep **as soon as** your head hits the pillow?	= very quickly after
j.	Mozart began to compose music **before** he was six.	= at an earlier time
k.	**By the time** they are six, most children know how to read.	They learn during the time before.
l.	I haven't played the piano **since** I injured my hand.	= from the beginning of the time, up to now
m.	Babies can't see as clearly as adults **until** they are several months old.	= up to that point

Avoid this common mistake with *until*:

n. *I have to get ready until six.* → I have to get ready by / before six. I have until six to get ready.

after examining the data

before continuing

9.7.3 Reduced adverbial clauses

Adverbial clauses with some conjunctions, especially *after* and *before* (*after I finished, before you leave*) can often be paraphrased by reduced clauses with an *–ing* from: *after finishing, before leaving.* Reduced clauses are correct if the subject of the main clause can be understood as the subject of the *–ing* form. When the subjects don't match, the mistake is sometimes called a dangling modifier.

a. *After examining the data, we changed our conclusion.*	**We** examined the data. **We** changed… We = We.
b. *Before continuing with the project, they need more funding.*	**They** will continue the project. **They** need funding. They = They.
~~*Before continuing with the project, more funding is needed.*~~	We will continue the project. **More funding** is needed. We ≠ More funding. (Dangling modifier.)
~~*After examining the data, our conclusion changed.*~~	**We** examined the data. **Our conclusion** changed. We ≠ Our conclusion. (Dangling modifier.)

Some conjunctions are used in reduced clauses and some are not.

Sometimes used in reduced clauses:	Not used in reduced clauses:
after before since when while	*as as soon as now that* *once by the time*
c. After doing a pilot study, we … (After we do …)	**As** ~~continuing~~, they …
d. Before stopping, they … (= Before they stop …)	**As soon as** ~~finishing~~, we …
e. Since changing my major, I … (Since I changed …)	**Now that** ~~living alone~~, I …
f. When shopping alone, men … (When men shop …)	**Once** ~~getting used to it~~, you …
g. Don't talk while chewing. (Don't talk while you …)	**By the time** ~~landing~~, the plane …
• Reduced clauses with an *–ing* form after *until* are possible but not usual.	

9.7.4 Time clauses about the future: *When I* ~~will~~…

Don't use *will* or past tense in time clauses about the future. Use present tenses (usually simple present or present perfect).

a. *Wait until the light is green.* (~~until the light will be green~~)
b. *You'll understand him better when you've known him a little longer.* (~~when you will know~~)
c. *I'll text you as soon as I* **arrive / have arrived**. (~~as soon as I will arrive, as soon as I arrived~~)

USAGE GUIDE: Time clauses

9.7.5 *When* or *while* or *as*?

When is the best choice to describe a period of time using a stative verb — for example, when we describe a period during a person's life.

   a. **When** *I was a child, I lived in Tokyo.* (As I was, While I was)
   b. *This house was in better shape* **when** *it belonged to the Changs.* (as, while)

As can also be used as a preposition: *As a child, I lived in Tokyo.*

While is usually best when we want to describe two actions taking place during the same limited period of time.

   c. *I want to travel the world while I'm still young.* (when, as)
   d. *You need to cancel your class while you still can do it without paying a fee.* (when, as)

As is the best choice for describing two changes that occur together over a period of time.

   e. *As I get older, I become more tolerant.* (When, While)
      (*When I get older* describes a future point or period, not a change over time.)

9.7.6 *Before* and *until*

Use *before* for the general meaning "at an earlier point in time than..." Use *until* for time up to an end point, especially when the end point represents a change. Don't use *until* when you describe an action that occurs at a point in time (d).

   a. *Add salt* **before** *the water boils.*
   b. *Heat some water* **until** *it boils.*
   c. *Can you buy alcohol before you are 21?* (until)
   d. *You have to move out of the dorm before the new semester begins.* (until)

Until is especially common when the main clause is negative. *Until* by itself is not negative. The negative is usually in the main clause. *Till* is sometimes used as a synonym for *until*.

   e. *In most states, you can't get* (can get) *a driver's license until you are 16.*

9.7.7 *By the time*, *before*, and *once*

In many cases, *before* and *by the time* are interchangeable.

   a. **Before / By the time** *they are six, most children know how to read.*

Don't use *by the time* (9.7.2) or *once* (9.7.10) as a substitute for *when*. Their meanings are more specific.

   b. *Kittens can't see* **when** *they are born.* (by the time)
   c. **When** *I graduated from high school, I was 17.* (Once)

9.7.8 *Two years after* and similar expressions

Clauses with *before* and *after* can be made more specific with words and phrases like *two years*, *just*, *right*, *long*, *not long*, and *soon* before the conjunction.

   a. *Can you exercise* **only a week after** *you've had surgery?*
   b. *Get to the airport* **two hours before** *your flight is scheduled to take off.*

USAGE GUIDE: Time clauses

9.7.9 Since before and until after

We can use *since before* for the idea of "since some time before" and *until after* for the idea of "until some time after."

a. *I've known Hannah **since before** we were in college.*
b. *The painter El Greco didn't become famous **until after** he died.* (until some time after)

9.7.10 Once and now that for stylistic variety

We can use special forms that combine time with reason or condition, as in *now that* (= "now and because") and *once* (= "after and because" or "after and if"). A clause introduced with *once* is usually before the main clause.

a. ***Now that** smart phones are so widespread, it's hard to imagine life without them.*	They are now widespread and because of that it's hard to imagine life without them.
b. *We never see you **now that** you have a job.*	We don't see you now because you have a job.
c. ***Once** you get used to it, the weather isn't so bad.*	After some time, if you are used to it, the weather isn't so bad.
d. ***Once** they became cheap enough, lots of people bought widescreen TVs.*	People bought them because they became cheaper at some point in time.

Once and *now that* can give your writing stylistic variety. In a clause introduced by *now that*, use present tenses (usually simple present or present perfect).

Instead of these:	Try these:
e. *You need to understand our concept of family, and then you will understand how we view divorce.*	f. *Once you understand our concept of family, you will understand how we view divorce.*
g. *I have described the problem. Now I will propose a solution.*	g. *Now that I have described the problem, I will propose a solution.*

Chapter 9 — Adverbial clauses

Test yourself: Time clauses

■ **Exercise 10** Choose the correct forms. More than one form may be correct.

1. When my rent _____ up, I'll have to get a roommate or move to a cheaper place.
   (a) goes   (b) is going   (c) went   (d) will go
2. _____ I've got a car, I don't get as much exercise as I used to.
   (a) As soon as   (b) Before   (c) Now that   (d) Until
3. She usually visits us _____ she comes to the city on a business trip.
   (a) as   (b) when   (c) whenever   (d) while
4. Elephants are becoming very rare in nature _____ their habitat gradually diminishes.
   (a) as   (b) as soon as   (c) by the time   (d) when
5. In most places you can't buy alcohol _____ you're twenty-one.
   (a) as soon as   (b) once   (c) until   (d) while
6. You'll know it's spring when the blossoms _____ on all the cherry trees.
   (a) appear   (b) appeared   (c) had appeared   (d) will appear
7. Do you like to unpack as soon ___ you get home from a trip?
   (a) after   (b) that   (c) when   (d) as
8. The Second World War ended ___ .
   (a) six years since it began   (b) after it began six years
   (c) after six years it began   (d) six years after it began

■ **Exercise 11** Complete these sentences with *when, while* or *as*.

1. Would you like a cup of coffee _____ you're waiting for your appointment?
2. _____ everything goes right, I don't normally need any help.
3. _____ people call you _____ you're eating, do you tell them to call back?
4. _____ time passes, even old people find it hard to imagine life without cell phones.
5. Did you like English _____ you were a child?

■ **Exercise 12** Complete each definition with *after* or *before* plus one of the verbs, checking a dictionary if you need to.

   die   finish   happen   study   take

1. A pretest is a test you take to determine how much you know ____ you ____ new material.
2. The afterlife is a religious concept referring to what happens to people ____ they ____ .
3. A postscript (or PS) is extra information you add to a letter ____ you ____ it.
4. A prerequisite is a course you have to pass ____ you ____ another course.
5. A premonition is a feeling that you know about something ____ it ____ .

■ **Exercise 13** Which sentences above can be paraphrased with reduced adverbial clauses?

■ **Exercise 14** Complete each adverbial clause so that it includes a conjunction from the list below, a subject pronoun, and one of the verbs below. For some of them, you may omit the subject pronoun and use an –*ing* form, to create a reduced adverbial clause (9.7.3).

after / before / since / until + subject pronoun + *buy / get / grade / leave / understand / win*

1. We tried to get home _____ too dark.
2. Lia's dog has really missed her _____ for college.
3. Do you always try clothing on _____ it?
4. Will your professor return the tests _____ them?
5. They explained the procedure to me again and again _____ it.
6. Senator Brown took office three weeks _____ he won the special election.

■ **Exercise 15** Rewrite each sentence with a complete time clause instead of the reduced clause.

Example: *Students must wear proper equipment when taking part in sports activities.*
➤ *Students must wear proper equipment when they take part in sports activities.*

1. You have to speak clearly when leaving a voicemail message.
2. Students should proofread their work carefully before handing it in.
3. Not long after graduating, Richard was offered a job at Google.
4. Since giving up her daily treat at Starbucks, Lola has saved a lot of money.
5. When deciding what courses to take, students often consult their peers.
6. After watching violent TV shows, are children more likely to act violently?
7. A huge oak tree stood on this spot for many years before being blown down in a storm.
8. After leaving the presidency, Jimmy Carter remained active in public life.

■ **Exercise 16** Add one pair of conjunctions to each description.

after / until   as / as   as soon as / when   when / while

1. Doppler radar allows forecasters to look inside large weather systems _____ they develop and to issue warnings _____ they start to become dangerous.
2. Most thermometers contain mercury, which expands _____ it gets warmer and contracts _____ it is cooling down.
3. _____ a large thunderstorm approaches you, it draws air into it, making the surface wind blow toward the storm _____ the storm is actually moving in the opposite direction.
4. _____ a computer model of the weather based on current calculations has been created, it can be used to predict future patterns. However, the effects of small errors in the original model grow over time _____ it no longer has accurate predictive power.

■ **Exercise 17** **One or two** underlined parts are wrong. Find and correct them.

Finding water in the desert near the coast of Namibia in southern Africa is not easy. However, the Namib beetle has found a way. <u>When</u> the early morning fog <u>drifts</u> across the desert from the ocean, the beetle is able to collect some of the moisture in a unique way. <u>Before</u> the sun <u>rises</u>, the beetle faces the ocean breeze and spreads its specially adapted wings to capture very small drops of water. <u>As</u> these tiny drops <u>will accumulate</u>, they form larger drops which become heavier until they <u>start</u> to trickle down to the beetle's waiting mouth. <u>By</u> the time the sun's heat <u>dissipating</u> the fog, the beetle has already collected its daily water supply.

9.8 Reason, result and purpose

Reason, result, and purpose are related ideas and are expressed with some of the same words.

a. *They succeeded **because** they worked hard.*	Hard work was the **reason** for their success.
b. ***Because** they worked hard, they succeeded.*	
c. *They worked hard, **so** they succeeded.*	Their success was the **result** of hard work.
d. *They worked hard **so that** they **could** succeed.*	Wanting success was their **purpose** for working. Note: so that and could succeed (not succeeded).

9.9 Reason clauses and phrases

To introduce a reason or cause, we usually use *because*. We sometimes use *since* and *as*, especially with the idea of "considering this fact" or "during this time." For present time, we can use *now that* to express both time (9.7) and cause. We can use some prepositions (9.9.2) with noun phrases, not clauses, to talk about reasons or causes.

9.9.1 Reason clauses

a. ***Because / Since / As** Shakespeare had little formal education, it's amazing that he wrote so brilliantly.*	= for that reason, considering this fact	**because**
b. *Are you studying grammar **because** you like it? (as, since)*	= Is that the reason? In this situation, we don't use *as* or *since*.	**since**
c. ***Since / As** costs have risen, universities are forced to raise tuition or reduce services.*	= during this time of rising costs and because of it	**as**
d. ***Since** I started exercising, I've lost weight.*	My weight loss has happened along with my exercising and probably because of it.	**now that**
e. ***Now that** everyone is here, we can begin.*	= now and for this reason	

9.9.2 Reason phrases with prepositions

a. ***Because of / Due to** distribution problems, people in many parts of the world go hungry.*	They go hungry because there are distribution problems.	**because of**
b. *Most food shortages are **due to** distribution problems. Shortages **due to** crop failure are less significant.*	*Due* is an adjective, so a phrase with *due to* can modify a noun. *Because of* is less commonly used in this way, especially in writing.	**due to**
c. ***Thanks to** abundant natural resources, Australia can meet a lot of its own energy needs.*	We usually use *thanks to* for things that people are grateful for. *They go hungry thanks to…*	**thanks to**

9.10 Result clauses with *so* and *so that*

So introduces a result (a). *So that* can also introduce a result, though it is less common (b). Clauses of result follow the main clause and are usually separated from it by a comma. (For *so* and *so that* to express purpose, see 9.12.)

a.	*Children learn languages naturally, so they don't have to study the rules.*	= Because they learn naturally, they don't have to study the rules. OR = and the result is
b.	*There has been an increased demand for oil, so that the price continues to rise.*	≈The increased demand has resulted in rising prices. OR = with the result that

The traffic was so bad that ...

9.11 Result clauses with separate parts

    so ... that   *such / such a ... that*   *so much / many ... that*

- We use the conjunctions *so ... that* and *such ... that* as separate parts. The first part, with *so* or *such*, is in the main clause. *That* introduces a subordinate clause.
- We use *so* before an adjective or adverb by itself (a, b, e).
- We use *such a* before an adjective plus a singular noun (f) and *such* before an adjective plus a plural (g) or uncountable noun (h).
- We use *so much* before an uncountable noun (c) and *so many* before a plural noun (d).
- The second part is introduced by *that* after the main clause. There is no comma.
- *So* followed by an adjective (*so good, so big, so fast*) is not correct if a noun comes after it (i).

a.	*The traffic was so bad ...*	... that we didn't get home till 11:00.	*so* + an adjective
b.	*The traffic moved so slowly ...*		*so* + an adverb
c.	*There was so much traffic ...*		*so much* + an uncountable noun
d.	*There were so many delays ...*		*so many* + a plural noun
e.	*J.S. Bach was so great ...*	... that he is called the father of Western music.	*o* + an adjective
f.	*J.S. Bach was such a great composer ...*		*such a* + an adjective + a singu- noun
g.	*J.S. Bach composed such great masterpieces ...*		*such* + an adjective + a plural noun or an uncountable noun
h.	*J.S. Bach composed such great music ...*		

Avoid this mistake:

i. WRONG: *She is so careful writer that she doesn't really need an editor.* ➤ *She is so careful that she ...* (like a and e above) / *She is such a careful writer that she ...* (like f)

9.12 Purpose clauses and phrases

    to   *in order to*   *so (that)*   *so as to*

Sit in front to hear better.

Sit in front so that you can hear better.

To introduce a purpose clause, we usually use a simple infinitive or an infinitive phrase with *in order to* (a, b). To introduce a different subject, we can use *for*, with or without *in order* (c, d). These phrases often introduce a condition that must be met before a result can be achieved.

So (that) also expresses purpose. We use *so (that)* when we have two subjects (e). A purpose clause with *so that* usually includes *can / could* or *will / would* (f–i). It is usually final, and there is usually no comma before it.

So as to (*so as* plus an infinitive) can also introduce a purpose (j). For negatives, we can use *so as not to* and *in order not to* (k). Instead of *not to,* we often use *avoid* plus a gerund (*not to do something* → *to avoid doing something*) (l).

a.	**To be** safe / **In order to be** safe, you need to be alert.	If you want to be safe, you need to be alert. (the same subject: *you*)
b.	I took astronomy (**in order**) **to satisfy** a requirement.	I took … I satisfied … (the same subject)
c.	**In order for** their children **to be** safe, their parents drove them everywhere.	*The children* is understood as the subject of *be safe*.
d.	**For / In order for** combustion **to occur**, fuel, heat, and oxygen are required.	Under those conditions, combustion may be the result.
e.	An academic paper includes a reference section **so (that)** readers can verify information or read more about the topic. (*a reference section to verify*)	The two subjects are different (*paper ≠ readers*) so we can't use an infinitive.
f.	We're taking the same class **so (that)** we can study together.	We want to study together.
g.	We went to the library **so (that)** we could study without distractions.	We wanted to study without distractions.
h.	I need to remove some items **so (that)** my luggage weighs less than 50 lbs.	I want to make it lighter.
i.	I removed some books **so that** my luggage would weigh less.	I wanted to make it lighter.
j.	Some holidays in the U.S. are always on Monday **so as to create** a three-day weekend.	The purpose is to create a three-day weekend.
k.	They listen to music with headphones **so as not to disturb** (**in order not to disturb**) the neighbors.	They don't want to disturb them.
l.	They listen to music with headphones **to avoid disturbing** their neighbors.	

9.13 *For* and *to* in descriptions of the purpose of an object or an action

To describe the purpose of an object, method, etc. we can use a phrase with *for ... to* (a) or an infinitive (b). We can also use *for*, sometimes followed by a gerund (c, d). (See also 8.20.)

a. These carts are **for** customers **to use** only inside the store.
b. We used to have to carry disks **to store** data.
c. Every company needs a system **for evaluating** employees.
d. A telescope is used **for viewing** distant objects.

I came here to go to grad school.

I came here for grad school.

We can use an infinitive or *for* plus a gerund in a purpose phrase after a **noun** (e). We usually use an infinitive, not *for* and a gerund, to describe the purpose of an **action** (f).

e. *I need a system **to remind** myself / **for reminding** myself of appointments.*	The purpose phrase modifies a noun: *system*.
f. *I wrote a note to remind myself of the appointment.* (*for reminding*)	The purpose phrase modifies an action: *I wrote a note*.

Avoid this common mistake.

g. I came here for ~~going to~~ grad school. ➤ I came here **to go** to grad school / **for** grad school.

9.14 *So little* and *so few... that* before a result clause

We can use *so little* with plural nouns and *so few* with uncountable nouns to emphasize the smallness of the amount or number, along with a result introduced by *that*.

*We had **so few** resources and **so little** time **that** we abandoned our project.*

USAGE GUIDE: Reason, purpose, and result clauses

9.15 *Such a disaster* and similar expressions before a result clause

We can use *such* a with singular nouns that express an evaluation (*disaster, genius, mess, success*) even when there is no adjective (a). If the noun is plural or not countable, we use only *such* (b).

a. *Bach was **such a** genius **that** he is often called the father of Western music.*
b. *The report was **such** nonsense **that** I couldn't take it seriously.*

USAGE GUIDE: Reason, purpose, and result clauses

9.16 Specific verbs with *for* phrases

thank someone for doing something

- The sentence *Thank you for not smoking* shows a typical pattern for expressing a reason after certain verbs.

Verb	Object	
admire *attack* *blame* *criticize* *discipline* *dislike* *envy* *hate* *honor* *like* *punish* *recognize* *reward* *praise* *thank*	someone her them me their leader etc.	*for something* *for doing something* *for not doing something*

- These verbs describe how people feel about (a, b), talk about (c, d), or respond to (e) the actions of others.
- If the reason is **lack** of action, we use a negative gerund: *not telling, not being*, etc. (f).
- If the verb is **passive** (Ch. 5), there is no object between the verb and *for* (g).
- With these verbs, we do not use a clause with *that* (h). (See 7.23)

a.	We admire him **for his dedication**.
b.	The villagers hate the army **for destroying** their crops.
c.	They blamed me **for the mistake**.
d.	I thanked her **for helping** us.
e.	The Nobel committee recognized Richard Thaler **for his work** behavioral economics.
f.	They blamed him for not telling the truth.
g.	Politicians are often criticized for not being consistent.
h.	They ~~criticized me that~~ I ... We ~~admire him that~~ he ... I ~~was punished that~~ I ...

■ **Exercise 18** Combine the sentences, using patterns from 9.16

1. I admire you. You stand up for your rights.
2. In a campaign debate, one of the candidates was attacked. He didn't release his tax returns.
3. Consumers often criticize advertisers. They don't tell the truth.
4. I sometimes have to discipline my son. He's mean to his sister.
5. At his retirement party, Frank was honored. He served the company more than 20 years.
6. I often praise my children. They work hard at school.
7. Sometimes I have to punish my dog. He chews on my shoes.
8. Martin Luther King, Jr., was recognized by the Nobel Committee. He promoted justice through nonviolent resistance.
9. Thank you. You are so helpful and you don't demand anything in return.

USAGE GUIDE: Reason, purpose, and result clauses

Tight writing can improve your style.

9.17 Using subordination to write more tightly: *so/such...*

In writing, subordination is often considered better style than other ways of connecting ideas because it often creates a tighter connection between clauses. *So / such ... that* allows writers to express a result in a way that makes a tight connection. Using subordination rather than coordination or separate sentences sometimes makes the writing more concise.

Looser style	Tighter style with subordination
a. *The violin is a very difficult instrument, so it takes many years to learn.* *So* is used as a coordinating conjunction.	*The violin is* **such a** *difficult instrument* **that** *it takes many years to learn.* Three changes are made: *A very* → *such a.* *So* → *that.* The comma is omitted.
b. *Jobs are very scarce. Therefore some unemployed workers have given up looking.* *Therefore* clearly introduces the result, but the sentences are short and simple.	*Jobs are so scarce that some unemployed workers have given up looking.* Three changes are made: *Very* → *so.* The result is expressed with *so...that* instead of *therefore.* The two sentences become one.
c. *Most people have cell phones. As a result, it's easy to call and let someone know if you're going to be late.*	**Because / Since** *most people have cell phones, it's easy to call and let someone know if you're going to be late.* Two changes are made: The result is expressed with *because* or *since* instead of *as a result*, and the two sentences become one sentence.

To answer this question ...

9.18 Purpose infinitives in front position

In writing, we often use purpose phrases with an infinitive at the beginning of a sentence, to connect a new idea to earlier content. (3.17 and Appendix D)

Poor flow from sentence to sentence:	Improved flow:
a. *How should children with autism be educated? We need to understand their characteristics.* The connection between the question and the following sentence is not clear.	*How should children with autism be educated?* **To answer this question,** *we need to understand their characteristics.* Adding a purpose phrase at the beginning makes the connection clear.
b. *Discipline is an important tool for guiding a child's development. It needs to be administered immediately after the child has misbehaved to be effective.* The purpose phrase is at the end.	*Discipline is an important tool for guiding a child's development.* **To be effective**, *it needs to be administered immediately after the child has misbehaved.* Moving the purpose phrase to the beginning makes the connection clearer.

Test yourself: Reason, result and purpose clauses

■ **Exercise 19** Choose the correct forms. More than one form may be correct.

1. Are you taking statistics __ you like it, or is it a requirement?
   (a) in order   (b) because of   (c) because   (d) as
2. __ tuition has gone up, many students have to look for part-time work.
   (a) As   (b) Because   (c) Since   (d) For
3. Can we begin the meeting __ everyone has arrived?
   (a) so   (b) so that   (c) now that   (d) so as
4. The ice caps have been melting, __ sea levels have been rising.
   (a) so as   (b) so   (c) that   (d) so that
5. Admission to some universities is __ only a tiny percentage of applicants get in.
   (a) so competitive that   (b) too competitive that
   (c) so competitive as   (d) very competitive that
6. Texas is __ that it takes more than a day to drive across it.
   (a) a very big state   (b) too big   (c) so big   (d) such a big state
7. __ safe when you travel, you should keep your passport well-concealed.
   (a) In order for   (b) To be   (c) For being   (d) In order to be
8. Most air travelers plan their flights __ minimize layovers.
   (a) to   (b) in order to   (c) so as to   (d) for
9. You need to register early __ can get into all the classes you want.
   (a) so you   (b) so that you   (c) as you   (d) so as
10. We haven't been able to make coffee or anything __ the power went out.
    (a) so that   (b) due to   (c) because of   (d) since
11. The rules were hard to apply ___ the way they were written.
    (a) because   (b) due to   (c) because of   (d) since
12. __ to improvements in automotive design, cars don't need service as often as they used to.
    (a) As   (b) Due   (c) Because   (d) Thanks
13. Most universities have a system __ teaching.
    (a) for evaluation   (b) to evaluate   (c) for evaluating   d) that evaluate
14. Does your college have a writing center __ get help with their papers?
    (a) in order to   (b) that students   (c) so as to   (d) for students to
15. I need to transfer to another school __ I can study hotel management.
    (a) that   (b) because   (c) so as   (d) so that
16. They painted their house so __ sell it for a higher price.
    (a) they could   (b) that they   (c) they   (d) to

■ **Exercise 20** Write a sentence that is similar in meaning, beginning with the adverbial clause or phrase.

1. My left knee became so painful that I had to stop running. *Because...*
2. Researchers use brain scanners so that they can track activity in the brain. *To...*
3. A person's chance of surviving cancer are better today because of improvements in early detection and treatment. *Thanks...*
4. I have trouble staying awake for an 8:00 class, so I always stop for coffee first. *Since...*
5. Please talk quietly so as not to disturb the other students. *To avoid...*

HIGH PRIORITY

■ **Exercise 21** Complete these sentences with one of the following:

> *because   because of   for   since   so   so that   to*

For some items, more than one answer is possible.

1. The StrengthsFinder was developed by the Gallup Organization ___ provide organizations with a new tool ___ improving the performance of teams of people.

2. The StrengthsFinder is an online assessment ___ helping people identify their talents ___ they can share them with others.

3. Organizations use it ___ promote a culture in which employees can take advantage of each others' strengths.

4. ___ the focus on strengths rather than weaknesses, employees are often eager to try it.

5. ___ the system was developed by a private company, organizations must pay ___ use it.

■ **Exercise 22** Rewrite each pair of sentences as a single sentence using *so... that* or *such... that*. In some cases you need to change or omit words (very, therefore).

1. Some rock musicians play very loudly. They damage their hearing.

2. The violin is a difficult instrument. It takes years to master it.

3. There are few jobs for unskilled workers. Therefore unemployment figures are likely to remain high.

4. Many students apply to this university. Only the top 10% are admitted.

5. Religion is a sensitive topic. Therefore people are often told to avoid it.

■ **Exercise 23** In the paragraph below there are mistakes in *one or two* of the underlined parts. Most of the parts have no mistakes. Find and fix the mistakes.

The U.S. system of government is often criticized <u>for being</u> too slow. Some of this slowness is <u>due to</u> the system of **checks and balances**. The founders of the country created the system of checks and balances <u>for ensuring</u> that no single branch of government has too much power, <u>because</u> the branches keep each other in check. For example, the legislative branch makes laws, but <u>in order for</u> a proposed piece of legislation to be adopted, the president — the head of the executive branch — must approve it. And <u>for</u> a law <u>to be</u> valid, it must be accepted as constitutional by the judicial branch of government. <u>Because</u> the way these three branches of government interact, some laws remain in doubt for many years.

9.19 Contrast and concession clauses

9.19.1 Contrast clauses

while

whereas

- We can use *while* to contrast two facts (a). A clause with *while* usually begins the sentence and is followed by a comma. Used in this way, *while* is very similar to *although* (9.19.2). For *while* in time clauses, see 9.7.1.
- We generally use *whereas* to contrast facts about similar types of things, such as two people, two places, or two theories (b), not as in (c). A clause with *whereas* is usually at the end. A comma usually separates the two clauses, no matter what the order is.

a.	**While** we agree that pollution is a problem, we disagree about how to solve it.	Our opinions are different.
b.	Cats are solitary animals, **whereas** dogs are social. / **Whereas** cats are solitary animals, dogs are social.	Cats and dogs are different in this way.
c.	**Not usual:** Whereas the university still offers Latin, few students take it.	→ *While* the university still offers Latin ... *Whereas* is not appropriate because we are not contrasting things of the same type.

9.19.2 Concession clauses

although

though

even though

even if

- We use *although* and *though* to introduce a clause with information that contrasts with the main clause. The clauses express two facts that usually don't go together (d, e).
- These are sometimes called concession clauses. (See also 3.12.)
- We usually use a comma between the clauses, especially if the concession is first.
- We use *even though* (two words, not one, and never ~~*even although*~~) in a similar way (f).
- Avoid confusing *even if* and *even though*. We use *even if* (g) to introduce a contrast when something might happen or sometimes happens (*Even if I'm wrong...*). We use *even though* (h) for things that are actually true or really happen (*Even though I'm young ...*).
- *Even* by itself is not a conjunction (i). Unusually *even if* or *even though* is correct.

d.	**Although** Mary is a vegetarian, she sometimes eats fish.	It's unexpected for a vegetarian to eat fish.
e.	I like the climate here, **though** the winters are pretty bad.	I like it except for the winters.
f.	**Even though** they lost the game, they had fun.	They lost, but they still had fun.
g.	Even if he's wrong, he won't admit it.	*Even if* is correct because he may be wrong. There is some doubt.
h.	Even though (~~even if~~) she's young, everyone looks to her for advice.	*Even though* is correct because she is in fact young. There is no doubt about that.
i.	WRONG: Even you're discouraged, you should do your best.	→ *Even if* / *Even though* / *Even when* (depending on the meaning)
• We also use *though* inside or at the end of a clause as a transition expression, similar to *however* in meaning. (See Appendix C.)		

as

just as

as if

as though

like

9.20 Manner clauses and phrases

- We use *as* and *just as* with a clause describing the way (the manner) in which something happens (a).
- We can use *as if* and *as though* to introduce a clause that expresses a comparison (b, c).
- We can also use *(just) like* plus a noun to make a comparison (d).
- We use *as* and a noun to mean "in the role of" (e).

a. *They make their living from the sea, **(just) as** their ancestors did.* (~~as their ancestors~~.)	= in the same way. Informally, we can say *like their ancestors* OR *like their ancestors did.*
b. *He walked in and sat down **as if / as though** he owned the place.*	= like a person who owned the place
c. *Some children talk to their parents **as if** they were servants.*	The parents are compared to servants.
d. *When there's a lot to do, I work like a slave.* (~~as~~)	I compare myself to a slave.
e. *The captives were forced to work **as** slaves.*	They were enslaved.

where

wherever

everywhere

9.21 Place clauses

- We use *where* to introduce a clause describing a definite place.
- We use *wherever* when we mean any place or "it doesn't matter where."
- We use *everywhere* for "in every place."

a. *I always sit **where** I can see all the action.*	I sit in a place with a good view.
b. ***Wherever** there are celebrities, there are photographers.*	It doesn't matter where.
c. ***Everywhere** we went, we found friendly people.*	They were friendly in all the places.
* *Where* can also introduce noun clauses (7.4) and relative clauses (8.7).	

USAGE GUIDE: Contrast, manner, and place clauses

9.22 Four ways of expressing contrast

although

despite

but

however

We can express contrast in four ways, with different punctuation. Be careful not to mix the different ways. In the examples below, the emphasis is on the idea that everyone had fun. The fact that it rained is less important.

	Less important information		More important information		
Adverbial clauses	Although / Though / Even though	it rained,	everyone had fun.		
Prepositional phrases	Despite / In spite of	the rain,			
Coordinating conjunctions		It rained,	but / yet	everyone had fun.	
Transition expressions		It rained. (Notice the period.)	However, / Nonetheless, / Nevertheless, / Even so,	everyone had fun.	

Despite ~~it rained~~, *everyone had fun.* → *the rain*
Although it rained, ~~but~~ *everyone had fun.*
It rained. ~~Although~~, *everyone had fun.* → *However / Even so*

- Also correct: *It rained, although everyone had fun.* This way emphasizes the rain, not the fun.

9.23 Verbs + *like*, *as if*, and *as though*

It looks like things are going our way.

We often use expressions such as *It looks like / as if / as though* with a clause to describe an impression. We use expressions such as *He acts like / as if / as though* to describe an impression of a person. After these verbs we can also use *like* followed by just a noun phrase. For the use of *as* before just a noun, see 9.7.5. See also 2.9 and 7.18.

It + verb + *like* / *as if* / *as though* + clause

It	feels / looks / seems / sounds	like / as if / as though	something is wrong.
	smells		something is burning.
	tastes		there is soap in this soup.
He	acts / behaves		he doesn't care.

Like + noun phrase

It / She	looks / sounds / seems	like (~~as~~)	a problem / an athlete.

The verb *treat* is used similarly.
    Like + a noun: *They treated us like royalty.*
    As if / as though + a clause: *She treated me as if / as though I knew nothing.*

USAGE GUIDE: Contrast, manner, and place clauses

Everything happened as expected.

9.24 Reduced clauses of contrast, manner, and place

We use some conjunctions plus an adjective or participle to create reduced clauses. We use present participles (e.g. *wondering*) for active verbs (*she wondered, she was wondering*) and past participles (e.g. *expected*) for passive verbs (*it was expected*).

a. *Wind power, **though** plentiful, is not easy to harness.*	= although / though it is plentiful
b. *She waited **as if** wondering what to do.*	= as if she **was wondering** (active)
c. *Everything happened **as** expected.*	= as **it was expected** to happen (passive)
d. *Buy bottled water **where** available.*	= where it is available

Test yourself: Contrast, manner and place clauses

■ **Exercise 24** Choose the correct forms. More than one form may be correct.

1. ___ I loved my home and family, I knew I had to go abroad for my studies.
   (a) Even though   (b) Though   (c) Although   (d) As though

2. You must follow each step in the procedure ___ I showed you.
   (a) as though   (b) even though   (c) just as   (d) as if

3. Many parking stalls are reserved, so you can't just park ___ you want.
   (a) as where   (b) where that   (c) whereas   (d) wherever

4. ___ single-parent families are increasingly common, it is still better financially to be in a family with two parents.
   (a) As if   (b) As though   (c) Even   (d) While

5. Other cars were speeding past me ___ I was standing still.
   (a) although   (b) as if   (c) as though   (d) even though

6. If you really want to relax, you should take your vacation ___ there is no Internet connection.
   (a) where   (b) whereas   (c) even   (d) while

7. Outdoor dining places are popular ___ they are sometimes noisy.
   (a) even   (b) even though   (c) as though   (d) despite

8. Even ___ English is not my native language, I like English movies.
   (a) although   (b) whereas   (c) while   (d) though

9. Science is based on observation, ___ religion is based on faith.
   (a) while   (b) whereas   (c) as if   (d) as though

10. Ants live in societies ___.
    (a) as people   (b) as people do   (c) like people   (d) as though people

11. Although junk food is tasty, ___ not very nutritious.
    (a) but it's   (b) however, it's   (c) it's   (d) is

12. ___ the cost, public transportation systems are usually a good investment in the long run.
    (a) Despite   (b) In spite of   (c) Even though   (d) While

13. We all want happiness, ___ we may define it differently.
    (a) however   (b) although   (c) even though   (d) though

14. Most people strive for success. ___, they may have different ideas of what success is.
    (a) However   (b) Although   (c) Even though   (d) Though

15. What's going on? It looks ___ there might have been an accident.
    (a) that   (b) as   (c) as if   (d) like

16. Everything happened as ___.
    (a) it was predicted   (b) it predicted   (c) predicted   (d) predicting

■ **Exercise 25** Complete these sentences with *as though, even though,* or *as*.

1. When you have a job interview, it's important to sound __ you know something about the company.
2. I like my physics class _____ the teacher is hard to understand sometimes.
3. They keep buying lottery tickets _____ they've never won anything.
4. When I lost my job, it felt _____ the world had come to an end.
5. Do most parents raise their children _____ they themselves were raised?

■ **Exercise 26** Rewrite the sentence so that it is similar in meaning, beginning with the words that are provided. In most items, you must omit some words.

1. Einstein's scientific work made nuclear weapons possible, but he often spoke against them. *Although...*
2. With celebrities, photographers are always close at hand. *Wherever there...*
3. The economy is slow even though there is growth in some sectors. *Despite...*
4. From the way Mark behaved, it seemed that he knew everyone at the meeting. *He acted...*
5. Americans tend to value individualism. Japanese are more focused on the group. *Whereas...*
6. The city of Washington is the center of government. However, its citizens have no representation in congress. *Even...*

■ **Exercise 27** Rewrite each sentence with a complete clause instead of the reduced clause.

1. The latest devices, though smaller and faster, are still quite expensive. *Although...*
2. Though not statistically significant, the findings are interesting. *Even...*
3. The president, though trying to be optimistic, talked about tough times ahead. *Though...*

■ **Exercise 28** Match the beginnings of sentences with the endings, using one of the expressions provided.

as   as if   like   though   whereas   wherever

1. We kept working ...	... she was expecting guests.
2. Her house was so clean it looked ...	... they went.
3. The travelers took pictures ...	... we were tired.
4. The mall near your house looks ...	... the boys were disappointed.
5. The girls were satisfied ...	... a good place to shop.
6. He behaved ...	... not very friendly.
7. They spent money ...	... they were rich.
8. Our new neighbor seems polite ...	... he didn't care what anyone thought.

■ **Exercise 29** Complete the text with six of these words and phrases.

although   as   as if   despite   however   whereas   wherever   while

_____ films and TV shows still celebrate a big wedding as one of the most exciting events in life, Americans no longer see marriage _____ their parents did. For the first time, according to the most recent Census report, married couples now represent less than half of all households. It seems _____ the traditional concept of a household, with mom, dad and kids under one roof, has fallen out of favor. The people who continue to have weddings tend to be well-educated (i.e. those with a college degree). This same group also has the lowest divorce rate, _____ people with less education are twice as likely to get divorced. Those with less education are also much more likely to have children without getting married. Only 6% of the babies of college-educated women were born outside marriage, _____ the figure for less educated women was 44%. The result is an expanding social division in the country in terms of how children experience and understand the concept of family. _____ frequent exposure in the media to the standard story of wedding bells and a married couple living "happily ever after," a new generation of Americans doesn't seem to be following the old script.

■ **Exercise 30** In each passage, one of the underlined parts includes a mistake. Find and fix the two mistakes.

1. *Red states* are states in which voters tend to vote for conservative candidates, <u>whereas</u> *blue states* tend to support more liberal candidates. <u>However</u>, the terms can be misleading. <u>Although</u> the majority of people in a state might vote for conservatives, <u>but</u> people in certain parts of the state, especially urban areas, might vote for liberals. <u>Wherever</u> you find conservatives, you can usually find liberals, too, <u>even if</u> they are in the minority.

2. The skills that a chief executive officer needs to run a company are very different from the skills that a president needs in a democracy. A CEO, <u>like</u> the president of a country, has to manage resources and people, <u>but</u> a CEO does not generally have to deal with strongly competing interests <u>as</u> a president does. And a CEO does not owe his or her position to the employees of the company <u>as if</u> the president owes his or her position to citizens. <u>While</u> the success of a business leader may make him or her an attractive presidential candidate, the differences between leading a business and leading a country are considerable.

Mixed exercises – Adverbial clauses and related structures

■ **Exercise 31** Complete the sentences. Key words from the chapter are underlined

1. <u>Once</u> you get used to it,
2. How do you feel about your grammar <u>now that</u>
3. <u>Before</u> handing in a paper,
4. <u>Before</u> grading students' papers,
5. <u>After</u> taking a difficult test,
6. You should always be careful <u>when</u>
7. Do you like to listen to music <u>while</u>
8. It's never a good idea to do something just <u>because</u>
9. The clothing they sell at this store is <u>so</u> expensive <u>that</u>
10. <u>Although</u> there are exceptions,
11. <u>Despite</u> the weather
12. Old people get their news from newspapers, <u>whereas</u>
13. You know what I mean! Don't act <u>as if</u>
14. Most people want to live <u>where</u>

Chapter 9 — Adverbial clauses

■ **Exercise 32** **Three or four** of the underlined parts are wrong. Find and fix the mistakes. Remember that since only three or four items have mistakes, some numbered items have no mistakes.

1. Should children be given money or other material rewards <u>when</u> they do well in school? Psychologists generally argue against such rewards, <u>whereas</u> economists and business people tend to support them.

2. <u>Though</u> most people would agree that students should study <u>because</u> they like learning, not <u>for getting</u> a monetary reward, the fact remains that rewards can motivate some students.

3. Some schools <u>reward</u> students not only <u>for doing</u> well academically but <u>to behave</u> well. <u>When</u> a child follows the rules consistently, she gets a ticket she can exchange for an item at a gift store.

4. People who favor rewards have a strong argument: <u>When</u> students are failing, schools should do anything they can <u>to reach</u> them. And <u>while</u> students may at first be motivated just by the rewards, their academic success might soon develop into a love of learning. <u>Because</u> arguments like these, rewards systems remain attractive to troubled schools.

5. Educators in troubled schools are so desperate <u>that</u> they are willing to try almost anything that promises success, and who can blame them <u>for trying</u> something new? Rewards systems are especially attractive <u>because</u> in some cases they are financially supported by business leaders.

6. <u>Where</u> rewards systems have been tried, there is some evidence of success, <u>though</u> it is not clear whether this success can continue. <u>Once</u> the rewards stop coming, some children may stop trying to learn.

7. <u>Before</u> adopt a reward system, psychologists say, schools should look for other ways of motivating students. And <u>even when</u> rewards are used, they don't have to be monetary rewards. All schools want to encourage reading, for example, <u>so</u> a book is a more appropriate reward than cash.

8. <u>Since</u> you are a student, you are very familiar with one kind of reward: grades. Although grades are very different from money, <u>but</u> they are a kind of reward, and almost every school system uses them. It <u>seems as if</u> schools don't trust students to study just <u>because</u> they want to.

9.25 Problems with adverbial clauses and related structures

Problems	Revisions	Comments
1. When that it's dry, the crops fail.	When it's dry, the crops fail.	After a subordinating conjunction, don't use *that* or any another conjunction. 9.3 (Exception: 9.7.9)
2. I study after when I get home.	I study after I get home. / I study when I get home.	
3. When the first time I tried skating, I was nervous.	When I first tried skating / When I tried skating the first time, I was nervous.	See 9.7.1.
	The first time I tried skating ...	See 8.7.
4. Despite the growing season is short, Iowa is an important agricultural state.	Despite the short growing season / Although the growing season is short, Iowa is an important agricultural state.	After a preposition (*because of, despite, during*), use only a noun phrase, not a clause. 9.4 After a conjunction (*although, because, while*), use a clause, with a subject and verb. 9.4
5. Products often have to be recalled because safety problems.	Products often have to be recalled because **they have** safety problems / because **of** safety problems.	
6. During having lunch, I got a call.	During lunch I got a call. While (I was) having lunch, I got a call.	Avoid *during* + a gerund. 9.4, 9.7.1, 9.7.7
7. Community colleges are thriving. Because they offer flexible programs.	Community colleges are **thriving because** they offer flexible programs.	Avoid fragments. 9.6, 2.19, Appendix C
8. When people are asked whether they consider themselves honest. Most people say yes.	When people are asked whether they consider themselves honest, most people say yes.	Subordinate conjunctions (*because, when, etc.*) introduce only a part of a sentence, not a whole sentence.
9. When the oldest living veteran will die, no one will remember the war.	When the oldest living veteran **dies**, no one will remember the war.	In a time clause, use present, not future, even for future events. 9.7.1
10. Before / after graduate from college, I hope to get a job.	Before **I graduate**, I hope to get a job. / Before **graduating**, I hope to get a job.	Use a full clause (with a subject and verb). 9.6.2 OR use a reduced clause (with an *–ing* form) 9.7.3.
11. After revising my paper, it was clearer.	After revising my paper, I felt that it was clearer. / After I revised my paper, it was clearer.	Avoid dangling modifiers. 9.7.3
12. I have to get ready until 6.	I have to get ready by/ before 6. I have until 6 to get ready.	
13. Now that he found a job, he can afford insurance.	Now that he **has** a job / **has found** a job / **is working**, he can afford insurance.	With *now that*, use present tenses. 9.7.10
14. After she graduated one year, she went back for a PhD.	One year after she graduated, she went back for a PhD.	Use a specific time expression in front of *before* or *after* 9.7.8

Problems	Revisions	Comments
15. He saved money that he was able to retire early.	He **saved money so that** he was able to retire early. / He **saved so much money that** he was able to retire early.	
16. The G.R.E. is so difficult test that many students have to take it more than once.	The G.R.E. is **so difficult** / that / **such a difficult** test that many students have to take it more than once.	Use *so* before just an adjective 9.11 Use *such* before an adjective + noun .9.11
17. I have to change this paragraph because it's clearer.	I have to change this paragraph so that it's clearer / because I want it to be clearer / (in order) to make it clearer.	Use *because* for a reason. 9.9.1 Use *so that* or *in order to* for purpose. 9.12
18. In order to survive endangered species, their habitat must be protected.	In order for endangered species to survive, their habitat must be protected.	In a purpose clause or phrase, use *for* or *in order for* to introduce a subject for the infinitive. 9.12
19. This pill is for help you sleep.	This pill is for helping you sleep. / This pill is to help you sleep.	Use a gerund after *for* (6.5), or use an infinitive without *for*. 9.12
20. I gave up smoking for improving my health.	I gave up smoking to improve my health.	Use an infinitive to express the purpose of an action. 9.13
21. They criticized that I hadn't prepared enough.	They criticized me for not preparing enough.	Use an object + *for* and a gerund after verbs like *criticize*. 9.16
22. It's important to keep learning even you are no longer a student.	It's important to keep learning even though / even if /even when you are no longer a student.	Don't use *even* by itself as a conjunction. Use **even as part of** a conjunction. 9.19.2.i
23. It's unwise to walk alone at night, especially you don't know the neighborhood.	It's unwise to walk alone at night, especially if / especially when you don't know the neighborhood.	Don't use *especially* as a conjunction. Use it before a conjunction.
24. Although / Even though / Though / planes sometimes crash, but flying is still safer than driving.	Although / Even though / Though planes sometimes crash, flying is still safer than driving. OR Planes sometimes crash, but...	Don't use *although* (or *even though* or *though*) with *but* ... Choose one. 9.5
25. Because the crops failed, so food prices rose.	Because the crops failed, food prices rose. / The crops failed, so food prices rose.	Don't use *Because ... so ...* Choose one. 9.5
26. Everything was double-checked. Although, some errors were overlooked.	Everything was double-checked, **although** some errors were overlooked. OR **However**, some errors... OR **Even so**, some errors...	Use *although* as a conjunction, not a transition expression. 9.19.2 OR Use a transition expression such as *however* or *even so*. 9.22

Chapter 10
Conditionals

IN THIS CHAPTER
Using *if* clauses and other structures to express predictions and describe hypothetical situations

Chapter 10
Conditionals

Chapter 10: Conditionals 303

10.1	Conditionals in context	305
10.2	What are conditionals?	305
10.3	Real conditionals	306
10.4	Unreal conditionals	307
10.5	Contrasting real and unreal conditionals	308
10.6	Conditionals with *can, could, may,* and *might*	311
10.7	*Were* in unreal conditionals	312
10.8	*Should* in conditionals	312
10.9	Inversion in *if* clauses	312
10.10	Negative conditions	313
10.11	Limited conditions	313
10.12	*Assuming, given that, in case*	314
10.13	Continuous verb phrases in conditionals	315
10.14	Mixed times in conditionals	315
10.15	When there is no condition: *no matter* and words with *-ever*	316
10.16	Usage guide Conditionals in paragraphs	317
10.17	Usage guide *Suppose* and *What if*	317
10.18	Usage guide Imperatives plus *and* or *or* to express conditions	318
10.19	Usage guide Special uses of *will* and *would* in *if* clauses	319
10.20	Usage guide *If I had ...* and *I wish (that) I had*	319
10.21	Problems with conditionals	321

Chapter 10   Conditionals   Grammar Advantage **305**

10.1 Conditionals in context

If someone's telephone rings during a concert, what goes through your mind? Would you feel angry if you were a performer in that situation? These are conditional sentences. They consist of a conditional clause beginning with *if* and a main clause.

KEY
Ch. 6 = Chapter 6
Ex. 23 = Exercise 23
5.2 = Chapter 5, section 2
2.14.3 = Chapter 2, section 14, subsection 3
(a) = an example

■ **Exercise 1** Based on what you already know about conditionals, can you identify the conditional sentences in the passage? Do you know any rules about how they are formed? (If you prefer, read 10.2 first.)

> In the days before cell phones, if you heard an unwelcome noise while attending a concert, it was usually someone coughing or dropping something. Times have changed. Not long ago, a businessman was attending a concert of a famous orchestra in New York when his cell phone rang with a marimba ring tone. If he had known it was his phone, he would have turned it off, of course, but he thought it was someone else's.
>
> If you were an orchestra conductor and a phone interrupted your concert, what would you do? Amazingly, the conductor stopped the orchestra and waited for the phone to be turned off. The man eventually realized it was his phone and turned it off, but only with great difficulty. It was a new and unfamiliar phone. If he ever goes to a concert again, no doubt he will leave his phone at home.

10.2 What are conditionals?

- Conditionals are sentences with clauses that begin with *if* (conditional clauses or *if* clauses), expressing the idea that one thing depends on another or that two situations always go together (a).
- An *if* clause may follow the main clause (a) or precede it (b). When the *if* clause is first, we put a comma after it (b).
- We can begin the main clause with *then* when we want to emphasize that it follows logically from the *if* clause (b).

a.	*Children can't concentrate **if they are hungry**.*	Hunger makes it impossible to concentrate.
b.	***If children do not eat breakfast**, then they do not do well in school* (OR *will not do well*).	Breakfast is necessary. Without it, they do not (OR will not) do well.

- We usually use *if* clauses when we talk about the possibility of an event (c) or when we are not sure whether something is or was true (d).
- When we are sure that something is or will be true, we use *when*, not if (e).
- When we express a generalization, we can use *if* in the same way as *when* or *whenever* (f).

c.	***If** I get a job with a good salary, I will get my own apartment.*	It is possible that I will get a job with a good salary.
d.	***If** I'm not mistaken, the world's largest city is Beijing.*	I don't know for sure.
	***If** you left a bag in the lab, you can get it in Room 42.*	Maybe you left it. We don't know.
e.	***When** I get a job, I will repay my student loans.*	I am certain that I will get a job.
f.	*The roof leaks / will leak **if / when / whenever** there is really heavy rain.*	This situation is generally true.

If I have time, I make coffee

10.3 Real conditionals

- We use real conditionals to talk about connections that are generally true, such as typical patterns, rules or habits, in the present (a, b) or past (c, d).
- We can also talk about connections that are likely to be true, such as future plans (e, f) or predictions (g), with *will* in the main clause.

a. If I **have** time, I **make** coffee in the morning. If I **don't have** time, I **don't make** coffee.	Sometimes I have time. Then I make coffee.
b. If your foot **touches** the line, you're out. If your foot **doesn't touch** the line, you're OK.	It's a rule of the game.
c. Our dog **used** to bark a lot if it **saw** a cat.	It sometimes happened.
d. During the nineties, I was often unemployed. If I **didn't have** a job, I **spent** my time hanging out with friends.	It sometimes happened.

- In the examples above, about present and past situations, *if* is more or less the same as *when*.

e. If you're **going** north, **you will** need a warm coat.	It will or may happen.
f. I **will do** the laundry later if I **have** time.	
g. If our currency **continues to decrease** in value, our exporters **will benefit**.	

- The examples in (a) and (b) are sometimes described as the factual or zero conditional. The examples in (e) through (g) are sometimes described as the predictive or first conditional.

■ **Exercise 2** Create sentences by matching words from the left box with words on the right. Between the parts, use *if*. For example: *What do you do at lunch time if you're not hungry?*

√ 1. What do you do at lunch time   you don't have a map?
   2. How do you get directions   someone asks "What's new?"
   3. How do you answer   *if*   you don't have a job
   4. How can you get money   you have to be absent?
   5. What do you call someone   √ you aren't hungry?
   6. What do you tell your teacher   you're feeling sad?
   7. How do you cheer yourself up   you can't remember their name?

Chapter 10 — Conditionals

10.4 Unreal conditionals

What would you do if you won the lottery?

- We use unreal conditionals to talk about remote possibilities (a, b) and imaginary future situations (c), with *if* + simple past for the condition and *would* in the main clause.
- When we talk about imaginary past situations (d) and regrets or blame for past events (e), we use *if* + past perfect (4.15) in the condition and *would have* in the main clause.
- We use *were*, not *was*, in unreal conditionals (f), except informally.

a. What **would happen** if an asteroid **crashed** into the planet?	Condition: simple past Main clause: *would* + base form
b. What **would** you **do** if you **won** the lottery?	
c. If people **ate** less junk food, they **would be** healthier.	
d. If you **had lived** in ancient Rome, you **would have spoken** Latin.	Condition: past perfect Main clause: *would have* + past participle
e. We **wouldn't have gotten** lost if you **had stopped** and asked for directions.	
f. I'm sure today is Sunday. If it **were** Monday, there would be more traffic. (Informal: If it was Monday ...)	If it were / if he were / if she were ... Except informally, we use *were*.

- The examples in (a) and (b) are sometimes described as the hypothetical or second conditional. The examples in (c) and (d) are sometimes described as the counterfactual or third conditional.

■ **Exercise 3** Answer the questions. Since these are unlikely or impossible situations, use *would*.

1. What would you do if you lost your wallet or purse?
2. If you had the chance to change your name, what name would you choose?
3. If you saw someone steal something in a store, what would you do?
4. If you had the opportunity to talk with a person from history, who would you choose?
5. What would happen if all the insects died?
6. What would your life be like if you lived in ___? (Name another country or city.)
7. What would happen if you looked directly at the sun during a solar eclipse?
8. How would your friends react if you suddenly stopped talking to them?

Real or unreal?

10.5 Contrasting real and unreal conditionals for future, present, and past

The difference between real and unreal conditionals is shown primarily in the main clause. The differences are shown in the chart. One important difference is in the use of past tense. In a real conditional about past time, we use past tense in the usual way: it refers to past time (Ch. 4). In an unreal conditional, past tense means "this isn't about a real situation".

In each of the large boxes, the first sentence is the **background** of the conditional. In other words, it describes the context in which the conditional is appropriate.

	Real conditionals – in *italics*	Unreal conditionals – in *italics*
Future time	(1) I might work tomorrow. *If I **work** tomorrow,* *I **will miss** class.* *If* clause: present tense Main clause: *will* (OR *can*, *may* or *might*)	(2) I will probably not work next Friday. *If I **worked** next Friday,* *I **would miss** a test.* *If* clause: past tense Main clause: *would* (OR *could* or *might*)
Present time	(3) I sometimes work at night. *If I **work** at night,* *I **miss** a lot of sleep.* *If* clause: present tense (*if* = when) Main clause: present tense	(4) I don't work all the time. *If I **worked** all the time,* *I **would miss** my freedom.* *If* clause: past tense Main clause: *would* (OR *could* or *might*)
Past time	(5) Years ago I worked at a bank, and I sometimes worked Saturday. *If I **worked** Saturday, I **missed** being able to hang out with my friends.* *If* clause: past tense (*if* = *when*) Main clause: past tense	(6) I did not work last week. *If I had **worked** last week,* *I **would have missed** the midterm exam.* *If* clause: past perfect Main clause: *would have* (OR *could have* or *might have*) + a past participle

■ **Exercise 4** Reconstruct the sentences from the chart 10.5. Read the **boldface** sentence first. It provides the **background**. To check your work, look back at 10.5.

	Real conditionals	Unreal conditionals
Future time	(1) **I might work tomorrow. (So I might miss class.)** If I _____ tomorrow, I _____ _____ class.	(2) **I will probably not work next Friday. (So I will not miss a test.)** If I _____ next Friday, I _____ _____ a test.
Present time	(3) **I sometimes work at night. (Then I miss a lot of sleep.)** If I _____ at night, I _____ a lot of sleep.	(4) **I don't work all the time. (So I don't miss my freedom.)** If I _____ all the time, I _____ _____ my freedom.
Past time	(5) **In the past I worked at a bank, and I sometimes worked Saturday. (Then I missed being able to hang out with my friends.)** If I _____ Saturday, I _____ being able to hang out with my friends.	(6) **I did not work last week. (So I did not miss the midterm exam.)** If I _____ last week, I _____ the midterm exam.

■ **Exercise 5** Choose the correct forms. More than one form may be correct.

1. In tennis, if the ball _____ any part of the line, it is treated as in, not out.
   (a) touches   (b) touched   (c) had touched   (d) will touch
2. I've always believed that if people work hard, _____ succeed.
   (a) they   (b) they'll   (c) they can   (d) they would
3. If _____ known it was going to be so cold, we would have brought warmer clothing.
   (a) we're   (b) we've   (c) we'd   (d) we'll
4. If children don't eat breakfast, they _____ do well in school.
   (a) won't   (b) wouldn't   (c) don't   (d) couldn't
5. It was a difficult lecture. I _____ it better if there had been more examples.
   (a) followed   (b) have followed   (c) will follow   (d) would have followed
6. We used to be able to walk out on the frozen lake if we _____ a really cold winter.
   (a) has   (b) had   (c) will have   (d) would have
7. If you had lived in ancient Rome, you _____ Latin.
   (a) would speak   (b) had spoken   (c) would have spoken   (d) were speaking
8. If I had to drop this class, I _____ it again next term.
   (a) take   (b) would take   (c) could take   (d) might take
9. If you treat customers well, _____ they remain loyal.
   (a) and   (b) so   (c) then   (d) if

310 Grammar Advantage   Chapter 10

■ **Exercise 6**   The passage below is confusing because *if* has been omitted in some sentences. Add *if* in three places, with appropriate punctuation (periods). Read carefully and think about the meaning.

Silent mode is convenient you wish to stop your phone from making noise when you are attending a performance or a lecture. You use silent mode the phone will vibrate and light up the external display. You want to exit silent mode you can press the display key again until "Normal profile" appears on the display.

■ **Exercise 7**   Identify the conditional sentences and determine where in chart 10.5 each one belongs. For example, is it real or unreal? Is it future, present or past?

In the days before cell phones, if you heard an unwelcome noise while attending a concert, it was usually someone coughing or dropping something. Times have changed. Not long ago, a businessman was attending a concert of a famous orchestra in New York when his cell phone rang with a marimba ring tone. If he had known it was his phone, he would have turned it off, of course, but he thought it was someone else's.

If you were an orchestra conductor and a phone interrupted your concert, what would you do? Amazingly, the conductor stopped the orchestra and waited for the phone to be turned off. The man eventually realized it was his phone and turned it off, but only with great difficulty. It was a new and unfamiliar phone. If he ever goes to a concert again, no doubt he will leave his phone at home.

■ **Exercise 8**   Complete each sentence in different ways by adding *if* and using one group of words from each column. Add an auxiliary verb or form of BE if it is needed, for example, in (1) *What will happen if the picnic tables are all in use?*

1	*We are planning to go by bus to a picnic in the park.* What will happen …?	the park	turn cold
		the weather	not have tables
		one of us	get sick
		the bus	all in use
		the picnic tables	not come
2	*We are talking about things we hope will never happen.* What would happen …?	everyone	strike the earth
		the economy	refuse to pay their taxes
		the university	collapse
		an asteroid	close down
3	*We lost the game, but it was very close.* What would have happened …?	we	not so muddy
		our coach	train us better
		the field	play on our own field
		the other team	make more errors
4	*Our neighborhood seems to be getting worse.* People will not want to live here …	the streets	too high
		apartment rents	overcrowded
		the schools	decreasing
		property values	not safe
5	*The business where I work is not doing well.* The company would make more money …	our competitors	not so reluctant to spend money
		our customers	go out of business
		our products	reduce our production costs
		we	not have to be shipped so far
6	*We saw a production of "Hamlet," and it was a disaster.* It wouldn't have been so bad …	the actors	take three hours
		people next to us	not whispering all the time
		the performance	more comfortable
		our seats	not forget their lines

Chapter 10

■ Exercise 9 Follow the examples, supplying the background (10.5) for the conditional sentences. Use the chart in 10.5 as a reference. The shaded boxes are done as examples.

Conditional sentences		Background
1. They would help me if I were stuck.	a.	Maybe I will…
2. They always helped me if I was stuck.	b.	Maybe I do…
3. If I offended you, I apologize.	c.	Sometimes I was…
4. If I figure out the answer, I will let you know.	d.	Maybe I did…
5. If I offended you, I would apologize.	e.	I wasn't…
6. If I seem nervous, it's because of the crowd.	1. f.	I am not *stuck*.
7. If I'd known you needed me, I would have come.	g.	I don't…
8. If I knew the answer, I would tell you.	10. h.	I did *offend* you.
9. If I'd been nervous, I wouldn't have done as well.	i.	I probably won't…
10. If I hadn't offended you, I wouldn't have felt so bad.	j.	I didn't…

10.6 Conditionals with *can, could, may,* and *might*

We can use alternatives to *will* and *would* in the main clause to show how certain we are about the connection between the main clause and the *if* clause.
- **Real** conditionals: Instead of *will*, we can use *can* (a) for opportunity or ability and *may, might* or *could* (b) for possibility.
- **Unreal** conditionals: Instead of *would*, we can use *could* (c, e) for opportunity, ability, or possibility and *might* (d, f) for possibility.

Real conditionals	Unreal conditionals
a. *If I don't wear my glasses, I can't read the small print in footnotes.* ≈ It's not possible.	Present time: c. *If I didn't have my glasses, I couldn't read this.* (~~can't~~) ≈ I would not have the ability.
b. *If I have time, I may / might / could take a nap.* ≈ Perhaps I will. (*Could* indicates a less likely action.)	d. *If weren't so busy, I might take a walk.* (~~may~~) ≈ It would be possible.
	Past time: e. *If I had gone to a bigger high school, I could have taken a wider variety of courses.* ≈ It would have been possible.
	f. *If I had gone to a big school, I might have had more friends.* (~~may~~) ≈ Perhaps I would have had more.

Above, *can* and *could* are in main clauses. We can also use them in *if* clauses: *can* in a real conditional (g) and *could* in an unreal conditional (h).

g. If I can use a calculator, I'll be more accurate.	≈ Maybe I can. (real conditional)
h. If I could avoid tests completely, I would.	≈ I can't. (unreal conditional)

If I could avoid tests, I would.

If I were ...

10.7 *Were* in unreal conditionals

We use *were*, not *was*, with all subjects in unreal conditionals, except in informal situations.

   a. *If I **were** illiterate, I wouldn't be able to read this sentence.* (Informal: *If I was ...*)
   b. *If it **were** easy to learn the violin, I would try it.* (Informal: *If it was easy ...*)

In unreal conditionals about the future, we can use *were to* (*were* and an infinitive) instead of a past tense (c). *Were to* is correct with any subject (d).

   c. *If you **were to get** a job, you could save more.* (≈ *If you got a job*)
   d. *What would happen if the economy **were to** collapse?* (≈ *if it collapsed*)

If anything should happen ...

10.8 *Should* in conditionals

We sometimes use *should* in an *if* clause to talk about an unlikely event (not the usual meaning of *should*). In the main clause, we can use *will*, *would* (a) or other modals (b). (See also 10.9.)

   a. *If the president **should become** ill, the vice-president **will / would take** over his duties.*
   b. *If it **should lose** your job, I **may / might be** able to help you.*

Had I known ...

10.9 Inversion in *if* clauses

In formal style, we can omit *if* and use **inversion** of the auxiliaries *had* (a), *should* (b) or *were* (c) with their subjects when we express a condition. (Inversion: see 2.13.)

Inversion, without *if*	Usual word order, with *if*
a. **Had I** known about the problem, I would have done something to help you.	≈ *If I had* known about the problem, I would have done something to help you.
b. **Should anything** go wrong, call me.	≈ *If anything should* go wrong, call me.
c. I'm afraid my car might break down. **Were** that to happen, I would be stranded.	≈ *If that were* to happen, I would be stranded.

■ **Exercise 10** Choose the correct answer(s). In some items, more than one is correct.

1. If Martin Luther King, Jr., __ alive today, would he support gay marriage?
 (a) could be   (b) had been   (c) were   (c) would be

2. __ happen to me, I'm counting on you to take care of my dog Napoleon.
 (a) Anything should   (b) Should anything   (c) If anything   (d) If anything should

3. The meeting would have been postponed __ been possible to find a different date.
 (a) if it has   (b) had it   (c) should it   (d) if it had

4. How would you get to school if the bus drivers __ on strike?
 (a) were to go   (b) should go   (c) went   (d) would go

5. If I had not been admitted to this university, I __ to look for a job instead of going to school.
 (a) might have decided   (b) might decide   (c) would have decided   (d) would decide

6. If dogs __ talk, what kinds of grammar mistakes would they make?
 (a) can   (b) were   (c) would   (d) could

7. If you ___ your seatbelt, the police can pull you over and give you a fine.
 (a) didn't wear   (b) don't wear   (c) hadn't worn   (d) aren't wearing

8. You weren't ready for the test. ____ you read the assigned material, you would have been ready.
 (a) If had   (b) Had   (c) Have   (d) Would

■ **Exercise 11** In the passage below, **two or three** of the underlined parts include a mistake. Find and fix the mistakes.

If you <u>have ever been</u> to a fast-food restaurant in the US, you <u>know</u> that the employees typically say the same things, such as "Would you like fries with that?" or "Is that for here or to go?"

A few years ago, I was attending a community college in a small U.S. city. I usually went home for lunch, but if I <u>didn't have</u> time, I <u>went</u> to a McDonald's near the campus. If there <u>had been</u> any other restaurants around, I <u>had tried</u> them, but McDonald's was the only one in those days.

The first time I went there, I was just a beginner in English. <u>Had I been</u> more experienced in fast food restaurants, I <u>might avoid</u> a silly mistake, but it was all new to me. The person at the counter asked me a question that I didn't understand until later: "For here or to go?" All I understood was that I had a choice. Since I was really hungry, I just said "Both!"

If you <u>should find</u> yourself in a similar situation, I <u>advise</u> you to try this phrase: "Sorry, could you repeat that more slowly?"

10.10 Negative conditions

unless

whether or not

We use *unless* to mean "except in the following situation" or "except if," often similar to *if … not* (a). We can use *if … not*, but not *unless*, when something is known to be true (b).

a. ***Unless** you trust the sender, it's not a good idea to open email attachments. Don't open them **unless** you're sure.*	≈ *If you don't trust …* ≈ *if you're not sure*
b. *I'd exercise more **if** it **didn't** take so much time.* (~~unless it~~)	≈ *it takes time.*

We use *whether … or* to mean "it doesn't matter if …" (c). We can put *or not* at the end of the clause (d). Sentences with *whether or not* can often be paraphrased by sentences with *even if + not* (e). See also 10.15.

   c. *It costs the same **whether** you use cash **or** a credit card.*
   d. *It's the same **whether or not** you use cash. It's the same **whether** you use cash **or not**.*
   e. ***Whether** you like it **or not**, it's yours.* ≈ ***Even if** you **don't** like it, it's yours.*

10.11 Limited conditions

only if

as long as

provided that

We can use *only if* to emphasize a limited condition, meaning "**only** in this situation" (a). We can put *only* in the main clause before the *if* clause (b). When we put *only if* at the beginning, we use inverted word order in the main clause and no comma (c). (See also 2.13.2.) We sometimes use *as long as* and *provided (that)* instead of *only if* (d).

   a. *Students can enroll in higher-level classes **only if** they have completed the prerequisites.*
   b. *Students can **only** enroll in higher-level classes **if** they have completed the prerequisites.*
   c. ***Only if** students have completed the prerequisites **can they** enroll in higher-level classes.*
   d. *Students can enroll in higher-level classes **as long as / provided (that)** they have completed the prerequisites.*

10.12 Assuming, given that, in case

We use *assuming (that)* to introduce a condition that is possibly true or could become true (a). We use *given that* to introduce a condition that we think is a fact (b). We use *in case* to mean "because of this possible situation" (c).

a.	**Assuming (that)** *the population continues to grow, what are the implications for the food supply?*	The population might continue to grow or probably will continue to grow.
b.	**Given that** *Hispanics are the fastest-growing ethnic group, it's not surprising that the Spanish language is growing in importance.*	It is a fact that they are the fastest-growing group.
c.	*You should always write down your password* **in case** *you forget it.*	You might forget it.

■ **Exercise 12** Add *only if* or *unless* to each sentence. Rewrite the sentence with the other form.

Example: I won't go ___ you go too. OR: *unless* OR: *I will go only if you go too.*

1. Get a new computer ___ you can afford it. OR:
2. He says he'd never eat chicken ___ he was starving. OR:
3. Don't go for a long hike ___ you take a lot of water. OR:
4. They'll let you use the library ___ you're a student. OR:

■ **Exercise 13** Add these conjunctions to the text.

as long as   assuming   in case   unless   whether

My mother complains that there's a light outside her window that's controlled by an automatic timer and comes on ___ anyone needs it or not. She's complained to the landlord about it, but he says it's needed ___ someone wants to go up or down the stairs after dark. She agrees with him, but the light doesn't have to be on ___ someone is actually using the stairs. All they need is an on/off switch. ___ nobody is using those stairs, the light can stay off and save electricity. However, the landlord has an answer to that. ___ someone comes and doesn't know there's a switch or can't find it, that might cause a serious problem, he says, and he doesn't want anyone to get injured on the stairs. He also says that motion sensor lights are unreliable.

■ **Exercise 14** Paraphrase each sentence using the words that are provided. The conditional clause may be first or last. Think carefully about which clause should be the conditional clause.

1. We can't prepare for the future if we don't remember the past. *unless*
2. They eat at 6 p.m. even if they're not hungry. *whether*
3. Answer (d) must be right. All the other answers are incorrect. *given*
4. Tuition is going to rise. More students will soon be looking for part-time jobs. *assuming*
5. You should keep your notes, You might need to review them. *in case* [Do not include *might*.]
6. You can't become president unless you were born in the U.S. *if*
7. You may take any course you want provided that you have passed the prerequisite. *as long as*
8. Only if we work together can we succeed. *unless*
9. *Paraphrase #1 using* only if *at the beginning*.
10. *Paraphrase #6 using* only if *at the beginning*.

10.13 Continuous verb phrases in conditionals

We use continuous verb phrases when we describe ongoing or temporary actions (4.7). We can use them in *if* clauses (*is looking*) and in main clauses (*will be looking, would be looking*).

a. If you **are looking** for a job, let me help. b. If I graduate on time, I **will be looking** for a job in June.	It is possible that you are looking or will be looking for a job (real present and future).
c. If I **were looking** for a job in sales, I would have a lot of competition. d. If I wanted to work in entertainment, I **would be looking** in Los Angeles.	I am not looking for a job in sales and I am not looking in Los Angeles (unreal present).
e. If you **had been looking** where you were going, you wouldn't have fallen. f. If I hadn't distracted you, you **would have been looking** ahead.	You were not looking (unreal past).

10.14 Mixed times in conditionals

With *will* in the main clause, we usually use present tense in the *if* clause (**10.3**), but we can also use a verb in the past (a) or present perfect (b) for an earlier condition.

a. You **will not get** accurate results in your experiment if you **didn't control** the temperature.	The experiment is past. I don't know if you controlled the temperature. (*If you don't control* would refer to a future experiment.)
b. If students **have completed** the core course requirements, they **will be allowed** to graduate.	Students who have already completed the requirements will be allowed to graduate.

We can connect an imaginary past situation (past perfect in an *if* clause) to another past event or to an imaginary present situation.

c. If demand for oil **hadn't increased**, prices **wouldn't have risen** and we **wouldn't be paying** so much for everything now.	The increase caused a past result (prices rose) and a present result (we are paying a lot now).
d. If I **had grown** up in England, I **would have learned** English from my parents and English **would be** my native language.	A past event is linked with a past result (I did not learn English from my parents) and a present result (English is not my native language.)

We can also connect an imaginary present situation (past tense in an *if* clause) with an imaginary past situation (*would have* and a past participle).

e. If I **liked** hot weather, I **would have gone** to a university in Florida.	I don't like hot weather (present situation). Past result: I did not go to a university in Florida.

Exercise 15 Choose the correct forms. More than one form may be correct.

1. If you had never come to this country, where _____ now?
   (a) are you   (b) have you been   (c) will you be   (d) would you be
2. If you _____ for a job, try using a social networking site.
   (a) are looking   (b) were looking   (c) will look   (d) would look
3. If I _____ in May, I will be looking for a job during the summer.
   (a) graduate   (b) graduated   (c) will graduate   (d) would graduate
4. If I _____ for a job in film production, I would have a lot of competition.
   (a) look   (b) have looked   (c) were looking   (d) will look
5. If I wanted to work in the stock market, I _____ for jobs in New York.
   (a) apply   (b) applied   (c) would be applying   (d) would have applied
6. If you had been watching where you were going, you _____ and hurt yourself.
   (a) didn't fall   (b) haven't fallen   (c) won't fall   (d) wouldn't have fallen
7. Sorry I distracted you! If I _____ you, you would have been paying more attention.
   (a) don't distract   (b) hadn't distracted   (c) won't distract   (d) wouldn't have distracted
8. If I liked hot weather, I _____ gone on vacation to the Caribbean.
   (a) had   (b) have   (c) will have   (d) would have

Exercise 16 Add the correct form of these verbs to the following sentences.

be   not feel   laugh   not drive   not need   stay   work

1. Tom arrived at the party in a gorilla suit, which made us all laugh. If you'd seen him, you __ too.
2. If you had been paying attention when we took the safety course the first time, you __ to go back last week and do the course again.
3. If I'd listened to my parents' advice, I __ in college instead of dropping out, and I __ a delivery van for a living now.
4. If we had saved some of the money we made, we __ able to take advantage of all these bargains now.
5. You __ so bad today if you hadn't drunk so much wine last night.
6. If I'd known then what I know now, I __ harder to save more and buy my own place instead of paying rent all those years.

No matter what happens ...

Whatever happens ...

10.15 When there is no condition

To express the idea that there is **no** condition, we can use expressions like *no matter what happens* and *no matter how I try*. Alternatively, we can use a *wh* word like *whatever* or *however*. The sentences on the right are paraphrases of the sentences on the left. See also 10.10.

a. *No matter what happens, don't give up.*	b. *Whatever happens, don't give up.*
c. *No matter what I say, you argue.*	d. *Whatever I say, you argue.*
e. *No matter how I try, I can't make you listen.*	f. *However I try, I can't make you listen.* (For *however* as a transition expression, see Chapter 3.)
g. *No matter who it is, don't answer.*	h. *Whoever it is, don't answer.*
i. *No matter where you live, you should get know your neighbors.*	j. *Wherever you live, you should get to know to your neighbors.* (See also 9.21.)

Usage Guide

10.16 Conditionals in paragraphs

An *if* clause may be associated with more than one sentence. For example, in a paragraph about **what would happen if you moved** to another country, you might include many consequences, marked with verb forms that are typical in the main clause of a conditional sentence.

> a. *If I **moved** to Canada, I **would** want to live in a big city, because that's where the job opportunities are. I would probably try living in Vancouver. I **could** look for work in the high-tech industry. I **might** take a class at the University of Vancouver. I like the idea of taking classes part-time, but it **would be** challenging to work and study at the same time.*

There is just one conditional clause, but *would*, *could*, and *might* are used in later sentences because they are all part of the same imaginary (unreal) future situation. Verbs that are not part of that imaginary situation (*that's where the job opportunities **are**; I **like** the idea*) are true in the real world, so they do not have conditional verb forms.

We can use *would* (b) and *would have* (c) in unreal main clauses when an *if* clause is implied.

> b. *They keep the animals in small cages. People **would be** disgusted.* (= if they saw them)
> c. *The party was great. You **would have liked** it.* (= if you had been there)

An *if* clause can go with more than one sentence.

10.17 *Suppose* and *What if*

Suppose followed by a *that* clause introduces a hypothetical situation in a complete sentence that can be used like an *if* clause. Using *suppose* in this way can be an effective way to introduce an extended discussion of a hypothetical situation. In (a), notice the use of a past tense after *Suppose* (*were required*) and *would* and *could* in later sentences.

> a. ***Suppose** students **were required** to turn off all electronic devices in lecture classes. How **would** the learning experience change? No cell phone rings **would** interrupt the lecture. No one **would** waste time checking Facebook updates. No one **could** play video games instead of listening to the lecture. At the same time, no one **could** use a laptop to take notes, and no one could access online information relevant to the lecture. To show students material on the course Web site, the professor **would** have to project an image of it. Granted, there **would** be fewer distractions, but opportunities **would** be lost as well.*

We can also use *Suppose* for a real situation, with a present tense (*are*) and *will*.

> b. ***Suppose** you **are** right in arguing that lowering taxes **will** stimulate development. **Will** that development continue or **will** it only be a short-term benefit?*

We can also use *What if* in a question to introduce alternative situations, real with the present tense (c), unreal future with the past tense (d), or unreal past with past perfect (e).

> c. ***What if** we **are** wrong about global warming? In many places the weather **is getting** cooler.*
> d. ***What if** students **were** required to turn off their cell phones? They **wouldn't be** happy.*
> e. ***What if** you **had been born** a century ago? Do you think you **would have liked** it?*

Usage Guide

■ **Exercise 17** Complete the text with appropriate forms of the verbs.

    be (x2)   *change*   *cope*   *happen*   *lose*

The Children of Men by P.D. James is based on a horrifying idea: What if the human race __ its ability to reproduce? If that __ , the people who are now alive, and any babies soon to be born, __ the last of their kind. How __ people __ with life under those circumstances? It __ the way we think and live. In spite of its grim subject matter, the novel __ a success.

■ **Exercise 18** Complete the text with appropriate forms of the verbs in real and unreal conditionals. More than one choice may be correct.

    behave   *find*   *give*   *not have*   *not have to*   *say*   *want*   *pay* (x2)

Suppose you had a meal in a restaurant and __ that you __ pay for your meal. Suppose the management __ , "The meal you had was worth $20. You can pay that if you __ to. But if you __ the money in your pocket, you don't have to pay." __ you __?

    This experiment has been tried at some Panera restaurants, and the company has found that about 80% of the customers pay what the meal is worth, while some __ more and some less, in about equal numbers. One conclusion is that most people, if you __ them a choice, __ honestly.

■ **Exercise 19** Complete each text with appropriate forms of one set of verbs.

    be / die / have / know   *end / happen / last / win*

1. For some countries, it is currently impossible to get completely accurate mortality information (information about deaths). However, suppose for a moment that we not only __ a complete count of deaths by year for a country, but we also __ the age and sex of each person when he or she __ . Then we __ in a much better position to calculate life expectancy at birth for that country.

2. In the U.S. Civil War, the North defeated the South, and slavery was abolished. But what if the South __ the war? What __ then? We have to believe that slavery __ at some point, but it probably __ many years in some states.

10.18 Imperatives plus *and* or *or* to express conditions

- A conditional can sometimes be paraphrased with an imperative (2.15.2) plus *and* (a, b).
- This pattern can be useful for adding variety to writing when you are making a generalization with *you* meaning "anyone."
- We can also use *or* to paraphrase a conditional with a negative in the *if* clause (c).

Imperatives with *and / or*	Similar conditional sentences
a. **Visit** a mall in any U.S. city, **and** you will see the same stores.	≈ If you visit a mall in any American city, you will see the same stores.
b. **Spend** one hour in front of the TV, **and** you will have been exposed to at least 14 minutes of advertising.	≈ If you spend one hour in front of the TV, you will have been exposed to at least 14 minutes of advertising.
c. **Be** careful **or** you'll fall.	≈ If you are **not** careful, you will fall.

Usage Guide

10.19 Special uses of *will* and *would* in *if* clauses

There are some special uses of *will* and *would* in conditional sentences. We can use *will* in an *if* clause when it has a meaning similar to "agree to" (a). We can use *would like* in the main clause as a polite way of saying "want" (b). We can also use *would* in the main clause to describe a typical behavior or habit in the past (c). (See also 4.11.)

a.	*If you **will** help me, I will help you.*	= If you agree to help me ...
b.	*If you are interested in the job, we **would like** you to begin immediately.*	= we want you to begin ...
c.	*I used to run most mornings. If I wasn't able to run in the morning, I **would** run at night.*	= I used to run at night ... (4.11)

10.20 *If* and *wish*

I wish I spoke Spanish.

If I spoke Spanish, I'd go to Mexico.

We can use *wish* plus a noun clause to talk about an unreal situation, as in an unreal conditional. We can use a sentence with wish and another sentence with would to talk about a present situation (a) or a past situation (b). We don't usually use wish for a future situation. Instead we use hope and a present tense verb (c). An exception: We sometimes use wish…would to express a very strong desire (d). See also 7.7.4.

Present situation: I don't speak Spanish.	
a. ***I wish (that) I spoke / could speak*** *Spanish. Then I **would** go to Mexico.*	≈ ***If I spoke / could speak*** *Spanish, I **would** go to Mexico.*
Past situation: I didn't speak to my advisor.	
b. ***I wish (that) I had spoken*** *to my advisor. Then I **would** know what to do. (now)* OR *Then I **would** have known what to do.*	≈ ***If I had spoken*** *to my advisor, I **would** know what to do.* OR *I **would** have known what to do.*
c. *I hope we win the prize.* (~~wish~~)	
d. *I wish this rain would stop!*	

■ **Exercise 20** Choose another clause (a-e) to follow each clause (1-5) and add *and, if,* or *or*.

1. Try this product
2. You'll get a full refund
3. Make your purchase today
4. Don't ignore this opportunity
5. You will receive a special gift

a. _____ you're not satisfied.
b. _____ you'll regret it.
c. _____ you order two or more.
d. _____ you'll be amazed.
e. _____ you'll get free shipping.

Usage Guide

■ **Exercise 21** For each sentence that uses an imperative, create a paraphrase using *if*. For each sentence that uses *if*, create a paraphrase using an imperative. (10.18)

1. If you try living without the Internet for 24 hours, you will discover that it's not easy.
2. Walk down any aisle in a modern supermarket, and you will find an astounding variety of competing products.
3. If you talk to three Americans about "the American dream," you will almost certainly get three different descriptions.
4. Follow the law or you will soon be in trouble.
5. Choosing a spouse is one of the most important decisions in a person's life. If you're not really careful, you might regret it for the rest of your life.

■ **Exercise 22** Complete these sentences with *will* or *would*. (10.19)

1. They said that if I'm selected, they _____ like me to join the team next week.
2. I wish the sun _____ come out. I hate cloudy days.
3. Everybody is hoping that the economic situation _____ improve this year.
4. Just stop and think about your basic needs and you _____ spend less.
5. Their children used to get up at about 5 in the morning and if nobody got up to look after them, they _____ make a horrible mess in the kitchen.

■ **Exercise 23** Complete the text with one word from each set. (10.19, 10.7)

   and / if / or   *ask / asked / asking*   *were / would be / will be*

___ anyone who remembers the 1960s ___ they will tell you that the Beatles were the greatest rock group of the day. After the group disbanded, John Lennon continued living and working in the U.S. until he was shot and killed in 1980. Many people still love his music and wish he ___ still writing and performing today.

Chapter 10 Conditionals

10.21 Problems with conditional sentences

Problems	Revisions	Comments
1. If anything will happen…	If anything **happens** …	Use present tense, not future, for future events in a real *if* clause. (10.3)
2. If anything happens, we would call.	If anything happens, we **will** call. (= It's possible.)	Use real *if* clauses with real main clauses (10.3), and unreal *if* clauses with unreal main clauses. (10.4)
3. If anything happened, we will call.	If anything happened, we **would** call. (= It's not likely.)	
4. If anything had happened, we would call.	If anything had happened, we **would have** called.	Use *would have* + a past participle for a past unreal situation. (10.4)
5. If I live to be 100, I never understand boxing.	If I live to be 100, I **will** never understand boxing.	In the main clause of a real conditional, use *will* or another future marker for future time unless the sentence is a generalization. (10.3)
6. People do not live forever. If they live forever…	If people **lived** forever …	For unreal situations, use verb forms that fit the background. (10.4)
7. I did not live in ancient Rome. If I lived at that time…	If I **had lived** at that time …	
8. Anything happens, they take care of it.	**If** anything happens, they take care of it.	Don't forget *if*. (10.2)
9. You can't vote unless if you are a citizen.	You can't vote **unless** you are a citizen.	Don't use two conjunctions. Choose one.
10. You can't vote if that you're not a citizen.	You can't vote **if** you're not a citizen.	
11. If a company that produces a valuable service, it will thrive.	If a **company produces** a valuable service, it will thrive. OR A **company that produces** a valuable service will thrive.	Don't mix these two ways of making a generalization: with a conditional (Ch. 10) or a sentence with a relative clause. (Ch. 8) See also 2.2.4.

Though we usually use real with real and unreal with unreal clauses, there are exceptions. In particular, *would* is sometimes used in a main clause that appears with a real *if* clause. Sometimes another condition is implied.

12. If you like suspense, you **will** love this movie.	This is the usual pattern: a real *if* clause with present tense and a real main clause with *will*. (10.3)
13. If you like French food, you **would** love Chez Paul.	*Would* is used with an implied condition, *If you went there*.

However, using only real with real and unreal with unreal clauses will usually help you avoid mistakes.

Appendix A

Tense overview — summary of forms and meanings (See also Ch. 4.)

The chart shows forms for affirmative statements (*sees*), negatives (*doesn't see*), and questions (*does...see?*). It includes both active voice (*sees, is seeing, has seen*) and passive voice (*is seen, is being seen, has been seen*).

	Simple	Continuous	Perfect	Perfect continuous
Present	*Active:* sees doesn't see Does ... see ...? *Passive:* is seen is not seen Is ... seen?	*Active:* is seeing is not seeing Is ... seeing ...? *Passive:* is being seen is not being seen Is ... being seen?	*Active:* has seen has not seen Has ... seen ...? *Passive:* has been seen has not been seen Has ... been seen?	*Active:* has been seeing has not been seeing Has ... been seeing ...? *Passive:* not important. The passive forms of the verb phrases above (e.g. *has been being seen*) are almost never needed.
Past	*Active:* saw didn't see did ... see ...? *Passive:* was seen was not seen Was ... seen?	*Active:* was seeing was not seeing was ... seeing ...? *Passive:* was being seen was not being seen Was ... being seen?	*Active:* had seen had not seen Had ... seen ...? *Passive:* Had been seen Had not been seen Had ... been seen?	*Active:* had been seeing had not been seeing Had ... been seeing ...? *Passive:* not important. The passive forms of the verb phrases above (e.g. *had been being seen*) are almost never needed.
Future with *will* and *be going to*	*Active:* will see is going to see will not see is not going to see Will ... see ...? Is ... going to see ...? *Passive:* will be seen is going to be seen will not be seen is not going to be ... Will ... be seen? Is ... going to be seen	*Active:* will be seeing is going to be seeing will not be seeing is not going to be seeing Will ... be seeing ...? Is ... going to be seeing ... *Passive:* not important. The passive form of the future continuous (e.g. *will be being seen*) is almost never used.	*Active:* will have seen will not have seen Will ... have seen ...? (*Going to* is not used much in future perfect.) *Passive:* will have been seen will not have been seen Will ... have been seen?	*Active:* will have been seeing will not have been seeing Will ... have been seeing ...? (*Going to* is not used much.) *Passive:* not important. The passive forms of the verb phrases above (e.g. *will have been being seen*) are almost never used.

Subject-verb agreement: Subject-verb agreement requires small changes in some forms above.
    does / do   is / are (am)   was / were   has / have

Forms with modal auxiliaries: Any modal auxiliary verb (*may, might, can, could, shall, should, will, would, must*) can replace *will* in the chart above, though the meanings are not necessarily future. For example, *She might need help* can mean *Maybe she **needs** help* (present) or *Maybe she **will** need help* (future). (See 4.4.)

Simple present   take, takes; do/does (not) take   is/are/am (not) taken   (4.6)

For present time

1. Repeated actions, habits, and routines: *My cat **sleeps** a lot. **Do** you enjoy your weekends? When I **overeat** I **get** sleepy. Our classrooms **are cleaned** daily.*

2. Note: Avoid this problem. *I am a nervous person. Whenever I* ~~had~~ *a presentation to make, I* ~~couldn't sleep~~ *the night before.* More usual: *Whenever I **have** a presentation to make, I **can't** sleep …* We prefer present tense in this situation, unless a past context is established (***When I was in college***, *I was always nervous in front of other people. Whenever I **had** a presentation to make, I **couldn't** sleep the night before.*)

3. General truths: *Water **boils** at 100 degrees Celsius. Rocks **don't float**. **Does** wheat **grow** in a wet climate? Arabic is **written** right to left.*

4. Present situations with stative verbs: *I **understand** French. **Do** you **see** what I **mean**? Is it true that a* ~~smile is~~ ***understood*** *everywhere?*

For future time (4.19):

5. Scheduled future actions, often with verbs like *arrive, leave*, etc. Usually a future time adverbial is needed. *We **leave** at 5:00 p.m. **tomorrow**.*

6. In a subordinate adverbial clause (often with *after, when,* or *before*): *Please call me as soon as you* ~~(will)~~ ***get*** *home. When he* gets ~~(will get)~~ *home tonight, he should call. When the doors **are opened**, people are going to race in to get the best seats.*

Simple past   took; did (not) take   was/were (not) taken   (See also 4.9.)

7. Completed past actions viewed as a whole: *Prices rose. I lived in France for two years. Mozart didn't drink Coke. How long did you work in the World Trade Center? The World Trade Center was attacked in 2001.*

8. Habitual actions in the past: *We took vacations every summer when I was a child. In the 1800s, whale oil was used in lamps.*

9. "Unreal" present time (in conditional sentences): *If I knew the answer, I would tell you. I wish I knew. If Alaska were divided into two states, they would the two biggest.*

Simple future (future with *will*)   will (not) take   will (not) be taken   (See also 4.18.)

10. Promises, offers, requests (with *I* and *you*): *I **will call** you tonight. **Will** you **help** me?*

11. Predictions (usually with certainty): *My birthday **will be** on a Sunday next year.*

12. Contingent future ("iffy" future): *Don't go so fast. You'**ll have** an accident. If you drive too fast, you **will endanger** yourself and others.*

Be going to future   is/are/am (not) going to take   is/are/am (not) going to be taken   (4.18)

13. Intentions: *I'm **going to take** five classes next term. (= I plan to take …) Is Art 101 **going to be offered** in the afternoon?*

14. Actions that are already "on the way": *My cousin **is going to have** a baby.*

Present continuous   is/are/am (not) taking   passive: is/are/am (not) being taken   (4.7, 4.8)

For present time

15. Action now, often with the idea that it is temporary. *Your request is being processed.* "Now" can be a moment—*Is the sun shining?*—or a long period: *Is the climate changing?*

For future time (4.19):

16. Scheduled future actions, often with verbs like *arrive, leave,* etc. Usually a future time adverbial is needed. *We're **leaving** at 5:00 tomorrow.*

17. Actions that are already "on the way": *My sister **is having** a baby.*

Past continuous *was/were (not) taking   was/were (not) being taken*   (See also 4.10.)

18. Actions in progress in the past (often as "background" for another action): *I **was watching** TV when the phone rang. In 1995, I **was living** in Rome. One day I went ... We had to take another route because the main road **was being repaired.***

Future continuous *will (not) be taking*   (See also 4.21.)

19. Actions in progress in the future, often as background for another action: *Call me tomorrow, but not between 6 and 7. I'**ll be watching** "The Simpsons."*

20. Especially in spoken English, this form is used very generally for future actions, when the action is viewed as "a matter of course" (taken for granted): *I'**ll be seeing** you. Next week we'**ll be working** on a new topic.*

Present perfect *has/have (not) taken   has/have (not) been taken*   (See also 4.12.)

21. Action that began in the past and continues now **with a duration phrase** (often with *for* or *since*). *We **have known** each other for five years. I'**ve worked** here since 2004.*

22. Past actions with no specified time. Very recent: *The rain **has stopped.** Hurry up. The show **has** already **started!*** Not recent: ***Have** you ever **met** a famous person? I don't want to see "Avatar." I've seen it 12 times already!*

23. Note: Do not use present perfect with a past-time adverbial (*last week, yesterday, when I was younger,* etc.): ***Last week** I have seen four movies.* Use past: *Last week I **saw** ...*

Past perfect *had (not) taken   had (not) been taken*   (See also 4.15.)

24. Past action before another past action: *We got married in '96; we **had known** each other five years. I looked outside; the rain had stopped. I didn't want to see "Avatar," because I **had already** seen it. When I got there, most of the work had already been done. Lucky me!* You usually need to mention a past event **first** (*We got married in '96*); only then does it make sense to use past perfect for the next action that you mention (*we had known...*). The most common mistake with past perfect is using it too much. Usually the simple past (sometimes the present perfect) is the tense you need.

25. For "unreal" past time (in hypothetical conditionals): *If I **had slept** well (really I didn't), I might have done better on my test.* (See "hypothetical conditionals" below.)

Future perfect *will (not) have taken*   (See also 4.22.)

26. Action that will be completed before a future time (often with *by*): *I plan to return to my country in June. I **will have graduated** by then, and I will be ready to look for a job.*

Present perfect continuous *has/have (not) been taking*   (See also 4.14)

27. Action that began in the past and continues now; a duration phrase is optional. *I'**ve been** studying French. I'**ve been studying** French for two years.*

Past perfect continuous *had (not) been taking*   (See also 4.16.)

28. Action that began in the past and continued until a past time, often as background for other actions. A **duration** phrase may or may not be included. *In 2002 I was living in Paris. I **had been studying** French. One day ... It's* a good idea to avoid this tense unless you have established a past time frame **earlier** in the sentence or paragraph.

29. Don't overuse the past perfect. Avoid this: *When I was a child, I ~~had often been~~ sick.* (⟶ *I was often sick.*) If you first establish a past time and then want to mention an action before it, past perfect may be a good choice: *I was feeling weak because I **had been** sick.*

Future perfect continuous *will (not) have been taking* (See also 4.23.)

30. Action stretching back in time from a future time. A **duration** phrase (like *for two hours*) is almost always included; often *by the time* is included: *By the time I return to my country, I **will have been living** in the U.S. for two years.* A rare tense; you'll almost never need it!

Special usages and expressions

Used to *used to take / didn't use to take* (See also 4.11.)

31. Habitual past: *I used to drive; now I take the bus. Used to* has no **present tense**. For habitual present, don't say *I ~~use to~~ take the bus.* Say *I **take*** or *I **usually take** the bus.*

32. A similar expression — **be** *used to* (+ an *-ing* word sometimes) — is related to **attitude** or **adjustment** to a situation, not to time. *He has lived here a long time, so he **is used to** the weather. He's **used to** driving in snow. When I lived in Minnesota, I didn't mind the weather. I **was used to** it. I **was** also **used to driving** on icy roads because I did it almost every day.*

***Would* for repeated past actions** *would (not) take   would (not) be taken* (4.11)

33. *I had a busy life in high school. I **would get up** at five and **go** to bed past midnight.*

Future in the past *would (was/were going to) take   would (was/were going to) be taken* (4.24)

34. Using *would* (as the past of *will*): *I hoped I **would win.***

35. Using *was/were going to*: *Did you think you **were going to win**?*

Lots of options for future actions (See also 4.18, 4.19, and 4.35.)

36. Often, there is more than one possibility for a future situation. *I'**m flying** to LA tomorrow. I **fly** to LA tomorrow. I **am going to fly** to LA tomorrow.* We also indicate future action by using verbs like *plan* or *have to* in the present. *I **have to fly** to LA tomorrow. I **plan to fly** to LA tomorrow. I **hope to graduate** in June.* Of course, these verbs add extra meaning.

Verbs with no tense (nonfinite verbs) (See also 4.5.)

37. Infinitives (I wanted **to go**), gerunds (I like **dancing**), and bare infinitives (He made me **laugh**) have no tense. The tense of the clause is in the earlier verb (*wanted, like,* and *made* in the examples).

Conditional forms (See also Ch. 10.)

38. For verbs in conditional sentences, especially unreal conditionals, see your text. *If I had not come to the U.S. I would (could, might) have gotten a job in the tourist industry.* The modal auxiliaries *would, could,* and *might* are especially important in the main clause of such a sentence.

APPENDIX B

Basic punctuation for joining clauses

We join clauses using coordinating conjunctions, subordinating conjunctions, and transition expressions. See also 2.19 and 9.6.

Coordinating conjunctions – usually *and, but,* or *so* (2.17.3)	
	Two independent clauses can be joined by a comma and a coordinating conjunction. There are six coordinating conjunctions: *and, but, so, or, nor, yet, for.*
a.	*I drink coffee, and you drink tea.*
b.	*I like tea, but I don't often drink it.* (NOT *I like tea. But, I don't ...*)
Subordinating conjunctions: *when, while, if, because, although,* etc. (2.17.2 and Ch. 9)	
	A subordinate clause at the beginning is followed by a comma and an independent clause. A subordinating conjunction introduces the first clause. If the clauses are reversed, there is usually no comma. The subordinate clauses below are in smaller type.
c.	*When I drink coffee, you drink tea.* *I drink coffee when you drink tea.*
d.	*I drink coffee because it helps me stay awake.* *Because it helps me stay awake, I drink coffee.*
Transition expressions: *however, as a result, in addition, in contrast,* etc. (Ch. 3)	
	Both parts are independent clauses. We use a period and then a comma.
e.	*Most people like green tea. However, it's not for everyone.* Sometimes we use a semicolon, not a period. *Most people like green tea; however, it ...* Sometimes we put the transition expression at the end: *It's not for everyone, however.*
f.	We often put a transition expression — especially *however* and *for example* – inside the second clause (usually after the first part of the sentence), with commas around it. *Most people like tea. Green tea, however, is not for everyone.*
Joining clauses without any connecting words	
	We can join independent clauses with just a semi-colon (;), especially when the two clauses are very similar.
g.	*I drink coffee; you drink tea.*
	We often use a colon (:) to introduce a series of words or phrases. The meaning of the colon is like "And here it is" or "And here they are." What follows the colon may be a phrase (or more than one phrase) or it may be an independent clause.
h.	*We serve three drinks: coffee, tea, and cocoa.* (NOT *We serve: coffee, tea, and cocoa.* The part before the colon must be complete.)
i.	*I have a bad habit: I spend too much at Starbucks.*

Errors to avoid (2.19 and 9.6)

	Avoid run-ons. Using no punctuation or connecting words between independent clauses creates a run-on.	Correct it with a period:
j.	*I drink coffee you drink tea.* →	*I drink coffee. You drink tea.*
	Avoid comma splices. Using just a comma between independent clauses creates a comma splice.	Correct it with a conjunction:
k.	*I like coffee, I love Starbucks.* →	*I like coffee, and I love Starbucks.*
l.	*I like coffee, I spend a lot at Starbucks.* →	*I like coffee, so I spend a lot at Starbucks.*
m.	*I like coffee, it helps me keep awake.* →	*I like coffee because it helps me keep awake.*
n.	An exception: We sometimes use just a comma between independent clauses when the first sentence tells what something is **not** and the second tells what it **is**: *It's not just a habit, it's a way of life.*	
	Avoid fragments. Using a subordinate clause or a phrase as if it were a sentence (with a capital and a period) creates a fragment.	Correct it by changing the punctuation, omitting the conjunction, or using another structure:
o.	*I need to stop drinking so much coffee. Because I'm spending too much and losing sleep.* →	*I need to stop drinking so much coffee because I'm spending too much and losing sleep.* OR *I need to stop drinking so much coffer. I'm spending too much and losing sleep.*
p.	*When you drink coffee all day and spend half your paycheck at Starbucks. You have a serious problem.* →	*When you drink coffee all day and spend half your paycheck at Starbucks, you have a serious problem.* OR *You drink coffee all day and spend half your paycheck at Starbucks. You have a serious problem.*
q.	*You drink coffee all day and spend half your paycheck at Starbucks. A problem that you need to do something about.* →	*You drink coffee all day and spend half your paycheck at Starbucks. You need to do something about this problem.*
r.	*There are other ways to stay awake. For example, by playing lively music or getting up and moving around from time to time.* →	*There are other ways to stay awake. For example, you can play lively music or get up and move around from time to time.* OR *There are other ways to stay awake, for example, by playing lively music or getting up and moving around from time to time.*
	Exceptions: Careful writers sometimes use fragments. For example, after a question, the answer can be stated acceptably as a fragment.	
s.	*Why do we drink coffee? Because we love it.*	The fragment is acceptable as an answer to the question.

APPENDIX C

Transition expressions word by word (See also Ch. 3.)

This list is arranged alphabetically. It includes some words that are not in the category of transition expressions, though they serve a similar function.

After — by itself is not a transition expression. It is a subordinating conjunction. Avoid mistakes like these: *I'm going to register for five classes. ~~After~~, I can drop one class if I'm too busy.* → *Later, I ... They washed the windows, vacuumed, and mowed the lawn. ~~After~~, they took a break.* → *Then they took ... / Afterward, they took ... / After washing the windows, vacuuming, and mowing the lawn, they took a break. / After they washed...*

After all — means something like "It is important to remember." *It's natural that you make mistakes in English. After all, it's not your native language.* Avoid this mistake: *You need to talk to your advisor, register, set up your email account, and buy your books. ~~After all~~, you are ready to go to class.* → *After that (After all of that), you are ready ...* (More concisely: *Then you are ready ...*) Though it includes the word *after*, the transition expression *after all* does not include the idea of "after."

All in all — can be used to sum something up, with the idea of "when you consider everything." For example, after a description of a bad day, you might write: *All in all, it was one of the worst days of my life. All in all* does not usually work well to introduce the conclusion of an essay.

All the same — marks contrast. *She apologized to everyone. All the same, some of us couldn't forgive her.*

Also — If you want your writing to be more idiomatic, use *also* **inside the sentence** (after the subject or the subject and the first auxiliary or BE verb), especially when the subjects of the two sentences are the same. *I worked hard. Also, I managed to save some money.* → *I also managed ...* Sometimes *also* at the beginning is the perfect choice, but more often it is used after the subject. Remember, too, that sometimes the most concise way is to use *and*. *I worked hard and managed to save some money.*

Although — is not a transition expression. Don't make the mistake of using *although* (or *even though*) in the same way as the transition expression *however* or *even so*. *The new copier is a great machine. ~~Although~~, it has one disadvantage.* → *The new copier is a great machine. However, it has ...* Or: *Although the new copier is a great machine, it has ... Our work went well. ~~Even though~~, we didn't get the recognition we hoped for.* → *Our work went well. Even so, we didn't get the recognition we hoped for. Although* and *even though* indicate a contrast, but they are subordinating conjunctions, not transition expressions.

Among other things **and** *for one thing* — You can use these transition expressions to add an example when you know there are more possible examples that you will not mention.
1. *I have a great deal of experience relevant to this job.* **Among other things**, *I held a very similar position at another company. In that setting ...*
2. *In "The World is Flat," Thomas Friedman examines globalization in the new century.* **Among other things**, *he argues that ...*

3. *People from other states often find it difficult to live in Minnesota.* **For one thing**, *the winters are hard to bear.*

These expressions are useful when you want to emphasize one thing while making it clear that you could mention other things as well.

Another   is useful for connecting, though it is not grammatically a transition expression. We use it before a noun (or a noun may just be implied), often in a series like this: **One problem** *with fossil fuels is that they're not sustainable.* **Another problem** *is that they pollute the air.* **Yet** (OR **still**) *another problem is that* ... Note the use of *still* or *yet* for the third item. See also 7.6.

As well **and** *too*   are useful at the end of a clause to indicate addition. *They export fruit and vegetables to the mainland. There is a developing market for fresh flowers* **as well / too**. They are rarely used at the beginning of a sentence.

At first, first, firstly   We use *at first* to introduce a situation that later changed or changes. *Automobiles began to be used in the late 19th century. At first, they were called "horseless carriages."* Use *first* (not *at first* or *firstly*) to introduce the first action of a series or the first of a series of points you wish to make. *Applying for financial aid requires a lot of work. First, you have to ...* (At first, Firstly)

At last **and** *finally*   We usually use *at last* to introduce the conclusion of something long or difficult. We can also use *finally* in this way. *The South surrendered in 1865, four years after the war began. At last / Finally, the War between the States was over.* Do not use *at last* if you are just introducing the final action of a series: *I did some product research, talked with friends who have cars, and test-drove two Toyotas and a Honda. Finally, (At last) I decided not to buy a car at all.*

At the same time   often indicates a contrast (1), but it may also indicate time (2) or simply addition (3).
1. *I want to live in a big city.* **At the same time,** *I want enough space for a garden.*
2. *During this last year, we've been adding employees.* **At the same time,** *we've been improving our facilities.*
3. *Hillary is very professional.* **At the same time,** *she's friendly and likeable.*

Besides   usually introduces another reason or argument to support a previous idea. *Improving crop yields will have to be accomplished by other means. More fertilizer is no longer the key to higher yields.* **Besides,** *the focus now is on better quality, not greater quantities.*

But   is a coordinating conjunction, not a transition expression. We usually use it inside a sentence. When you have short, simple sentences, don't punctuate like this: *I was born in Japan. But I never learned the language.* → *... Japan, but I ...* When the first part is long and complicated, we often end it with a period and begin the next sentence with *but*. *I was born in Japan and lived there for a few years. My mother worked at a university and I went to a private school. But I never learned the language.* Do not punctuate *but* as a transition expression *... blah blah. But, blah ...* → *... blah blah, but blah ...* OR *... blah blah. But blah ...* If you don't like beginning a sentence with *but* (some teachers advise against it), you can often use *however*. See also 2.17.3 (g).

By the way	In speaking and informal writing, we often introduce an addition with *by the way*, especially if the information is digressive (not central to the main point). In academic writing, we usually avoid this expression. *By the way* is like "Oh, and I almost forgot …" In careful writing, when we forget something we go back and revise, so we don't need *by the way*.
Even so	introduces a contrast. Don't use *even though* in the same situation. *Our work went well. Even so, we didn't get the recognition we hoped for.* (~~Even though~~) See *Though*.
Except for	means something like "not including." *Except for physics, all my classes are in the afternoon.* Do not use *except* when you mean *in addition*. *In addition to* (not ~~Except~~) *physics, I'm taking history and math.*
First, firstly	*First* (not *firstly*) is usually correct. See also *At First, First, Firstly*.
For example	(and *for instance*) can introduce a phrase or a clause, but be sure to punctuate correctly. If the example is not a sentence, don't punctuate it as a sentence: *Lots of tourist attractions are not only entertaining but educational.* ~~For example, Disney World in Florida.~~ Possible revisions: *For example, you can learn a lot at Disney World in Florida. One good example is Disney World in Florida. Lots of tourist attractions, for example (,) Disney World in Florida, are not only entertaining but educational.*
Fortunately	or *unfortunately* (sometimes after *but*) may be a good alternative to *however*. *I had no sales experience. However, I learned quickly.* → *Fortunately, I learned… I liked my job. However, there were no opportunities for advancement.* → *I liked my job, but unfortunately …* (*However* is not a mistake; the revisions are just other options.)
For one thing	See *Among other things*.
However	• Punctuation: The most common mistake with *however* is a comma splice (2.19 and Appendix B). *The big tourist attractions of Florida are well-known, however, there are wonderful smaller ones as well …* → *… known. However, there are …* OR *… known, but there …* • Placement: More than any other transition expression, *however* often appears after the first element of a sentence. *College used to be primarily for young men. In recent years,* **however**, *women have outnumbered men in higher education.* *Over the years, it has often been claimed that coffee is bad for you.* **Recent research, however,** *has called that into question.* We place *however* inside the sentence only if the part before presents contrasting information. *I play the piano and sing. However, I don't like to perform in public.* (~~I, however,~~ …) *My sister loves to perform in public. I, however, do not.* • Alternatives: If you want to avoid using *however* again and again, you may find that *fortunately* or *unfortunately* works. *At the same time* may work. If *however* is too heavy, *but* is often a good option, with appropriate punctuation. See also *like* and *unlike*.
In a word	means "in one word." *The new play is well-written, lavishly produced, and brilliantly acted. In a word, it is phenomenal.* We usually don't use *in a word* to sum up something unless we can actually sum it up in a single word.
In conclusion	Skilled writers generally avoid using *in conclusion*, especially in a short essay. The placement and the content of a conclusion usually make *in conclusion* unnecessary. (It can be useful, however, in an oral presentation.)

Like* and *unlike are similar to expandable transition expressions like *as a result (of)* and *in addition (to)* (3.4). The difference is that they **must** be expanded. *Unlike* can help you avoid overusing transition expressions like *in contrast* and *however*.
Using *in contrast*: *Korea is about 50 percent Christian. In contrast, Japan has not embraced Christianity deeply.*
Using *unlike*: *Unlike Korea, which is about 50% Christian, Japan has not embraced Christianity deeply.*
Like and *unlike* can help you improve the style of sentences like these: *Education is a practical field of study, and so is business.* → *Business, like education, is a practical field of study.* OR *Education, like business, is a practical field of study.*
Avoid this mistake: ~~Unlike Americans move~~ *from place to place frequently, families in my country tend to stay in the same village or town for generations.* → *Unlike Americans, who move from place to place frequently, families ...* OR *Unlike Americans, families in my country tend to stay ...*

Likewise* and *similarly introduce a parallel example. *Hearing difficulties prevent some children from participating fully in classes. Likewise / Similarly, children with physical disabilities cannot easily participate in sports.*

Not only that, but... is useful for showing addition. *Participating in peer review teaches you to look critically at things your read. Not only that, but it improves your ability to identify problems in your own work.*

On the contrary is usually used to correct a misconception, after a negative sentence or a question. (The question or negative statement implies that some people have the wrong idea about something). (3.11)
• *Coffee is not bad for you. On the contrary, some research suggests it has health benefits.*
• *Does a child's learning begin in school? On the contrary, the most important learning takes place in the years before school.*
For a contrast, *in contrast* is usually the best choice. *High schools in my country don't give students lots of choices. In contrast, (~~On the contrary,~~) students in U.S. schools can choose lots of electives.*

On the other hand is useful for weighing contrasting points. Sometimes we introduce the first point with *on (the)one hand*. *Deciding to immigrate was a tough decision. On the one hand, we knew it would improve our economic prospects. On the other hand, it meant leaving behind all our relatives and friends.*

Otherwise means something like "in a different situation" or "if not." *Early registration is advised. Otherwise, you risk not getting into the courses you want.* Don't use *otherwise* for a simple contrast. *Most people spend weekends with their families. ~~Otherwise~~, some people go the office.* → *Others go to ... / Some people go...* Don't use *otherwise* for *in addition*. *I have five classes and a part-time job. In addition (~~otherwise~~), I volunteer at a hospital.*

Similarly See *Likewise*.

So at the beginning of a sentence usually has no comma after it. *Most cyclists don't compete in races. They run errands by bike, ride for pleasure, or commute to school or work. So the average biker has no need for an expensive racing bike.* When the part before *so* is short and simple, it's usually best to write the information as one sentence, with a comma before *so*. *Most cyclists don't compete in races, so the average biker has no need for an expensive racing bike.*

Still	marks a contrast. *English spelling has many irregularities. Still, it's not completely chaotic. Still* is also useful in combination with *another*. See *Another*.
Such as	Don't use a clause after *such as*. Use a noun phrase after *such as* or use *for example* instead. *There are lots of risks associated with smoking, such as smokers are more likely to get lung cancer.* → *... risks associated with smoking. For example, smokers are more likely ...* OR *... risks associated with smoking, such as a greater likelihood of lung cancer.*
Then	usually has no comma after it. *People used to make their own music at home or go out to enjoy it. Then radio and recording technologies were invented, and everything changed.* When initial *then* has a comma after it, it is usually because another element appears before the main part of the sentence. *Then, with the invention of radio and the phonograph, everything changed.*
Therefore and **thus**	are used in similar ways to introduce a result. We use *therefore* to introduce a logical result, where one thing necessarily follows from another. We use *thus* (= "in this way") to introduce a result based on information already given. We also use *thus* (not *therefore*) as part of a participial phrase introducing a result. • *We know the number of students, their gender and their final scores.* ***Therefore*** *we can calculate the average scores for males and females.* • *Our initial sample of 400 subjects was reduced by a number of students who missed a session or dropped out of the study completely.* ***Thus*** *the final sample consisted of 366 subjects.* • *In the new version they have increased the number of applications,* ***thus*** *making the device more versatile.* Note that these uses of *therefore* and *thus* do not require a comma.
Though	is sometimes used (usually in speaking) at the end of a clause with the meaning of *however*. *You look like the president. You have better hair, though.* Except for this usage, *though* (sometimes *even though*) is a subordinating conjunction. Avoid this mistake: *You look a little like the president.* ~~Though~~, / ~~Even though~~, *your hair is better.* → *You look like the president, (even) though your hair is better.* *Although* is like *though* except that we don't use it at the end of a clause or after *even*.
Unlike	See *Like*.
What is more	is a useful way to introduce an addition, similar to *moreover*. *In the digital age libraries are still an important resource. Librarians are experts at helping patrons sift through overwhelming amounts of published material.* ***What's more****, some references are available only in physical form in libraries, not online.*

APPENDIX D

KEY
Ch. 6 = Chapter 6
Ex. 23 = Exercise 23
5.2 = Chapter 5, section 2
2.14.3 = Chapter 2, section 14, subsection 3
(a) = an example

Principles for ordering information in sentences (See also 3.17-3.19)

How are these different?

If you are seriously interested in a career in business, it's best to get some real-world experience before graduation.

It's best to get some real-world experience before graduation if you are seriously interested in a career in business.

Both are correct, and if there is no context, one is as good as the other. In most contexts, however, the two are not interchangeable. This is because we tend to follow certain **principles for ordering information**. These principles tell us that one part or another should be first.

We can identify a handful of principles. There is overlap among them, and sometimes some of them conflict with others. In other words, they're not always simple to apply. But they may help you write sentences that flow better.

1. Put the important information at the end of the sentence. Usually this means the **main** clause will be at the end.

When you were a beginner in English, all your sentences probably began with the subject:

Everyone spends more time outside enjoying the sun when summer finally arrives.

But putting the main clause at the end is often a good choice. It emphasizes the information in the main clause. Then the first clause just gives information like time or condition.

When summer finally arrives, everyone spends more time outside enjoying the sun.

2. Put the information that you plan to **develop** at the end of the sentence.

In fact, the information you are going to develop is the important information, so this principle agrees with the first one.

You can see these principles in action below:

When I was at the university, I was active in Student Senate. As a member of the senate, I played a key role in getting several policies changed. Among these policies was the "no refund" policy, which stipulated that ...

The important information in the first sentence is "I was active..." This is also the information that is developed in the next sentence. Thus, the best place for this information is at the end of the sentence. Similarly, "I played a key role in getting several policies changed" is the important information—and the information that will be developed—so it is at the end.

Principles #1 and 2 do not mean that the main clause is always at the end, as this example shows:

Mozart began writing music when he was only 10. People were amazed ...

Here the important information is "when he was only 10," and this is also the information that is developed in the next sentence. In this case, the subordinate clause has this information, so it is at the end. (Another option: *When Mozart began writing music, he was only 10. People were amazed ...*)

3. At or near the beginning of the sentence, use **words that show how your sentence is linked** with what comes before.

Transition expressions such as *however, moreover,* and *therefore* can provide this link. So can content-specific phrases such as *In spite of these limitations* and *As a result of this disaster* (3.4).

> *If you ask a police officer whether the police discriminate, he or she is likely to answer that they do not. An ordinary citizen,* **however***, might give you a different answer.*

However marks the relationship of contrast. (It could be the first word, but we often prefer to delay it a little.) Here's an example with a content-specific connecting phrase:

> *If you ask a police officer whether the police discriminate, he or she is likely to answer that they do not.* **In spite of such denials***, cases of discrimination have been well documented.*

4. Put **old information near the beginning** of the sentence (2.22.2, 3.17).

Phrases with old information are phrases that refer to things already mentioned or repeat information already implied. For example:

> *When I was a high school student, I was active in the Student Senate.* **As a member of the senate,** *I played a key role in getting several rules changed.*

"As a member of the senate" is old information because the previous sentence says, "I was active in the student senate." It would be a mistake (in style) to put "as a member of the senate" at the end of the sentence. It is the linking information, the old information, so it should be first. (It is also *not* the most important information, so it should not be last, following principle 1.)

Which of the two orderings below seems best?

> *The strictest teacher I ever had was Ms. Lee. I met her when I was six years old.*
> *The strictest teacher I ever had was Ms. Lee. When I was six years old, I met her.*

If you follow the principle of "old before new," the first is better. "I met her" is old information; "when I six ..." is new. (Notice, too, that this is another case in which the subordinate clause is last. *Information* principles are more important than grammar.)

If your sentence includes no old information and does not include words that signal the relationship with what came before (like transitions), consider adding something — following one of the principles above.

Below is a paragraph about the benefits of requiring students to wear uniforms. The content is acceptable, but the flow is weak. How could you improve it following the principles above?

> *The benefits of uniforms are well known. It is often said that uniforms predispose children to take school seriously. Learning as much as possible is the main goal of education. Uniforms eliminate fashion differences that lead to teasing and bullying among students. Bad behavior is a serious problem in many schools today, but students are more likely to treat each other equally if they all dress alike. When students leave the school grounds, they are easily identified if they wear uniforms. Owners of nearby businesses can call the school if they see a truant student.*

GLOSSARY OF GRAMMAR TERMS

For some of the terms, definitions are given. Others you can understand through examples. For some, you are directed to another part of the book.

Active voice and **passive voice** (Ch. 5): See **passive**. In active voice, the subject performs the action: *Brazilians speak Spanish.* Passive voice: *Spanish is spoken in Brazil.*

Adverbs and **adverbials** (2.20): words that add information about *when, where, how, how often, to what degree,* etc. **Adverbial clauses** Ch. 3.

An **adjective** modifies (gives information about) a noun. An adjective is usually before a noun or after a linking verb such as BE: *An **old** person can still be **active**.*

Adjective clause: another term for *relative clause.* See **Relative clause.**

Agreement: See **subject-verb agreement** (below and in 2.2.5) and **pronoun agreement** (below and in 2.16.3).

An **appositive** (8.15): *Thomas Jefferson, **the third president**, was a Virginian. Mount Rushmore, **the home that Jefferson designed for himself**, is a museum today.*

Articles: *The* (definite) and *a/an* (indefinite).

Attributive adjective: An adjective when it is used before a noun. The adjective *hard* is used as an attributive adjective in the phrase *a hard time. Predicate adjective* refers to an adjective when it is not used before a noun: *This is hard.* Most adjectives can be used in both ways. A few adjectives, such as *asleep* and *alive*, are not used as attributive adjectives. We say a *sleeping girl (an asleep girl)*. We say *a live lobster (an alive lobster)*. A few adjectives, such as *main*, are used only as attributive adjectives: *the main idea, the main reason,* etc.

Attributive clause: another term for *relative clause.* See **Relative clause**.

Auxiliary verbs (4.1) are verbs that precede the main verb: ***didn't*** *look,* ***is*** *looking,* ***have been*** *looking,* ***can*** *look,* etc. These include modals (*can, could,* etc.), forms of DO used in the simple tenses, forms of BE used in the continuous tenses and the passive voice, and forms of HAVE used in the perfect tenses.

BE refers to any of these forms: *be, am, is, are, was, were, been, being.*

A **clause** (2.2, 2.17) is a subject and verb along with other parts that complete the meaning. A sentence can consist of a single clause (*I know it*) or more than one: *When it rains, it pours. I know you're right, but I don't care.* Ch. 7 (noun clauses), Ch. 8 (relative clauses), and Ch. 9 (adverbial clauses).

A **comma splice** (2.19 and Appendix B) is a type of error in which a comma appears between independent clauses. Change the comma to a period or a semicolon or restructure the sentence. *There are 10 chapters, they are all important.* ⟶ *... chapters. They ... / ... chapters; they ... / ... chapters, and ... The train is convenient, it's rather expensive* ⟶ *... convenient, but it's ... Though the train is convenient, it ...*

Common noun: any ordinary noun. See also **Noun** and **Proper noun**.

Comparison is the expression of similarities and differences.

-er, more, -est, and *most*
a. With short, common adjectives: *He's tall. She's taller. I'm the tallest (of all).*
b. Irregular forms: *bad, worse, the worst; good, better, the best (of all)*
c. With adverbs (2.20): *work more quickly, work harder*
d. With longer adjectives: *more important, the most important (of all)*
e. With nouns: *more money, the most money*
f. With verbs and BE *worth*: *A costs a lot. B costs more. C costs the most. A is worth a lot. B is worth more. C is worth the most.*
Less, the least, fewer, the fewest
g. *He had less trouble. She had the least trouble.*
h. *He had few errors. She had fewer errors… I had the fewest errors.*
As….as
i. With adjectives: *Are cats as smart as dogs?*
j. With adverbs: *I don't react as quickly as I used to.*
k. With *much* and *many*: *A didn't make as much progress as B. B doesn't have as many advantages as A.*

Comparison mistakes to avoid
l. *A is large / interesting than B.* ⟶ *is larger than / more interesting than, etc.* When you use *than*, you usually need a comparative word earlier in the sentence.
m. ~~more~~ *tall*, ~~more~~ *taller*, *tall* ~~more than~~ …, *the* ~~most tall~~, *the most* ~~tallest~~ ⟶ *taller, the tallest*
n. *She had trouble more than I did.* ⟶ *had more trouble / had trouble more often*

A **complement** is a phrase or clause that follows a noun (*They promote the idea **that people should be equal***), verb (*They want **people to be equal***) or adjective (*I'm sorry **that I hurt you***), completing its meaning. Noun and adjective complements: 6.23, 7.81, 7.82). Verb complements: 6.6.

A **concise** sentence, paragraph, or essay is one that uses no unnecessary words. See **wordiness**.

A **conditional** sentence (Ch. 10) consists of a main clause and a clause beginning with *if*. **Real conditionals** (10.3): *I will call if I need you. If something happens, I will call.* **Unreal conditionals** (10.4): *I would call if I needed you. If something happened, I would call.*

Conjunctions join sentences or sentence parts. **Coordinating conjunctions** (2.17.3) are *and, but, or, nor, so, for, yet*. **Subordinating conjunctions** (2.17.2) include *when, while, as soon as, if, because, although* and many more (Ch. 9).

Continuous verb phrases (also called progressive) include BE followed by an *–ing* form: *is working / was working,* etc. (4.7, 4.10, 4.14, 4.16)

Contractions, used mainly to represent speech, are words like *it's (it is), he's (he is),* and *aren't (are not)*. Note that *It's* means "It is." For the possessive form of *it*, use *its*: *This book isn't as good as its title.*

Count and **noncount nouns** **Count** (countable) **nouns** can be either singular or plural: *cat / cats; idea / ideas.* Normally a singular count noun is preceded by a determiner (*the, a/an, my, this,* etc.). ~~in dictionary~~ ⟶ *in the / a dictionary.* **Noncount** (uncountable) **nouns** don't normally have *–s*, are used with singular verbs, and can be used with singular words like *this* and *that*: *This advice is useful.* (~~These advices are~~ …), *I found information …* (*an* ~~information, informations~~)

Coordination (2.17.3): joining parts (words, phrases, clauses) with a coordinating conjunctions: *and, but, or, nor, so, for, yet.* See also **Parallelism**.

Demonstratives: *this, that, these* and *those*, used as pronouns *(This is your pen)* or as the first word of a noun phrase *(**This pen** is yours)*.

	Near	Far
Singular	*I got this tattoo when I was 18.*	*That cloud looks ominous.*
Plural	*I got these tattoos when I was 18.*	*Those clouds look ominous.*

Determiners are words like *the* (articles), *this* (demonstratives), and *my* (possessives) at the beginning of a noun phrase: *the earth, this chapter, my first trip abroad.*

A **direct object** (2.4.1) is a noun or noun phrase that directly follows a verb (a transitive verb), receiving the action of the verb. *The snake ate **the rabbit**.*

Faulty parallelism (2.18) is a mistake in which words, phrases, or clauses joined by *and* do not have similar forms and functions.

Faulty parallelism mistakes	Revisions with correct parallel structure
I like playing basketball and watch movies.	*I like **playing** basketball and **watching** movies.* (parallel verbs) *I like **basketball** and **movies**.* (parallel nouns)
She asked us to choose a topic and wrote about it for five minutes.	*She asked us to **choose** a topic and write about it for five minutes.* (parallel verbs) *She **asked** us to choose a topic and **had** us write about it…* (parallel verbs)
The clerk helped us promptly and very polite.	*The clerk **helped** us promptly and **was** very politely.* (parallel verbs) *The clerk **helped** us **promptly** and very **politely**.* (parallel adverbs)

A **fragment** (2.19, 9.6, Appendix B) is a kind of mistake. It is punctuated as a sentence (with a capital letter and a period) but it is not structurally a sentence. Fragments can be fixed in various ways.

Fragments (in **boldface**)	Revisions
English spelling is hard. **Because there are so many exceptions.**	*English spelling is hard (,) because there are …* *English spelling is hard. There are …*
When I was ten. *My family moved to the countryside*	*When I was ten, my family …*
It's hard to find parking near the campus. **Especially on days when there is a football game.**	*It's hard to find parking near the campus, especially on days when there is a football game.*
To be effective, a supervisor needs a variety of strengths. **For example, the ability to inspire employees to do their best, which is essential to the success of a business.**	*To be effective, a supervisor needs a variety of strengths. For example, the ability to inspire employees to do their best is essential to the success of a business.*

A **gerund** (6.2) is a verb plus *–ing* used as a noun: ***Interrupting*** *people is rude* (6.4). *I avoid **interrupting** people* (6.6).

An **idiom** is a phrase whose meaning cannot be understood from the meanings of the parts, such as *take place* (= happen), and *keep an eye on* (= watch carefully). The language as native speakers use it can be described as ***idiomatic***, meaning natural. See also **Idiomatic language**.

Idiomatic language is language as native speakers use it. It's the natural way to speak or write. **Unidiomatic** language is language unlike what native speakers use, such as *go to my home* (correct but unidiomatic) instead of *go home* (both correct and idiomatic).

Imperative is another word for *command*: *Stop! Don't worry*, etc. See 2.15.2.

Indirect **objects** (2.6)

We brought **our neighbors** some cookies.	We brought some cookies **to our neighbors**.
We brought **them** some cookies.	

An **infinitive** (6.2) is *to* followed by a base form verb.
   An infinitive subject (6.7): **To balance** *parenting and a career is not easy.*
   An infinitive as a delayed subject (6.7): *It is not easy* **to balance** *parenting and a career.*
   An infinitive as a complement of a verb (6.10): *I want* **to help** *you.*
   An infinitive of purpose (9.12): **To find** *a job, you need to do some networking.*
   An infinitive in a structure like a relative clause (6.18, 8.20): *The papers* **to sign** *are on the table.*

An **intransitive** verb (2.4.3, 5.7) is a verb — like *happen, live, participate*, and *stay* — that is never followed by a direct object (a noun or noun phrase right after it). *We stayed* ~~a good hotel~~ *for two weeks.* → *We stayed* **at** *a good hotel ... / We stayed for two weeks.* An intransitive verb can never be passive (~~was happened~~, ~~has been lived~~, ~~are participated~~, ~~was stayed~~). In contrast, a **transitive** verb may have an object (*The storm destroyed the town*) and may be passive (*The town was destroyed*).

Inversion is the process of switching (inverting) the order of a subject and an auxiliary verb (or form of BE.)

Normal order (statement order)		Inverted order (question order)	
Subject	Verb	Auxiliary or BE	Subject
This	*is*	*Is*	*this...?*
It	*is...*	*Is*	*it...?*
The problem	*has become...*	*Has*	*the problem become...?*
Studying a language	*can be....*	*Can*	*studying a language be...?*
The government	*spends...*	*Does*	*the government spend...?*
Thomas Edison	*invented...*	*Did*	*Thomas Edison invent...?*

Irregular verbs are verbs that have past tense forms and past participles that are not formed with *–ed*. For the forms of irregular verbs, check a dictionary.

	Base forms	Past tenses	Past participles
Irregular verbs:	*begin, keep, write, etc.*	*began, kept, wrote, etc.*	*begun, kept, written, etc.*
Regular verbs:	*play, work, study, etc.*	*played, worked, studied, etc.*	

Lexical grammar (2.4.2, 2.8.1, 5.13, 6.28, 7.23, 9.23) is the grammar of individual words. It may relate to forms (for example, *go, went, gone*) or patterns (for example, the choice of gerunds or infinitives after verbs).

Linking verbs (2.8) can be followed by adjectives (as well as other structures). The most important linking verb is BE. *She* **is** *late. I* **became** *angry. This* **feels** *wrong. He* **seems** *friendly.*

The **main verb** in a verb phrase (4.1): *I don't* **care**. *Are you* **coming**? *Has it* **stopped** *raining? Can I* **join** *you? It* **hurts**.

Modal auxiliaries, also called modals (4.4), are verbs that appear first in a verb phrase, followed by a base form verb: **can** *swim,* **could** *swim,* **may** *happen,* **might** *work,* **must** *try,* **shall** *go,* **should** *leave,* **will** *take,* **would** *take.* **Ought** is also a modal, though it is followed by an infinitive: *ought to know.*

Modify: give more information about.
   Adjectives modify nouns: *She's a* **good** *doctor.*
   Adverbs modify verbs (and more; see **Adverbs**): *She responded* **quickly**.
   A relative clause modifies a noun or noun phrase: *Where's that magazine* **that you were looking at**?

Negative usually refers to a form like *not* or *never* (a kind of adverb) or to a sentence with a negative form. The process of making a sentence negative is negation.

A **modifier** is a word or group of words that modifies another word or words. See **Modify**.

A **noun** refers to a person (*queen, cousin*), place (*kitchen, beach*), or thing (*toy, idea, sugar*). A proper noun, written with a capital letter, is the name of a person, group, or place: *Elizabeth, the New York Yankees, California*. A noun can be a subject (**History** *is interesting*), the object of a verb or preposition (*I like* **history**. *Are you interested in* **history**?) or a modifier of another noun (*a* **history** *book, a* **California** *beach*). See also **count nouns**.

Noun clauses (Ch. 7): *We knew* **(that) something was wrong**. *We didn't know* **what was wrong**.

A **noun phrase** is a group of words that functions as a noun. It can be a single noun or pronoun, a noun plus modifiers, or a noun clause.

An **object** (2.4) is a noun or noun phrase that directly follows the verb and receives the action: *The teacher evaluated* **the students**. *The students took* **a test**. Many verbs, to complete their meaning, require a preposition and a noun: *listen* **to music**, *depend* **on others**. For these, we do not use the term *object*. The object of a verb is a noun or noun phrase that **directly** follows it.

We also use the term *object* for a word or phrase that follows a preposition: *to* **New York**, *for* **my family**, *from* **me**.

An **object complement**: a noun or adjective that follows a direct object after certain verbs.

	Direct object	Object complement
They call	*their grandfather*	*Boppa.*
The delay made	*everyone*	*angry.*
We should elect	*her*	*class president.*
I painted	*my bedroom door*	*orange.*

Parallelism (parallel construction; 2.18): When we join elements with *and*, those elements must be of the same general form and function. See **Faulty parallelism** (a mistake in which words joined by *and* do not have similar forms and functions).

Paraphrasing means expressing the same idea in different words. For example, *Someone stole my bike* can be paraphrased as *My bike was stolen* or *I lost my bike to a thief*. *There are no windows in our classroom* can be paraphrased as *Our classroom has no windows* or *We meet in a windowless classroom*.

Part of speech: the name for a major category of words. The most important are *verbs, nouns, pronouns, adjectives, verbs, adverbs, prepositions,* and *conjunctions*. Less important categories are *demonstratives, particles* and *quantifiers*. Most categories have subgroups. Nouns: *countable, uncountable; proper, common*. Verbs: *Auxiliary verbs, action verbs, stative verbs, phrasal verbs*. All of these terms have entries in this glossary.

Participles   **Past participles**: *given, spoken, written,* etc. (irregular); *talked, worked,* etc. (regular). **Present participles**: *giving, talking,* etc.

Particles (2.10) are adverbs and prepositions (*away, back, in, off, up,* etc.) that often combine with verbs to form **phrasal verbs** (*go on, put up, run out*).

Passive voice (Ch. 5): *Portuguese* **is spoken** *in Brazil. The rabbit* **was killed** *by a fox.* (In **active** voice, the subject performs the action: *They speak Portuguese in Brazil, A fox killed the rabbit*).

Past tense (simple past; 4.9): *explained, exaggerated,* etc. (regular); *spoke, built,* etc. (irregular).

Past continuous (4.10): *was* or *were* plus an *–ing* form: *was sleeping, were shopping*

Past perfect (4.15): *had* plus a past participle. *I finished my paper at midnight. I* **had worked** *on it all day.*

Perfect gerund (6.21): *having worked, having been, having taken; not having worked,* etc. *They apologized for **having misunderstood** our request. They felt bad about **not having been** more perceptive.*

Perfect infinitive (6.21) *to have worked, to have taken, to have been, not to have worked,* etc. (*to have* + a past participle). *They seem **to have misunderstood**. They seem **not to have noticed** the problem.*

Perfect tenses: verbs consisting of *have* plus a past participle: *has/have worked, had worked.* See **Present perfect, Past perfect, Perfect infinitives,** and **Perfect gerunds**.

Phrasal verbs (2.10) are verbs that consist of a verb plus a particle and sometimes a preposition: *put away, run out of,* etc. The term is also used for verb + preposition combinations like *long for* (= want very much) and idiomatic expressions like *take place* (= happen).

Phrasal prepositions: *according to, ahead of, along with, because of, due to, instead of, out of, with regard to,* etc.

Plural and singular: See **Singular** and **plural.**

Possessive forms are words like *my* and *Adam's*. **Possessive pronouns:** ***my*** *house,* ***his*** *efforts,* ***their*** *country*. **Possessive nouns:** ***Adam's*** *father, my* ***country's*** *history, the* ***boys'*** *names, the* ***children's*** *teacher*

The **predicate** of a sentence is the rest of the sentence, apart from the subject: *We **tried**. We **did our best**. We **did everything we could do**.* See 2.2.4.

Predicate adjective refers to an adjective when it is not used before a noun: *This is hard*. See also **attributive adjective**.

Prepositions (*at, for, from, in, on, to, with,* etc.) are followed by nouns or noun phrases or pronouns to form. **Prepositional phrases:** *at 1600 Pennsylvania Avenue, for my friends, from where I live.*

Present tense (simple present; 4.6)
Present tense, active voice (4.6): *It usually **works**. Does it work **well**? It **doesn't** always **work**.*
Present tense, passive voice (5.3): *It **is explained** on page 50. Is it **explained** clearly? It **isn't explained** completely.*

Present continuous (4.7): *is* or *are* + an *–ing* form: *We **are working**. Is the copy machine **working**?*

Present perfect (4.12): *has* or *have* + a past participle: *We **have lived** here a long time. **Has** the game **been canceled**?*

Progressive: See **Continuous**.

Pronouns (*I, me, my, mine, she, her,* etc.) take the place of a noun. A pronoun usually **refers to** (points to) a noun that comes before it. *Cindy turned **her** paper in on time, but **it** wasn't complete. **She** has to do more work on **it**.* Most pronouns that refer to people, along with *it,* are **personal pronouns. Indefinite** pronouns are words like *any, anything, nothing,* and *something*.

Personal pronouns	Subject pronouns	Object pronouns	Possessive Before a noun	pronouns With no noun	Reflexive Pronouns
1st person singular:	*I*	*me*	*my* name	This is *mine*.	I see *myself*.
2nd person singular:	*you*		*your* name	This is *yours*.	You see *yourself*.
3rd person singular:	*she*	*her*	*her* name	This is *hers*.	She sees *herself*.
	he	*him*	*his* name	This is *his*.	He sees *himself*.
	it		*its* name		It sees *itself*.
1st person plural:	*we*	*us*	*our* names	This is *ours*.	We see *ourselves*.
2nd person plural:	*you*		*your* names	This is *yours*.	You see *yourselves*.
3rd person plural:	*they*	*them*	*their* names	This is *theirs*.	They see *themselves*.
	• *They, them,* and *their* can refer to people or things.				

Pronoun agreement and **reference** (2.16) A pronoun **refers** to a noun that (usually) comes before it. A pronoun **agrees** with the noun it refers to. Number agreement: *My eyes are red, but **they don't** (~~it doesn't~~) hurt. **They agrees** in number with eyes and don't.* Gender agreement: *My **sister** told me **she** (~~he~~) is doing well in her (~~his~~) job. **She** agrees in gender with my sister.*

Proper noun: a noun starting with a capital letter that refers uniquely to a person, group, or place: *Batman, Italians, Gotham.*

Punctuation marks

'	an apostrophe (*That's Kim's dog.*)	—	a long dash	?	a question mark
A, a	a capital letter, a lower-case letter	!	an exclamation point	" "	quotation marks, double
:	a colon	( )	parentheses	' '	quotation marks, single
,	a comma	.	a period (a full stop)	;	a semi-colon

Quantifiers are used before nouns and sometimes alone as indefinite pronouns: *any, all, few, only a few, little, only a little, lots of (a lot of), more, most, no, some.*

Reduced clauses

Reduced adverbial clauses (9.7.3, 9.24)	
When in Rome, do as the Romans do.	= *When **you are** in Rome…*
*It's dangerous to text **while driving**.*	= *…while **you are** driving.*
*Doctors wash their hands **before and after examining a patient**.*	= *…before and after **they examine**…*
*Wind power, **though plentiful**, is not easy to harness.*	= *…though **it is** plentiful*
*They waited **as if wondering** what to do.*	= *…as if **they were** wondering….*
Reduced relative clauses (8.12)	
*Students **planning to graduate in June** must file a form.*	= *Students **who are** planning….*
*On the wall was a chart **showing how sales had grown**.*	= *…a chart **that showed**…*
*A thank-you note **written by hand** is a rare thing these days.*	= *A thank you note **that** is written…*

Reflexive pronouns replace the usual object pronouns (*me, him,* etc.) when the object (of a verb or a preposition) refers to the same person as the subject: *I hurt myself (~~me~~). Do you live by yourself?* A reflexive pronoun can immediately follow a subject pronoun for emphasis: *I **myself** don't have a bike, but I use my brother's. Several students were late, and the **teacher himself** barely made it on time.* For a complete list, see **Pronouns**.

Regular verbs: See **irregular verbs**

Relative clauses (Ch. 8): *We helped a woman **who/that was lost**. The map **that she was using** was out of date. She was lost in an area **where there was lots of construction**.*

A **run-on** sentence (2.19 and Appendix B) is a sentence with no punctuation where a period is needed. *Maria is from Mexico she was born in Puebla.* → *Maria is from Mexico. She was born in Puebla.*

Singular and **plural**
    Singular words refer to just one: *cat, house, child, this, that, someone.* **Plural** words refer to more than one: *cats, houses, children, these, those, some people.* **Singular verbs:** *(she) **is, has, works**,* etc. **Plural verbs:** *(They) **are, were, have, work**,* etc.

A **stative passive** verb phrase (5.11) looks like passive voice (BE + past participle) but is more like an expression with BE and an adjective: ***Are** they **married**? I think we **are lost**.*

A **stative** verb names a state or relationship rather than an action: *know, own, seem,* etc. See 4.7.

The **subject** of a sentence (2.2) does (or sometimes experiences) the action of the verb.

The police *rescued the child.* (active voice)	The subject (*the police*) did the action.
The child *was rescued by the police.* (passive voice; see Chapter 5)	The subject (*the child*) experienced the action.
We *heard a crash.*	The subject (*we*) experienced the action.
Living with a roommate *is new to me.*	A subject can be a thing or an action, not only a person.
What happened *surprised everyone.*	The subject is a clause.
Last summer ***we*** *had lots of rain.*	The subject is not always first in the sentence.
Last summer ***there*** *were some big storms.*	Existential *there* (2.12) serves as a subject.
It's *fun to live with a roommate.*	Empty *it* (2.11) serves as a subject.
Did ***the police*** *rescue the child?*	
Is ***living with a roommate*** *new to you?*	In a question, the subject follows an auxiliary verb.
Were ***there*** *storms last summer?*	
Is ***it*** *fun to live with a roommate?*	
Everyone *knows that* ***the climate*** *is changing.*	Each clause has its own subject.

Subject-verb agreement (2.2.5): Third-person singular subjects (*it, she, he, the earth*) go with verbs ending in *–s: it is, she was, he has, the earth rotates*, etc.) when they are used in present tenses. Other subjects (*you, they, we, the planets*) use *are, have, do, rotate*, etc.

Tenses (verb tenses; Ch. 4) express present, past, and future time (*calls, called, will call*) as well as notions like action in progress (*is calling, was calling, will be calling*) and completed action (*has called, had called, will have called*).

A **transition** is a "bridge" that helps readers or listeners understand connections between parts. We use **transition expressions** (*for example, moreover, nevertheless*) for transitions, but a transition can also be a sentence (*My experience provides an example, Good examples are easy to find*) or even a short paragraph.

Transition expressions (Ch. 3), also called conjunctive adverbs, are words and phrases that show how a clause or sentence relates to the information before it in terms of meaning. They express notions like addition (*in addition, moreover*), contrast (*however, nonetheless*), and result (*as a result, therefore*).

A **transitive verb** (2.4.1) is a verb that can (sometimes must) have an object (a noun or noun phrase that directly follows it): *The storm **destroyed** the town. We **eat** lunch at noon.*

Uncountable noun (noncount noun): See **Count and noncount nouns**.

Verbs name actions (*participate, work*), states (*believe, want*), and relationships (*correlate, own*).

A **verb phrase** (Ch. 4) is a main verb and any auxiliary verbs that go with it: *We **are studying** clams. Someone **has been using** my phone. We **don't work** on Sundays. You **shouldn't have worried**.*

Wh words: *what, who, whom, whose, when, where, why, how, whether*

Word choice mistakes are mistakes in which the wrong word — not just the wrong form of a word — is used. *I did a mistake* → *I made a mistake. Say the truth* → *Tell the truth. You would better be careful.* → *You had better be …*

Word forms are the different shapes that a single word can have: *take, took, taken, takes, taking*. The different forms are sometimes different parts of speech: *succeed* (verb), *success* (noun), *successful* (adjective). See also **Parts of speech**.

Wordiness is the problem of using unnecessary words. The opposite is conciseness. Wordy: *In my opinion, I think this is wrong.* More concise: *I think this is wrong.* Even more concise: *This is wrong.*

Word order is important in a variety of grammar patterns, starting with basic sentence structure (subject + verb).

	Problems	Revisions	Comments
a.	We were waiting for the bus when appeared a taxi.	We were waiting for the bus when a taxi appeared.	Subject + verb (Ch. 2)
b.	Why they don't they care? How you can say that?	Why don't they like care? How can you say that?	Follow word order rules for questions. (2.14)
c.	I wonder where is she. Do you know where is she?	I wonder where she is. Do you know where she is?	In a noun clause, don't follow word order rules for questions. (7.4)
d.	Never this has happened before.	Never has this happened before.	When a negative element is moved to the front, use inverted word order. (2.13.2)
e.	It was too rainy for an outdoor game, so they called off it.	It was too rainy for an outdoor game, so they called it off.	When a phrasal verb has a pronoun object, put the pronoun between the parts. (2.10)
f.	We have every week a quiz.	We have a quiz every week.	We usually do not put any words between verb and its object. (2.20)
g.	The book was from the library that I chose.	The book that I chose was from the library.	Put a relative clause immediately after the noun it modifies. (8.2)
h.	When I was in high school, I was active in the student senate. I played a key role in getting several rules changed as a member of the senate.	When I was a high school student, I was active in the Student Senate. As a member of the senate, I played a key role in getting several rules changed.	Consider using old before new information. (2.22.2, 3.17, and Appendix D)
i.	In my country, high school students don't have a lot of choices. **Students** sometimes have lots of options to choose from in big U.S. schools.	In my country, high school students don't have a lot of choices. **In big U.S. schools**, students sometimes have lots of options to choose from.	Start with information that will help your reader follow your thinking. Sometimes starting with a subject is not the best way. (2.22 and Appendix D)

EDITING GUIDE

Teachers may use this to interpret feedback on students' work. Corrections are in the column on the right.

ASK	**Ask** about this. Talking about it may help you revise the sentence.	
?? or UNCL	**Unclear.** It may be a problem in grammar, vocabulary, or thinking. Try another way.	
Do you mean...? I did everything best. *Do you mean you did your best?*	Use the words after *Do you mean* (maybe with small changes) if that is what you mean. If not, try another way.	I did my best.
I am studying at University of Minnesota.	Add a word: maybe an article, a preposition, or a verb.	... at the University of Minnesota.
How important to be punctual?	Add two words.	How important is it to be punctual?
Although I fell, but I wasn't hurt.	These parts can't go together. Use only one.	Although I fell, I didn't get hurt. I fell, but I didn't get hurt.
Most of people are right-handed.	Omit this.	Most people are...
My all friends are students.	Reverse these parts.	All my friends are students.
I go everyday. This is my every day cap.	Write this as two words or write this as one word.	...go every day... my everyday cap.
# There are lots of bikes trail.	Number: change singular to plural or plural to singular.	There are lots of bike trails.
A/P or P/A The iPad introduce in 2010. Apple was introduced the iPad in 2010.	Use passive voice with the proper forms (BE + a past participle); don't use active voice. Or use active voice instead of passive voice. (Ch. 5)	Passive: the iPad was introduced in 2010. Active: Apple introduced the iPad in 2010.
ART We are the same.	Add a **article**: *a, an* or *the*, depending on the context.	I have the same problem.
BW This is a poem I made.	There may be a **better word** to use.	This is a poem I wrote.
C/N or N/C I followed their advices.	A problem related to a **countable** and **uncountable nouns** (count and noncount nouns)	their advice / their suggestions
CONJ I don't have a job. I don't want one.	Use a **conjunction** (usually *and, but* or *so*)	I don't have a job, and I don't...
CS I don't have a job. I don't want one.	A **comma splice**. Don't use only a comma between independent clauses. Use a period or a semi-colon or add a conjuction. (2.20, Ch. 5)	I don't have a job. I don't want one. I don't have a job, and I don't... I don't have a job because I don't...
FP I want fame and successful.	**Faulty parallelism**: The parts you joined (usually with *and*) don't work together because they are not the same type of thing. Join sentences and sentences, predicates and predicates, noun phrases and noun phrases, etc. (2.18)	I want fame and success. (N + N.) I want to be famous and successful. (Adj. + adj.) I want to be famous, and I want to be successful. (Independent clauses.)
FRAG This is a serious problem. Because it affects everyone.	This "sentence" is a **fragment**, not a proper sentence; it's only part of a sentence. Change the punctuation, omit something, or add something. (2.20, Ch. 5)	This is a serious problem because... This is a serious problem, because... This is a serious problem. It affects...
G We've already known that.	A **grammar** or word choice problem. Try another way. (4.25)	We already know that. We've already studied / learned that.
GER Write a paper is hard work.	Used a **gerund**: a verb + *-ing* used as a noun (6.4)	Writing a paper is hard work.
ICB I see bee.	Don't use a singular countable noun with no determiner. Add a determiner (usually *a / an* or *the*) or make the noun plural, depending on the meaning.	I see a bee. I see the bee. I see bees. (ICB) Sometimes a determiner like *my* or *this* is needed.
INF My goal is retire in 2050.	Use an **infinitive**: *to* + base form verb.	My goal to retire in 2050.
ING I heard a baby cried.	Use the word with *-ing* (a present participle or a gerund)	I heard a baby crying. (6.7)

Editing Guide

LG	I consider it's important to be on time.	**Lexical grammar** problems involve grammar that is associated with particular words, especially verbs. You need to learn the grammar of the word.	I consider it important to be on time.
NN	In the article "College Pressures," the author William Zinsser argues…	**Not needed.** To make it better (more concise or maybe just more correct), omit this.	In "College Pressures," William Zinsser argues…
NOUN	This school is strict. They have to follow lots of rules.	Use a **noun** or noun phrase, not a pronoun.	The students have to follow lots of rules.
OBJ	I went to a party, but I didn't enjoy.	Add an **object**, usually a pronoun: *it, him, them,* etc.	…enjoy it. / …enjoy myself.
POSS	My teacher wife has own business.	Use a **possessive** (e.g. *teacher's, their, his*)	My teacher's wife has her own…
PREP	We talked everything.	Add a **preposition**: *about, at, by, for, from, in, of, to,* etc.	We talked about everything.
PRF	They donot care.	**Proofread** to see if you can fix an obvious mistake, usually in grammar, spelling, or punctuation.	They do not care. They don't care.
PRO	I like cars because cars are…	Use a **pronoun**, like *he* (*him*), *they* (*them*), or *it*.	I like cars because they are…
PRO AG	If you have extra books, sell it.	Make your **pronoun agree** with the noun it refers to.	…extra books, sell them.
PUNC or **P**	What will the future bring. We can only wait and see	Add, remove, or change **punctuation** — for example, a period (.), comma (,), or a question mark (?).	What will the future bring? We can only wait and see.
QC	What it means?	Apply the rules for the grammar of questions.	What does it mean?
REF or **PRO REF**	This school is strict. They have to follow lots of rules.	A **reference** problem. Clarify who or what you are referring to.	The students have to follow… The teachers have to follow…
R-O	There are five parts each one has four pages.	A **run-on** sentence. Separate the clauses with a period or a comma and a conjunction.	…five parts. Each… …five parts, and each…
SP	There is no easy anser.	Fix the **spelling**. A spell-checking program may help.	There is no easy answer.
SS	In this chapter covers many topics. The man who won he was only 33. It may not true, but people believe it.	**Sentence structure.** Does the sentence have all the parts it needs and no extra part? Read it slowly to make sure the parts go together well. (Does the end fit the beginning?) There are usually various ways to fix it.	This chapter covers… In this chapter, the author covers… The man who won was only 33. It may not be true…
SV	Every problem have a solution.	**Subject-verb** agreement (is / are, get / gets, etc.)	Every problem has…
UNCL		**Unclear.** It may be a problem in grammar, vocabulary, or thinking. Try another way.	
UNID	I go to my home after class.	**Unidiomatic.** There is a more idiomatic (usual) way.	I go home after class.
VT	At first I hate it, but now I start to like it.	Choose a different **verb tense**: past instead of present, present instead of past, future instead of present, etc.	At first I hated it, but now I'm starting… At first I hated it, but now I have started… At first I hated it, but last week I started…
WC	Always say the truth. We have the similar custom.	**Word choice.** Use a different word (not just a different form of the same word).	Always tell the truth. We have a similar custom.
WF	At an university, it can be difficulty to developing friendships.	Change the **word form**. The change may involve a different part of speech (noun, adjective, adverb, etc.)	At a university, it can be difficult to develop friendships.
WO	The article was long that we read. We speak always English.	**Word order.** Move this or rearrange the parts of it.	The article that we read was… We always speak English.
WORDY	In my opinion, I think it's true.	Be concise (don't waste words).	I think it's true. / In my opinion, it's true. / It's true.

INDEX

KEY
Ch. 6 = Chapter 6
Ex. 23 = Exercise 23
5.2 = Chapter 5, section 2
2.14.3 = Chapter 2, section 14, subsection 3
(a) = an example

above all 3.8; 3.11
according to 7.15
actually 3.8, 3.10, 3.11
addition expressed with transitional expressions 3.8
adjective: glossary
adjective + *that* clause 7.8.2
adjectives and prepositional phrases after nouns 8.16
adjectives like *easy* 6.16 (*You're easy to talk to*) and 6.7 (*It's easy to make pancakes*)
adjectives with infinitive complements 6.23.2
admittedly 3.12
active and passive voice Ch. 5, glossary
adverb 2.20, glossary
adverb, conjunctive: See transition expressions.
adverbial, beginning sentences with an adverbial 2.22.1; in reporting 7.10, glossary
adverbial clauses Ch. 9
    compared to prepositional phrases 9.4
    concession clauses 9.19.2
    conditional clauses 9.2, Ch. 10
    connecting an adverbial clause and a main clause 9.5
    contrast and concession clauses 9.19
    contrast clauses 9.19.1, usage guide 9.22, reduced clauses of contrast 9.24
    fragments and adverbial clauses 9.6
    manner clauses 9.21, usage guide 9.22, reduced clauses of manner 9.24
    meanings that adverbial clauses express 9.2
    place clauses 9.21, usage guide 9.22, reduced clauses of place 9.24
    problems with adverbial clauses 9.25
    purpose clauses and phrases 9.12, usage guide 9.15
    reason clauses 9.91
    reason, result, and purpose clauses 9.8
    reduced adverbial clauses of time 9.7.3
    time clauses 9.7
    adverbials of place and *-ing* phrases indicating "at the same time" 4.34
agreement, subject-verb agreement 2.3.5
agreement of pronouns 2.16.3
after 9.7.2 and 9.7.3
after that, afterwards 3.9
also 3.8
all the same 3.10
among other things 3.8
and 2.18.1
and starting a sentence 3.14
appositives 8.15, glossary
articles: glossary
as...as: See comparison in the glossary.
as 9.7.1
as a consequence 3.9
as a matter of fact 3.8
as a result (of) 3.4, 3.9, 3.13
as if, as though, and *like* 9.21
as soon as 9.7.2
ask 2.6.2, 6.10
assuming, in case, and *given that* 10.12
at the same time 3.10

KEY
Ch. 6 = Chapter 6
Ex. 23 = Exercise 23
5.2 = Chapter 5, section 2
2.14.3 = Chapter 2, section 14, subsection 3
(a) = an example

INDEX

attribution phrases 7.15
attributive adjective: glossary
attributive clause: See relative clauses.
auxiliary verbs 4.1, 4.4
bare infinitives after *let, make,* and *help* 6.16, after perception verbs 6.14
BE *like* 2.8.3
BE *used to* and *used to* 4.11
because and *because of* 9.4
before 9.7.2 and 9.7.3
before and *until* 9.7.6
beginning and ending sentences 2.2.2
besides 3.8
bore, bored, boring and similar words 5.12
but and *however* 3.6
but and *or* 2.18.4
but starting a sentence 3.14
buy someone something, buy something for someone 2.6.2
by with passive voice 5.4
by the time 9.7.2, 9.7.7
can in conditionals 10.6
choppiness 2.23.1
clauses, independent and subordinate clauses 2.17.1; see also adverbial clauses, noun clauses, and relative clauses and the glossary.
comma splice (comma fault) 2.19, Appendix B, glossary
commands 2.15.2
commands, requests, exclamatory sentences 2.15
comparison: glossary
complement, noun and adjective complements with *that* 7.8, glossary
completing the meaning of a verb 2.4, avoiding verb completion mistakes 2.4.7
concession clauses 9.19.2
condition expressed with transition expressions 3.13
conditionals Ch. 10
    can, could, may, and *might* in conditionals 10.6
    conditionals and *wish* 10.20,
    conditionals in paragraphs 10.16
    continuous verb phrases in conditionals 10.13
    contrasting real and unreal conditionals 10.5
    limited conditions 10.11
    mixed times 10.14
    negative conditions 10.11
    no condition 10.15
    problems with conditionals 10.21
    real conditionals 10.3, 10.5
    unreal conditionals 10.4, 10.5
    conjunctions, coordinating conjunctions 2.17.3; subordinating conjunctions 2.17.2
    conjunctive adverbs: See transition expressions.
    connecting, five ways 3.19
    connectors: See transition expressions and conjunctions.
consequently 3.9
consider, find, regard, and *see* 7.20
continuous verb phrases, present continuous 4.7; past continuous 4.10; present perfect continuous 4.14; future continuous 4.21; future perfect continuous 4.22; continuous verb phrases in conditionals 10.13

INDEX

contractions: glossary
contrast clauses 9.9.2, usage guide 9.22, 9.24; reduced clauses of contrast 9.24
contrast expressed with *but* 2.17.3, 3.6
contrast expressed with transition expressions 3.10
coordination and coordinating conjunctions 2.17.3; the algebra of coordination 2.18.3
could in conditionals 10.6
count and noncount nouns: glossary
delayed infinitive subjects 6.7
demonstratives: glossary
determiners: glossary
direct object 2.4.1, 2.6, glossary
direct reporting 7.9
during 9.4
easy + infinitive 6.16 (*You're easy to talk to*) and 6.7 (*It's easy to make pancakes*)
editing guide
embedded questions 7.4.1
empty *it* as an object 6.9
empty *it*, common expressions with empty it 6.8
empty *it* subjects 2.11; 6.7
enough and *too* with infinitives 6.15
-er: See comparison in the glossary.
ergative verbs 5.9
even so 3.10
eventually 3.8
exclamatory sentences 2.15.3
extra BE problem 5.8
the fact that and similar expressions 7.8
faulty parallelism, avoiding faulty parallelism 2.18.2, glossary
feel like, look like, sound like, and *seem like* 7.18
finally 3.9
first 3.9, Appendix C
for, beginning sentences with *for* 2.22.4
for a start 3.9
for example 3.8, 3.15
for in purpose phrases 9.13
for instance 3.8
for one thing 3.8
for phrases after verbs like *thank* 9.16
fortunately Appendix C
fragments, run-ons, and comma splices 2.19, glossary
fragments with adverbial clauses 9.6
furthermore 3.8
gender bias, avoiding gender bias in pronoun choice, 2.24
gerunds 6.2, glossary
gerunds in expressions like *have difficulty walking* and *go swimming* 6.26
gerunds after perception verbs 6.14
gerunds after prepositions 6.5
gerunds after verbs 6.6
gerunds and infinitives Ch. 6, perfect gerunds and infinitives 6.21, usage guide 6.24, lexical grammar 6.28, problems with gerunds and infinitives, 6.29
gerunds and possessives 6.27
gerund subjects 6.4
get someone to do something, get something done 6.13.3
give someone something, give something to someone (two-object verbs) 2.6.1

KEY

Ch. 6 = Chapter 6
Ex. 23 = Exercise 23
5.2 = Chapter 5, section 2
2.14.3 = Chapter 2, section 14, subsection 3
(a) = an example

KEY

Ch. 6 = Chapter 6
Ex. 23 = Exercise 23
5.2 = Chapter 5, section 2
2.14.3 = Chapter 2, section 14, subsection 3
(a) = an example

INDEX

given that, in case, and *assuming* 10.12
go biking, go shopping, and similar expressions 6.21.2
grammar terms 1.4, glossary
granted 3.12
have, causative HAVE 6.13
have difficulty walking and similar expressions 6.26
headless relative clauses 8.19
help 6.16
hence 3.9
hope and *wish* 7.7.4
however, as a transition expression 3.10, punctuation and placement 3.5 and 3.15, as a subordinating conjunction 10.15
idiom, idiomatic language: glossary
if 10.2
if so 3.13
if and *whether* 7.4
imperative 2.15.2, 10.18, glossary
impersonal *you* and *one* in generalizations 2.25
implied subjects with infinitives and phrases like *for someone to do something* 6.19
in addition 3.8
in case, assuming, and *given that* 10.12
in that case 3.13
in conclusion 3.9
in contrast 3.10
in fact 3.8, 3.11
in order to 9.13
in other words 3.8
in particular 3.8
in sum 3.9
in the same way 3.8
indirect object 2.4.1, 2.6, glossary
indirect reporting 7.9
indirect reporting and paraphrasing 7.22
infinitives 6.2, glossary
infinitives after BE 6.7
infinitives after verbs and verb + object combinations 6.10, 6.11
infinitives and gerunds Ch. 6
infinitives and *wh* words 6.17
infinitives in phrases like *for someone to do something* 6.19
infinitives of purpose in front position 9.18
infinitive phrases that function like relative clauses 6.18
infinitive subjects 6.7
instead 3.10
intransitive verbs (verbs without objects) 2.4.4, glossary
inversion 2.13; in questions 2.14; with fronted negative elements 2.13.2; in if clauses 10.9, glossary
-ing word, beginning a sentence with an *-ing* word 2.22.5
it as an empty object 6.9
it as an empty subject 2.11, 6.7. 6.8, and 6.9
later 3.9
less, least: See comparison in the glossary.
let 6.16
lexical grammar 2.4.2, 2.8.1, 5.1.3, 6.28

INDEX

linking verbs 2.8, glossary
like, as if, and *as though* 9.21
like it that 7.19
likewise 3.8
look like, seem like, and *sound like* 2.9
main verb: glossary
make 6.16
manner clauses 9.21, usage guide 9.23; reduced clauses of manner 9.24
may and *might* in conditionals 10.6
mismatches 2.3.3
modal auxiliaries and semi-modals 4.4; reporting and modals 7.10, glossary
modify, modifier: glossary
more, most: See comparison in the glossary.
more/most important(ly) 3.8
moreover 3.8
negative: glossary
next 3.9
nevertheless 3.10
noncount and count nouns: glossary
nonetheless 3.10
nonrestrictive and restrictive relative clauses 8.8, 8.17
noun, count and noncount nouns: glossary
noun clauses Ch. 7, problems with noun clauses 7.26, usage guide 7.14, glossary
    and lexical grammar 7.23
    and relative clauses 7.24
    and preciseness in writing 7.25
    and punctuation 7.4.3
    and reporting Ch. 7
    beginning with *that* 7.6, 7.7
    beginning with *wh* words 7.4
    with *that* or no marker 7.3
noun + *of* + gerund 6.22
noun phrase: glossary
noun phrases, beginning with a noun phrase 2.22.3
nouns with infinitive complements 6.23
now that in adverbial clauses 9.7.10
objects 2.4.1, 2.6, glossary
object complement with *consider* and *find* 7.20, glossary
of course 3.12
old before new information 2.22.2, 3.17, Appendix D
on the contrary 3.11
on the other hand 3.10
once in adverbial clauses 9.7.10
one and *you* as impersonal pronouns 2.25
otherwise 7.4
paraphrasing: glossary
paraphrasing and indirect reporting 7.22
parallelism, parallel structure 2.18; parallel structure and repetition 3.18, glossary
part of speech 2.3, glossary
particles 2.10, glossary
participles in passive verb phrases Ch. 5, glossary
participles in perfect tenses 4.12, 4.14, 4.15, 4.16 glossary
passive and active voice Ch. 5, glossary
    by phrases 5.4
    comparing passive and active 5.2

KEY

Ch. 6 = Chapter 6
Ex. 23 = Exercise 23
5.2 = Chapter 5, section 2
2.14.3 = Chapter 2, section 14, subsection 3
(a) = an example

KEY

Ch. 6 = Chapter 6
Ex. 23 = Exercise 23
5.2 = Chapter 5, section 2
2.14.3 = Chapter 2, section 14, subsection 3
(a) = an example

INDEX

    intransitive verbs, 5.7.2
    passive and the dictionary 5.13
    passive gerunds and infinitives 6.20
    passive in different tenses and with modal auxiliaries, 5.3, Appendix A
    problems with passive and active voice 5.16
    stative passives 5.11
    uses of the passive voice 5.10, 5.14
    verb + preposition combinations that allow passive voice 5.7.2
    verbs that are never passive 5.7
    visualizing passive and active voice 5.5
past tense, past simple 4.9; past tenses in contrast 4.17; past tenses in unreal conditionals and after *wish* 4.29, glossary
perception verbs 6.14
perfect gerunds and infinitives 6.21
phrasal verbs 2.10
place adverbials and *-ing* phrases indicating "at the same time" 4.34
place clauses 9.21
possessive, possessives before a gerund 6.27, glossary
predicate 2.2.4, glossary
predicate noun: glossary
prepositions after nouns but not verbs 2.5
prepositions and prepositional phrases Ch. 2.4, compared with conjunctions 9.4, glossary
prepositional phrases after nouns 8.16
prevent someone from doing something 6.25
principles for ordering information in sentences Appendix D
probability with *be likely to* and *be sure to* 6.24
problems with adverbial clauses 9.25
problems with comparison: See comparison in the glossary.
problems with conditionals 10.21
problems with gerunds and infinitives, 6.29
problems with noun clauses 7.26
problems with passive and active voice 5.16
problems with questions 2.14.5
problems with relative clauses 8.28
problems with sentence structure 2.27
problems with tenses 4.39
problems with transition expressions 3.20
problems with verb completion 2.4.7
problems with word order: See word order in the glossary.
progressive: See continuous.
pronouns 2.16, glossary
pronoun agreement 2.16.3, glossary
pronoun forms 2.16.2, glossary
pronoun reference 2.16, glossary
punctuation for joining clauses Appendix B
punctuation with *so, yet, but* and *and* 3.14
purpose clauses and phrases 9.12
purpose infinitives in front position 9.18
purpose phrases with *for* and *to* 9.13
questions 2.14, *yes/no* questions 2.14.1, *wh* questions 2.14.2, *What is it like? / How is it?* 2.14.4, problems with questions 2.14.5
reason, result, and purpose clauses 9.8, usage guide 9.15
reason clauses and phrases 9.9.1
reduced relative clauses, 8.12

INDEX

reference 2.16.1, glossary
relative clauses Ch. 8; see also reduced relative clauses.
    after a pronoun (*one that will fit me*) 8.18
    compared to other structures that modify nouns 8.22
    definitions with relative clauses 8.26
    details expressed in relative clauses 8.24
    grammar checkers and relative clauses 8.23
    infinitive phrases that are like relative clauses (*a book for you to read*) 8.20
    modifying a sentence 8.9
    problems with relative clauses 8.28
    restrictive and nonrestrictive 8.8
    sentence structure and relative clauses 8.21
    tight writing 8.27
    usage guide 8.23
    with a subject relativizer: *a woman who was lost* 8.3
    with an object relativizer: *the woman (that) we helped* 8.4
    with a preposition: *the friends (that) we stayed with* 8.5
    with and without commas (nonrestrictive and restrictive) 8.8
    with *of whom* and *of which* 8.10
    with *whose* C8.6
    with *where, when, why,* and *the way* 8.7
    wordy relative clauses, avoiding 8.25
repetition and parallel structure 3.18
repetitiveness, avoiding repetitiveness by using pronouns 2.16.5
reporting, 7.9, tenses, modals, and adverbials in reporting 7.10
reporting commands and requests 7.12
reporting questions 7.11
restrictive (no commas) and nonrestrictive (with commas) relative clauses 8.8
result clauses with separate parts 9.11
result clauses with *so* and *so that* 9.10
run-on sentences 2.19, Appendix B, glossary
semi-modals 4.4.2
sentences and clauses 2.17
sentence flow Ch. 3, five ways of achieving sentence flow 3.19; Appendix D
sentence structure Ch. 2; problems with sentence structure 2.27, usage guide 2.22
sentence structure and relative clauses 8.21
sentence types 2.15.1; traditional sentence types 2.23.1
sentence variety in your writing 2.23
shifting points of view 2.26
should in conditionals 10.7
similarly 3.8
since 9.4, 9.7
since before 9.7.9
singular and plural 2.3.5, glossary
so and *yet* punctuation 3.14
so as a transition expression 3.9 and 3.14, as a coordinating conjunction 2.18.3
so few/little 9.14
so much/many 9.11
specifically 3.8
stative verb 4.7, 4.30, glossary
stative passives 5.11, glossary
still 3.10
subject 2.2, glossary
subjects and verbs 2.2

KEY

Ch. 6 = Chapter 6
Ex. 23 = Exercise 23
5.2 = Chapter 5, section 2
2.14.3 = Chapter 2, section 14, subsection 3
(a) = an example

KEY
Ch. 6 = Chapter 6
Ex. 23 = Exercise 23
5.2 = Chapter 5, section 2
2.14.3 = Chapter 2, section 14, subsection 3
(a) = an example

INDEX

subject-verb agreement 2.2.5, glossary
subjunctive (*demand that he leave*) 7.7.3
subordination and subordinating conjunctions 2.17.2, tight writing 9.17
such 9.11
such as 3.8
suppose and *what if* 10.17
tenses Ch. 4
    continuous tenses with stative verbs 4.20
    continuous verb phrases in conditionals 10.13
    future continuous 4.21
    future in the past 4.23
    future perfect 4.22
    future perfect continuous 4.22
    future with *will* and *be going to* 4.18
    future-oriented verbs 4.35
    generalizations 4.38
    modal auxiliaries and semi-modals 4.4
    overview Appendix A
    passive verb phrases 4.3, 5.3
    past continuous 4.10
    past perfect 4.15
    past perfect continuous 4.16
    past simple 4.9
    past tenses in contrast 4.17
    past tenses in unreal conditionals and after *wish* 4.29
    present perfect 4.12; in contrast to simple past 4.13, glossary
    present perfect continuous 4.14
    present continuous 4.7, continuous tenses with stative verbs 4.20, continuous tenses for change over time 4.31, continuous tenses with verbs that describe momentary actions 4.22, continuous tenses with *always* to express emotion 4.33, place adverbials and *-ing* phrases indicating "at the same time" 4.34
    present simple 4.6, in contrast with present continuous 4.8, for reporting what an author says 4.26, with performative verbs 4.17, present tense for future time in subordinate clauses 4.20
    problems with tenses 4.39
    tense chart 4.2, tense overview Appendix A
    tense choice and verb choice 4.25
    tense shifts, 4.38
    time reference in reduced clauses 4.36, 8.12
    unanchored past tenses, 4.28
    used to and *would* for past actions, *used to* and BE *used to* 4.11
that: See demonstratives in the glossary.
that, omitting *that* in a noun clause 7.3 and 7.17, omitting *that* in a relative clause 8.4
that clauses (see also noun clauses) glossary
    after BE 7.6
    after adjectives 7.8.2
    after nouns 7.8.1
    after verbs 7.7
    noun clauses compared to relative clauses 8.22
    subjunctive 7.7.3
    when to include *that* in a noun clause 7.17
    when you can omit *that* in a relative clause 8.4
    wish and *hope* 7.7.4
that is, that is to say 3.8

INDEX

then 3.9, 3.1, 10.2
there is (existential *there*) 2.12
there is no doubt that 3.12
therefore 3.9
these: See demonstratives in the glossary.
this: See demonstratives in the glossary.
thus 3.9
time clauses 9.7, usage guide 9.7.5
time expressions in the form of noun phrases 2.21
to, purpose phrases 9.13
to be sure 3.12
to begin with 3.9
to infinitives 6.3,
to sum up 3.9
too and *enough* with infinitives 6.15
transition: glossary
transition expressions Ch. 3, glossary
    addition, examples, details, and restatement 3.8
    alphabetical listing 3.3; see also Appendix C.
    and conjunctions 3.6
    and sentence flow Ch. 3
    concession 3.12
    condition 3.13
    contrast 3.10
    correcting a misconception Ch. 11
    expanded transition expressions 3.4, 3.16
    meanings, 3.7
    placement and punctuation, 3.5
    problems with transition expressions 3.20
    punctuation with *so* and *yet* 3.14
    result, time, and text structure 3.9
    usage guide Ch. 3
    word by word Appendix C
transitive verbs (verbs with objects) 2.4.1, glossary
transitive verbs that are also intransitive 2.4.5
true, it is true that 3.12
two-object verbs 2.6
unanchored past tenses, 4.28
uncountable noun: See count noun in the glossary.
until 9.4, 9.7
until after 9.7.9
variety, sentence variety 2.23
verbs (See also tenses.)
    main verb: glossary
    tense choice and verb choice 4.25
    verb + gerund, 6.6
    verb + infinitive, Ch. 6.10
    verbs + noun clause with *that* 7.7
    verb phrase: glossary
    verbs that are never passive 5.7
    verbs + *wh* clauses 7.4.7
    verbs with no tense 4.5, 6.2
verb tenses: See tenses Ch. 4.

KEY

Ch. 6 = Chapter 6
Ex. 23 = Exercise 23
5.2 = Chapter 5, section 2
2.14.3 = Chapter 2, section 14, subsection 3
(a) = an example

KEY

Ch. 6 = Chapter 6
Ex. 23 = Exercise 23
5.2 = Chapter 5, section 2
2.14.3 = Chapter 2, section 14, subsection 3
(a) = an example

INDEX

were in unreal conditionals 10.7
wh words and infinitives 6.17, 7.4.6, glossary
what if and *suppose* 10.17
when or *while* or *as*? 9.7.5
when, *while*, and *as* 9.7.1
whenever 9.7.1
whereas and *while* for contrast 9.19.1,
whether in an adverbial clause 10.10
whether in a noun clause 7.4.2
while and *whereas* for contrast 9.19.1
wish and *hope* 7.7.4, *wish* and conditionals 10.20
will and *would* special uses in *if* clauses 10.19
word choice: glossary
word forms 2.3.1, glossary
word forms and parts of speech 2.3, glossary
word order Ch. 2, 2.10, 2.14, 2.20, 7.4, 8.2, 9.18
wordiness, avoiding wordy relative clauses 8.25, glossary
would and *used to* for past actions 4.11
would and *will* special uses in *if* clauses 10.19
yes, *but* arguing 3.12
yet 3.10.
yet, punctuation with *so* and *yet* 3.14
you and *one* as impersonal pronouns 2.25

www.ingramcontent.com/pod-product-compliance
Lightning Source LLC
Chambersburg PA
CBHW051350070526
44584CB00025B/3702